CIMA

STUDY TEXT

Foundation Paper 3c

Business Mathematics

IN THIS JULY 2002 EDITION

- Targeted to the **syllabus** and **learning outcomes**

- **Quizzes** and **questions** to check your understanding

- Clear layout and style designed to save you time

- Plenty of **exam-style questions**

- **Chapter roundups** and summaries to help revision

- **Mind maps** to integrate the key points

NEW IN THIS JULY 2002 EDITION

- **Question Bank** for **paper-based exams** with full answers

- **Question Bank** for **computer-based assessments** with full answers

BPP's **MCQ cards** and **i-Learn** and **i-Pass** products also support this paper.

BPP Publishing
July 2002

First edition 2000
Third edition July 2002

ISBN 0 7517 3754 2 (previous edition 0 7517 3158 7)

British Library Cataloguing-in-Publication Data
A catalogue record for this book
is available from the British Library

Published by

BPP Publishing Ltd
Aldine House, Aldine Place
London W12 8AW

www.bpp.com

Printed in Great Britain by W M Print
45-47 Frederick Street
Walsall, West Midlands
WS2 9NE

We are grateful to the Chartered Institute of Management Accountants for permission to reproduce past examination questions and questions from the pilot paper. The suggested solutions to the illustrative questions have been prepared by BPP Publishing Limited.

Contents

MULTIPLE CHOICE QUESTION CARDS

Multiple choice questions form a large part of the exam. To give you further practice in this style of question, we have produced a bank of **150 multiple choice question cards**, covering the syllabus. This bank contains exam style questions in a format to help you revise **on the move**.

COMPUTER-BASED LEARNING PRODUCTS FROM BPP

For **self-testing**, try **i-Pass,** which offers a large number of objective test questions, particularly useful where **objective test questions** form part of the exam.

See the order form at the back of this text for details of these innovative learning tools.

VIRTUAL CAMPUS

The Virtual Campus uses BPP's wealth of teaching experience to produce a fully **interactive** e-learning resource **delivered via the Internet**. The site offers comprehensive **tutor support** and features areas such as **study**, **practice**, **email service**, **revision** and **useful resources**.

Visit our website www.bpp.com/virtualcampus/cima to sample aspects of the campus free of charge.

LEARNING TO LEARN ACCOUNTANCY

BPP's ground-breaking **Learning to learn accountancy** book is designed to be used both at the outset of your CIMA studies and throughout the process of learning accountancy. It challenges you to consider how you study and gives you helpful hints about how to approach the various types of paper which you will encounter. It can help you **get your studies both subject and exam focused**, enabling you to **acquire knowledge, practice and revise efficiently and effectively**.

THE BPP STUDY TEXT

Aims of this Study Text

To provide you with the knowledge and understanding, skills and application techniques that you need if you are to be successful in your exams

This Study Text has been written around the **Business Mathematics** syllabus.

- It is **comprehensive**. It covers the syllabus content. No more, no less.

- It is written at the **right level**. Each chapter is written with CIMA's precise learning outcomes in mind.

- It is targeted to the **exam**. We have taken account of pilot material, papers and assessments set to date, questions put to the examiner and assessment methodologies.

To allow you to study in the way that best suits your learning style and the time you have available, by following your personal Study Plan (see page (viii))

You may be studying at home on your own until the date of the exam, or you may be attending a full-time course. You may like to (and have time to) read every word, or you may prefer to (or only have time to) skim-read and devote the remainder of your time to question practice. Wherever you fall in the spectrum, you will find the BPP Study Text meets your needs in designing and following your personal Study Plan.

To tie in with the other components of the BPP Effective Study Package to ensure you have the best possible chance of passing the exam (see page (vi))

BPP STUDY TEXTS AND THE CIMA CERTIFICATE IN BUSINESS ACCOUNTING

In supporting your Foundation level studies, this text is your passport to success in the **CIMA Certificate in Business Accounting**, awarded from May 2002 to students who complete their Foundation level exams.

BPP PUBLISHING

Recommended period of use	Elements of the BPP Effective Study Package
From the outset and throughout	**Learning to learn accountancy** Read this invaluable book as you begin your studies and refer to it as you work through the various elements of the BPP Effective Study Package. It will help you to acquire knowledge, practice and revise, both efficiently and effectively.
Three to twelve months before the exam	**Study Text** Use the Study Text to acquire knowledge, understanding, skills and the ability to use application techniques.
Throughout	**Virtual Campus** Study, practice, revise and take advantage of other useful resources with BPP's fully interactive e-learning site with comprehensive tutor support.
Throughout	**MCQ cards and i-Pass** Revise your knowledge and ability to use application techniques, as well as practising this key exam question format, with 150 multiple choice questions. **i-Pass**, our computer-based testing package, provides objective test questions in a variety of formats and is ideal for self-assessment.
One to six months before the exam	**Practice & Revision Kit** Try the multiple choice questions and objective test questions for your chosen assessment format. Then attempt the mock paper-based exam or the mock computer based assessment.
From three months before the exam until the last minute	**Passcards** Work through these short, memorable notes which are focused on what is most likely to come up in the exam you will be sitting.
One to six months before the exam	**Success Tapes** These audio tapes cover the vital elements of your syllabus in less than 90 minutes per subject. Each tape also contains exam hints to help you fine tune your strategy.
Three to twelve months before the exam	**Breakthrough Videos** Use a Breakthrough Video to supplement your Study Text. They give you clear tuition on key exam subjects and allow you the luxury of being able to pause or repeat sections until you have fully grasped the topic.

HELP YOURSELF STUDY FOR YOUR CIMA EXAMS

Exams for professional bodies such as CIMA are very different from those you have taken at college or university. You will be under **greater time pressure before** the exam - as you may be combining your study with work. There are many different ways of learning and so the BPP Study Text offers you a number of different tools to help you through. Here are some hints and tips: they are not plucked out of the air, but **based on research and experience**. (You don't need to know that long-term memory is in the same part of the brain as emotions and feelings - but it's a fact anyway.)

The right approach

1   The right attitude

Believe in yourself	Yes, there is a lot to learn. Yes, it is a challenge. But thousands have succeeded before and you can too.
Remember why you're doing it	Studying might seem a grind at times, but you are doing it for a reason: to advance your career.

2   The right focus

Read through the Syllabus and learning outcomes	These tell you what you are expected to know and are supplemented by Exam Focus Points in the text.
Study the Exam Paper section	Past papers are a reasonable guide of what you should expect in the exam.

3   The right method

The big picture	You need to grasp the detail - but keeping in mind how everything fits into the big picture will help you understand better. • The **Introduction** of each chapter puts the material in context. • The **Syllabus content, learning outcomes** and **Exam focus points** show you what you need to **grasp**. • **Mind Maps** show the links and key issues in key topics.
In your own words	To absorb the information (and to practise your written communication skills), it helps to **put it into your own words.** • **Take notes.** • Answer the **questions** in each chapter. As well as helping you absorb the information, you will practise the assessment formats used in the exam and your written communication skills, which become increasingly important as you progress through your CIMA exams. • Draw **mind maps**. We have some examples. • Try 'teaching' a subject to a colleague or friend.

Give yourself cues to jog your memory	The BPP Study Text uses **bold** to **highlight key points** and **icons** to identify key features, such as **Exam focus points** and **Key terms**. • Try **colour coding** with a highlighter pen. • Write **key points** on cards.

4   The right review

Review, review, review	It is a **fact** that regularly reviewing a topic in summary form can **fix it in your memory**. Because **review** is so important, the BPP Study Text helps you to do so in many ways. • **Chapter roundups** summarise the key points in each chapter. Use them to recap each study session. • The **Quick quiz** is another review technique to ensure that you have grasped the essentials. • Go through the **Examples** in each chapter a second or third time.

Developing your personal Study Plan

One thing that the BPP Learning to learn accountancy book emphasises is the need to prepare a study plan (and to use it!). Planning and sticking to the plan are key elements of learning success.

There are four steps you should work through.

Step 1. How do you learn?

First you need to be aware of your style of learning. The BPP Learning to learn accountancy book commits a chapter to this **self-discovery** at the outset. What types of intelligence do you display when learning? You might be advised to brush up on certain study skills before launching into this Study Text.

> BPP's **Learning to learn accountancy** book helps you to identify what intelligences you show more strongly and then identifies how you can tailor your study process through your preferences. It also includes handy hints on how to develop intelligences you exhibit less strongly, which might be needed as you study accountancy.

Are you a **theorist** or more **practical**? If you would rather get to grips with a theory before trying to apply it in practice, you should follow the study sequence below. If the reverse is true (you like to know learning theory before you do so), you might be advised to flick through your Study Text chapter and look at questions, case studies and examples (Steps 7, 8 and 9 in the **Suggested Study sequence** below) before reading through the detail of theory.

Step 2. **How much time do you have?**

Work out the time you have available per week, given the following.

- The standard you have set yourself
- The time you need to set aside later for work on the Practice & Revision Kit and Passcards
- The other exam(s) you are sitting
- Very importantly, practical matters such as work, travel, exercise, sleep and social life

Note your time available in box A.

A [ ] Hours

Step 3. **Allocate your time**

- Take the time you have available per week for this Study Text shown in box A, multiply it by the number of weeks available and insert the result in box B.

B [ ]

- Divide the figure in Box B by the number of chapters in this text and insert the result in box C.

C [ ]

Remember that this is only a rough guide. Some of the chapters in this book are longer and more complicated than others, and you will find some subjects easier to understand than others.

Step 4. **Implement**

Set about studying each chapter in the time shown in box C, following the key study steps in the order suggested by your particular learning style.

This is your personal **Study Plan**. You should try and combine it with the study sequence outlines below. You may want to modify the sequence a little (as has been suggested above) to adapt it to your **personal style**.

Suggested study sequence

It is likely that the best way to approach this Study Text is to tackle the chapters in the order in which you find them. Taking into account your individual learning style, you could follow this sequence.

Key study steps	Activity
Step 1 **Topic list**	Each numbered topic is a numbered section in the chapter.
Step 2 **Introduction**	This gives you the **big picture** in terms of the **context** of the chapter, the **content** you will cover, and the **learning outcomes** the chapter assesses - in other words, it sets your **objectives for study.**
Step 3 **Knowledge brought forward boxes**	In these we highlight information and techniques that it is assumed you have 'brought forward' with you from your earlier studies. If there are topics which have changed recently due to legislation for example, these topics are explained in more detail.
Step 4 **Explanations**	Proceed methodically through the chapter, reading each section thoroughly and making sure you understand.

BPP
PUBLISHING

Key study steps	Activity
Step 5 **Key terms and** **Exam focus** **points**	• **Key terms** can often earn you *easy marks* if you state them clearly and correctly in an appropriate exam answer (and they are highlighted in the index at the back of the text). • **Exam focus points** give you a good idea of how we think the examiner intends to examine certain topics.
Step 6 **Note taking**	Take brief notes, if you wish. Avoid the temptation to copy out too much. Remember that being able to put something into your own words is a sign of being able to understand it. If you find you cannot explain something you have read, read it again before you make the notes.
Step 7 **Examples**	Follow each through to its solution very carefully.
Step 8 **Case examples**	Study each one, and try to add flesh to them from your own experience – they are designed to show how the topics you are studying come alive (and often come unstuck) in the real world.
Step 9 **Questions**	Make a very good attempt at each one.
Step 10 **Answers**	Check yours against ours, and make sure you understand any discrepancies.
Step 11 **Chapter roundup**	Work through it very carefully, to make sure you have grasped the major points it is highlighting.
Step 12 **Quick quiz**	When you are happy that you have covered the chapter, use the **Quick quiz** to check how much you have remembered of the topics covered and to practise questions in a variety of formats.
Step 13 **Question(s) in the** **Question banks**	Either at this point, or later when you are thinking about revising, make a full attempt at the **Question(s)** suggested at the very end of the chapter. You can find these at the end of the Study Text, along with the **Answers** so you can see how you did. If you have purchased the **MCQ cards** or **i-Pass**, use these too.

Short of time: Skim study technique?

You may find you simply do not have the time available to follow all the key study steps for each chapter, however you adapt them for your particular learning style. If this is the case, follow the **skim study** technique below (the icons in the Study Text will help you to do this).

• Study the chapters in the order you find them in the Study Text.

• For each chapter, follow the key study steps 1-3, and then skim-read through step 4. Jump to step 11, and then go back to step 5. Follow through steps 7 and 8, and prepare outline answers to questions (steps 9/10). Try the Quick quiz (step 12), following up any items you can't answer, then do a plan for the Question (step 13), comparing it against our answers. You should probably still follow step 6 (note-taking), although you may decide simply to rely on the BPP Passcards for this.

Moving on...

However you study, when you are ready to embark on the practice and revision phase of the BPP Effective Study Package, you should still refer back to this Study Text, both as a source of **reference** (you should find the index particularly helpful for this) and as a way to **review** (the Chapter roundups and Quick quizzes help you here).

And remember to keep careful hold of this Study Text – you will find it invaluable in your work.

BPP
PUBLISHING

SYLLABUS AND LEARNING OUTCOMES

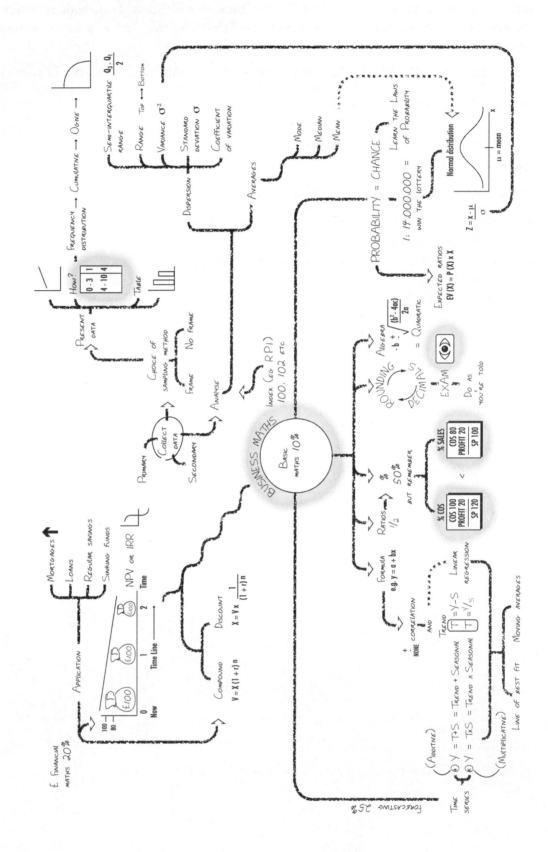

Syllabus overview

This is a foundation level study in mathematical and statistical concepts and techniques. The first two sections, Basic Mathematics and Summarising and Analysing Data, include techniques which are fundamental to the work for the Management Accountant. The third section covers basic probability and is needed because Management Accountants need to be aware of and be able to estimate the risk and uncertainty involved in the decisions they make. The fourth section is an introduction to financial mathematics, a topic that is important to the study of financial management. Finally, there is an introduction to the mathematical techniques needed for forecasting, necessary in the area of business planning.

Aims

This syllabus aims to test the student's ability to:

- Explain and demonstrate the use of basic mathematics including formulae and ratios
- Identify reasonableness in the calculation of answers
- Identify and apply techniques for summarising and analysing data
- Explain and demonstrate the use of probability where risk and uncertainty exist
- Explain and apply financial mathematical techniques
- Explain and demonstrate techniques used for forecasting

Assessment

Assessment is either by means of a paper-based exam or by computer-based assessment. Further information of these assessment methods is given on pages (xviii) to (xxiii).

Learning outcomes and syllabus content

3c(i) Basic mathematics – 10%

Learning outcomes

On completion of their studies students should be able to:

- Demonstrate the order of operations in formulae, including the use of brackets, negative numbers, powers and roots

- Calculate percentages and proportions

- Calculate answers to appropriate significant figures or decimal places

- Calculate maximum absolute and relative errors

- Solve simple equations, including 2 variable simultaneous equations and quadratic equations

- Prepare graphs of linear and quadratic equations

BPP
PUBLISHING

Syllabus content

		Covered in chapter
•	Use of formulae	1
•	Percentages and ratios	1
•	Rounding of numbers	1
•	Basic algebraic techniques and the solution of equations – including simultaneous and quadratic equations	2

3(ii) Summarising and analysing data - 25%

Learning outcomes

On completion of their studies students should be able to:

- Explain the difference between data and information
- Explain the characteristics of good information
- Explain the difference between primary and secondary data
- Identify the sources of secondary data
- Explain the different methods of sampling and identify where each is appropriate
- Tabulate data and explain the results
- Prepare a frequency distribution from raw data
- Prepare and explain the following graphs and diagrams: bar charts, time series graphs (not Z charts), scatter diagrams, histograms and ogives
- Calculate and explain the following summary statistics for ungrouped data: arithmetic mean, median, mode, range, standard deviation and variance
- Calculate and explain the following summary statistics for grouped data: arithmetic mean, median (graphical method only), mode (graphical method only), range, semi-interquartile range (graphical method only), standard deviation and variance
- Calculate and explain a simple index number, a fixed base and chain base series of index numbers
- Use index numbers to deflate a series and explain the results
- Calculate a simple weighted index number. Candidates will not have to decide whether to use base or current weights

Syllabus content

	Covered in chapter
• Data and information	4
• Primary and secondary data	4
• Probability sampling (simple random sampling, stratified, systematic, multi-stage, cluster) and non-probability sampling (quota)	4
• Tabulation of data	5
• Frequency distributions	5
• Graphs and diagrams: bar charts, time series graphs (not Z charts), scatter diagrams, histograms and ogives	5
• Summary measures for both grouped and ungrouped data	6, 7
• Coefficient of variation	7
• Index numbers	8

3c(iii) Probability - 20%

Learning outcomes

On completion of their studies students should be able to:

- Calculate a simple probability
- Demonstrate the use of the addition and multiplication rules of probability
- Calculate a simple conditional probability
- Calculate and explain an expected value
- Demonstrate the use of expected values to make decisions
- Explain the limitations of expected values
- Demonstrate the use of normal distribution and the CIMA tables
- Demonstrate the application of the normal distribution to calculate probabilities

Syllabus content

	Covered in chapter
• The relationship between probability, proportion and percent	9
• The addition and multiplication rules	9
• Expected values	9
• Normal distribution	10

BPP PUBLISHING

3c(iv) Financial Mathematics - 20%

Learning outcomes

On completion of their studies students should be able to:

- Calculate future values of an investment using both simple and compound interest

- Calculate an Annual Percentage Rate of interest given a quarterly or monthly rate

- Calculate the present value of a future cash sum, using both a formula and CIMA tables

- Calculate the present value of an annuity using both a formula and CIMA tables

- Calculate loan/mortgage repayments and the value of an outstanding loan/mortgage

- Calculate the present value of a perpetuity

- Calculate the future value of regular savings (sinking funds) or find the savings given the future value, if necessary, using the sum of a geometric progression

- Calculate the NPV of a project and use this to decide whether a project should be undertaken, or to choose between mutually exclusive projects

- Calculate and explain the use of the IRR of a project

Syllabus content

	Covered in chapter
Simple and compound interest	11
Discounting to find the present value	12
Annuities and perpetuities	12
Loans and mortgages	11, 12
Sinking funds and savings funds	11, 12
Simple investment appraisal	12

3c(v) Forecasting - 25%

Learning outcomes

On completion of their studies students should be able to:

- Calculate the correlation coefficient between 2 variables and explain the value

- Calculate the rank correlation coefficient between 2 sets of data and explain the value

- Explain the meaning of $100r^2$ (the coefficient of determination)

- Demonstrate the use of regression analysis between 2 variables to find the line of best fit, and explain its meaning

- Calculate a forecast of the value of the dependent variable, given the value of the independent variable

- Prepare a time series graph and identify trends and patterns

- Identify the components of a time series model

- Calculate the trend using a graph, moving averages or linear regression and be able to forecast the trend

- Calculate the seasonal variations for both additive and multiplicative models

- Calculate a forecast of the actual value using either the additive or the multiplicative model

- Explain the difference between the additive and multiplicative models, and when each is appropriate

- Calculate the seasonally adjusted values in a time series

- Explain the reliability of any forecasts made

Syllabus content

	Covered in chapter
• Correlation	14
• Simple linear regression	14
• Time series analysis – graphical analysis	13
• Calculation of trend using graph, moving averages and linear regression	13
• Seasonal variations – additive and multiplicative	13
• Forecasting	13

BPP PUBLISHING

THE PAPER-BASED EXAM

Format of the paper-based exam

		Number of marks
Section A:	Multiple choice questions	50
Section B:	Scenario-based objective test questions	50
		100

Time allowed: 2 hours

Multiple choice questions

Detailed guidance on how to tackle multiple choice questions is given on page (xxii).

Scenario-based objective test questions

Section B will be comprised of two or more scenarios and you will be asked several OT questions about each scenario.

There will be **no optional questions**, you will have to attempt all the questions in both sections.

CIMA has offered the following **guidance** about OT questions in the exam.

- **Only your answers will be marked**, not workings or any justifications.

- If you **exceed a specified limit on the number of words** you can use in an answer, you will **not be awarded any marks**.

- If you make **more than one attempt** at a question, clearly **cross through** any answers that you do not want to submit. If you don't do this, only your first answer will be marked.

We strongly suggest therefore, that you **take note of the guidance given above when answering OT questions in the paper-based exam.**

Further information relating to OTs is given on page (xxiii).

The Question Bank (paper-based exam) contains a selection of scenario-based objective test questions similar to the ones that you are likely to meet in your paper-based exam. When you have completed each chapter, try the relevant question(s) in the paper-based exam Question Bank – these are clearly indicated at the end of each chapter. If you have enough time, have a go at the OTs in the computer-based assessment Question Bank as well.

Analysis of papers

The analysis below shows the topics which have been examined under the current syllabus and included in the pilot paper for *Business Mathematics*. Note that the format of the paper-based exam changed with effect from the May 2002 sitting.

May 2002

Section A

1   Twenty five multiple choice questions covering various business mathematics topics

Section B

2   Investment appraisal
3   Time series analysis
4   Averages and dispersion; probability; correlation and index numbers

November 2001

Section A

1   Twenty five multiple choice questions covering various business mathematics topics

Section B

2   Regression analysis
3   Data presentation; averages and dispersion
4   Investment appraisal

May 2001

Section A

1   Twenty five multiple choice questions covering various business mathematics topics

Section B

2   Discounting
3   Times series analysis
4   Expected values

Pilot paper

Section A

1   Twenty five multiple choice questions covering various business mathematics topics.

Section B

2   Data presentation, averages and dispersion
3   Interest, discounting and index numbers
4   Correlation and regression

BPP PUBLISHING

COMPUTER-BASED ASSESSMENT

Format of the computer-based assessment (CBA)

The CBA will not be divided into sections. There will be a total of forty objective test questions and you will need to answer **ALL** of them in the time allowed, 1½ hours.

Frequently asked questions about CBA

Q   What are the main advantages of CBA?

A   • Assessments can be offered on a continuing basis rather than at six-monthly intervals

 • Instant feedback is provided for candidates by displaying their results on the computer screen

Q   Where can I take CBA?

A   • CBA must be taken at a 'CIMA Accredited CBA Centre'. For further information on CBA, you can email CIMA at cba@cimaglobal.com.

Q   How does CBA work?

A   • Questions are displayed on a monitor

 • Candidates enter their answers directly onto a computer

 • Candidates have 1½ hours to complete the *Business Mathematics* examination

 • The computer automatically marks the candidate's answers when the candidate has completed the examination

 • Candidates are provided with some indicative feedback on areas of weakness if the candidate is unsuccessful.

Q   What sort of questions can I expect to find in CBA?

Your exam will comprise entirely of a number of different types of **objective test question**. Here are some possible examples.

• **MCQs.** Read through the information on page (xxii) about MCQs and how to tackle them.

• **Data entry.** This type of OT requires you to provide figures such as the correct figure for creditors in a balance sheet.

• **Hot spots.** This question format might ask you to identify which cell on a spreadsheet contains a particular formula or where on a graph marginal revenue equals marginal cost.

• **Multiple response.** These questions provide you with a number of options and you have to identify those which fulfil certain criteria.

• **Matching.** This OT question format could ask you to classify particular costs into one of a range of cost classifications provided, to match descriptions of variances with one of a number of variances listed, and so on.

This text provides you with **plenty of opportunities to practise** these various question types. You will find OTs **within each chapter** in the text, the **Quick quizzes** at the end of each chapter are full of them. The Question Bank (computer-based assessment) contains more than fifty five objective test questions similar to the ones that you are likely to meet in your CBA.

Further information relating to OTs is given on page (xxiii).

The **Practice and Revision Kit** for this paper was published in **January 2002** and is **full of OTs,** providing you with vital revision opportunities at the fundamental techniques and skills you will require in the exam.

BPP PUBLISHING

TACKLING MULTIPLE CHOICE QUESTIONS

The MCQs in your exam contain four possible answers. You have to **choose the option that best answers the question**. The three incorrect options are called distracters. There is a skill in answering MCQs quickly and correctly. By practising MCQs you can develop this skill, giving you a better chance of passing the exam.

You may wish to follow the approach outlined below, or you may prefer to adapt it.

Step 1.   Skim read all the MCQs and identify what appear to be the easier questions.

Step 2.   Attempt each question – **starting with the easier questions** identified in Step 1. Read the question thoroughly. You may prefer to work out the answer before looking at the options, or you may prefer to look at the options at the beginning. Adopt the method that works best for you.

Step 3.   Read the four options and see if one matches your own answer. Be careful with numerical questions, as the distracters are designed to match answers that incorporate common errors. Check that your calculation is correct. Have you followed the requirement exactly? Have you included every stage of the calculation?

Step 4.   You may find that none of the options matches your answer.

- Re-read the question to ensure that you understand it and are answering the requirement

- Eliminate any obviously wrong answers

- Consider which of the remaining answers is the most likely to be correct and select the option

Step 5.   If you are still unsure make a note and continue to the next question.

Step 6.   Revisit unanswered questions. When you come back to a question after a break you often find you are able to answer it correctly straight away. If you are still unsure have a guess. You are not penalised for incorrect answers, so **never leave a question unanswered!**

After extensive practice and revision of MCQs, you may find that you recognise a question when you sit the exam. Be aware that the detail and/or requirement may be different. If the question seems familiar read the requirement and options carefully – do not assume that it is identical.

TACKLING OBJECTIVE TEST QUESTIONS

What is an objective test question?

An objective test (**OT**) question is made up of some form of **stimulus,** usually a question, and a **requirement** to do something.

(a) **Filling in a blank or blanks in a sentence**

(b) **Listing items in rank order**

(c) **Stating a definition**

(d) **Identifying a key issue, term or figure**

(e) **Calculating a specific figure**

(f) **Completing gaps in a set of data where the relevant numbers can be calculated from the information given**

(g) **Identifying points/zones/ranges/areas on graphs or diagrams**

(h) **Matching items or statements**

(i) **Stating whether statements are true or false**

(j) **Writing brief (in a specified number of words) explanations to the data given**

Multiple choice questions (MCQs) – selecting the most appropriate option from a number of options provided – are the most common form of OT question. We looked at them in detail on page (xxii).

BPP PUBLISHING

Part A
Basic mathematics

Chapter 1

BASIC MATHEMATICAL TECHNIQUES

Topic list		Syllabus reference	Ability required
1	Integers, fractions and decimals	(i)	Application
2	Order of operations	(i)	Application
3	Percentages and ratios	(i)	Application
4	Roots and powers	(i)	Application
5	Geometric progressions	(iv)	Application

Introduction

Business mathematics is a foundation level paper which is designed to provide you with a number of mathematical and statistical concepts and techniques that you will need as you progress through your intermediate and final level papers.

This Study Text is divided into five sections. An outline of each section and why it is important for your CIMA Studies is shown below.

PART A: BASIC MATHEMATICS

PART B: SUMMARISING AND ANALYSING DATA

These two sections cover a number of techniques which are **fundamental** to your work as a management accountant.

PART C: PROBABILITY

Management accountants need to be aware of and to be able to estimate any **risk** and **uncertainty** which may be associated with the decisions that they make.

PART D: FINANCIAL MATHEMATICS

This section is an introduction to financial mathematics - a topic which is vitally important to the study of **financial management**.

PART E: FORECASTING

Finally, Part E introduces you to the mathematical techniques that are needed for forecasting - you will find these invaluable in your studies and work associated with **business planning**.

Many students do not have a mathematical background and so this chapter is intended to cover the basic mathematics that you will need for the **Business Mathematics** exam.

Even if you have done mathematics in the past don't ignore this chapter. Skim through it to make sure that you are aware of all the concepts and techniques covered. Since it provides the foundation for much of what is to follow it is an **extremely important chapter**.

BPP PUBLISHING

Learning outcomes covered in this chapter

- **Demonstrate** the order of operations in formulae, including the use of brackets, negative numbers, powers and roots
- **Calculate** percentages and proportions
- **Calculate** answers to appropriate significant figures or decimal places

Syllabus content covered in this chapter

- Use of formulae
- Percentages and ratios
- Rounding of numbers

---

1 INTEGERS, FRACTIONS AND DECIMALS

KEY TERMS

- An **integer** is a whole number and can be either positive or negative.
- **Fractions** and **decimals** are ways of showing parts of a whole.

1.1 Examples of integers are ..., –5, –4 , –3 , –2, –1, 0, 1, 2, 3, 4, 5, ...

Examples of fractions are ½, ¼, 19/35, 10/377, ...

Examples of decimals are 0.1, 0.25, 0.3135, ...

1.2 A fraction has a numerator (the number on the top line) and a denominator (the number on the bottom line).

$$\text{FRACTION} = \frac{\text{NUMERATOR}}{\text{DENOMINATOR}}$$

For example, the fraction ½ has a numerator equal to 1 and a denominator of 2.

1.3 A fraction can be turned into a decimal by dividing the numerator by the denominator. For example, the fraction ½ equates to 0.5, and the fraction ¼ equates to 0.25. When turning decimals into fractions, you need to remember that places after the decimal point stand for tenths, hundredths, thousandths and so on.

Significant figures and decimal places

1.4 Before we go any further, we should say something about significant figures and decimal places.

1.5 Sometimes a decimal number has too many figures in it for practical use. For example consider the fraction 6/9 which when turned into a decimal = 0.666666 recurring. This problem can be overcome by rounding the decimal number to a specific number of **significant figures** by discarding figures using the following rule.

If the first figure to be discarded is greater than or equal to five then add one to the previous figure. Otherwise the previous figure is unchanged.

1.6   Let's look at the fraction 6/9 again.

6/9 = 0.66666 (the dot above the last 6 means 'recurring' and tells us that there are an infinite number of 6s after the decimal point).

We could express 6/9 as a decimal in the following ways.

- Correct to three decimal places

  6/9 = 0.667

- Correct to three significant figures

  6/9 = 0.67

- Correct to four decimal places

  6/9 = 0.6667

- Correct to four significant figures

  6/9 = 0.667

Now have a look at the following examples which should reinforce the concepts of **significant figures** and **decimal places**.

1.7   EXAMPLE: SIGNIFICANT FIGURES

(a) 187.392 correct to five significant figures is 187.39

   Discarding a 2 causes nothing to be added to the 9.

(b) 187.392 correct to four significant figures is 187.4

   Discarding the 9 causes one to be added to the 3.

(c) 187.392 correct to three significant figures is 187

   Discarding a 3 causes nothing to be added to the 7.

1.8   EXAMPLE: DECIMAL PLACES

(a) 49.28723 correct to four decimal places is 49.2872

   Discarding a 3 causes nothing to be added to the 2.

(b) 49.28723 correct to three decimal places is 49.287

   Discarding a 2 causes nothing to be added to the 7.

(c) 49.28723 correct to two decimal places is 49.29

   Discarding the 7 causes 1 to be added to the 8.

(d) 49.28723 correct to one decimal place is 49.3

   Discarding the 8 causes 1 to be added to the 2.

Question 1

Using your calculator convert the fraction 29/35 into a decimal. Round your answer in the following ways.

(a) Correct to five significant figures
(b) Correct to four significant figures
(c) Correct to three significant figures

(d) Correct to two significant figures
(e) Correct to one significant figure
(f) Correct to five decimal places
(g) Correct to four decimal places
(h) Correct to three decimal places
(i) Correct to two decimal places
(j) Correct to one decimal place

Answer

29/35 = 0.82857142857

(a)	0.8286	(Discarding the 7 causes 1 to be added to the 5)
(b)	0.829	(Discarding the 5 causes 1 to be added to the 8)
(c)	0.83	(Discarding the 8 causes 1 to be added to the 2)
(d)	0.8	(Discarding the 2 causes nothing to be added to the 8)
(e)	1	(Discarding the 8 causes 1 to be added to the 0)
(f)	0.82857	(Discarding the 1 causes nothing to be added to the 7)
(g)	0.8286	(Discarding the 7 causes 1 to be added to the 5)
(h)	0.829	(Discarding the 5 causes 1 to be added to the 8)
(i)	0.83	(Discarding the 8 causes 1 to be added to the 2)
(j)	0.8	(Discarding the 2 causes nothing to be added to the 8)

Exam focus point

It is vitally important that you are able to perform calculations correct to a given number of significant figures or decimal places since examination questions will often state this as a requirement of the question. If you did not get all parts of Question 1 correct, work through Section 1 again and retry the question. Do not underestimate the importance of understanding significant figures and decimal places.

2 ORDER OF OPERATIONS

Brackets

2.1 Brackets are commonly used to indicate which parts of a mathematical expression should be grouped together, and calculated before other parts. In other words, brackets can indicate a **priority**, or an **order** in which calculations should be made. The rule is as follows.

(a) Do things in brackets before doing things outside them.

(b) Subject to rule (a), do things in this order.

- Powers and roots
- Multiplications and divisions, working from left to right
- Additions and subtractions, working from left to right

2.2 Brackets are used for the sake of clarity. Here are some examples.

(a) $3 + 6 \times 8 = 51$. This is the same as writing $3 + (6 \times 8) = 51$.

(b) $(3 + 6) \times 8 = 72$. The brackets indicate that we wish to multiply the sum of 3 and 6 by 8.

(c) $12 - 4 \div 2 = 10$. This is the same as writing $12 - (4 \div 2) = 10$ or $12 - (4/2) = 10$.

(d) $(12 - 4) \div 2 = 4$. The brackets tell us to do the subtraction first.

2.3 A figure outside a bracket may be multiplied by two or more figures inside a bracket, linked by addition or subtraction signs. Here is an example.

$5(6 + 8) = 5 \times (6 + 8) = 5 \times 6 + 5 \times 8 = 70$

This is the same as $5(14) = 5 \times 14 = 70$

The multiplication sign after the 5 can be omitted, as shown here $(5(6 + 8))$, but there is no harm in putting it in $(5 \times (6 + 8))$ if you want to.

Similarly:

$5(8 - 6) = 5(2) = 10$; or

$5 \times 8 - 5 \times 6 = 10$

2.4   When two sets of figures linked by addition or subtraction signs within brackets are multiplied together, each figure in one bracket is multiplied in turn by every figure in the second bracket. Thus:

$(8 + 4)(7 + 2) = (12)(9) = 108$ or

$8 \times 7 + 8 \times 2 + 4 \times 7 + 4 \times 2 = 56 + 16 + 28 + 8 = 108$

Negative numbers

2.5   When a negative number $(-p)$ is **added** to another number (q), the net effect is to **subtract** p from q.

     (a) $10 + (-6) = 10 - 6 = 4$ (b) $^-10 + (-6) = -10 - 6 = -16$

2.6   When a negative number $(-p)$ is **subtracted** from another number (q), the net effect is to **add** p to q.

     (a) $12 - (^-8) = 12 + 8 = 20$ (b) $-12 - (^-8) = -12 + 8 = -4$

2.7   When a negative number is **multiplied** or **divided** by another negative number, the result is a **positive** number.

     (a) $-8 \times (-4) = +32$ (b) $-18/(-3) = +6$

2.8   If there is only **one negative number** in a multiplication or division, the result is **negative**.

     (a) $^-8 \times 4 = -32$ (b) $3 \times (-2) = ^-6$ (c) $12/(^-4) = ^-3$ (d) $-20/5 = -4$

Question 2

Work out the following.

(a) $(72 - 8) - (-2 + 1)$ (c) $8(2 - 5) - (4 - (-8))$

(b) $\dfrac{88 + 8}{12} + \dfrac{(29 - 11)}{-2}$ (d) $\dfrac{-36}{9 - 3} - \dfrac{84}{3 - 10} - \dfrac{-81}{3}$

Answer

(a) $64 - (-1) = 64 + 1 = 65$ (c) $-24 - (12) = -36$

(b) $8 + (-9) = -1$ (d) $-6 - (-12) - (-27) = -6 + 12 + 27 = 33$

Reciprocals

> **KEY TERM**
>
> The **reciprocal** of a number is just 1 divided by that number.

2.9 For example, the reciprocal of 2 is 1 divided by 2 = $^1/_2$. The reciprocal of 3 is 1 divided by 3 = $^1/_3$.

Extra symbols

2.10 We will come across several other mathematical signs in this book but there are five which you should learn **now**.

(a) > means 'greater than'. So 46 > 29 is true, but 40 > 86 is false.
(b) ≥ means 'is greater than or equal to'. So 4 ≥ 3 and 4 ≥ 4.
(c) < means 'is less than'. So 29 < 46 is true, but 86 < 40 is false.
(d) ≤ means 'is less than or equal to'. So 7 ≤ 8 and 7 ≤ 7.
(e) ≠ means 'is not equal to'. So we could write 100.004 ≠ 100.

Question 3

Work out all answers to four decimal places, using a calculator.

(a) $(43 + 26.705) \times 9.3$

(b) $(844.2 \div 26) - 2.45$

(c) $\dfrac{45.6 - 13.92 + 823.1}{14.3 \times 112.5}$

(d) $\dfrac{303.3 + 7.06 \times 42.11}{1.03 \times 111.03}$

(e) $\dfrac{7.6 \times 1,010}{10.1 \times 76,000}$

(f) $(43.756 + 26.321) \div 171.036$

(g) $(43.756 + 26.321) \times 171.036$

(h) $171.45 + (-221.36) + 143.22$

(i) $66 - (-43.57) + (-212.36)$

(j) $\dfrac{10.1 \times 76,000}{7.6 \times 1,010}$

(k) $\dfrac{21.032 + (-31.476)}{3.27 \times 41.201}$

(l) $\dfrac{-33.33 - (-41.37)}{11.21 + (-24.32)}$

(m) $\dfrac{-10.75 \times (-15.44)}{-14.25 \times 17.15} + \left(\dfrac{16.23}{8.4 + 3.002}\right)$

(n) $\dfrac{-7.366 \times 921.3}{10,493 - 2,422.8} - \left(\dfrac{8.4 + 3.002}{16.23}\right)$

Answer

(a) 648.2565

(b) 30.0192

(c) 0.5313

(d) 5.2518

(e) 0.01

(f) 0.4097

(g) 11,985.6898

(h) 93.31

(i) –102.79

(j) 100 (Note that this question is the reciprocal of part (e), and so the answer is the reciprocal of the answer to part (e).)

(k) –0.0775

(l) –0.6133

(m) 0.7443

(n) –1.5434

3 PERCENTAGES AND RATIOS

3.1 Percentages are used to indicate the **relative size** or **proportion** of items, rather than their **absolute** size. For example, if one office employs ten accountants, six secretaries and four supervisors, the **absolute** values of staff numbers and the **percentage** of the total work force in each type would be as follows.

	Accountants	*Secretaries*	*Supervisors*	*Total*
Absolute numbers	10	6	4	20
Percentages	50%	30%	20%	100%

3.2 The idea of percentages is that the whole of something can be thought of as 100%. The whole of a cake, for example, is 100%. If you share it out equally with a friend, you will get half each, or 100%/2 = 50% each.

3.3 To turn a percentage into a fraction or decimal you divide by 100%. To turn a fraction or decimal back into a percentage you multiply by 100%. Consider the following.

(a) $0.16 = 0.16 \times 100\% = 16\%$
(b) $^4/_5 = 4/5 \times 100\% = {}^{400}/_5\% = 80\%$
(c) $40\% = {}^{40\%}/_{100\%} = {}^2/_5 = 0.4$

3.4 You may encounter a number of situations involving percentages. Here are some examples.

(a) **Find X% of Y**

   Question: What is 40% of £64?

   Answer: 40% of £64 = 0.4 × £64 = £25.60.

(b) **Express X as a percentage of Y**

   Question: What is £16 as a percentage of £64?

   Answer: £16 as a percentage of £64 $= \dfrac{16}{64} \times 100\% = \dfrac{1}{4} \times 100\% = 25\%$

   In other words, put the £16 as a fraction of the £64, and then multiply by 100%.

(c) **Find the original value of X, given that after a percentage increase of Y% it is equal to X_1**

   Question: Fred Bloggs' salary is now £60,000 per annum after an annual increase of 20%. What was his annual salary before the increase?

   Answer:
Fred Bloggs' salary *before* increase (original)	100%
Salary increase	20%
Fred Bloggs' salary after increase (final)	120%

   We know that Fred's salary after the increase (final) also equals £60,000.

   Therefore 120% = £60,000.

   We need to find his salary *before* the increase (original), ie 100%.

   We can do this as follows.

Step 1.   **Calculate 1%**

If 120% = £60,000

1% = $\dfrac{£60,000}{120}$

1% = £500

Step 2.   **Calculate 100% (original)**

If 1% = £500

100% = £500 × 100

100% = £50,000

Therefore, Fred Bloggs' annual salary before the increase was £50,000.

(d) **Find the final value of A, given that after a percentage increase/decrease of B% it is equal to A$_1$**

Question: If sales receipts in year 1 are £500,000 and there was a percentage decrease of 10% in year 2, what are the sales receipts in year 2?

Answer: Adopt the step-by-step approach used in part (c) as follows.

Sales receipts - year 1 (original)	100%
Percentage decrease	–10%
Sales receipts - year 2 (final)	90%

This question is slightly different to that in part (c) because we have the original value (100%) and not the final value as in part (c).

We know that sales receipts in year 1 (original) also equal £500,000.

We need to find the sales receipts in year 2 (final). We can do this as follows.

Step 1.   **Calculate 1%**

If 100% = £500,000

1% = £5,000

Step 2.   **Calculate 90% (original)**

If 1% = £5,000

90% = £5,000 × 90

90% = £450,000

Therefore, sales receipts in year 2 are £450,000.

3.5 You might think that the calculations involved in parts (c) and (d) above are long-winded but it is vitally important that you understand how to perform these types of calculation. As you become more confident with calculating percentages you may not need to go through all of the steps that we have shown. The key to answering these types of question correctly is to be very clear about which values represent the **original** amount (100%) and which values represent the **final** amount (100 + x%).

	Increase	*Decrease*
	%	%
ORIGINAL VALUE	100	100
INCREASE/(DECREASE)	x	–x
FINAL VALUE	100 + x	100 – x

3.6 You might also be required to calculate the value of the **percentage change**, ie in 3.4(c) you may have been required to calculate the percentage increase in Fred Bloggs' salary, or in part (d) you may have been required to calculate the percentage decrease of sales receipts in year 2 (as compared with year 1).

The formula required for calculating the **percentage change** is as follows.

$$\text{Percentage change} = \frac{\text{'Change'}}{\text{Original}} \times 100\%$$

Note that it is the **original value** that the change is compared with and not the final value when calculating the percentage change.

Discounts

3.7 The calculation of discounts requires an ability to manipulate percentages. The example which follows will illustrate the technique.

3.8 EXAMPLE: DISCOUNTS

A travel agent is offering a 17% discount on the brochure price of a particular holiday to America. The brochure price of the holiday is £795.

Required

Calculate the price being offered by the travel agent.

3.9 SOLUTION

Let 100% = £795

$$\therefore 1\% = \frac{100\%}{100} = \frac{£795}{100} = £7.95$$

$$\therefore 17\% = 17 \times 1\% = 17 \times £7.95 = £135.15$$

$$\therefore \text{Price offered} = £(795 - 135.15) = £659.85$$

Alternatively, price offered = £795 × (100 – 17)% = £795 × 83% = £795 × 0.83 = £659.85

Question 4

A television has been reduced from £490.99 to £340.99. What is the percentage reduction in price to three decimal places?

| A | 30.550 | B | 30.551 | C | 43.990 | D | 43.989 |

Answer

Difference in price = £(490.99 – 340.99) = £150.00

$$\text{Percentage reduction} = \frac{\text{change}}{\text{original price}} \times 100\% = \frac{150}{490.99} \times 100\% = 30.551\%$$

The correct answer is B.

Question 5

Three years ago a retailer sold action man toys for £17.50 each. At the end of the first year he increased the price by 6% and at the end of the second year by a further 5%. At the end of the third year the selling price was £20.06. The percentage price change in year three was

| A | −3% | B | +3% | C | −6% | D | +9% |

Answer

Selling price at end of year 1 =   £17.50 × 1.06 = £18.55

Selling price at end of year 2 =   £18.55 × 1.05 = £19.48

Change in selling price in year 3 =   £(20.06 − 19.48) = £0.58

∴ Percentage change in year 3 was $\dfrac{£0.58}{£19.48}$ × 100% = £2.97%, say 3%

The correct answer is B.

Profits

3.10   You may be required in your examination to calculate profit, selling price or cost of sale of an item or number of items from certain information. To do this you need to remember the following crucial formula.

	%
Cost of sales	100
Plus Profit	25
Equals Sales	125

Profit may be expressed either as a percentage of **cost of sales** (such as 25% ($^{25}/_{100}$) mark-up) or as a percentage of **sales** (such as 20% ($^{25}/_{125}$) margin).

If profit is expressed as a percentage of sales (**margin**) the following formula is also useful.

	%
Selling price	100
Profit	20
Cost of sales	80

It is best to think of the selling price as 100% if profit is expressed as a **margin** (percentage of sales). On the other hand, if profit is expressed as a percentage of cost of sales (**mark-up**) it is best to think of the cost of sales as being 100%. The following examples should help to clarify this point.

3.11 EXAMPLE: PROFITS AND PERCENTAGES

Delilah's Dresses sells a dress at a 10% margin. The dress cost the shop £100. Calculate the profit made by Delilah's Dresses.

3.12 SOLUTION

The margin is 10% (ie ($^{10}/_{100}$))

∴ Let selling price = 100%

∴ Profit = 10%

∴ Cost   = 90% = £100

∴ 1%   = (£100/90)

∴ 10% = profit = £100/90 × 10 = £11.11

3.13 EXAMPLE: PERCENTAGES AND PROFITS

Trevor's Trousers sells a pair of trousers for £80 at a 15% mark-up.

Required

Calculate the profit made by Trevor's Trousers.

3.14 SOLUTION

The markup is 15%.

∴ Let cost of sales = 100%
∴ Profit = 15%
∴ Selling price   = 115% = £80
∴ 1% = (£80/115)
∴ 15% = profit = (£80/115) × 15 = £10.43

Proportions

> ### KEY TERM
>
> A **proportion** means writing a percentage as a proportion of 1 (that is, as a decimal).
>
> 100% can be thought of as the whole, or 1. 50% is half of that, or 0.5.

3.15 Suppose there are 14 women in an audience of 70. What proportion of the audience are men?

Number of men = 70 − 14 = 56

Proportion of men = $\frac{56}{70}$ = $\frac{8}{10}$ = 80% = 0.8

- The **fraction** of the audience made up of men is $^8/10$ or $^4/5$.
- The **percentage** of the audience made up of men is 80%.
- The **proportion** of the audience made up of men is 0.8.

Question 6

There are 30 students in a class room, 17 of whom have blonde hair. What proportion of the students (to four decimal places) do not have blonde hair (delete as appropriate).

0.5667	0.5666
0.4334	0.4333

Answer

~~0.5667~~	~~0.5666~~
~~0.4334~~	0.4333

$(30 - 17)/30 \times 100\% = 43.33\% = 0.4333$

Question 7

A skirt which cost the retailer £75 is sold at a profit of 25% on the selling price. The profit is therefore

A	£18.75	B	£20.00	C	£25.00	D	£30.00

Answer

Let selling price = 100%

Profit = 25% of selling price

∴ Cost = 75% of selling price

Cost = £75 = 75%

$$\therefore 1\% = \frac{£75}{75}$$

$$\therefore 25\% = \text{profit} = \frac{£75}{75} \times 25 = £25$$

The correct answer is C.

Ratios

3.16 Suppose Tom has £12 and Dick has £8. The **ratio** of Tom's cash to Dick's cash is 12:8. This can be cancelled down, just like a fraction, to 3:2. Study the following examples carefully.

3.17 EXAMPLE: RATIOS

Suppose Tom and Dick wish to share £20 out in the ratio 3:2. How much will each receive?

3.18 SOLUTION

Because $3 + 2 = 5$, we must divide the whole up into five equal parts, then give Tom three parts and Dick two parts.

(a) £20 ÷ 5 = £4 (so each part is £4)

(b) Tom's share = 3 × £4 = £12

(c) Dick's share = 2 × £4 = £8

(d) **Check:** £12 + £8 = £20 (adding up the two shares in the answer gets us back to the £20 in the question)

This method of calculating ratios as amounts works no matter how many ratios are involved.

3.19 EXAMPLE: RATIOS AGAIN

A, B, C and D wish to share £600 in the ratio 6:1:2:3. How much will each receive?

3.20 SOLUTION

(a) Number of parts = 6 + 1 + 2 + 3 = 12

(b) Value of each part   = £600 ÷ 12 = £50

(c) A: 6 × £50   = £300
     B: 1 × £50   = £50
     C: 2 × £50   = £100
     D: 3 × £50   = £150

(d) **Check:** £300 + £50 + £100 + £150 = £600

Question 8

Tom, Dick and Harry wish to share out £800. Calculate how much each would receive if the ratio used was:

(a) 3 : 2 : 5
(b) 5 : 3 : 2
(c) 3 : 1 : 1

Answer

(a) Total parts = 10
     Each part is worth £800 ÷ 10 = £80
     Tom gets   3 × £80 = £240
     Dick gets   2 × £80 = £160
     Harry gets   5 × £80 = £400

(b) Same parts as (i) but in a different order.
     Tom gets   £400
     Dick gets   £240
     Harry gets   £160

(c) Total parts = 5
     Each part is worth £800 ÷ 5 = £160
     Therefore Tom gets £480
     Dick and Harry each get £160

---

4   ROOTS AND POWERS

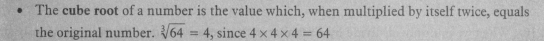

KEY TERMS

- The **square root** of a number is a value which, when multiplied by itself, equals the original number. $\sqrt{9} = 3$, since $3 \times 3 = 9$

- The **cube root** of a number is the value which, when multiplied by itself twice, equals the original number. $\sqrt[3]{64} = 4$, since $4 \times 4 \times 4 = 64$

- The **nth root** of a number is a value which, when multiplied by itself $(n - 1)$ times, equals the original number.

4.1 **Powers** work the other way round to roots.

Thus the 6th power of $2 = 2^6 = 2 \times 2 \times 2 \times 2 \times 2 \times 2 = 64$.

Similarly, $3^4 = 3 \times 3 \times 3 \times 3 = 81$.

Since $\sqrt{9} = 3$, it also follows that $3^2 = 9$, and since $\sqrt[3]{64} = 4$, $4^3 = 64$.

Part A: Basic mathematics

4.2 When a number with an index (a 'to the power of' value) is multiplied by the **same** number with the same or a different index, the result is that number to the power of the **sum** of the indices.

(a) $5^2 \times 5 = 5^2 \times 5^1 = 5^{(2+1)} = 5^3 = 125$

(b) $4^3 \times 4^3 = 4^{(3+3)} = 4^6 = 4{,}096$

4.3 Similarly, when a number with an index is divided by the **same** number with the same or a different index, the result is that number to the power of the first index **minus** the second index.

(a) $6^4 \div 6^3 = 6^{(4-3)} = 6^1 = 6$

(b) $7^8 \div 7^6 = 7^{(8-6)} = 7^2 = 49$

4.4 When a number with an index x is raised to the power y, the result is the number raised to the power xy.

The powers are simply multiplied together.

(a) $(2^2)^3 = 2^{2\times3} = 2^6 = 64$

(b) $(5^3)^3 = 5^{3\times3} = 5^9 = 1{,}953{,}125$

4.5 Any figure to the power of one always equals itself: $2^1 = 2$, $3^1 = 3$, $4^1 = 4$ and so on.

4.6 Any figure to the power of **zero** always equals **one**. $1^0 = 1$, $2^0 = 1$, $3^0 = 1$, $4^0 = 1$ and so on.

4.7 One to any power always equals one. $1^2 = 1$, $1^3 = 1$, $1^4 = 1$ and so on.

4.8 An index can be a **fraction**, as in $16^{\frac{1}{2}}$. What $16^{\frac{1}{2}}$ means is the square root of 16 ($\sqrt{16}$ or 4). If we multiply $16^{\frac{1}{2}}$ by $16^{\frac{1}{2}}$ we get $16^{(\frac{1}{2}+\frac{1}{2})}$ which equals 16^1 and thus 16.

Similarly, $216^{\frac{1}{3}}$ is the cube root of 216 (which is 6) because $216^{\frac{1}{3}} \times 216^{\frac{1}{3}} \times 216^{\frac{1}{3}} = 216^{(\frac{1}{3}+\frac{1}{3}+\frac{1}{3})} = 216^1 = 216$.

4.9 An index can be a **negative** value. The negative sign represents a **reciprocal**. Thus 2^{-1} is the reciprocal of, or one over, 2^1.

$$2^{-1} = \frac{1}{2^1} = \frac{1}{2}$$

Likewise $2^{-2} = \frac{1}{2^2} = \frac{1}{4}$; $2^{-3} = \frac{1}{2^3} = \frac{1}{8}$; $5^{-6} = \frac{1}{5^6} = \frac{1}{15{,}625}$

4.10 When we multiply or divide by a number with a negative index, the rules previously stated still apply.

(a) $9^2 \times 9^{-2} = 9^{(2+(-2))} = 9^0 = 1$ (That is, $9^2 \times \frac{1}{9^2} = 1$)

(b) $4^5 \div 4^{-2} = 4^{(5-(-2))} = 4^7 = 16{,}384$

(c) $3^8 \times 3^{-5} = 3^{(8-5)} = 3^3 = 27$

(d) $3^{-5} \div 3^{-2} = 3^{-5-(-2)} = 3^{-3} = \frac{1}{3^3} = \frac{1}{27}$. (This could be re-expressed as $\frac{1}{3^5} \div \frac{1}{3^2} = \frac{1}{3^5} \times 3^2 = \frac{1}{3^3}$.)

4.11 A fraction might have a power applied to it. In this situation, the main point to remember is that the power must be applied to both the top and the bottom of the fraction.

(a) $(2^{1}/_{3})^{3} = (\frac{7}{3})^{3} = \frac{7^{3}}{3^{3}} = \frac{343}{27}$

(b) $(5^{2}/_{5})^{-4} = (\frac{27}{5})^{-4} = \frac{1}{(27/_{5})^{4}} = \frac{1}{27^{4}/_{5^{4}}} = \frac{5^{4}}{27^{4}} = \frac{625}{531,441}$

4.12 The main rules relating to roots and powers can be summarised as follows.

(a) When **multiplying** the same number with the same or different index, **add the powers together** $(2^{2} \times 2^{2} = 2^{2+2} = 2^{4})$

(b) When dividing the same number with the same or different index, **subtract the powers** $(2^{3} \div 2^{2} = 2^{3-2} = 2^{1})$

(c) When raising one power to another, the **powers are multiplied together** $((2^{2})^{3} = 2^{2 \times 3} = 2^{6})$

(d) $x^{0} = 1$ (always)

(e) $x^{1} = x$ (always)

(f) $1^{x} = 1$ (always)

(g) A **negative index** represents a **reciprocal** and is the same as a positive index divided by 1 $(2^{-3} = \frac{1}{2^{3}})$

(h) When index numbers are applied to fractions, apply the power to both the top and the bottom of the fraction $((2^{1}/_{2})^{2} = (^{5}/_{2})^{2} = {^{5^{2}}}/_{2^{2}})$

Question 9

Work out the following, using your calculator as necessary.

(a) $(18.6)^{2.6}$

(b) $(18.6)^{-2.6}$

(c) $\sqrt[2.6]{18.6}$

(d) $(14.2)^{4} \times (14.2)^{\frac{1}{4}}$

(e) $(14.2)^{4} + (14.2)^{\frac{1}{4}}$

Answer

(a) $(18.6)^{2.6} = 1{,}998.64$

(b) $(18.6)^{-2.6} = \left(\frac{1}{18.6}\right)^{2.6} = 0.0005$

(c) $= \sqrt[2.6]{18.6} = 3.078$

(d) $(14.2)^{4} \times (14.2)^{\frac{1}{4}} = (14.2)^{4.25} = 78{,}926.98$

(e) $(14.2)^{4} + (14.2)^{\frac{1}{4}} = 40{,}658.69 + 1.9412 = 40{,}660.631$

BPP PUBLISHING

5   GEOMETRIC PROGRESSIONS

KEY TERM

A **geometric progression** is a sequence of numbers in which there is a common or constant ratio between adjacent terms. An algebraic representation of a **geometric progression** is as follows.

$A, AR, AR^2, AR^3, AR^4, ..., AR^{n-1}$

where   A   is the first term
           R   is the common ratio
           n   is the number of terms

5.1   Examples of geometric progressions are as follows.

(a)   2, 4, 8, 16, 32, where there is a common ratio of 2.

(b)   121, 110, 100, 90.91, 82.64, where (allowing for rounding differences in the fourth and fifth terms) there is a common ratio of $1/1.1 = 0.9091$.

5.2   EXAMPLE: A GEOMETRIC PROGRESSION

A sales manager has reported that sales in the next year will amount to 5,000 units of product. He also estimates that sales will then increase in volume by 40% a year until year 6. What sales volume would be expected in year 6?

5.3   SOLUTION

We require the sixth term in the geometric progression.

A   =   year 1 sales = 5,000
R   =   rate of growth = 140% (Note that R = 140% or 1.4, not 40% or 0.4.)
n   =   6
T_6 = $5,000 \times 1.4^{(6-1)}$
     = $5,000 \times 5.37824$
     =   26,891.2 units (say 26,891 units)

The sum of a geometric progression

5.4   It is sometimes necessary to calculate the sum of the terms in a geometric progression. For example, suppose that a factory expects to produce 4,000 units in week 1 and to increase output by 20% each week for three more weeks.

Total output in the four weeks = 4,000 + 4,800 + 5,760 + 6,912 = 21,472 units

5.5   The calculation is relatively straightforward when the progression consists of a small number of terms. However, when we wish to calculate the sum of longer geometric progressions, it is easier to use a formula.

FORMULA TO LEARN

The formula for the sum (S) of a **geometric progression** is derived as follows.

$$S = A + AR + AR^2 + AR^3 + \ldots + AR^{n-1} \quad (1)$$

Multiply both sides of the equation by R to give:

$$RS = AR + AR^2 + AR^3 + \ldots + AR^n \quad (2)$$

Subtract (1) from (2).

$$RS - S = AR^n - A$$

$$\therefore S(R - 1) = A(R^n - 1)$$

$$\therefore S = \frac{A(R^n - 1)}{R - 1}$$

5.6   In the example in Paragraph 5.4, we have the following.

$$S = 4{,}000 + 4{,}000 \times 1.2 + 4{,}000 \times 1.2^2 + 4{,}000 \times 1.2^3$$

$$1.2S = 4{,}000 \times 1.2 + 4{,}000 \times 1.2^2 + 4{,}000 \times 1.2^3 + 4{,}000 \times 1.2^4$$

$$1.2S - S = (4{,}000 \times 1.2^4) - 4{,}000$$

$$S = \frac{4{,}000(1.2^4 - 1)}{(1.2 - 1)}$$

$$= +21{,}472 \text{ units}$$

Exam focus point

You are unlikely to encounter a whole question based on the topics covered in this chapter - but you will find that many questions will draw on these skills.

Chapter roundup

- **Brackets** indicate a priority or an order in which calculations should be made.

- The **negative number rules** are as follows.

  $-p + q = q - p$

  $q - (-p) = q + p$

  $-p \times -q = pq$ and $^{-p}/_{-q} = {}^p/_q$

  $-p \times q = -pq$ and $^{-p}/_q = -{}^p/_q$

- The **reciprocal** of a number is 1 divided by that number.

- **Percentages** are used to indicate the relative size or proportion of items, rather than their absolute size. To turn a percentage into a fraction or decimal you divide by 100%. To turn a fraction or decimal back into a percentage you multiply by 100%.

- A **percentage increase** or **reduction** is calculated as (difference ÷ initial value) × 100%.

- A **proportion** means writing a percentage as a proportion of 1 (that is, as a decimal).

- **Ratios** show relative shares of a whole.

- The **nth root** of a number is a value which, when multiplied by itself $(n-1)$ times, equals the original number. Powers work the other way round.

- The main rules to apply when dealing with powers and roots are as follows.

  ○ $2^x \times 2^y = 2^{x+y}$

  ○ $2^x \div 2^y = 2^{x-y}$

  ○ $(2^x)^y = 2^{x \times y} = 2^{xy}$

  ○ $x^0 = 1$

  ○ $x^1 = x$

  ○ $1^x = 1$

  ○ $2^{-x} = \frac{1}{2}^x$

  ○ $(1\frac{1}{2})^x = (\frac{3}{2})^x = \frac{3^x}{2^x}$

- A **geometric progression** is a sequence of numbers in which there is a common ratio between adjacent terms.

Quick quiz

1   $3^3/_4$ is an **integer/fraction/decimal**

2   1004.002955 to nine significant figures is …………

3   The product of a negative number and a negative number is

Positive   ☐

Negative   ☐

4   $217 \le 217$

True   ☐

False   ☐

5   To turn a percentage into a fraction or decimal you must

    A   Divide by 100%
    B   Multiply by 100%
    C   Divide by 100
    D   Multiply by 100

6   3^{-1} can also be written as

    A 3^{-1}
    B 3^{1}
    C $^{1}/_{3}$
    D -1^{3}

Answers to quick quiz

1   Fraction

2   1004.00296

3   Positive

4   True

5   A

6    $C = {}^{1}/_{3}$

Now try the following objective test questions

Question bank	Question numbers	Page
Paper-based exam	1	271
Computer-based assessment	1	291

BPP PUBLISHING

Chapter 2

FORMULAE AND EQUATIONS

Topic list		Syllabus reference	Ability required
1	Formulae and equations	(i)	Application
2	Linear equations	(i)	Application
3	Linear equations and graphs	(i)	Application
4	Simultaneous and non-linear equations	(i)	Application

Introduction

You are over the moon. You have just been awarded a £1,000 pay rise. If the man on the Clapham omnibus asks you to explain your new salary in terms of your old salary, what would you say? You might say something like 'my new salary equals my old salary plus £1,000'. Easy. What would you say, on the other hand, to the mathematics professor who asks you to give a mathematical equation which describes your new salary in terms of your old salary? Like many students, you may be perfectly capable of answering the man on the omnibus, but not the professor. Your reply to the professor should be something like 'y = x + 1,000' but many students get completely confused when they have to deal with mathematical symbols and letters instead of simple words. There is, however, no need to worry about equations: they are simply a shorthand method of expressing words. Work through this chapter and it should help to make things clearer.

Learning outcomes covered in this chapter

- **Solve** simple equations, including two variable simultaneous equations and quadratic equations

- **Prepare** graphs of linear and quadratic equations

Syllabus content covered in this chapter

- Basic algebraic techniques and the solution of equations - including simultaneous and quadratic equations

1 FORMULAE AND EQUATIONS

Formulae

1.1 So far all our problems formulated entirely in terms of specific numbers. However, think back to when you were calculating powers with your calculator in Chapter 1. You probably used the x^y key on your calculator. x and y stood for whichever numbers we happened to have in our problem, for example, 3 and 4 if we wanted to work out 3^4. When we use letters like this to stand for any numbers we call them **variables**. When we work out 3^4, x stands for 3. When we work out 7^2, x will stand for 7: its value can vary.

1.2   The use of variables enables us to state general truths about mathematics.

For example:

- x   =   x
- x^2 =   x × x
- If y   =   0.5 × x, then x = 2 × y

These will be true **whatever** values x and y have. For example, let y = 0.5 × x

- If y = 3, x = 2 × y = 6
- If y = 7, x = 2 × y = 14
- If y = 1, x = 2 × y = 2, and so on for any other choice of a value for y.

1.3   We can use **variables** to build up useful **formulae**, we can then put in values for the variables, and get out a value for something we are interested in.

1.4   Let us consider an example. For a business, profit = revenue – costs. Since revenue = selling price × units sold, we can say that

profit = selling price × units sold – costs.

'Selling price × units sold – costs' is a formula for profit.

We can then use single letters to make the formula quicker to write.

Let   x   =   profit
      p   =   selling price
      u   =   units sold
      c   =   cost

Then x = p × u – c.

If we are then told that in a particular month, p = £5, u = 30 and c = £118, we can find out the month's profit.

Profit   =   x = p × u – c = £5 × 30 – £118
         =   £150 – £118 = £32

1.5   It is usual when writing formulae to leave out multiplication signs between letters. Thus p × u – c can be written as pu – c. We will also write (for example) 2x instead of 2 × x.

Equations

1.6   In the above example, pu – c was a formula for profit. If we write x = pu – c, we have written an **equation**. It says that one thing (profit, x) is **equal** to another (pu – c).

1.7   Sometimes, we are given an equation with numbers filled in for all but one of the variables. The problem is then to find the number which should be filled in for the last variable. This is called **solving the equation**.

1.8   (a)   Returning to x = pu – c, we could be told that for a particular month p = £4, u = 60 and c = £208. We would then have the **equation** x = £4 × 60 – £208. We can solve this easily by working out £4 × 60 – £208 = £240 – £208 = £32. Thus x = £32.

   (b)   On the other hand, we might have been told that in a month when profits were £172, 50 units were sold and the selling price was £7. The thing we have not been told is the month's costs, c. We can work out c by writing out the equation.

BPP
PUBLISHING

$$£172 = £7 \times 50 - c$$
$$£172 = £350 - c$$

We need c to be such that when it is taken away from £350 we have £172 left. With a bit of trial and error, we can get to c = £178.

The rule for solving equations

1.9 To solve an equation, we need to get it into the following form.

Unknown variable = something with just numbers in it, which we can work out.

We therefore want to get the unknown variable on one side of the = sign, and everything else on the other side.

1.10 **The rule is that you can do what you like to one side of an equation, so long as you do the same thing to the other side straightaway. The two sides are equal, and they will stay equal so long as you treat them in the same way.**

1.11 For example, you can do any of the following: add 37 to both sides; subtract 3x from both sides; multiply both sides by –4.329; divide both sides by (x + 2); take the reciprocal of both sides; square both sides; take the cube root of both sides.

We can do any of these things to an equation either before or after filling in numbers for the variables for which we have values.

1.12 (a) If £172 = £350 – c   (as in Paragraph 1.8) we can then get

           £172 + c = £350   (add c to each side)

           c = £350 – £172   (subtract £172 from each side)

           c = £178   (work out the right hand side)

    (b)   450 = 3x + 72   (initial equation: x unknown)

        450 – 72 = 3x   (add 72 to each side)

$$\frac{450 - 72}{3} = x \qquad \text{(divide each side by 3)}$$

        126 = x   (work out the left hand side)

    (c)   3y + 2 = 5y – 7   (initial equation: y unknown)

         3y + 9 = 5y   (add 7 to each side)

              9 = 2y   (subtract 3y from each side)

           4.5 = y   (divide each side by 2)

    (d)

$$\frac{\sqrt{3x^2 + x}}{2\sqrt{x}} = 7 \qquad \text{(initial equation: x unknown)}$$

$$\frac{3x^2 + x}{4x} = 49 \qquad \text{(square each side)}$$

$$(3x + 1)/4 = 49 \qquad \text{(cancel x in the numerator and the denominator of the left hand side: this does not affect the value of the left hand side, so we do not need to change the right hand side)}$$

          3x + 1 = 196   (multiply each side by 4)

              3x = 195   (subtract 1 from each side)

                x = 65   (divide each side by 3)

(e)   Our example in Paragraph 1.6 was x = pu – c. We could change this, so as to give a formula for p.

$$x = pu - c$$

$$x + c = pu \qquad \text{(add c to each side)}$$

$$\frac{x+c}{u} = p \qquad \text{(divide each side by u)}$$

$$p = \frac{x+c}{u} \qquad \text{(swap the sides for ease of reading)}$$

Given values for x, c and u we can now find p. We have rearranged the equation to give p in terms of x, c and u.

(f)   Given that $y = \sqrt{3x + 7}$, we can get an equation giving x in terms of y.

$$y = \sqrt{3x + 7}$$

$$y^2 = 3x + 7 \qquad \text{(square each side)}$$

$$y^2 - 7 = 3x \qquad \text{(subtract 7 from each side)}$$

$$x = \frac{y^2 - 7}{3} \qquad \text{(divide each side by 3, and swap the sides for ease of reading)}$$

1.13   In equations, you may come across expressions like 3(x + 4y – 2) (that is, 3 × (x + 4y – 2)). These can be re-written in separate bits without the brackets, simply by multiplying the number outside the brackets by each item inside them. Thus 3(x + 4y – 2) = 3x + 12y – 6.

Question 1

(a)   If 47x + 256 = 52x, then x =

(b)   If $4\sqrt{x}$ + 32 = 40.6718, then x =

(c)   If $\dfrac{1}{3x + 4} = \dfrac{5}{2.7x - 2}$, then x =

Answer

(a)

| x = 51.2 |

$$47x + 256 = 52x$$

$$256 = 5x \qquad \text{(subtract 47x from each side)}$$

$$51.2 = x \qquad \text{(divide each side by 5)}$$

(b)

| x = 4.7 |

$$4\sqrt{x} + 32 = 40.6718$$

$$4\sqrt{x} = 8.6718 \qquad \text{(subtract 32 from each side)}$$

$$\sqrt{x} = 2.16795 \qquad \text{(divide each side by 4)}$$

$$x = 4.7 \qquad \text{(square each side).}$$

(c)

| x = –1.789 |

BPP PUBLISHING

$$\frac{1}{3x+4} = \frac{5}{2.7x-2}$$

$3x + 4 = \dfrac{2.7x-2}{5}$ (take the reciprocal of each side)

$15x + 20 = 2.7x - 2$ (multiply each side by 5)

$12.3x = -22$ (subtract 20 and subtract 2.7x from each side)

$x = -1.789$ (divide each side by 12.3).

Question 2

(a) Rearrange $x = (3y - 20)^2$ to get an expression for y in terms of x.
(b) Rearrange $2(y - 4) - 4(x^2 + 3) = 0$ to get an expression for x in terms of y.

Answer

(a) $x = (3y - 20)^2$

     $\sqrt{x} = 3y - 20$ (take the square root of each side)

     $20 + \sqrt{x} = 3y$ (add 20 to each side)

     $y = \dfrac{20 + \sqrt{x}}{3}$ (divide each side by 3, and swap the sides for ease of reading)

(b) $2(y - 4) - 4(x^2 + 3) = 0$

     $2(y - 4) = 4(x^2 + 3)$ (add $4(x^2 + 3)$ to each side)

     $0.5(y - 4) = x^2 + 3$ (divide each side by 4)

     $0.5(y - 4) - 3 = x^2$ (subtract 3 from each side)

     $x = \sqrt{0.5(y - 4) - 3}$ (take the square root of each side, and swap the sides for ease of reading)

     $x = \sqrt{0.5y - 5}$

2   LINEAR EQUATIONS

> ### KEY TERM
>
> A **linear equation** has the general form $y = a + bx$
>
> where   y   is the **dependent variable**, depending for its value on the value of x
>
>   x   is the **independent variable** whose value helps to determine the corresponding value of y
>
>   a   is a **constant**, that is, a fixed amount
>
>   b   is also a **constant**, being the **coefficient** of x (that is, the number by which the value of x should be multiplied to derive the value of y)

2.1   EXAMPLE: ESTABLISHING BASIC LINEAR EQUATIONS

(a) Let us establish some basic linear equations. Suppose that it takes Joe Bloggs 15 minutes to walk one mile. How long does it take Joe to walk two miles? Obviously it takes him 30 minutes. How did you calculate the time? You probably thought that if the distance is doubled then the time must be doubled. How do you explain (in words) the relationships between the distance walked and the time taken? One explanation would be that every mile walked takes 15 minutes. Now let us try to explain the relationship with an equation.

(b) First you must decide which is the **dependent variable** and which is the **independent variable**. In other words, does the time taken depend on the number of miles walked or does the number of miles walked depend on the time it takes to walk a mile? Obviously the time depends on the distance. We can therefore let y be the dependent variable (time taken in minutes) and x be the independent variable (distance walked in miles).

(c) We now need to determine the **constants a** and **b**. There is no fixed amount so a = 0. To ascertain b, we need to establish the number of times by which the value of x should be multiplied to derive the value of y. Obviously y = 15x where y is in minutes. If y were in hours then y = $^x/_4$.

2.2 EXAMPLE: DERIVING A LINEAR EQUATION

A salesman's weekly wage is made up of a basic weekly wage of £100 and commission of £5 for every item he sells. Derive an equation which describes this scenario.

2.3 SOLUTION

x = number of items sold and y = weekly wage

a = £100 (fixed weekly wage paid however many items he sells) and b = £5 (variable element of wage, depends on how many items he sells)

∴   y = 5x + 100

2.4 Note that the letters used in an equation do not have to be x and y. It may be sensible to use other letters, for example we could use p and q if we are describing the relationship between the price of an item and the quantity demanded.

3 LINEAR EQUATIONS AND GRAPHS

3.1 One of the clearest ways of presenting the relationship between two variables is by plotting a **linear equation** as a **straight line** on a graph.

The rules for drawing graphs

3.2 A graph has a **horizontal axis**, the **x axis** and a **vertical axis**, the **y axis**. The x axis is used to represent the **independent variable** and the y axis is used to represent the **dependent variable**. If calendar time is one variable, it is always treated as the independent variable. When time is represented on the x axis of a graph, we have the graph of a **time series**.

3.3 (a) If the data to be plotted are derived from calculations, rather than given in the question, make sure that there is a neat table in your working papers.

(b) The scales on each axis should be selected so as to use as much of the graph paper as possible. Do not cramp a graph into one corner.

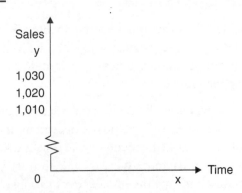

(c) In some cases it is best not to start a scale at zero so as to avoid having a large area of wasted paper. This is perfectly acceptable as long as the scale adopted is clearly shown on the axis. One way of avoiding confusion is to break the axis concerned, as follows.

(d) The scales on the x axis and the y axis should be marked. For example, if the y axis relates to amounts of money, the axis should be marked at every £1, or £100 or £1,000 interval or at whatever other interval is appropriate. The axes must be marked with values to give the reader an idea of how big the values on the graph are.

(e) A graph should not be overcrowded with too many lines. Graphs should always give a clear, neat impression.

(f) A graph must always be given a title, and where appropriate, a reference should be made to the source of data.

3.4   EXAMPLE: DRAWING GRAPHS

Plot the graph for y = 4x + 5.

Consider the range of values from x = 0 to x = 10.

3.5   SOLUTION

The first step is to draw up a table for the equation. Although the problem mentions x = 0 to x = 10, it is not necessary to calculate values of y for x = 1, 2, 3 etc. A graph of a linear equation can actually be drawn from just two (x, y) values but it is always best to calculate a number of values in case you make an arithmetical error. We have calculated five values. You could settle for three or four.

x	y
0	5
2	13
4	21
6	29
8	37
10	45

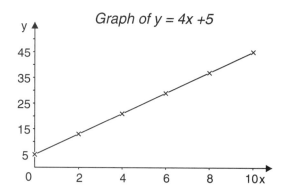

Graph of y = 4x +5

The intercept and the slope

3.6 The graph of a linear equation is determined by two things.

- The gradient (or slope) of the straight line
- The point at which the straight line crosses the y axis

KEY TERMS

- The **intercept** is the point at which a straight line crosses the y-axis.

- The **gradient** of the graph of a linear equation is $(y_2 - y_1)/(x_2 - x_1)$ where (x_1, y_1) and (x_2, y_2) are two points on the straight line.

3.7 The intercept of $y = 4x + 5$ is $(0, 5)$. It is no coincidence that the intercept is the same as the constant represented by a in the general form of the equation $y = a + bx$. a is the value y takes when $x = 0$, in other words a constant, and so is represented on a graph by the point $(0, a)$.

3.8 The slope of $y = 4x + 5 = (21 - 13)/(4 - 2) = 8/2 = 4$ where $(x_1, y_1) = (2, 13)$ and $(x_2, y_2) = (4, 21)$.

Question 3

If y = 10 – x, the gradient =

Answer

The gradient = –1

If y = 10 – x, then a = 10 and b = –1 (–1 × x = –x).

Therefore gradient = –1

3.9 Note that the gradient of $y = 4x + 5$ is positive whereas the gradient of $y = 10 - x$ is negative.

- A positive gradient slopes upwards from left to right.
- A negative gradient slopes downwards from left to right.
- The greater the value of the gradient, the steeper the slope.

3.10 Just as the intercept can be found by inspection of the linear equation, so can the gradient. It is represented by the coefficient of x (b in the general form of the equation). The slope of the graph $y = 7x - 3$ is therefore 7 and the slope of the graph $y = 3{,}597 - 263x$ is -263.

Question 4

Calculate the intercept and slope of the graph of $4y = 16x - 12$.

	Intercept	Slope
A	−3	+4
B	−4	+3
C	+3	−4
D	+4	−3

Answer

$4y = 16x - 12$

Equation must be in the form $y = a + bx$

$$y = -\frac{12}{4} + \frac{16}{4}x = -3 + 4x$$

Intercept = a = −3 ie (0, −3)

Slope = 4

Therefore the correct answer is A.

If you selected option D, you have obviously confused the intercept and the slope. Remember that with an equation in the form $y = a + bx$, a = intercept (ie where the line of the graph crosses the y axis) and b = the slope or gradient of the line.

4 SIMULTANEOUS AND NON-LINEAR EQUATIONS

Simultaneous equations

KEY TERM

Simultaneous equations are two or more equations which are satisfied by the same variable values.

4.1 The following two linear equations both involve the unknown values x and y. There are as many equations as there are unknowns and so we can find the values of x and y.

$$y = 3x + 16$$
$$2y = x + 72$$

Graphical solution

4.2 One way of finding a solution is by a **graph**. If both equations are satisfied together, the values of x and y must be those where the straight line graphs of the two equations **intersect**.

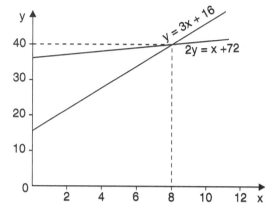

Since both equations are satisfied, the values of **x** and **y** must lie on both the lines. Since this happens only once, at the intersection of the lines, the value of **x** must be 8, and of **y** 40.

Algebraic solution

4.3   A more common method of solving simultaneous equations is by **algebra**.

(a)   Returning to the original equations, we have:

$$y = 3x + 16 \qquad\qquad (1)$$
$$2y = x + 72 \qquad\qquad (2)$$

(b)   Rearranging these, we have:

$$y - 3x = 16 \qquad\qquad (3)$$
$$2y - x = 72 \qquad\qquad (4)$$

(c)   If we now multiply equation (4) by 3, so that the coefficient for x becomes the same as in equation (3) we get:

$$6y - 3x \ = 216 \qquad\qquad (5)$$
$$y - 3x \quad = 16 \qquad\qquad (3)$$

(d)   Subtracting (3) from (5) we get:

$$5y \ = 200$$
$$y \quad = 40$$

(e)   Substituting 40 for y in any equation, we can derive a value for x. Thus substituting in equation (4) we get:

$$2(40) - x \ = 72$$
$$80 - 72 \quad = x$$
$$8 \qquad\quad = x$$

(f)   The solution is y = 40, x = 8.

Question 5

Solve the following simultaneous equations using algebra.

$$5x + 2y \ = 34$$
$$x + 3y \quad = 25$$

BPP PUBLISHING

Answer

$5x + 2y = 34$	(1)	
$x + 3y = 25$	(2)	
$5x + 15y = 125$	(3)	$5 \times (2)$
$13y = 91$	(4)	$(3) - (1)$
$y = 7$		
$x + 21 = 25$		Substitute into (2)
$x = 25 - 21$		
$x = 4$		

The solution is $x = 4$, $y = 7$.

Non-linear equations

4.4 So far we have looked at equations in which the highest power of the unknown variable(s) is one (that is, the equation contains x, y but not x^2, y^3 and so on).

4.5 We are now going to turn our attention to **non-linear equations** in which one variable varies with the nth power of another, where $n > 1$. The following are examples of non-linear equations.

$$y = x^2; \quad y = 3x^3 + 2; \quad 2y = 5x^4 - 6; \quad y = -x^{12} + 3$$

4.6 It is common for a non-linear equation to include a number of terms, all to different powers. Here are some examples.

$$y = x^2 + 6x + 10 \qquad\qquad y = -12x^9 + 3x^6 + 6x^3 + 3x^2 - 1$$
$$2y = 3x^3 - 4x^2 - 8x + 10 \qquad\qquad 3y = 22x^8 + 7x^7 + 3x^4 - 12$$

4.7 Non-linear equations can be expressed in the form

$$y = ax^n + bx^{n-1} + cx^{n-2} + dx^{n-3} + \ldots + \text{constant}.$$ Consider the following equation.

$$y = -12x^9 + 3x^6 + 6x^3 + 2x^2 - 1,$$

In this equation $a = -12$, $b = 0$, $c = 0$, $d = 3$, $e = 0$, $f = 0$, $g = 6$, $h = 2$, $i = 0$, constant $= -1$ and $n = 9$.

Graphing non-linear equations

4.8 The graph of a **linear equation**, as we saw earlier, is a **straight line**. The graph of a **non-linear equation**, on the other hand, **is not a straight line**. Let us consider an example.

4.9 EXAMPLE: GRAPHING NON-LINEAR EQUATIONS

Graph the equation $y = -2x^3 + x^2 - 2x + 10$.

4.10 SOLUTION

The graph of this equation can be plotted in the same way as the graph of a linear equation is plotted. Take a selection of values of x, calculate the corresponding values of y, plot the pairs of values and join the points together. The joining must be done using as smooth a curve as possible.

x	-3	-2	-1	0	1	2	3
$-2x$	6	4	2	0	-2	-4	-6
x^2	9	4	1	0	1	4	9
$-2x^3$	54	16	2	0	-2	-16	-54
10	10	10	10	10	10	10	10
y	79	34	15	10	7	-6	-41

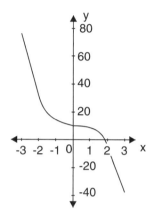

Quadratic equations

KEY TERM

Quadratic equations are a type of non-linear equation in which one variable varies with the square (or second power) of the other variable. They can be expressed in the form $y = ax^2 + bx + c$.

4.11 A **quadratic equation** may include both a term involving the square and also a term involving the **first power** of a variable. Here are some examples.

$$y = x^2 \qquad\qquad y = x^2 + 6x + 10 \qquad\qquad 2y = 3x^2 - 4x - 8 \qquad\qquad y = 5x^2 + 7$$

4.12 In the equation $y = 3x^2 + 2x - 6$, $a = 3$, $b = 2$, $c = -6$.

Graphing a quadratic equation

4.13 The graph of a quadratic equation can be plotted using the same method as that illustrated in Paragraph 4.10.

4.14 EXAMPLE: GRAPHING A QUADRATIC EQUATION

Graph the equation $y = -2x^2 + x - 3$

4.15 SOLUTION

x	-3	-2	-1	0	1	2	3
$-2x^2$	-18	-8	-2	0	-2	-8	-18
-3	-3	-3	-3	-3	-3	-3	-3
y	-24	-13	-6	-3	-4	-9	-18

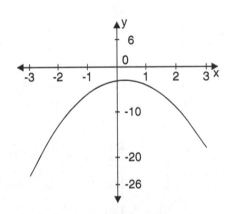

4.16 Graphs shaped like that in Paragraph 4.15 are sometimes referred to as **parabolas** and both illustrate a number of points about the graph of the equation $y = ax^2 + bx + c$.

(a) The constant term 'c' determines the value of y at the point where the curve crosses the y axis (the intercept). In the graph above, c = –3 and the curve crosses the y axis at y = –3.

(b) The sign of 'a' determines the way up the curve appears.

- If 'a' is **positive**, the curve is shaped like a **ditch**
- If 'a' is **negative**, as in Paragraph 4.15, the curve is shaped like a **bell**

A ditch-shaped curve is said to have a **minimum point** whereas a bell-shaped curve is said to have a **maximum point**.

(c) The graph enables us to find the values of x when y = 0 (if there are any). In other words the graph allows us to solve the quadratic equation $0 = ax^2 + bx + c$. For the curve in Paragraph 4.15 we see that there are no such values (that is, $0 = -2x^2 + x - 3$ cannot be solved).

Solving quadratic equations

4.17 The graphical method is not, in practice, the most efficient way to determine the solution of a quadratic equation. Many quadratic equations have two values of x (called '**solutions for x**' or '**roots of the equation**') which satisfy the equation for any particular value of y. These values can be found using the following formula.

FORMULA TO LEARN

If $ax^2 + bx + c = 0$ then $x = \dfrac{-b \pm \sqrt{(b^2 - 4ac)}}{2a}$

4.18 EXAMPLE: QUADRATIC EQUATIONS

Solve $x^2 + x - 2 = 0$.

4.19 SOLUTION

For the equation $x^2 + x - 2 = 0$

$a = 1$

$b = 1$

$c = -2$

We can insert these values into the following formula which is used to solve quadratic equations.

$$x = \frac{-b \pm \sqrt{(b^2 - 4ac)}}{2a}$$

$$x = \frac{-1 \pm \sqrt{(1^2 - (4 \times 1 \times (-2)))}}{2 \times 1} = \frac{-1 \pm \sqrt{(1 + 8)}}{2} = \frac{-1 \pm 3}{2}$$

$\therefore \quad x = \quad \dfrac{-4}{2}$ or $\dfrac{2}{2}$ ie $x = -2$ or $x = 1$

Quadratic equations with a single value for x

4.20 Sometimes, $b^2 - 4ac = 0$, and so there is only one solution to the quadratic equation. Let us solve $x^2 + 2x + 1 = 0$ using the formula above where $a = 1$, $b = 2$ and $c = 1$.

$$x = \frac{-2 \pm \sqrt{(2^2 - (4 \times 1 \times 1))}}{2} = \frac{-2 \pm 0}{2} = -1$$

This quadratic equation can only be solved by one value of x.

Exam focus point

One of the learning outcomes stated in the Business Mathematics syllabus is that, 'on completion of their studies, students should be able to solve **simple equations**, including **2 variable simultaneous equations** and **quadratic equations**'.

The ability to solve equations is a skill that is required at all levels of your CIMA studies.

4.21 Attempt the following questions to make sure that you have got to grips with the contents of this chapter so far.

Question 6

A company manufactures a product. The total fixed costs are £75 and the variable cost per unit is £5.

Required

(a) Find an expression for total costs (c) in terms of q, the quantity produced.
(b) Use your answer to (a) to determine the total costs if 100 units are produced.
(c) Prepare a graph of the expression for total costs.
(d) Use your graph to determine the total cost if 75 units are produced.

BPP PUBLISHING

Answer

(a)   Let   C = total costs

C = total variable costs + total fixed costs

C = 5q + 75

(b)   If q = 100, C = (5 × 100) + 75 = £575

(c)   If q = 0,   C = £75

If q = 100,   C = £575

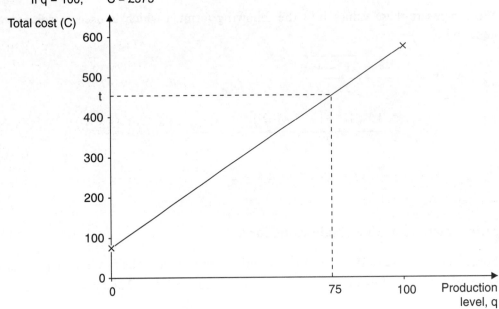

Total cost (C)

(d)   From graph above, if q = 75, C = £450

Question 7

A company manufactures a product, the total cost function for the product being given by C = (25 – q)q, where q is the quantity produced and C is in £.

Required

(a)   Calculate the total costs if 15 units are produced.

(b)   Draw a graph of the total cost function and use it to calculate the total cost if 23 units are produced.

Answer

(a)   C = (25 – q)q

If q = 15, C = (25 – 15) × 15 = 10 × 15 = £150

(b)

q	C
0	0
5.0	100.00
10.0	150.00
12.5	156.25
15.0	150.00
20.0	100.00
25.0	0

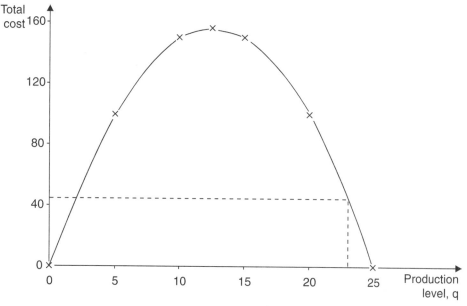

From the graph, if 23 units are produced the total cost is approximately £45.

Exam focus point

One of the learning outcomes in the **Business Mathematics** syllabus states that students should be able to **prepare graphs of linear and quadratic equations** on completion of their studies.

Chapter roundup

- When we use letters to stand for any numbers we call them **variables**. The use of variables enables us to state general truths about mathematics.

- The **general rule for solving equations** is that you can do what you like to one side of an equation, so long as you do the same thing to the other side straightaway.

- A **linear equation** has the general form **y = a + bx**, where x is the independent variable and y the dependent variable, and a and b are fixed amounts.

- The **graph of a linear equation is a straight line**. The intercept of the line on the y axis is a in
  y = a + bx and the slope of the line is b.

- **Simultaneous equations** are two or more equations which are satisfied by the same variable values. They can be solved graphically or algebraically.

- In **non-linear equations**, one variable varies with the nth power of another, where n> 1. The graph of a non-linear equation is *not* a straight line.

- **Quadratic equations** are **non-linear equations** in which one variable varies with the square of the other variable.

- The graphs of quadratic equations are parabolas, the sign of 'a' in the general form of the quadratic equation (y = ax^2 + bx + c) determining the way up the curve appears.

- Quadratic equations can be solved by the formula

$$x = \frac{-b \pm \sqrt{(b^2 - 4ac)}}{2a}$$

BPP PUBLISHING

Part A: Basic mathematics

Quick quiz

1   A linear equation has the general form y = a + bx where

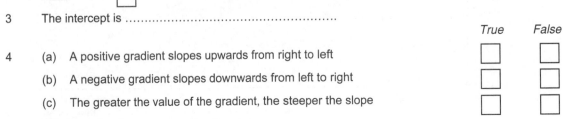

2   The horizontal axis on a graph is known as the y axis.

True   ☐

False   ☐

3   The intercept is ....

4   (a)   A positive gradient slopes upwards from right to left

     (b)   A negative gradient slopes downwards from left to right

     (c)   The greater the value of the gradient, the steeper the slope

	True	*False*
(a)	☐	☐
(b)	☐	☐
(c)	☐	☐

5   What are simultaneous equations?

6   In what form are quadratic equations usually expressed?

7   Consider the equation $y = -4x^2 + 3x - 2$

     (a)   The graph of the equation is shaped like a ditch/bell

     (b)   The graph of the equation has a minimum/maximum point

     (c)   The point at which the curve crosses the y axis is ....

8   Use the symbols and numbers below to construct the formula for solving a quadratic equation.

     $x, -b, -4, a, a, \sqrt{}, =, \pm, b^2, c, 2$

Answers to quick quiz

1   y = dependent variable
    x = independent variable
    b = constant (coefficient of x)
    a = constant (fixed amount)

2   False

3   The point at which a straight line crosses the y-axis

4   (a)   False
    (b)   True
    (c)   True

5   Two or more equations which are satisfied by the same variable values

6    $y = ax^2 + bx + c$

7   (a)   bell
    (b)   maximum point
    (c)   –2

8    $x = \dfrac{-b \pm \sqrt{(b^2 - 4ac)}}{2a}$

Now try the following objective test questions

Question bank	Question numbers	Page
Paper-based exam	2	271
Computer-based assessment	2	291

Chapter 3

ACCURACY AND APPROXIMATION

Topic list	Syllabus reference	Ability required
1 Rounding	(i)	Application
2 Maximum errors	(i)	Application
3 Errors and calculations	(i)	Application

Introduction

Having covered basic mathematical ideas and techniques in the first two chapters, we are now going to turn our attention to a number of concepts which you must bear in mind when you read the remaining chapters in this Study Text. These concepts relate to **approximation**.

Approximation arises for two principal reasons. It is often not possible to obtain an accurate value for a large number (such as the population of a town) and some figures may only be easily measurable to the nearest whole number (for example the speed of a car). Sometimes, on the other hand, it may not be necessary or desirable to express data as accurately as they can be measured. In such circumstances numbers are **rounded**.

Obviously when calculations are made using rounded data, errors may be introduced into the results of the calculations and any subsequent conclusions drawn. Having looked at how numbers can be rounded we will turn our attention to the types of errors that can occur and look at how we can take account of such errors in calculations using rounded data.

Once you have completed this chapter we will be moving away from basic mathematics on to specific quantitative methods, beginning with ways of summarising and analysing data.

Learning outcome covered in this chapter

- **Calculate** maximum, absolute and relative errors

1   ROUNDING

1.1   There are three methods of rounding and these will be illustrated using the figure 18,600.

(a) **Rounding up**. 18,600 would be expressed as 19,000 to the nearest thousand above.

(b) **Rounding down**. 18,600 would be expressed as 18,000 to the nearest thousand below.

(c) **Rounding to the nearest round amount**. 18,600 would be expressed as 19,000 to the nearest thousand. This is the most commonly used method.

In rounding to the **nearest unit**, a value ending in 0.5 is usually rounded up. Thus 3.5 rounded to the nearest unit would be 4.

1.2 Rounding can be specified to the **nearest whole unit** (as above), by the **number of decimal places** (3.94712 to 2 decimal places is 3.95), or by the **number of significant figures** (as covered in Chapter 1).

Question 1

(a) What is £482,365.15 to the nearest:

(i)	£1	
(ii)	£100	
(iii)	£1,000	
(iv)	£10,000	

(b) What is 843.668 correct to:

(i)	one decimal place	
(ii)	two decimal places?	

Answer

(a)

(i)	£1	£482,365
(ii)	£100	£482,400
(iii)	£1,000	£482,000
(iv)	£10,000	£480,000

(b)

(i)	843.7
(ii)	843.67

Spurious accuracy

KEY TERM

Spurious accuracy arises when a statistic gives the impression that it is more accurate than it really is.

1.3 EXAMPLE: SPURIOUS ACCURACY

Suppose we see stated in a magazine '24.68% of women over the age of 30 are smokers'. This result is probably based on a sample and so we know that it cannot be as accurate as it seems: the two decimal places have arisen simply because of the arithmetic of the calculations. It would be less misleading to state 'approximately 25% of women over the age of 30 are smokers'. This removes the spurious accuracy implied by the decimal places.

2   MAXIMUM ERRORS

Absolute errors

2.1   Suppose that the population of a country is stated as 40 million. It is quite likely that this figure has been rounded to the nearest million. We could therefore say that the country's population is 40 million ± 500,000 where 40 million is the **estimate** of the population and 500,000 is the **maximum absolute error.**

2.2   In general terms an estimate with a maximum absolute error can be expressed as a ± b.

Relative errors

2.3   The error in the population of the country could also be expressed as 40 million ± 1.25%, where 500,000 is 1.25% of 40 million. In this instance the maximum error is a **maximum relative error** and is calculated as $\dfrac{\text{maximum absolute error}}{\text{estimate}} \times 100\%$.

3   ERRORS AND CALCULATIONS

3.1   If calculations are made using values that have been rounded then the results of such calculations will only be **approximate**. However, provided that we are aware of the maximum errors that can occur, we can still draw conclusions from the results of the calculations.

3.2   There are two rules to remember when performing calculations involving rounded or approximate numbers.

(a)   **Addition/subtraction.** When two or more rounded or approximate numbers are added or subtracted the **maximum absolute error** in the result equals the sum of the individual maximum absolute errors.

(b)   **Multiplication/division.** When two or more rounded or approximate numbers are multiplied or divided, the **approximate maximum relative error** in the result is obtained by adding the individual maximum relative errors.

3.3   EXAMPLE: ERRORS

A chemical producer plans to sell 50,000 litres (to the nearest 1,000 litres) of a particular chemical at a price of £10 (to the nearest pound) per litre.

The cost of materials used to produce the chemicals is expected to be £100,000 but depending on wastage levels this is subject to an error of ± 5%. Labour costs are estimated to be £300,000 ± 10%, depending on overtime working and pay negotiations.

Required

Calculate the maximum absolute error and the maximum relative error in revenue and costs of production.

3.4 SOLUTION

	Estimate	Maximum absolute error	Maximum relative error %
Quantity sold	50,000 litres	500 litres*	1
Price	£10	£0.50**	5
Materials	£100,000	£5,000	5
Labour	£300,000	£30,000	10

*   This is because 41,500 litres would be rounded up to 42,000 litres but 41,499 litres would be rounded down to 41,000 litres.

**   This is because £9.50 would be rounded up to £10 but £9.49 would be rounded down to £9.00.

(a) **Revenue**   = quantity sold × price
        = $(50,000 \pm 1\%) \times (£10 \pm 5\%)$
        = $(50,000 \times £10) \pm (1\% + 5\%)$
        = $£500,000 \pm 6\%$
        = $£500,000 \pm £30,000$

∴ Approximate maximum absolute error = £30,000

Approximate maximum relative error = 6%

Note that we need to use relative errors when doing multiplication/division calculations.

(b) **Costs of production**   = material + labour
        = $(£100,000 \pm £5,000) + (£300,000 \pm £30,000)$
        = $(£100,000 + £300,000) \pm (£5,000 + £30,000)$
        = $£400,000 \pm £35,000$
        = $£400,000 \pm 8.75\%$

∴   Maximum absolute error = £35,000

Maximum relative error = 8.75%

Note that we need to use absolute errors when doing addition/subtraction calculations.

3.5 The rule in Paragraph 3.2(b) above only gives an approximate **maximum relative error**. Let's see what the actual error would have been in Paragraph 3.4(a) above.

Maximum revenue   = maximum quantity × maximum price
        = $(50,000 + 1\%) \times (£10 + 5\%)$
        = $50,500 \times £10.50$
        = $£530,250$

∴ Our approximation of the maximum absolute error was correct to within £(530,250 − 530,000) = £250.

Question 2

The management accountant for Kent Ltd has established the cost of materials for a unit of product T as £10 to the nearest £1.

What are the maximum absolute and the maximum relative errors in the cost?

	Maximum absolute error	Maximum relative error
A	£0.50	10%
B	£0.50	5%
C	£1.00	10%
D	£1.00	5%

Answer

The maximum absolute error = 50p = £0.50 because £9.50 would be rounded up to £10.00 but £9.49 would be rounded down to £9.00.

The maximum relative error $= \dfrac{\text{maximum absolute error}}{\text{estimate}} \times 100\%$

$$= \frac{£0.50}{£10.00} \times 100\% = 5\%$$

The correct answer is B.

Chapter roundup

- **Approximation** arises if it is not possible to obtain an accurate figure or if a number has been rounded. Rounding can be specified to the **nearest whole unit**, by the **number of decimal places** or by the **number of significant figures**.

- **Spurious accuracy** arises when a statistic gives the impression that it is more accurate than it really is.

- **Maximum errors** can be **absolute** or **relative**.

- When two or more rounded or approximate numbers are added or subtracted, the maximum absolute error in the result equals the sum of the individual maximum absolute errors.

- When two or more rounded or approximate numbers are multiplied or divided, the **approximate** maximum relative error in the result is obtained by adding the individual relative errors.

- You can determine the actual error in calculations involving only a few values/variables without using the two rules.

Quick quiz

1   What are the three main methods of rounding?

2   Maximum relative error $= \dfrac{a}{b} \times 100\%$

    where   a =
            b =

3   Mr Wong has estimated the cost of a 'venus' to be £20 to the nearest £1.

    What are the maximum absolute and the maximum relative errors in the cost?

	Maximum absolute error	Maximum relative error
A	£0.50	2.5%
B	£0.50	5.0%
C	£1.00	2.5%
D	£1.00	5.0%

Answers to quick quiz

1 (a)   Rounding up
  (b)   Rounding down
  (c)   Rounding to the nearest round amount

2 a = maximum absolute error
  b = estimate

3 A

The maximum absolute error = 50p = £0.50 because £19.50 would be rounded up to £20.00 but £19.49 would be rounded down to £19.00.

$$\text{The maximum relative error} = \frac{\text{maximum absolute error}}{\text{estimate}} \times 100\%$$

$$= \frac{£0.50}{£20.00} \times 100\% = 2.5\%$$

Now try the following objective test questions

Question bank	Question numbers	Page
Paper-based exam	3	271
Computer-based assessment	3	291

Part B
Summarising and analysing data

Chapter 4

THE COLLECTION OF DATA

Topic list	Syllabus reference	Ability required
1 Data and information	(ii)	Comprehension
2 Types of data	(ii)	Comprehension
3 Sources of data	(ii)	Comprehension
4 Primary data	(ii)	Comprehension
5 Secondary data	(ii)	Comprehension
6 Sampling	(ii)	Comprehension
7 Probability sampling methods	(ii)	Comprehension
8 Non-probability sampling methods	(ii)	Comprehension

Introduction

The words 'quantitative methods' often strike terror into the hearts of students. They conjure up images of complicated mathematical formulae, scientific analysis of reams of computer output and the drawing of strange graphs and diagrams. Such images are wrong. Quantitative methods simply involves:

- **Collecting data**
- **Presenting the data in a useful form**
- **Inspecting the data**

A study of the subject will demonstrate that quantitative methods is nothing to be afraid of and that a knowledge of it is extremely advantageous in your working environment.

We will start our study of quantitative methods by looking at **data collection**. In Chapter 5 we will consider how to **present data** once they have been collected.

Learning outcomes covered in this chapter

- **Explain** the difference between data and information
- **Explain** the characteristics of good information
- **Explain** the difference between primary and secondary data
- **Identify** the sources of secondary data
- **Explain** the different methods of sampling and **identify** where each is appropriate

Syllabus content covered in this chapter

- Data and information
- Primary and secondary data
- Probability sampling (simple random sampling, stratified, systematic, multi-stage, cluster) and non-probability sampling (quota)

BPP PUBLISHING

1   DATA AND INFORMATION

What are data?

> ## KEY TERM
>
> **Data** is a 'scientific' term for facts, figures, information and processing. Data are the raw materials for data processing.

1.1   Examples of data include the following.

- The number of tourists who visit Hong Kong each year
- The sales turnovers of all restaurants in Salisbury
- The number of people (with black hair) who pass their driving test each year

What is information?

> ## KEY TERM
>
> **Information** is data that has been processed in such a way as to be meaningful to the person who receives it. Information is anything that is communicated.

1.2   **Information** is sometimes referred to as processed data. The terms 'information' and 'data' are often used interchangeably. Let us consider the following situation in which data is **collected** and then **processed** in order to produce meaningful information.

1.3   Many companies providing a product or service like to research consumer opinion, and employ market research organisations to do so. A typical market research survey employs a number of researchers who request a sample of the public to answer questions relating to the product. Several hundred questionnaires may be completed. The questionnaires are input to a system. Once every questionnaire has been input, a number of processing operations are performed on the data. A report which summarises the results and discusses their significance is sent to the company that commissioned the survey.

1.4   Individually, a completed questionnaire would not tell the company very much, only the views of one consumer. In this case, the individual questionnaires are **data**. Once they have been processed, and analysed, the resulting report is **information**. The company will use it to inform its decisions regarding the product. If the report revealed that consumers disliked the product, the company would scrap or alter it.

1.5   The **quality of source data** affects the value of information. Information is worthless if the source data is flawed. If the researchers filled in questionnaires themselves, inventing the answers, then the conclusions drawn from the processed data would be wrong, and poor decisions would be made.

Quantitative and qualitative data

> **KEY TERM**
>
> **Quantitative data** are data that can be measured (think of measuring quantities).
>
> A **variable** is a word commonly used in mathematics meaning 'something which can be measured'.

1.6 Examples of quantitative data include the following.

- The temperature on each day of January in Singapore. This can be **measured** in degrees Fahrenheit or Celsius.

- The time it takes you to swim 50 lengths. This can be **measured** in hours and minutes.

> **KEY TERM**
>
> **Qualitative data** are data that cannot be measured but which reflect some quality of what is being observed. The data are said to have **attributes**.
>
> An **attribute** is something an object has either got or not got. It cannot be measured.

1.7 An example of **qualitative data** is whether someone is male or female. Whether you are male or female is an **attribute** because the sex of a person cannot be measured.

Quantitative and qualitative information

1.8 Just as data may be quantitative or qualitative, so too may information.

> **KEY TERMS**
>
> - **Quantitative information** is information which is capable of being expressed in numbers. It is usually financial in nature.
>
> - **Qualitative information** is information which may not be expressed very easily in terms of numbers. Information of this nature is more likely to reflect the quality of something.

1.9 An example of **quantitative information** is 'The Chairman of the company has announced that the turnover for the year is **£4 million.**' You can see how this information is easily expressed in numerical terms.

1.10 An example of **qualitative information** is 'The standard of the books produced was **very high.**' This information cannot easily be expressed in terms of numbers, as the standard of something is usually described as being very high, quite low, or average and so on.

Characteristics of good information

1.11 Whether information is quantitative or qualitative, it should have the following characteristics.

- It should be **relevant** for its purpose.
- It should be **complete** for its purpose.
- It should be sufficiently **accurate** for its purpose.
- It should be **clear** to the user.
- The user should have **confidence** in it.
- It should be **communicated** to the right person.
- It should not be excessive - its **volume** should be manageable.
- It should be **timely** - in other words communicated at the most appropriate time.
- It should be communicated by an appropriate **channel** of communication.
- It should be provided at a **cost** which is less than the value of its benefits.

1.12 Let us look at these characteristics in more detail.

(a) **Relevance**. Information must be relevant to the purpose for which a manager wants to use it. In practice, far too many reports fail to 'keep to the point' and contain purposeless, irritating paragraphs which only serve to vex the managers reading them.

(b) **Completeness**. An information user should have all the information he needs to do his job properly. If he does not have a complete picture of the situation, he might well make bad decisions.

(c) **Accuracy**. Information should obviously be accurate because using incorrect information could have serious and damaging consequences. However, information should only be accurate enough for its purpose and there is no need to go into unnecessary detail for pointless accuracy.

(d) **Clarity**. Information must be clear to the user. If the user does not understand it properly he cannot use it properly. Lack of clarity is one of the causes of a breakdown in communication. It is therefore important to choose the most appropriate presentation medium or channel of communication.

(e) **Confidence**. Information must be trusted by the managers who are expected to use it. However not all information is certain. Some information has to be certain, especially operating information, for example, related to a production process. Strategic information, especially relating to the environment, is uncertain. However, if the assumptions underlying it are clearly stated, this might enhance the confidence with which the information is perceived.

(f) **Communication**. Within any organisation, individuals are given the authority to do certain tasks, and they must be given the information they need to do them. An office manager might be made responsible for controlling expenditures in his office, and given a budget expenditure limit for the year. As the year progresses, he might try to keep expenditure in check but unless he is told throughout the year what is his current total expenditure to date, he will find it difficult to judge whether he is keeping within budget or not.

(g) **Volume**. There are physical and mental limitations to what a person can read, absorb and understand properly before taking action. An enormous mountain of information, even if it is all relevant, cannot be handled. Reports to management must therefore be **clear** and **concise** and in many systems, control action works basically on the 'exception' principle.

(h) **Timing**. Information which is not available until after a decision is made will be useful only for comparisons and longer-term control, and may serve no purpose even then. Information prepared too frequently can be a serious disadvantage. If, for example, a decision is taken at a monthly meeting about a certain aspect of a company's operations, information to make the decision is only required once a month, and weekly reports would be a time-consuming waste of effort.

(i) **Channel of communication**. There are occasions when using one particular method of communication will be better than others. For example, job vacancies should be announced in a medium where they will be brought to the attention of the people most likely to be interested. The channel of communication might be the company's in-house journal, a national or local newspaper, a professional magazine, a job centre or school careers office. Some internal memoranda may be better sent by 'electronic mail'. Some information is best communicated informally by telephone or word-of-mouth, whereas other information ought to be formally communicated in writing or figures.

(j) **Cost**. Information should have some value, otherwise it would not be worth the cost of collecting and filing it. The benefits obtainable from the information must also exceed the costs of acquiring it, and whenever management is trying to decide whether or not to produce information for a particular purpose (for example whether to computerise an operation or to build a financial planning model) a cost/benefit study ought to be made.

2   TYPES OF DATA

2.1   We have already seen how data can be classified as being **quantitative** (can be measured (variables)) or qualitative (cannot be measured, has an **attribute**). We shall now consider the ways in which data may be further classified as follows.

- Primary and secondary data
- Discrete and continuous data
- Sample and population data

Primary and secondary data

> **KEY TERMS**
>
> - **Primary data** are data collected especially for the purpose of whatever survey is being conducted. Raw data are primary data which have not been processed at all, and which are still just a list of numbers.
>
> - **Secondary data** are data which have already been collected elsewhere, for some other purpose, but which can be used or adapted for the survey being conducted.

Discrete and continuous data

2.2   Quantitative data may be further classified as being **discrete** or **continuous**.

BPP PUBLISHING

KEY TERMS

- **Discrete data** are data which can only taken on a finite or countable number of values within a given range.

- **Continuous data** are data which can take on any value. They are measured rather than counted.

2.3 **Discrete data** are the number of goals scored by Arsenal against Chelsea in the FA Cup Final: Arsenal could score 0, 1, 2, 3 or even 4 goals (**discrete variables** =0, 1, 2, 3, 4), but they cannot score 1½ or 2½ goals.

2.4 **Continuous data** include the heights of all the members of your family, as these can take on any value: 1.542m, 1.639m and 1.492m for example. **Continuous variables** = 1.542, 1.639, 1.492.

Sample and population data

KEY TERMS

- **Sample data** are data arising as a result of investigating a sample. A sample is a selection from the population.

- **Population data** are data arising as a result of investigating the population. A population is the group of people or objects of interest to the data collector.

2.5 The following diagram should help you to remember the ways in which data may be classified.

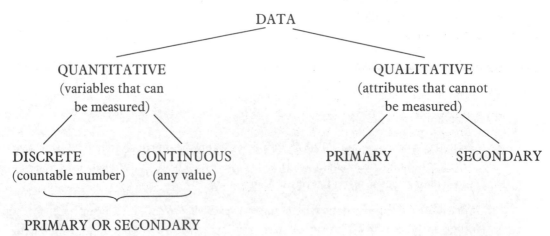

Question 1

Look through the following list of surveys and decide whether each is collecting qualitative data or quantitative data. If you think the data is quantitative, indicate whether it is discrete or continuous.

(a) A survey of accountancy textbooks, to determine how many diagrams they contain.

(b) A survey of greetings cards on a newsagent's shelf, to determine whether or not each has a price sticker on it.

(c)   A survey of the results in a cost accounting examination, to determine what percentage of marks the students obtained.

(d)   A survey of heights of telegraph poles in Papua New Guinea, to find out if there is any variation across the country.

(e)   A survey of swimmers to find out how long they take to swim a kilometre.

Answer

(a)   The number of diagrams in an accountancy text book is an example of **quantitative** data, because it can be measured. Because the number of diagrams can only be counted in whole number steps, the resulting data is **discrete.** You cannot for example have 42½ diagrams, but you can have 42 or 43 diagrams.

(b)   Whether or not a greetings card has a price sticker on it is not something that can be measured. This is therefore an example of **qualitative** data, as a greetings card either has a price sticker on it, or it does not have a price sticker on it.

(c)   The results of a cost accounting examination can be measured, and are therefore an example of **quantitative** data. The examination results can only take on whole number values between 0% and 100%, and the data are therefore **discrete.** (It may be possible to score 62½%, or 64½%, but it is not possible to score 62.41%, so the variable is not continuous.)

(d)   The heights of telegraph poles is an example of **quantitative** data as they can be measured. Since the telegraph poles may take on any height, the data is said to be **continuous.**

(e)   The time taken to swim a kilometre may be measured and is therefore **quantitative** data. Because the time recorded can take on any value, in theory, the data is said to be **continuous.**

2.6   Now we know what sorts of data we may come across, and how it is classified, we can take a look at the different **sources of data.**

3   SOURCES OF DATA

3.1   Data may be obtained from either an **internal** source or from an **external** source.

Internal sources of data

The financial accounting records

3.2   There is no need for us to give a detailed description of the constituents of the financial accounting records. You are by now very familiar with the idea of a system of sales ledgers and purchase ledgers, general ledgers, cash books and so on. These records provide a history of an organisation's monetary transactions. Some of this data is of great value outside the accounts department, for example sales data for the marketing function. Other data, like cheque numbers or employees' PAYE codes, is of purely administrative value within the accounts department.

3.3   You will also be aware that to maintain the integrity of its financial accounting records, an organisation of any size will have systems for and controls over transactions. These also give rise to valuable data. A stock control system is the classic example. Besides actually recording the monetary value of purchases and stock in hand for external financial reporting purposes, the system will include purchase orders, goods received notes, goods returned notes and so on, and these can be analysed to provide management information about speed of delivery, say, or the quality of supplies.

Other internal sources

3.4 Much of the data that are not strictly part of the financial accounting records are in fact closely tied in to the accounting system.

    (a) Data relating to personnel will be linked to the payroll system. Additional data may be obtained from this source if, say, a project is being costed and it is necessary to ascertain the availability and rate of pay of different levels of staff, or the need for and cost of recruiting staff from outside the organisation.

    (b) Much data will be produced by a production department about machine capacity, fuel consumption, movement of people, materials, and work in progress, set up times, maintenance requirements and so on. A large part of the traditional work of cost accounting involves ascribing costs to the physical information produced by this source.

    (c) Many service businesses - notably accountants and solicitors - need to keep detailed records of the time spent on various activities, both to justify fees to clients and to assess the efficiency of operations.

External sources of data

3.5 We hardly need say that an organisation's files are also full of invoices, letters, advertisements and so on received from customers and suppliers. These documents provide data from an external source. There are many occasions when an active search outside the organisation is necessary.

    (a) A **primary source** of data is, as the term implies, as close as you can get to the origin of an item of data: the eyewitness to an event, the place in question, the document under scrutiny.

    (b) A **secondary source**, again logically enough, provides 'second-hand' data: books, articles, verbal or written reports by someone else.

3.6 The next section of this chapter will take a closer look at primary data.

4 PRIMARY DATA

4.1 You will remember that **primary data** are data collected especially for the purpose of whatever survey is being conducted.

Advantage

The investigator knows where the data came from and is aware of any inadequacies or limitations in the data.

Disadvantage

It can be very expensive to collect primary data.

4.2 **Main sources of primary data**

    • Personal investigation
    • Teams of investigators
    • Interviews
    • Postal questionnaires
    • Telephone surveys

Personal investigation

4.3 Personal investigation involves the investigator collecting all the data himself, for example by interviewing people, or by looking through historical records.

4.4 This method of collecting data is **time consuming, expensive** and **limited to the amount of data a single person can collect**. On the other hand, personal investigation has the advantage that the data collected are likely to be **accurate** and **complete**, because the investigator knows exactly what he wants and how to get it. He is not relying on other people to do the survey work.

Teams of investigators

4.5 A survey could be carried out by a team of investigators who collect data separately and then pool their results.

4.6 A team of investigators can cover a larger field than personal investigation but will still be **expensive**. The members of the team must be carefully briefed to ensure that the data they collect are satisfactory. This method is sometimes called **delegated personal investigation**.

Questionnaires

4.7 With a questionnaire, the questions which need to be answered for the survey are listed and are either sent to a number of people (so that they can fill in their answers and send the questionnaires back) or used by investigators to interview people (perhaps by approaching people in the street and asking them the questions).

Comparison of interviews and postal questionnaires

4.8 We are using the term **postal questionnaire** to cover all methods in which the questionnaire is given to the respondent and returned to the investigator without personal contact. Such questionnaires could be posted but might also be left in pigeonholes or on desks.

4.9 Postal questionnaires have the following advantages over personal interviews.

(a) The cost per person is likely to be less, so more people can be sampled.

(b) It is usually possible to ask more questions because the people completing the forms (the respondents) can do so in their own time.

(c) All respondents are presented with questions in the same way. There is no opportunity for an interviewer to influence responses (interviewer bias) or to misrecord them.

(d) It may be easier to ask personal or embarrassing questions in a postal questionnaire than in a personal interview.

(e) Respondents may need to look up information for the questionnaire. This will be easier if the questionnaire is sent to their homes or places of work.

4.10 On the other hand, the use of personal interviews does have certain advantages over the use of postal questionnaires.

(a) Large numbers of postal questionnaires may not be returned or may be returned only partly completed. This may lead to biased results if those replying are not representative of all people in the survey. Response rates are likely to be higher with personal interviews, and the interviewer can encourage people to answer all questions. Low response rates are a major problem with postal questionnaires.

(b) Misunderstanding is less likely with personal interviews because the interviewer can explain questions which the interviewee does not understand.

(c) Personal interviews are more suitable when deep or detailed questions are to be asked, since the interviewer can take the time required with each interviewee to explain the implications of the question. Also, the interviewer can probe for further information and encourage the respondent to think deeper.

Measures to improve the response rate for postal questionnaires

4.11 (a) Provide a stamped and addressed envelope or a prominently sited box for the return of the questionnaire.

(b) Give a date by which you require the completed questionnaire.

(c) Consider providing an incentive such as a lottery number for those who return questionnaires on time.

Enumerators

4.12 A cheaper alternative to interviews is the use of an enumerator who will deliver the questionnaire and encourage the respondent to complete it. He will later visit the respondent again to collect the completed questionnaire and perhaps to help with the interpretation of difficult questions. This method results in a better response rate than for postal questionnaires.

Telephone surveys

4.13 There are a number of advantages and disadvantages in conducting telephone interviews.

Advantages

(a) The response is rapid.
(b) A wide geographical area can be covered fairly cheaply.
(c) It may be easier to ask sensitive or embarrassing questions.

Disadvantages

(a) A **biased** sample may result from the fact that a large proportion of people do not have telephones and many of those who do are ex-directory.

(b) It is not possible to use 'showcards' or pictures.

(c) The refusal rate is much higher than with face-to-face interviews.

(d) It is not possible to see the interviewee's expressions or to develop the rapport that is possible with personal interviews.

(e) The interview must be short.

5 SECONDARY DATA

5.1 **Secondary data** are data which have already been collected elsewhere, for some other purpose, but which can be used or adapted for the survey being conducted.

Advantage of secondary data	Disadvantage of secondary data
They are cheaply available	Since the investigator did not collect the data, he is therefore unaware of any inadequacies or limitations of the data.

5.2 Secondary data sources may be satisfactory in certain situations, or they may be the only convenient means of obtaining an item of data. It is essential that there is good reason to believe that the secondary data used is **accurate** and **reliable**.

5.3 External sources of data may have been obtained for many different reasons, and care should be taken to ensure that it is used properly. This is because the data will have been collected for a specific purpose, and then used as secondary data.

5.4 Despite the limitations of secondary data, they can be very valuable in many situations. The main secondary data sources are as follows.

- Governments
- Banks
- Newspapers
- Trade journals

Governments

5.5 One of the most important external sources of data in many countries are official statistics which are supplied by many Governments. In Great Britain, official statistics are supplied by the Office for National Statistics (ONS), and include the following.

(a) The *Annual Abstract of Statistics*

This is a general reference book for the United Kingdom which includes data on climate, population, social services, justice and crime, education, defence, manufacturing and agricultural production.

(b) The *Monthly Digest*

This is an abbreviated version of the *Annual Abstract of Statistics.*

(c) *Financial Statistics*

This is a monthly compilation of financial data. It includes statistics on Government income, expenditure and borrowing, financial institutions, companies, the overseas sector, the money supply, exchange rates, interest rates and share prices.

(d) *Economic Trends* and *Regional Trends*

The main purpose of these publications is to indicate trends using tables, maps and charts.

(e) *The United Kingdom National Accounts (The Blue Book)*

This publication is an essential source of data on the gross national product, the gross national income and the gross national expenditure. It gives a clear indication of how the nation makes and spends its money.

(f) *The United Kingdom Balance of Payments (The Pink Book)*

This annual publication gives data on the inflows and outflows of private capital in the United Kingdom.

BPP
PUBLISHING

(g) *Social trends*

This annual publication provides data on the population, income, householders, families and many other aspects of British life and work.

5.6 Monthly statistics are also published by many Government departments. For example, the Department of Employment in Britain publishes *The Department of Employment Gazette* which gives details of retail prices, employment, unemployment, unfilled job vacancies and other statistics relating to employment.

5.7 Retail prices are very important to a wide variety of users.

(a) For the Government, the Retail Prices Index (RPI) indicates the degree of success there has been in fighting inflation.

(b) For employees, the RPI may give an indication of how much wages need to rise to keep pace with inflation.

(c) For consumers, the RPI indicates the increases to be expected in the prices of goods in shops.

(d) For businesses, the RPI may give a broad indication of how much costs should have been expected to rise over recent years and months.

(e) For pensioners and social security recipients, the movement in the RPI is used to update benefit levels.

5.8 The Department of Trade and Industry in Britain publishes *British Business* on a weekly basis. It includes data on production, prices and trade.

5.9 Population data is published by many Governments around the world, and includes data on that country's population, such as population numbers, births, deaths, marriages and so on. In Britain the Government carries out a full census of the whole population every ten years, the results of which are published.

Banks

5.10 The Bank of England issues a quarterly magazine which includes data on banks in the UK, the money supply and Government borrowing and financial transactions.

Financial newspapers

5.11 There are a number of financial newspapers which contain detailed business data and information. Financial newspapers include the *Financial Times,* the *Wall Street Journal,* the *Singapore Business Times* and the *Nikkei Weekly.* Such newspapers provide data on foreign exchange rates, interest rates, gilts and other stock prices. They are a valuable source of data which are relevant to the business world.

Trade journals

5.12 Most industries are served by one or more trade journals which can provide invaluable data to those working within the industry.

Journals contain data on new developments in the industry, articles about competitors' products, details of industry costs and prices and so on.

Other sources

5.13 There are a number of other sources of secondary external data. The main sources include the following.

(a) *Advice or information bureaux.* These provide information in the form of advice, information leaflets or fact sheets.

(b) *Consultancies.* These include general market research organisations such as MORI and Gallup. There are also specialist market research companies which provide data on specific industries.

(c) *Specific reference works.* Different businesses will have different reference works or so called 'bibles' which are always used as a point of reference.

(d) *Libraries and information services.* Most countries have free public library systems. Educational institutes and business organisations may also provide library services which are available to their members.

(e) *Electronic sources* such as local and national radio and TV, teletext and the internet.

Exam focus point

A typical objective test question on the collection of data might be as follows.

Secondary data is:

A   data that does not provide any information
B   data collected for another purpose
C   data collected specifically for the purpose of the survey being undertaken
D   data collected by post or telephone, not by personal interview

Did you get the right answer (B)? If not look back at Section 5 and revise the topic of secondary data!

Question 2

Which of the following are secondary external sources of data.

I   *Economic Trends* (published by the Office for National Statistics in the United Kingdom).

II   The *Singapore Business Times*.

III   Data collected for a survey which was commissioned in order to determine whether Donald Ltd should launch a new product.

IV   Historical records of expenditure on canteen costs in a hospital in order to prepare current forecasts.

A   I and II only
B   I, II and III only
C   I, II and IV only
D   I, II, III and IV

Answer

The correct answer is C.

Economic Trends and the *Singapore Business Times* are both sources of secondary external data. Historic expenditure data of canteen costs were not collected specifically for the preparation of forecasts, and are therefore also secondary data. Data collected through personal interview for a particular project are primary data.

6   SAMPLING

6.1   In many situations, it will not be practical to carry out a survey which considers every item of the **population**. For example, if a poll is taken to try to predict the results of an election, it would not be possible to ask all eligible voters how they are going to vote. To ask the whole population would take far too long and cost too much money.

6.2   In such situations where it is not possible to survey the whole population, a **sample** is selected. The results obtained from the sample are used to estimate the results of the whole population.

6.3   In situations where the whole population is examined, the survey is called a **census**. This situation is quite rare, which means that the investigator must chose a **sample.**

6.4   **Disadvantages of a census**

- The high cost of a census may exceed the value of the results obtained.
- It might be out of date by the time you complete it.

6.5   **Advantages of a sample**

(a)   It can be shown mathematically that once a certain sample size has been reached, very little accuracy is gained by examining more items. The larger the size of the sample, however, the more accurate the results.

(b)   It is possible to ask more questions with a sample.

The choice of a sample

6.6   One of the most important requirements of sample data is that they should be **complete.** That is, the data should **cover all areas** of the population to be examined. If this requirement is not met, then the sample will be **biased**.

Sampling methods

6.7   Sampling methods are categorised as follows.

- **Probability** sampling methods
- **Non-probability** sampling methods

7   PROBABILITY SAMPLING METHODS

> **KEY TERM**
>
> A **probability sampling method** is a sampling method in which there is a known chance of each member of the population appearing in the sample.

7.1   **Probability sampling methods**

- Random sampling
- Stratified random sampling
- Systematic sampling
- Multistage sampling
- Cluster sampling

Random sampling

> **KEY TERM**
>
> A **simple random sample** is a sample selected in such a way that every item in the population has an equal chance of being included.

7.2   If a sample is selected using random sampling, it will be free from bias (since every item will have an equal chance of being selected). Once the sample has been selected, valid inferences about the population being sampled can be made.

7.3   For example, if you wanted to take a random sample of library books, it would not be good enough to pick them off the shelves, even if you picked them at random. This is because the books which were out on loan would stand no chance of being chosen. You would either have to make sure that all the books were on the shelves before taking your sample, or find some other way of sampling (for example, using the library index cards).

7.4   **A random sample is not necessarily a perfect sample.** For example, you might pick what you believe to be a completely random selection of library books, and find that every one of them is a detective thriller. It is a remote possibility, but it could happen. The only way to eliminate the possibility altogether is to take **100% survey (a census)** of the books, which, unless it is a tiny library, is impractical.

Sampling frames

7.5   If random sampling is used then it is necessary to construct a **sampling frame**.

> **KEY TERM**
>
> A **sampling frame** is a numbered list of all items in a population.

Once a numbered list of all items in the population has been made, it is easy to select a random sample, simply by generating a list of random numbers.

7.6   For instance, if you wanted to select a random sample of children from a school, it would be useful to have a list of names:

0   J Absolam
1   R Brown
2   S Brown
...

Now the numbers 0, 1, 2 and so on can be used to select the random sample. It is normal to start the numbering at 0, so that when 0 appears in a list of random numbers it can be used.

7.7   Sometimes it is not possible to draw up a sampling frame. For example, if you wanted to take a random sample of Americans, it would take too long to list all Americans.

BPP PUBLISHING

7.8 A sampling frame should have the following characteristics.

- **Completeness.** Are all members of the population included on the list?
- **Accuracy.** Is the information correct?
- **Adequacy.** Does it cover the entire population?
- **Up to dateness.** Is the list up to date?
- **Convenience.** Is the sampling frame readily accessible?
- **Non-duplication.** Does each member of the population appear on the list only once?

7.9 Two **readily available sampling frames** for the human population of Great Britain are the **council tax register** (list of dwellings) and the **electoral register** (list of individuals).

Random number tables

7.10 Assuming that a sampling frame can be drawn up, then a random sample can be picked from it by one of the following methods.

- The lottery method (picking numbered pieces of paper out of a box).
- The use of random number tables.

7.11 Set out below is part of a typical random number table.

93716	16894	98953	73231
32886	59780	09958	18065
92052	06831	19640	99413
39510	35905	85244	35159
27699	06494	03152	19121
92962	61773	22109	78508
10274	12202	94205	50380
75867	20717	82037	10268
85783	47619	87481	37220

You should note the following points.

(a) The sample is found by selecting groups of random numbers with the number of digits depending on the total population size, as follows.

Total population size	Number of random digits
1 - 10	1
1 - 100	2
1 - 1,000	3

The items selected for the sample are those corresponding to the random numbers selected.

(b) The starting point on the table should be selected at random. After that, however, numbers must be selected in a consistent manner. In other words, you should use the table row by row or column by column. By jumping around the table from place to place, personal bias may be introduced.

(c) In many practical situations it is more convenient to use a computer to generate a list of random numbers, especially when a large sample is required.

7.12 EXAMPLE: RANDOM NUMBER TABLES

An investigator wishes to select a random sample from a population of 800 people, who have been numbered 000, 001, ...799. As there are three digits in 799 the random numbers will be selected in groups of three. Working along the first line of the table given earlier, the first few groups are as follows.

937   161   689   498   953   732

Numbers over 799 are discarded. The first four people in the sample will therefore be those numbered 161, 689, 498 and 732.

Drawbacks of random sampling

7.13   (a)   Selected items are subject to the full range of variation inherent in the population.
          (b)   An unrepresentative sample may result.
          (c)   An adequate sampling frame might not exist.
          (d)   The numbering of the population might be laborious.
          (e)   It might be difficult to obtain the data if the selected items cover a wide area.
          (f)   It might be costly to obtain the data if the selected items cover a wide area.

Stratified random sampling

7.14   A variation on the random sampling method is **stratified random sampling**.

> **KEY TERM**
>
> **Stratified random sampling** is a method of sampling which involves dividing the population into strata or categories. Random samples are then taken from each stratum or category.

7.15   In many situations, stratified sampling is the best method of choosing a sample. Stratified sampling is best demonstrated by means of an example.

7.16   EXAMPLE: STRATIFIED SAMPLING

The number of cost and management accountants in each type of work in a particular country are as follows.

Partnerships	500
Public companies	500
Private companies	700
Public practice	800
	2,500

If a sample of 20 was required the sample would be made up as follows.

		Sample
Partnerships	$\dfrac{500}{2,500} \times 20$	4
Public companies	$\dfrac{500}{2,500} \times 20$	4
Private companies	$\dfrac{700}{2,500} \times 20$	6
Public practice	$\dfrac{800}{2,500} \times 20$	6
		20

7.17 **Advantages and disadvantages of stratification** are as follows.

Advantages	Disadvantages
The sample selected will be representative since it guarantees that every important category will have elements in the final sample.	The main **disadvantage** of stratification is that it requires **prior knowledge of each item in the population**; sampling frames do not always contain such information.
The structure of the sample will reflect that of the population if the same proportion of individuals is chosen from each stratum.	
Each stratum is represented by a randomly chosen sample and therefore **inferences can be made about each stratum**.	
Precision is increased. Sampling takes place within strata and, because the range of variation is less in each stratum than in the population as a whole and variation between strata does not enter as a chance effect, higher precision is obtainable.	

Systematic sampling

KEY TERM

Systematic sampling is a sampling method which works by selecting every nth item after a random start.

7.18 If it were decided to select a sample of 20 from a population of 800, then every 40th (800 ÷ 20) item after a random start in the first 40 should be selected. The starting point could be found using the lottery method or random number tables. If (say) 23 was chosen, then the sample would include the 23rd, 63rd, 103rd, 143rd ... 783rd items. The gap of 40 is known as the **sampling interval**.

7.19 **Advantages and disadvantages of systematic sampling**

Advantages	Disadvantages
It is easy to use	It is possible that a biased sample might be chosen if there is a regular pattern to the population which coincides with the sampling method.
It is cheap	It is not completely random since some samples have a zero chance of being selected.

Multistage sampling

> **KEY TERM**
>
> **Multistage sampling** is a probability sampling method which involves dividing the population into a number of sub-populations and then selecting a small sample of these sub-populations at random.
>
> Each sub-population is then divided further, and then a small sample is again selected at random. This process is repeated as many times as is necessary.

7.20   Multistage sampling is best demonstrated by means of an example.

7.21   EXAMPLE: MULTISTAGE SAMPLING

A survey of spending habits is being planned to cover the whole of Britain. It is obviously **impractical to draw up a sampling frame**, so **random sampling is not possible**. Multistage sampling is to be used instead.

The country is divided into a number of areas and a small sample of these is selected at random. Each of the areas selected is subdivided into smaller units and again, a smaller number of these is selected at random. This process is repeated as many times as necessary and finally, a random sample of the relevant people living in each of the smallest units is taken. A fair approximation to a random sample can be obtained.

Thus, we might choose a random sample of eight areas, and from each of these areas, select a random sample of five towns. From each town, a random sample of 200 people might be selected so that the total sample size is $8 \times 5 \times 200 = 8,000$ people.

7.22   **Advantages and disadvantages of multistage sampling**

Advantages	Disadvantages
Fewer investigators are needed	There is the **possibility of bias** if, for example, only a small number of regions are selected.
It is not so costly to obtain a sample	The method is **not truly random** as once the final sampling areas have been selected the rest of the population cannot be in the sample.
	If the population is heterogeneous, the areas chosen should reflect the **full range of the diversity**. Otherwise, choosing some areas and excluding others (even if it is done randomly) will result in a biased sample.

Cluster sampling

KEY TERM

Cluster sampling is a non-random sampling method that involves selecting one definable subsection of the population as the sample, that subsection taken to be representative of the population in question.

7.23 For example, the pupils of one school might be taken as a cluster sample of all children at school in one county.

7.24 **Advantages and disadvantages of cluster sampling**

Advantages	Disadvantages
It is a good alternative to multistage sampling if a satisfactory sampling frame does not exist.	The potential for considerable bias.
It is inexpensive to operate.	

Question 3

Describe four methods a brewery could employ to test the market for a new canned beer. Discuss the relative advantages and disadvantages of each method chosen.

Answer

(a) The brewery could try to supply the beer to a **random sample** of beer drinkers, and then ask for their views. Such samples are taken in such a way that every member of the population (in this case, all beer drinkers and perhaps all potential beer drinkers) has an equal chance of being selected for the sample. The main advantage of random sampling is that it allows mathematical analysis of the data to be carried out. The main disadvantage is that a random sample can be difficult and expensive to collect. The brewery may well find that it is impossible to compile a list of all beer drinkers from which to select a sample.

(b) **Stratified sampling** may well be appropriate. The population would first be divided into groups, perhaps by age or by weekly beer consumption, and then samples would be selected from each group (reflecting the proportion of the population in the group). The main advantage of stratified sampling is that it ensures that each group is represented in the sample. The main disadvantage is that preliminary work is needed to determine which groupings are likely to be useful and the proportion of the population in each group.

(c) **Cluster sampling** may well be a practical alternative, giving some of the benefits of both random sampling and stratified sampling. The population could be divided geographically into beer drinkers at public houses in different regions of the country and beer purchasers at off licences within these regions. A sample of regions could be selected, and a sample of public houses and off licences in each selected region could be chosen. All consumers at the chosen public houses and off licences would then form the sample. The main advantage of cluster sampling is its relative cheapness. The main disadvantage is that the sample obtained will not be truly random, so some forms of statistical analysis will not be possible.

(d) **Quota sampling** has the advantage of being even cheaper than cluster sampling, but the disadvantage of producing a sample which is even further from being random. Researchers would simply visit a selection of public houses and off licences and interview the first beer drinkers they met until they had fulfilled some quota (say ten men and ten women).

Question 4

Which of the following are disadvantages of systematic sampling? Tick as appropriate.

☐ The sample chosen might be biased

☐ Some samples have a zero chance of being selected so sampling method is not completely random

☐ Prior knowledge of each item in the population is required

Answer

☑ The sample chosen might be biased

☑ Some samples have a zero chance of being selected so sampling method is not completely random

☐ Prior knowledge of each item in the population is required

8 NON-PROBABILITY SAMPLING METHODS

> **KEY TERM**
>
> A **non-probability sampling method** is a sampling method in which the chance of each member of the population appearing in the sample is not known.

8.1 The only non-probability sampling method that you need to know about for your Business Mathematics studies is **quota sampling.**

Quota sampling

> **KEY TERM**
>
> In **quota sampling,** randomness is forfeited in the interests of cheapness and administrative simplicity. Investigators are told to interview all the people they meet up to a certain quota.

8.2 EXAMPLE: QUOTA SAMPLING

Consider the figures in Paragraph 7.16, but with the following additional information relating to the sex of the cost and management accountants.

	Male	Female
Partnerships	300	200
Public companies	400	100
Private companies	300	400
Public practice	300	500

An investigator's quotas might be as follows.

	Male	Female	Total
Partnerships	30	20	50
Public companies	40	10	50
Private companies	30	40	70
Public practice	30	50	80
			250

Using quota sampling, the investigator would interview the first 30 male cost and management accountants in partnerships that he met, the first 20 female cost and management accountants in partnerships that he met and so on.

8.3 Advantages and disadvantages of quota sampling

Advantages	Disadvantages
It is **cheap** and **administratively easy**.	The method can result in certain **biases**. For example, an interviewer in a shopping centre may fill his quota by only meeting people who can go shopping during the week.
A much larger sample can be studied, and hence more information can be gained at a faster speed for a given outlay than when compared with a fully randomised sampling method.	The non-random nature of the method rules out any valid estimate of the **sampling error** (a concept you will meet later in your studies) in estimates derived from the sample.
Although a fairly detailed knowledge of the characteristics of a population is required, **no sampling frame is necessary** because the interviewer questions every person he meets up to the quota.	
It may be the **only possible approach** in certain situations, such as television audience research.	
Given suitable, trained and properly briefed field workers, quota sampling **yields enough accurate information** for many forms of commercial market research.	

Exam focus point

The type of objective test question on sampling that you might meet in an exam is shown below.

Identify which of the following sampling methods does *not* require a sampling frame.

- Random
- Stratified
- Quota
- Systematic

The correct answer was of course quota sampling which is the only non-probability sampling method covered in this topic of data collection.

Would you have got the right answer? It was worth 2 marks!

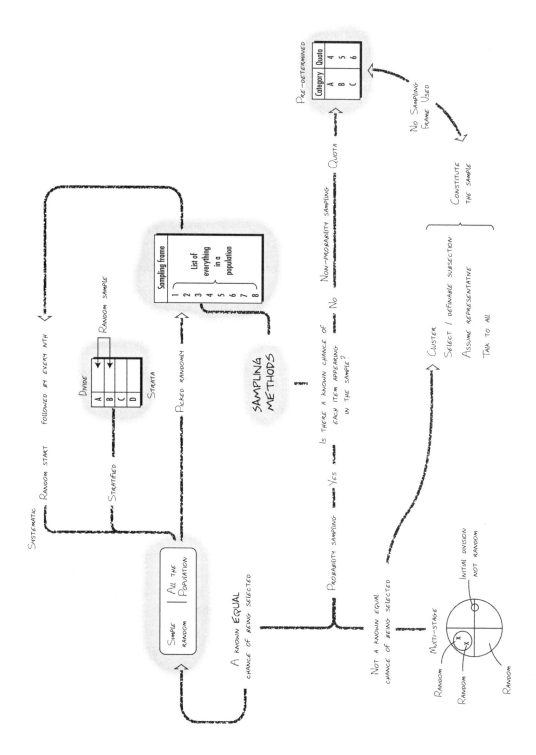

BPP
PUBLISHING

Chapter roundup

- **Data** are the raw materials for data processing. **Information** is data that has been processed.

- **Quantitative data** are data that can be measured. A 'variable' is something which can be measured.

- **Qualitative data** cannot be measured, but have **attributes** (an attribute is something an object either has or does not have).

- Data may be **primary** (collected specifically for the purpose of a survey) or **secondary** (collected for some other purpose).

- The main **characteristics of good information**

Relevance	Confidence-inspiring
Completeness	Properly communicated
Accuracy	Clarity

- **Discrete** data/variables can only take on a countable number of values. **Continuous** data/ variables can take on any value.

- Data may be obtained from an **internal** source or an **external** source.

- The main sources of **primary data** are: personal investigation; teams of investigators; interviews; postal questionnaires and telephone surveys.

- The main sources of **secondary data** are: Governments; banks; newspapers; trade journals; information bureaux; consultancies; libraries and information services.

- Data are often collected from a **sample** rather than from a population. If the whole population is examined, the survey is called a **census**.

- A **probability sampling method** is a sampling method in which there is a known chance of each member of the population appearing in the sample.

  Probability sampling methods

  - Random
  - Stratified random
  - Systematic
  - Multistage
  - Cluster

- Random sampling requires the construction of a **sampling frame**. A sampling frame is a numbered list of all items in a population.

- A **non-probability sampling method** is a sampling method in which the chance of each member of the population appearing in the sample is not known, for example, **quota sampling**.

- You must be aware of the characteristics and advantages and disadvantages of the sampling methods covered in this chapter.

- Once data have been collected they need to be **presented** and **analysed** It is important to remember that if data have not been collected properly, no amount of careful presentation or analysis can remedy this defect.

Quick quiz

1 **Fill in the blanks** in the statements below using the words in the box.

Data can be either (1) .... (have variables) or (2) .... (have (3) ....). Variables can be either (4) .... (eg 0, 1, 2, 3) or (5) .... (eg 0.54, 0.612, 0.117). Data may also be classified as (6) .... (collected for a specific survey) or (7) .... (collected for some other purpose).

• Quantitative	• Continuous	• Attributes	• Primary
• Secondary	• Qualitative	• Discrete	

2 List four main secondary data sources.

3 What is the main advantage of using primary data over secondary data?

4 Identify the following as either primary or secondary data.

Primary data   **Secondary data**

Annual Abstract of Statistics

Wall Street Journal

Investigator's survey

Survey questionnaire

Management Accounting

BPP's website

5 Fill in the blanks in the boxes below using the words in the box.

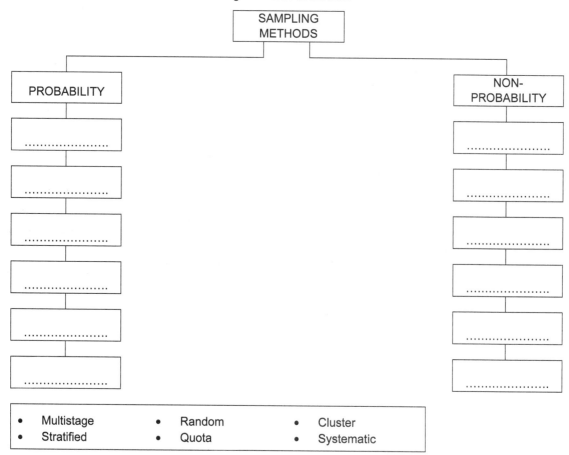

• Multistage	• Random	• Cluster	
• Stratified	• Quota	• Systematic	

6   A simple random sample is a sample selected in such a way that every item in the population has an equal chance of being included.

True ☐

False ☐

7   I   If a sample is selected using random sampling, it will be free from bias

       II   A sampling frame is a numbered list of all items in a sample

       III   Cluster sampling is a non-probability sampling method

       IV   In quota sampling, investigators are told to interview all the people they meet up to a certain quota

Which of the above statements are true?

A   I, II, III and IV
B   I, II and IV only
C   I and II only
D   I and IV only

8   The essence of systematic sampling is that

A   Each element of the population has an equal chance of being chosen
B   Members of various strata are selected by the interviewers up to predetermined limits
C   Every nth item of the population is selected
D   Every element of one definable sub-section of the population is selected

Answers to quick quiz

1   (1) Quantitative   (2) Qualitative   (3) Attributes

       (4) Discrete   (5) Continuous   (6) Primary

       (7) Secondary

2   • Governments
     • Banks
     • Newspapers
     • Trade journals

3   The user of the information knows where it came from, the circumstances under which it was collected and any limitations or inadequacies in it.

4   **Primary data**   **Secondary data**

       Investigator's survey   Wall Street Journal

       Survey questionnaire   *Annual Abstract of Statistics*

                                Management Accounting

                                  BPP's website

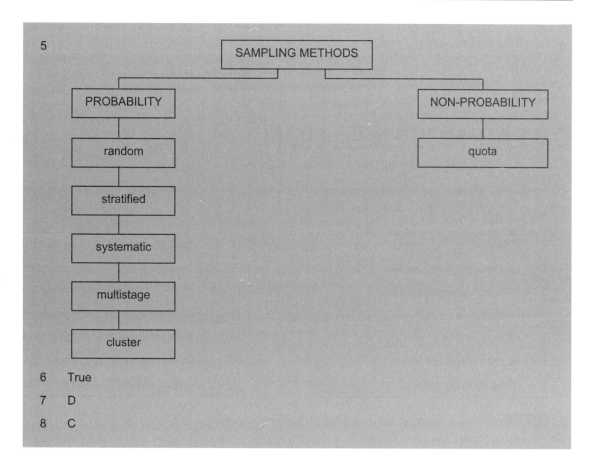

6   True

7   D

8   C

Now try the following objective test questions

Question bank	Question numbers	Page
Paper-based exam	4	272
Computer-based assessment	4	291

BPP PUBLISHING

Chapter 5

DATA PRESENTATION

Topic list		Syllabus reference	Ability required
1	Tables	(ii)	Comprehension and application
2	Bar charts	(ii)	Comprehension and application
3	Frequency distributions	(ii)	Application
4	Histograms	(ii)	Comprehension and application
5	Ogives	(ii)	Comprehension and application
6	Scatter diagrams	(ii)	Comprehension and application
7	Time series graphs	(ii)	Comprehension and application

Introduction

You now know how to collect data. So what do we do now? We have to **present** the data we have collected so that they can be of use. This chapter begins by looking at how data can be presented in **tables** and **charts**. Such methods are helpful in presenting key data in a **concise** and **easy to understand way**.

Data that are a mass of numbers can usefully be summarised into a **frequency distribution**. **Histograms** and **ogives** are the **pictorial representation** of grouped and cumulative frequency distributions. Data recorded over time can be presented as **time series graphs**.

Learning outcomes covered in this chapter

- **Tabulate** data and **explain** the results

- **Prepare** a frequency distribution from raw data

- **Prepare** and **explain** the following graphs and diagrams: bar charts, time series graphs, scatter diagrams, histograms and ogives

Syllabus content covered in this chapter

- Tabulation of data

- Frequency distributions

- Graphs and diagrams: bar charts, time series graphs, scatter diagrams, histograms and ogives

1   TABLES

1.1   **Raw data** (the list of results from a survey) need to be **summarised** and **analysed,** to give them meaning. One of the most basic ways is the preparation of a **table**.

KEY TERMS

- **Tabulation** means putting data into tables.

- A **table** is a matrix of data in rows and columns, with the rows and the columns having titles.

1.2 Since a table is **two-dimensional**, it can only show **two variables**. To tabulate data, you need to recognise what the two dimensions should represent, prepare **rows** and **columns** accordingly with suitable **titles**, and then **insert the data** into the appropriate places in the table.

1.3 EXAMPLE: TABLES

The total number of employees in a certain trading company is 1,000. They are employed in three departments: production, administration and sales. 600 people are employed in the production department and 300 in administration. There are 110 males under 21 in employment, 110 females under 21, and 290 females aged 21 years and over. The remaining employees are males aged 21 and over.

In the production department there are 350 males aged 21 and over, 150 females aged 21 and over and 50 males under 21, whilst in the administration department there are 100 males aged 21 and over, 110 females aged 21 and over and 50 males aged under 21.

Draw up a table to show all the details of employment in the company and its departments and provide suitable secondary statistics to describe the distribution of people in departments.

1.4 SOLUTION

The basic table required has the following two dimensions.

- Departments
- Age/sex analysis

In this example we are going to show the percentage of the total workforce in each department.

Analysis of employees

	Production		Administration		Sales			Total		
	No	%	No	%	No		%	No		%
Males 21 yrs +	350	58.4	100	33.3	40	★★	40.0	490	★	49.0
Females 21 yrs +	150	25.0	110	36.7	30	★★	30.0	290		29.0
Subtotals 21 yrs +	500	83.4	210	70.0	70		70.0	780		78.0
Males under 21	50	8.3	50	16.7	10	★★	10.0	110		11.0
Females under 21	50 ★	8.3	40 ★	13.3	20	★★	20.0	110		11.0
Subtotals under 21	100	16.6	90	30.0	30		30.0	220		22.0
Total	600	100.0	300	100.0	100		100.0	1,000		100.0

★   Balancing figure to make up the column total
★★ Balancing figure then needed to make up the row total

Guidelines for tabulation

1.5 The example above illustrates certain guidelines which you should apply when presenting data in tabular form. These are as follows.

- The table should be given a **clear title**.
- All columns should be **clearly labelled**.
- Where appropriate, there should be **clear sub-totals**.
- A **total column** may be presented; this would usually be the right-hand column.
- A **total figure** is often advisable at the bottom of each column of figures.
- Tables should not be packed with so much data that reading information is difficult.
- Non-essential information should be eliminated.
- Consider ordering columns/rows by order of importance/magnitude.

Explaining the results of tabulated data

1.6 In an examination you may be asked to extract and interpret key information from tabulated data. Look back at the table in paragraph 1.4, and study the following comments which could be made about the information presented.

(a) 49% of the total workforce is made up of males who are 21 years old or more, and 29% of the total workforce is made up of females who are 21 years old or more. The workforce is therefore made up primarily of workers who are 21 years old or more.

(b) The percentage of the workforce who are under 21 years old is 22. (Males and females in this age group both make up 11% of the total workforce.) We may conclude that most of the employees making up the workforce are 21 years old or more.

(c) The production department is made up of 58.4% of males who are 21 years old or more, and 25% of females who are 21 years old or more. There are therefore significantly more males than females employed in the production department (just over twice as many in fact).

Males and females employed in the production department who are under 21 years of age form only 16.6% of the total employees in this department. Males and females employed in this age group both make up 8.3%.

(d) 70% of the employees of both the administration and the sales departments are aged 21 years or more. This is slightly less than the corresponding figure of 83.4% in the production department. The production department therefore employs a higher number of employees who are 21 years old or more than both the administration and sales departments. The administration department employs more females than males who are aged under 21 years old.

(e) The sales department employs slightly more males than females who are 21 years old or more, in contrast the administration department employs slightly more females than males in this age group. The sales department employs twice as many females than males who are under 21 years old.

1.7 Make sure that you can present data in a tabulated form, and then explain the results obtained.

Question 1

By 20X9, Healthy Healthfoods Ltd had been in business for ten years. It now employs 20,770 people, of whom the largest group (36%) were sales staff, the next largest group (21%) were buyers and the third largest group (18%) were administrative staff. Other groups of employees made up the rest of the staff.

Things had been very different when the company first began operations in 20X0. Then, it had just 4,200 employees, of whom the 1,260 buyers were the biggest group; there were 1,176 sales staff and just 840 administrative staff.

By 20X3, the company had nearly doubled in size, employing 7,650 people, of whom 2,448 were buyers, 2,372 were sales staff and 1,607 were administrators.

By 20X6, the company employed 12,740 people, and the growth in numbers had been most noticeable amongst sales staff, of whom there were 4,840. There were 3,185 buyers. Administrative staff had increased substantially in number to 2,550.

The company's managing director has been very pleased with the growth in business over the past nine years, but has tried to limit the growth in the numbers of staff who are not sales staff, buyers or administrative staff.

Required

Present the given data in tabular form.

Are there any comments you would make about what the information in the table should tell the managing director of the company?

Answer

The two dimensions of the table should be:

(a) years
(b) each group of employees, including a category for 'others'

It would also be possible to include percentage growth over the years.

The entries in the 'cells' of the table could be actual numbers of employees, percentages of the total work force or both.

Analysis of employee groups at Healthy Healthfoods Ltd

	20X0		20X3			20X6			20X9		
	Number empl'd	*% of total*	*Number empl'd*	*% of total*	*% growth in total*	*Number empl'd*	*% of total*	*% growth in total*	*Number empl'd*	*% of total*	*% growth in total*
Sales staff	1,176	28	2,372	31	102	4,840	38	104	7,477	36	54
Buyers	1,260	30	2,448	32	94	3,185	25	30	4,362	21	37
Administrative staff	840	20	1,607	21	91	2,550	20	59	3,739	18	47
Other groups	924	22	1,223	16	32	2,165	17	77	5,192	25	140
Total	4,200	100	7,650	100	82	12,740	100	67	20,770	100	63

The table shows that there has been a substantial increase in the number of sales staff over the years, with the percentage of employees who are sales staff rising from under 30% in 20X0 to 36% in 20X9. There has been a decrease in the proportion of employees who are buyers, and a small decrease in the proportion who are administrative staff. The managing director's concern about the rapid growth in other groups of employees might be justified. The percentage increase in their numbers between 20X6 and 20X9 suggests that efforts to control their numbers have not yet had much success.

2   BAR CHARTS

2.1   Instead of presenting data in a table, it might be preferable to give a **visual display** in the form of a **chart**. The purpose of a chart is to convey the data in a way that will demonstrate its meaning more clearly than a table of data would. Charts are not always more appropriate than tables, and the most suitable way of presenting data will depend on the following.

(a) **What the data are intended to show.** Visual displays usually make one or two points quite forcefully, whereas tables usually give more detailed information.

(b) **Who is going to use the data.** Some individuals might understand visual displays more readily than tabulated data.

Bar charts

KEY TERM

The **bar chart** is one of the most common methods of presenting data in a visual form. It is a chart in which quantities are shown in the form of bars.

2.2 There are three main types of bar chart.

- Simple bar charts
- Component bar charts, including percentage component bar charts
- Multiple (or compound) bar charts

KEY TERM

A **simple bar chart** is a chart consisting of one or more bars, in which the length of each bar indicates the magnitude of the corresponding data item.

2.3 EXAMPLE: A SIMPLE BAR CHART

A company's total sales for the years from 20X1 to 20X6 are as follows.

Year	Sales
	£'000
20X1	800
20X2	1,200
20X3	1,100
20X4	1,400
20X5	1,600
20X6	1,700

The data could be shown on a simple bar chart as follows

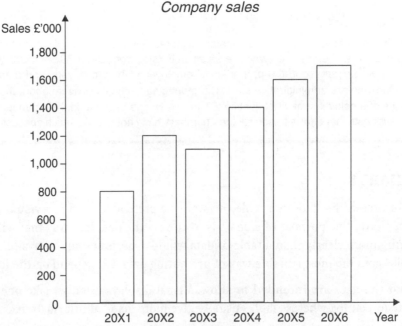

Each axis of the chart must be clearly labelled, and there must be a scale to indicate the magnitude of the data. Here, the y axis includes a scale for the amount of sales, and so readers of the bar chart can see not only that sales have been rising year by year (with 20X3 being an exception) but also what the actual sales have been each year.

2.4 Simple bar charts serve two purposes.

- The actual magnitude of each item is shown.
- The lengths of bars on the chart allow magnitudes to be compared.

KEY TERM

A **component bar chart** is a bar chart that gives a breakdown of each total into its components. The total length of each bar and each component on a component bar chart indicates magnitude (a bigger amount is shown by a longer bar).

2.5 EXAMPLE: A COMPONENT BAR CHART

Charbart plc's sales for the years from 20X7 to 20X9 are as follows.

	20X7	20X8	20X9
	£'000	£'000	£'000
Product A	1,000	1,200	1,700
Product B	900	1,000	1,000
Product C	500	600	700
Total	2,400	2,800	3,400

A component bar chart would show the following.

- How total sales have changed from year to year
- The components of each year's total

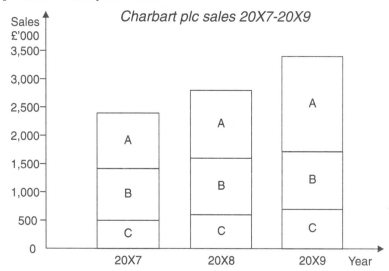

In this diagram the growth in sales is illustrated and the significance of growth in product A sales as the reason for the total sales growth is also fairly clear.

KEY TERM

A **percentage component bar chart** is a component barchart which does not show **total magnitudes** - if one or more bars are drawn on the chart, the total length of each bar is the same. The lengths of the sections of the bar however, do vary, and it is these lengths that indicate the **relative sizes** of the components.

2.6 EXAMPLE: A PERCENTAGE COMPONENT BAR CHART

The information in the previous example of sales of Charbart plc could have been shown in a **percentage component bar chart** as follows.

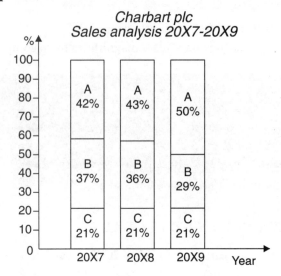

Working

	20X7		20X8		20X9	
	£'000	%	£'000	%	£'000	%
Product A	1,000	42	1,200	43	1,700	50
Product B	900	37	1,000	36	1,000	29
Product C	500	21	600	21	700	21
Total	2,400	100	2,800	100	3,400	100

This chart shows that sales of C have remained a steady proportion of total sales, but the proportion of A in total sales has gone up quite considerably, while the proportion of B has fallen correspondingly.

KEY TERM

A **multiple bar chart** (or **compound bar chart**) is a bar chart in which two or more separate bars are used to present sub-divisions of data.

2.7 EXAMPLE: A MULTIPLE BAR CHART

The data on Charbart plc's sales could be shown in a multiple bar chart as follows.

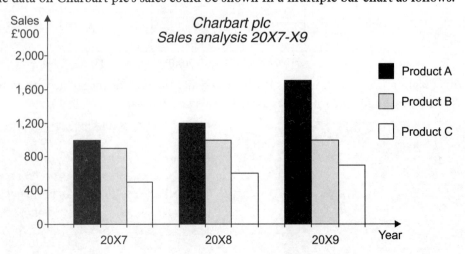

A multiple bar chart uses several bars for each total. In this multiple bar chart, the sales in each year are shown as three separate bars, one for each product, A, B and C.

2.8 Multiple bar charts present similar information to component bar charts, except for the following.

(a) Multiple bar charts do not show the grand total whereas component bar charts do.

(b) Multiple bar charts illustrate the comparative magnitudes of the components more clearly than component bar charts.

2.9 **Multiple bar charts are sometimes drawn with the bars horizontal instead of vertical.**

Question 2

Income for Canary Bank in 20X0, 20X1 and 20X2 is made up as follows.

	20X0	20X1	20X2
	£'000	£'000	£'000
Interest income	3,579	2,961	2,192
Commission income	857	893	917
Other income	62	59	70

Using the above data complete the following graphs.

(a)

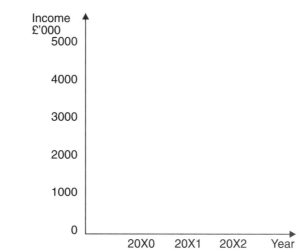

(b)

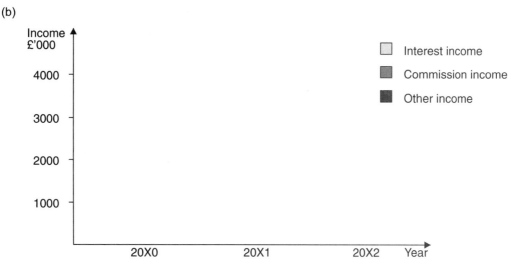

Answer

Workings

	20X0	20X1	20X2
	£'000	£'000	£'000
	3,579	2,961	2,192
	857	893	917
	62	59	70
	4,498	3,913	3,179

(a)

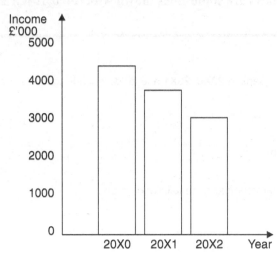

(b)

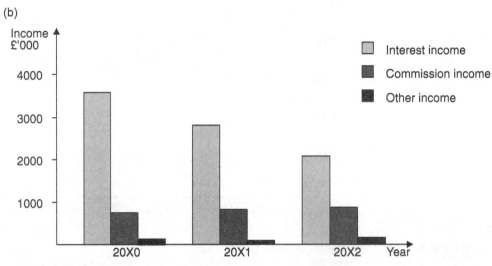

---

3   FREQUENCY DISTRIBUTIONS

3.1   Frequently the data collected from a statistical survey or investigation is simply a mass of numbers.

65	69	70	71	70	68	69	67	70	68
72	71	69	74	70	73	71	67	69	70

3.2   The raw data above yields little information as it stands; imagine how much more difficult it would be if there were hundreds or even thousands of data items. The data could, of course, be arranged in **order size** (an **array**) and the lowest and highest data items, as well as typical items, could be identified.

3.3 Many sets of data, however, contain a limited number of data values, even though there may be many occurrences of each value. It can therefore be useful to organise the data into what is known as a **frequency distribution** (or **frequency table**) which records the number of times each value occurs (the **frequency**). A frequency distribution for the data in Paragraph 3.1 (the output in units of 20 employees during one week) is as follows.

Output of employees in one week in units

Output Units	*Number of employees (frequency)*
65	1
66	0
67	2
68	2
69	4
70	5
71	3
72	1
73	1
74	1
	20

3.4 When the data are arranged in this way it is immediately obvious that 69 and 70 units are the most common volumes of output per employee per week.

Grouped frequency distributions

3.5 If there is a large set of data or if every (or nearly every) data item is different, it is often convenient to group frequencies together into **bands** or **classes**. For example, suppose that the output produced by another group of 20 employees during one week was as follows, in units.

1,087	850	1,084	792
924	1,226	1,012	1,205
1,265	1,028	1,230	1,182
1,086	1,130	989	1,155
1,134	1,166	1,129	1,160

3.6 The range of output from the lowest to the highest producer is 792 to 1,265, a **range** of 473 units. This range could be divided into classes of say, 100 units (the **class width** or **class interval**), and the number of employees producing output within each class could then be grouped into a single frequency, as follows.

Output Units	*Number of employees (frequency)*
700 - 799	1
800 - 899	1
900 - 999	2
1,000 - 1,099	5
1,100 - 1,199	7
1,200 - 1,299	4
	20

3.7 **Note, however, that once items have been 'grouped' in this way their individual values are lost.**

3.8 As well as being used for **discrete variables** (as above), grouped frequency distributions (or grouped frequency tables) can be used to present data for **continuous variables**.

3.9 EXAMPLE: A GROUPED FREQUENCY DISTRIBUTION FOR A CONTINUOUS VARIABLE

Suppose we wish to record the heights of 50 different individuals. The information might be presented as a grouped frequency distribution, as follows.

	Number of individuals
Height	*(frequency)*
cm	
Up to and including 154	1
Over 154, up to and including 163	3
Over 163, up to and including 172	8
Over 172, up to and including 181	16
Over 181, up to and including 190	18
Over 190	4
	50

3.10 Note the following points.

(a) It would be wrong to show the ranges as 0 - 154, 154 - 163, 163 - 172 and so on, because 154 cm and 163 cm would then be values in two classes, which is not permissible. Although each value should only be in one class, we have to make sure that each possible value can be included. Classes such as 154-162, 163-172 would not be suitable since a height of 162.5 cm would not belong in either class. Such classes could be used for discrete variables, however.

(b) **There is an open ended class at each end of the range.** This is because heights up to 154 cm and over 190 cm are thought to be uncommon, so that a single 'open ended' class is used to group all the frequencies together.

3.11 **To prepare a grouped frequency distribution, a decision must be made about how wide each class should be.** You should observe the following guidelines if you are not told how many classes to use or what the class interval should be.

(a) The size of each class should be appropriate to the nature of the data being recorded, and the most appropriate class interval varies according to circumstances.

(b) The upper and lower limits of each class interval should be suitable 'round' numbers for class intervals which are in multiples of 5, 10, 100, 1,000 and so on. For example, if the class interval is 10, and data items range in value from 23 to 62 (discrete values), the class intervals should be 20-29, 30-39, 40-49, 50-59 and 60-69, rather than 23-32, 33-42, 43-52 and 53-62.

(c) With **continuous variables**, either:

(i) the **upper limit** of a class should be '**up to and including ...**' and the **lower limit** of the next class should be '**over ...**'

(ii) the **upper limit** of a class should be '**less than...**', and the **lower limit** of the next class should be '**at least ...**'

Question 3

The commission earnings for May 20X0 of the assistants in a department store were as follows (in pounds).

60	35	53	47	25	44	55	58	47	71
63	67	57	44	61	48	50	56	61	42
43	38	41	39	61	51	27	56	57	50

55	68	55	50	25	48	44	43	49	73
53	35	36	41	45	71	56	40	69	52
36	47	66	52	32	46	44	32	52	58
49	41	45	45	48	36	46	42	52	33
31	36	40	66	53	58	60	52	66	51
51	44	59	53	51	57	35	45	46	54
46	54	51	39	64	43	54	47	60	45

Required

Prepare a grouped frequency distribution classifying the commission earnings into categories of £5 commencing with '£25 and under £30'.

Answer

We are told what classes to use, so the first step is to identify the lowest and highest values in the data. The lowest value is £25 (in the first row) and the highest value is £73 (in the fourth row). This means that the class intervals must go up to '£70 and under £75'.

We can now set out the classes in a column, and then count the number of items in each class using tally marks.

Class interval	Tally marks	Total
£25 and less than £30	///	3
£30 and less than £35	////	4
£35 and less than £40	ΗΗ ΗΗ	10
£40 and less than £45	ΗΗ ΗΗ ΗΗ	15
£45 and less than £50	ΗΗ ΗΗ ΗΗ ///	18
£50 and less than £55	ΗΗ ΗΗ ΗΗ ΗΗ	20
£55 and less than £60	ΗΗ ΗΗ ///	13
£60 and less than £65	ΗΗ ///	8
£65 and less than £70	ΗΗ /	6
£70 and less than £75	///	3
	Total	100

3.12 You should be able to interpret a grouped frequency distribution and express an interpretation in writing. In the example in Paragraph 3.9, an interpretation of the data is fairly straightforward.

(a) Most heights fell between 154 cm and 190 cm.

(b) Most heights were in the middle of this range, with few people having heights in the lower and upper ends of the range.

Cumulative frequency distributions

3.13 A cumulative frequency distribution (or cumulative frequency table) can be used to show the total number of times that a value above or below a certain amount occurs.

3.14 There are two possible cumulative frequency distributions for the grouped frequency distribution in Paragraph 3.6.

	Cumulative frequency		*Cumulative frequency*
≥ 700	20	< 800	1
≥ 800	19	< 900	2
≥ 900	18	<1,000	4
≥ 1,000	16	<1,100	9
≥ 1,100	11	<1,200	16
≥ 1,200	4	<1,300	20

(a) The symbol > means 'greater than' and ≥ means 'greater than or equal to'. The symbol < means 'less than' and ≤ means 'less than or equal to'. These symbols provide a convenient method of stating classes.

(b) The first cumulative frequency distribution shows that of the total of 20 employees, 19 produced 800 units or more, 18 produced 900 units or more, 16 produced 1,000 units or more and so on.

(c) The second cumulative frequency distribution shows that, of the total of 20 employees, one produced under 800 units, two produced under 900 units, four produced under 1,000 units and so on.

3.15 Students often find frequency distributions tricky. The following summary might help to clarify the different types of frequency distribution we have covered in this section.

(a) **Frequency distribution**. Individual data items are arranged in a table showing the frequency each **individual** data item occurs.

(b) **Grouped frequency distribution - discrete variables**. Data items (which are discrete variables, eg the number of marks obtained in an examination) are divided into classes of say 10 marks. The numbers of students (frequencies) scoring marks within each band are then grouped into a single frequency.

(c) **Grouped frequency distribution - continuous variables**. These are similar to the grouped frequency distributions for discrete variables (above.) However, as they are concerned with **continuous** variables note the following points.

   (i) There is an open-ended class at the end of the range.

   (ii) Class intervals must be carefully considered so that they capture all of the data once (and only once!).

(d) **Cumulative frequency distribution**. These distributions are used to show the number of times that a value above or below a certain amount occurs. Cumulative frequencies are obtained by adding the individual frequencies together.

4   **HISTOGRAMS**

KEY TERM

A **histogram** is a chart that looks like a bar chart except that the bars are joined together. On a histogram, frequencies are represented by the **area** covered by the bars (compare this with a bar chart where the frequencies are represented by the heights of the bars).

4.1   **A frequency distribution can be represented pictorially by means of a histogram.**

Histograms of frequency distributions with equal class intervals

4.2 **If all the class intervals are the same,** as in the frequency distribution in Paragraph 3.6, **the bars of the histogram all have the same width and the heights will be proportional to the frequencies. The histogram looks almost identical to a bar chart except that the bars are joined together. Because the bars are joined together, when presenting discrete data the data must be treated as continuous so that there are no gaps between class intervals.** For example, for a cricketer's scores in various games the classes would have to be ≥ 0 but < 10, ≥ 10 but < 20 and so on, instead of 0-9, 10-19 and so on.

4.3 A histogram of the distribution in Paragraph 3.6 would be drawn as follows.

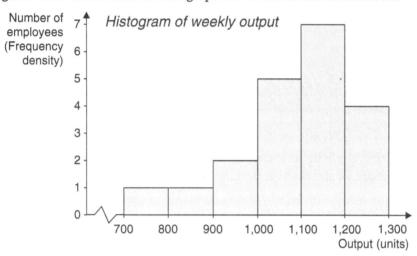

4.4 Note that the discrete data have been treated as continuous, the intervals being changed to >700 but ≤ 800, >800 but ≤ 900 and so on.

Histograms of frequency distributions with unequal class intervals

4.5 **If a distribution has unequal class intervals, the heights of the bars have to be adjusted for the fact that the bars do not have the same width.**

4.6 EXAMPLE: A HISTOGRAM WITH UNEQUAL CLASS INTERVALS

The weekly wages of employees of Salt Lake Ltd are as follows.

Wages per employee	*Number of employees*
Up to and including £60	4
> £60 ≤ £80	6
> £80 ≤ £90	6
> £90 ≤£120	6
More than £120	3

The class intervals for wages per employee are not all the same, and range from £10 to £30.

4.7 **A histogram is drawn as follows.**

(a) **The width of each bar on the chart must be proportionate to the corresponding class interval.** In other words, the bar representing wages of $> £60 \leq £80$, a range of £20, will be oncewide as the bar representing wages of $> £80 \leq £90$, a range of only £10.

(b) **A standard width of bar must be selected.** This should be the size of class interval which occurs most frequently. In our example, class intervals £10, £20 and £30 each occur once. An interval of £20 will be selected as the standard width.

(c) **Open-ended classes must be closed off.** It is usual for the width of such classes to be the same as that of the adjoining class. In this example, the class 'up to and including £60' will become >£40 ≤ £60 and the class 'more than £120' will become >£120 ≤ £150.

(d) **Each frequency is then multiplied by (standard class width ÷ actual class width)** to obtain the height of the bar in the histogram.

(e) The height of bars no longer corresponds to **frequency** but rather to **frequency density** and hence the vertical axis should be labelled **frequency density**.

(f) Note that the data is considered to be **continuous** since the gap between, for example, £79.99 and £80.00 is very, very small.

4.8

Class interval	Size of interval	Frequency	Adjustment	Height of bar
> £40 ≤ £60	20	4	× 20/20	4
> £60 ≤ £80	20	6	× 20/20	6
> £80 ≤ £90	10	6	× 20/10	12
> £90 ≤ £120	30	6	× 20/30	4
> £120 ≤ £150	30	3	× 20/30	2

(a) The first two bars will be of normal height.

(b) The third bar will be twice as high as the class frequency (6) would suggest, to compensate for the fact that the class interval, £10, is only half the standard size.

(c) The fourth and fifth bars will be two thirds as high as the class frequencies (6 and 3) would suggest, to compensate for the fact that the class interval, £30, is 150% of the standard size.

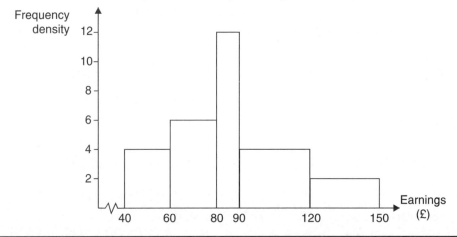

Histogram of weekly earnings: Salt Lake Ltd

Question 4

In a histogram in which one class interval is one and a half times as wide as the remaining classes, the height to be plotted in relation to the frequency for that class is

A × 1.5   B × 1.00   C × 0.75   D × 0.67

Answer

If a distribution has unequal class intervals, the heights of the bars have to be adjusted for the fact that the bars do not have the same width. If the width of one bar is one and a half times the standard width, we must divide the frequency by one and a half, ie multiply by 0.67 (1/1.5 = 2/3 = 0.67).

The correct answer is D.

Question 5

The following grouped frequency distribution shows the performances of individual sales staff in one month.

Sales	Number of sales staff
Up to £10,000	1
> £10,000 ≤ £12,000	10
> £12,000 ≤ £14,000	12
> £14,000 ≤ £18,000	8
> £18,000 ≤ £22,000	4
> £22,000	1

Required

Draw a histogram from this information.

Answer

This is a grouped frequency distribution for continuous variables.

Before drawing the histogram, we must decide on the following.

(a) A **standard class width**: £2,000 will be chosen.

(b) An **open-ended class width**. In this example, the open-ended class width will therefore be £2,000 for class 'up to £10,000' and £4,000 for the class '> £22,000'.

Class interval	Size of width £	Frequency	Adjustment	Height of block
Up to £10,000	2,000	1	× 2/2	1
> £10,000 ≤ £12,000	2,000	10	× 2/2	10
> £12,000 ≤ £14,000	2,000	12	× 2/2	12
> £14,000 ≤ £18,000	4,000	8	× 2/4	4
> £18,000 ≤ £22,000	4,000	4	× 2/4	2
> £22,000	4,000	1	× 2/4	½

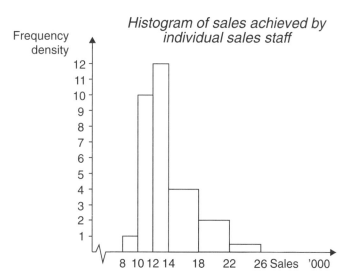

Frequency polygons

4.9 A histogram is not a particularly accurate method of presenting a frequency distribution because, in grouping frequencies together in a class interval, it is assumed that these frequencies occur evenly throughout the class interval, which is unlikely. To overcome this criticism, we can convert a histogram into a **frequency polygon**, which is drawn on the assumption that, within each class interval, the frequency of occurrence of data items is not evenly spread. There will be more values at the end of each class interval nearer the histogram's peak (if any), and so the flat top on a histogram bar should be converted into a rising or falling line.

4.10 A frequency polygon is drawn from a histogram, in the following way.

Step 1. Mark the mid-point of the top of each bar in the histogram.

Step 2. Join up all these points with straight lines.

Step 3. The ends of the diagram (the mid-points of the two end bars) should be joined to the base line at the mid-points of the next class intervals outside the range of observed data. These intervals should be taken to be of the same size as the last class intervals for observed data.

4.11 EXAMPLE: A FREQUENCY POLYGON

The following grouped frequency distribution relates to the number of occasions during the past 40 weeks that a particular cost has been a given amount.

Cost £	Number of occasions
> 800 ≤ 1,000	4
> 1,000 ≤ 1,200	10
> 1,200 ≤ 1,400	12
> 1,400 ≤ 1,600	10
> 1,600 ≤ 1,800	4
	40

Required

Prepare a frequency polygon.

4.12 SOLUTION

A histogram is first drawn, in the way described earlier. All classes are of the same width.

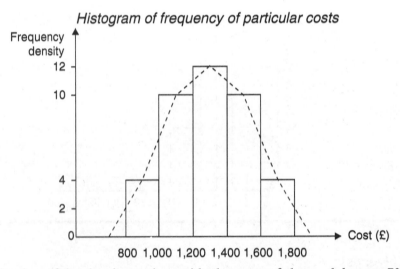

Histogram of frequency of particular costs

The mid-points of the class intervals outside the range of observed data are 700 and 1,900.

Frequency curves

4.13 Because a frequency polygon has straight lines between points, it too can be seen as an inaccurate way of presenting data. One method of obtaining greater accuracy would be to make the class intervals smaller. If the class intervals of a distribution were made small enough the frequency polygon would become very smooth. It would become a curve.

5   OGIVES

5.1   Just as a grouped frequency distribution can be graphed as a histogram, a cumulative frequency distribution can be graphed as an ogive. An ogive shows the cumulative number of items with a value less than or equal to, or alternatively greater than or equal to, a certain amount.

5.2   EXAMPLE: OGIVES

Consider the following frequency distribution.

Number of faulty units rejected on inspection	Frequency	Cumulative frequency
> 0, ≤ 1	5	5
> 1, ≤ 2	5	10
> 2, ≤ 3	3	13
> 3, ≤ 4	1	14
	14	

An ogive would be drawn as follows.

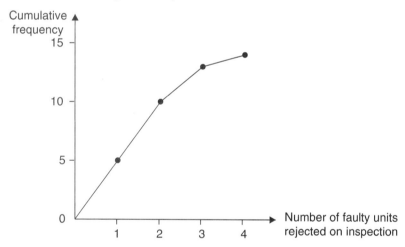

Ogive of rejected items

The ogive is drawn by plotting the cumulative frequencies on the graph, and joining them with straight lines. Although many ogives are more accurately curved lines, you can use straight lines in drawing an ogive in an examination. **An ogive drawn with straight lines may be referred to as a cumulative frequency polygon (or cumulative frequency diagram) whereas one drawn as a curve may be referred to as a cumulative frequency curve.**

For grouped frequency distributions, where we work up through values of the variable, the cumulative frequencies are plotted against the **upper limits** of the classes. For example, for the class 'over 2, up to and including 3', the cumulative frequency should be plotted against 3.

Question 6

A grouped frequency distribution for the volume of output produced at a factory over a period of 40 weeks is as follows.

Output (units)	Number of times output achieved
> 0 ≤ 200	4
>200 ≤ 400	8
>400 ≤ 600	12
>600 ≤ 800	10
>800 ≤1,000	6
	40

Required

Draw an appropriate ogive, and estimate the number of weeks in which output was 550 units or less.

Answer

Upper limit of interval	Frequency	Cumulative frequency
200	4	4
400	8	12
600	12	24
800	10	34
1,000	6	40

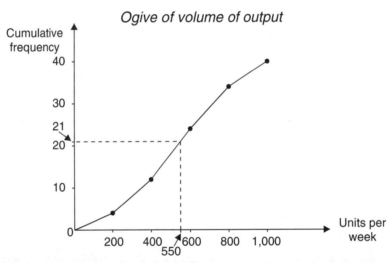

Ogive of volume of output

The dotted lines indicate that output of up to 550 units was achieved in 21 out of the 40 weeks.

5.3 We can also draw ogives to show the cumulative number of items with values greater than or equal to some given value.

5.4 EXAMPLE: DOWNWARD-SLOPING OGIVES

Output at a factory over a period of 80 weeks is shown by the following frequency distribution.

Output per week Units	Number of times output achieved
> 0 ≤ 100	10
> 100 ≤ 200	20
> 200 ≤ 300	25
> 300 ≤ 400	15
> 400 ≤ 500	10
	80

5.5 If we want to draw an ogive to show the number of weeks in which output **exceeded** a certain value, the cumulative total should begin at 80 and drop to 0. In drawing an ogive when we work down through values of the variable, the **descending cumulative frequency** should be plotted against the **lower limit** of each class interval.

Lower limit of interval	Frequency	Cumulative ('more than') frequency
0	10	80
100	20	70
200	25	50
300	15	25
400	10	10
500	0	0

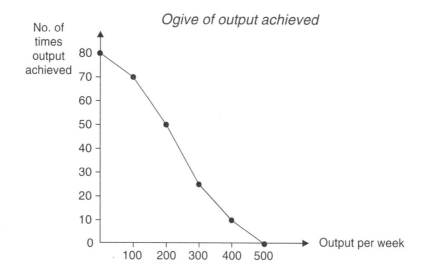

Ogive of output achieved

Make sure that you understand what this curve shows.

For example, 350 on the x axis corresponds with about 18 on the y axis. This means that output of 350 units or more was achieved 18 times out of the 80 weeks.

6 SCATTER DIAGRAMS

KEY TERM

Scatter diagrams are graphs which are used to exhibit data, rather than equations which produce simple lines or curves, in order to compare the way in which two variables vary with each other.

6.1 The x axis of a scatter diagram is used to represent the independent variable and the y axis represents the dependent variable.

93

6.2   To construct a scatter diagram or scattergraph, we must have several pairs of data, with each pair showing the value of one variable and the corresponding value of the other variable. Each pair is plotted on a graph. The resulting graph will show a number of pairs, scattered over the graph. The scattered points might or might not appear to follow a trend.

6.3   EXAMPLE: SCATTER DIAGRAM

The output at a factory each week for the last ten weeks, and the cost of that output, were as follows.

Week	1	2	3	4	5	6	7	8	9	10
Output (units)	10	12	10	8	9	11	7	12	9	14
Cost (£)	42	44	38	34	38	43	30	47	37	50

The data could be shown on a scatter diagram as follows.

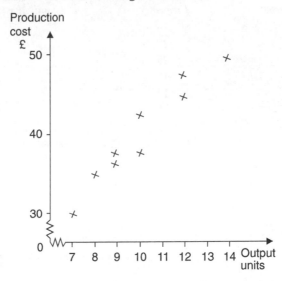

(a)   The cost depends on the volume of output: volume is the independent variable and is shown on the x axis.

(b)   You will notice from the graph that the plotted data, although scattered, lie approximately on a rising trend line, with higher total costs at higher output volumes. (The lower part of the y axis has been omitted, so as not to waste space. The break in the y axis is indicated by the jagged line.)

Curve fitting

6.4   For the most part, scatter diagrams are used to try to identify **trend lines**.

6.5   If a trend can be seen in a scatter diagram, the next step is to try to draw a trend line. Fitting a line to scatter diagram data is called **curve fitting**.

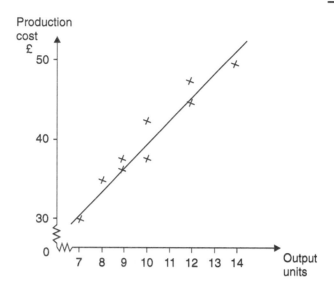

6.6   The reason for wanting to do this is to make predictions.

(a)   In the previous example, we have drawn a trend line from the scatter diagram of output units and production cost. This trend line might turn out to be, say, y = 10 + 3x. We could then use this trend line to establish what we think costs ought to be, approximately, if output were, say, 10 units or 15 units in any week. (These 'expected' costs could subsequently be compared with the actual costs, so that managers could judge whether actual costs were higher or lower than they ought to be.)

(b)   If a scatter diagram is used to record sales over time, we could draw a trend line, and use this to forecast sales for next year.

6.7   The trend line could be a straight line, or a curved line. The simplest technique for drawing a trend line is to make a visual judgement about what the closest-fitting trend line seems to be.

6.8   Here is another example of a scatter diagram with a trend line added.

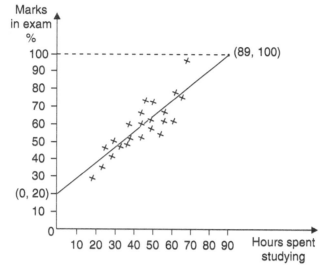

The line passes through the point x = 0, y = 20, so if its equation is y = a + bx, we have a = 20. The line also passes through x = 89, y = 100, so:

100   = 20 + (b × 89)

b   = $\dfrac{(100-20)}{89}$

= 0.9.

The line is y = 20 + 0.9x.

Question 7

The quantities of widgets produced by WDG Ltd during the year ended 31 October 20X9 and the related costs were as follows.

Month	Production Thousands	Factory cost £'000
20X8		
November	7	45
December	10	59
20X9		
January	13	75
February	14	80
March	11	65
April	7	46
May	5	35
June	4	30
July	3	25
August	2	20
September	1	15
October	5	35

You may assume that the value of money remained stable throughout the year.

Required

(a) Draw a scatter diagram related to the data provided above, and plot on it the line of best fit.

(b) Now answer the following questions.

    (i) What would you expect the factory cost to have been if 12,000 widgets had been produced in a particular month?

    (ii) What is your estimate of WDG's monthly fixed cost?

Answer

Your answers to parts (b) and (c) may have been slightly different from those given here, but they should not have been very different, because the data points lay very nearly along a straight line.

(a) *WDG Ltd - Scatter diagram of production and factory costs, November 20X8-October 20X9*

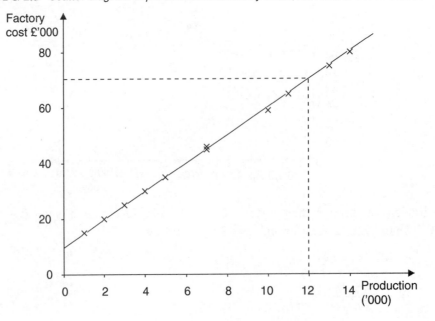

(b) (i) The estimated factory cost for a production of 12,000 widgets is £70,000.

    (ii) The monthly fixed costs are indicated by the point where the line of best fit meets the vertical axis (costs at zero production). The fixed costs are estimated as £10,000 a month.

7 TIME SERIES GRAPHS

KEY TERMS

- A **time series** is a series of figures or values recorded over time such as monthly sales over the last two years.

- A **historigram** is a graph of a time series. The horizontal axis of a historigram is always chosen to represent time and the vertical axis represents the values of the data recorded. The graph will give some indication of the trend in the data over time.

7.1 EXAMPLE: TIME SERIES

The following data show the sales of a product in the period 20X6-X8.

Year	Quarter 1 '000	Quarter 2 '000	Quarter 3 '000	Quarter 4 '000
20X6	86	42	57	112
20X7	81	39	55	107
20X8	77	35	52	99

Required

Plot a time series of the above data.

7.2 SOLUTION

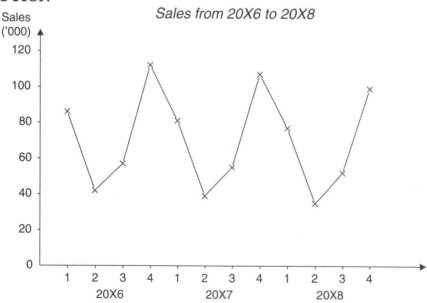

7.3 We will be looking at time series analysis in some detail in Chapter 13.

Exam focus point

Remember that you can always pick up easy marks in an examination for drawing charts and graphs neatly. Always use a ruler, label your axes and use an appropriate scale.

Chapter roundup

- **Tables** are a simple way of presenting information about two variables.

- **Charts** often convey the meaning or significance of data more clearly than would a table.

- There are three main **types of bar chart**: **simple**, **component** (including **percentage component**) and **multiple** (or **compound**).

- **Frequency distributions** are used if values of particular variables occur more than once. Make sure that you know the difference between **grouped frequency** and **cumulative frequency** distributions.

- A **frequency distribution** can be represented pictorially by means of a **histogram**. The number of observations in a class is represented by the **area** covered by the bar, rather than by its height. **Frequency polygons** and **frequency curves** are perhaps more accurate methods of data presentation than the standard histogram.

- An **ogive** shows the cumulative number of items with a value less than or equal to, or alternatively greater than or equal to, a certain amount.

- **Scatter diagrams** are graphs which are used to exhibit data, (rather than equations) in order to compare the way in which two variables vary with each other.

- The graph of a time series is called a **historigram**.

Quick quiz

1   What are the main guidelines for tabulation?

2   What are the two purposes served by simple bar charts?

3   When selecting a standard width of bar when calculating the heights of the bars in a histogram you would select the size of the class interval which occurs most frequently.

   True   ☐

   False ☐

4   The steps involved in drawing a frequency polygon from a histogram are

   Step 1. ....

   Step 2. ....

   Step 3. ....

5   A grouped frequency distribution can be drawn as a(n) histogram/ogive, whereas a cumulative frequency distribution can be graphed as a(n) ogive/histogram.

6   A scatter diagram has an x axis and a y axis which represent dependent and independent variables as follows.

   x axis ⎤ ? ⎡ independent variable
   y axis ⎦   ⎣ dependent variable

7   What is the name given to the graph of a time series?

Histogram	Scattergram
Ogive	Historigram

8   How do downward-sloping ogives differ from upward-sloping ogives?

Answers to quick quiz

1. • The table should have a clear title
   • All columns should be clearly labelled
   • Clear sub-totals should be included
   • Columns should be totalled showing a total figure
   • Tables should be spaced out so information presented may be read easily

2. • The magnitude of each item is shown
   • The lengths of bars on the chart allow magnitudes to be compared

3. True

4. ***Step 1.*** Mark mid-points of each bar at the top

   Step 2. Join all these points with straight lines

   Step 3. Estimate the mid-points of the class intervals outside the range of observed data and joint up with the midpoints of the two end bars

5. A grouped frequency distribution can be drawn as a histogram, whereas a cumulative frequency distribution can be graphed as an ogive.

6. x axis $\longrightarrow$ independent variable
   y axis $\longrightarrow$ dependent variable

7. Historigram

8. **Upward-sloping ogive**

   • Work up through grouped frequency distributions

   • Plot ascending cumulative frequency distributions against upper limits of each class interval

   Downward-sloping ogive

   • Work down through grouped frequency distributions

   • Plot descending cumulative frequency distributions against lower limits of each class interval

Now try the following objective test questions

Question bank	Question numbers	Page
Paper-based exam	5	274
Computer-based assessment	5	292

BPP
PUBLISHING

Chapter 6

AVERAGES

Topic list	Syllabus reference	Ability required
1 The arithmetic mean	(ii)	Comprehension and application
2 The mode	(ii)	Comprehension and application
3 The median	(ii)	Comprehension and application

Introduction

In Chapter 5 we saw how data can be summarised and presented in tabular, chart and graphical formats. Sometimes you might need more information than that provided by diagrammatic representations of data. In such circumstances you may need to apply some sort of numerical analysis, for example you might wish to calculate a **measure of centrality** and a **measure of dispersion**. In Chapter 7 we will look at measures of dispersion, in this chapter measures of centrality, or averages.

An **average** is a representative figure that is used to give some impression of the size of all the items in the population. There are three main types of average.

- Arithmetic mean
- Mode
- Median

We will be looking at each of these averages in turn, their calculation, advantages and disadvantages. In the next chapter we will move on to the second type of numerical measure, measures of dispersion.

Learning outcomes covered in this chapter

- **Calculate** and **explain** the following summary statistics for ungrouped data: arithmetic mean, median and mode

- **Calculate** and **explain** the following summary statistics for grouped data: arithmetic mean, median (graphical method only) and mode (graphical method only)

Syllabus content covered in this chapter

- Summary measures for both grouped and ungrouped data

1   **THE ARITHMETIC MEAN**

FORMULA TO LEARN

Arithmetic mean of ungrouped data $= \dfrac{\text{Sum of values of items}}{\text{Number of items}}$

The arithmetic mean of a variable x is shown as $\bar{x}$ ('x bar').

1.1 EXAMPLE: THE ARITHMETIC MEAN

The demand for a product on each of 20 days was as follows (in units).

3 12 7 17 3 14 9 6 11 10 1 4 19 7 15 6 9 12 12 8

The arithmetic mean of daily demand is $\bar{x}$.

$$\bar{x} = \frac{\text{Sum of demand}}{\text{Number of days}} = \frac{185}{20} = 9.25 \text{ units}$$

1.2 In the above example, demand on any one day is never actually 9.25 units. The arithmetic mean is merely an **average representation** of demand on each of the 20 days.

Finding the arithmetic mean of data in a frequency distribution

1.3 It is more likely in an exam that you will be asked to calculate the arithmetic mean of a **frequency distribution**. In our previous example, the frequency distribution would be shown as follows.

Daily demand	Frequency	Demand × frequency
x	f	fx
1	1	1
3	2	6
4	1	4
6	2	12
7	2	14
8	1	8
9	2	18
10	1	10
11	1	11
12	3	36
14	1	14
15	1	15
17	1	17
19	1	19
	20	185

$$\bar{x} = \frac{185}{20} = 9.25$$

Sigma, Σ

> **KEY TERM**
>
> Σ means 'the sum of' and is used as shorthand to mean 'the sum of a set of values'.

1.4 In the previous example:

(a) Σ f would mean the sum of all the frequencies, which is 20

(b) Σ fx would mean the sum of all the values of 'frequency multiplied by daily demand', that is, all 14 values of fx, so Σ fx = 185

PUBLISHING

> ## EXAM FORMULA
>
> The **arithmetic mean of grouped data**, $\bar{x} = \dfrac{\Sigma fx}{n}$ or $\dfrac{\Sigma fx}{\Sigma f}$ where n is the number of values recorded, or the number of items measured.

Finding the arithmetic mean of grouped data in class intervals

1.5 You might also be asked to calculate (or at least approximate) the arithmetic mean of a frequency distribution, where the frequencies are shown in class intervals.

1.6 EXAMPLE: THE ARITHMETIC MEAN OF GROUPED DATA

Using the example in Paragraph 1.3, the frequency distribution might have been shown as follows.

Daily demand	Frequency
> 0 ≤ 5	4
> 5 ≤ 10	8
>10 ≤ 15	6
>15 ≤ 20	2
	20

1.7 There is, of course, an extra difficulty with finding the average now; as the data have been collected into classes, a **certain amount of detail has been lost** and the values of the variables to be used in the calculation of the mean are **not clearly specified**.

To calculate the arithmetic mean of grouped data we therefore need to decide on **a value which best represents all of the values in a particular class interval**. This value is known as the **mid-point**.

1.8 The **mid-point** of each class interval is conventionally taken, on the assumption that the frequencies occur **evenly** over the class interval range. In the example above, the variable is **discrete**, so the first class includes 1, 2, 3, 4 and 5, giving a mid-point of 3. With a **continuous** variable, the mid-points would have been 2.5, 7.5 and so on. Once the value of x has been decided, the mean is calculated using the formula for the arithmetic mean of grouped data.

Daily demand	Mid point x	Frequency f	fx
> 0 ≤ 5	3	4	12
> 5 ≤ 10	8	8	64
>10 ≤ 15	13	6	78
>15 ≤ 20	18	2	36
		$\Sigma f = 20$	$\Sigma fx = 190$

Arithmetic mean $\bar{x} = \dfrac{\Sigma fx}{\Sigma f} = \dfrac{190}{20} = 9.5$ units

1.9 Because the assumption that frequencies occur evenly within each class interval is not quite correct in this example, our approximate mean of 9.5 is not exactly correct, and is in error by 0.25 (9.5 – 9.25). **As the frequencies become larger, the size of this approximating error should become smaller.**

1.10 EXAMPLE: THE ARITHMETIC MEAN OF COMBINED DATA

Suppose that the mean age of a group of five people is 27 and the mean age of another group of eight people is 32. How would we find the mean age of the whole group of 13 people?

$$\text{Arithmetic mean} = \frac{\text{Sum of values of items}}{\text{Number of items}}$$

The sum of the ages in the first group is $5 \times 27 \quad = 135$

The sum of the ages in the second group is $8 \times 32 = 256$

The sum of all 13 ages is $135 + 256 \quad = 391$

The mean age is therefore $\frac{391}{13} = 30.07$ years.

Question 1

The mean weight of 10 units at 5 kgs, 10 units at 7 kgs and 20 units at X kgs is 8 kgs.

The value of X is [   ]

Answer

The value of X is [10]

Workings

$$\text{Mean} = \frac{\text{Sum of values of items}}{\text{Number of items}}$$

Sum of first 10 units = $5 \times 10 = 50$ kgs

Sum of second 10 units = $7 \times 10 = 70$ kgs

Sum of third 20 units = $20 \times X = 20X$

Sum of all 40 units = $50 + 70 + 20X = 120 + 20X$

$\therefore$ Arithmetic mean $= 8 = \dfrac{120 + 20X}{40}$

$\therefore \qquad 8 \times 40 \quad = \qquad 120 + 20X$

$\qquad 320 - 120 \quad = \qquad 20X$

$\qquad\qquad 10 \quad = \qquad X$

The advantages and disadvantages of the arithmetic mean

1.11 The **advantages** of the arithmetic mean are as follows.

- It is easy to calculate.
- It is widely understood.
- It is representative of the whole set of data.
- It is supported by mathematical theory and is suited to further statistical analysis.

1.12 The **disadvantages** of the arithmetic mean are as follows.

(a) **Its value may not correspond to any actual value.** For example, the 'average' family might have 2.3 children, but no family has exactly 2.3 children.

(b) **An arithmetic mean might be distorted by extremely high or low values.** For example, the mean of 3, 4, 4 and 6 is 4.25, but the mean of 3, 4, 4, 6 and 15 is 6.4. The high value, 15, distorts the average and in some circumstances the mean would be a misleading and inappropriate figure.

Question 2

For the week ended 15 November, the wages earned by the 69 operators employed in the machine shop of Mermaid Ltd were as follows.

Wages	Number of Operatives
under £ 60	3
£60 and under £70	11
£70 and under £80	16
£80 and under £90	15
£90 and under £100	10
£100 and under £110	8
Over £110	6
	69

Required

Calculate the arithmetic mean wage of the machine operators of Mermaid Ltd for the week ended 15 November.

Answer

The mid point of the range 'under £60' is assumed to be £55 and that of the range over £110 to be £115, since all other class intervals are £10. This is obviously an approximation which might result in a loss of accuracy; nevertheless, there is no better alternative assumption to use. Because wages can vary in steps of 1p, they are virtually a continuous variable and hence the mid-points of the classes are halfway between their end points.

Mid-point of class	Frequency	
x	f	fx
£		
55	3	165
65	11	715
75	16	1,200
85	15	1,275
95	10	950
105	8	840
115	6	690
	69	5,835

$$\text{Arithmetic mean} = \frac{\Sigma fx}{\Sigma f} = \frac{£5,835}{69} = £84.57$$

2   THE MODE

KEY TERM

The **mode** or **modal value** is an average which means 'the most frequently occurring value'.

2.1   EXAMPLE: THE MODE

The daily demand for stock in a ten day period is as follows.

Demand Units	Number of days
6	3
7	6
8	$\frac{1}{10}$

The mode is 7 units, because it is the value which occurs most frequently.

Finding the mode of a grouped frequency distribution

2.2   **The mode of a grouped frequency distribution can be calculated from a histogram.**

2.3   EXAMPLE: FINDING THE MODE FROM A HISTOGRAM

Consider the following grouped frequency distribution

Value		Frequency
At least	Less than	
0	10	0
10	20	50
20	30	150
30	40	100

(a)   The modal class (the one with the highest frequency) is 'at least 20, less than 30'. But how can we find a single value to represent the mode?

(b)   What we need to do is draw a histogram of the frequency distribution.

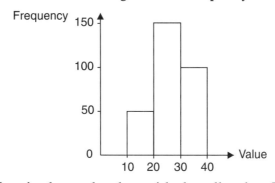

The modal class is always the class with the tallest bar. This may not be the class with the highest frequency if the classes do not all have the same width.

(c)   We can estimate the mode graphically as follows.

Step 1.   Join with a straight line the top left hand corner of the bar for the modal class and the top left hand corner of the next bar to the right.

Step 2.   Join with a straight line the top right hand corner of the bar for the modal class and the top right hand corner of the next bar to the left.

(d)   Where these two lines intersect, we find the **estimated modal value**. In this example it is approximately 26.7.

Histogram showing mode

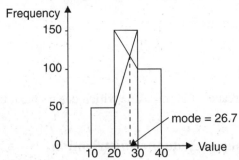

(e) We are assuming that the frequencies occur evenly within each class interval but this may not always be correct. It is unlikely that the 150 values in the modal class occur evenly. Hence **the mode in a grouped frequency distribution is only an estimate.**

The advantages and disadvantages of the mode

2.4 The **advantages** of the mode are as follows.

- It is easy to find.
- It is not influenced by a few extreme values.
- It can be used for data which are not even numerical (unlike the mean and median).
- It can be the value of an actual item in the distribution.

2.5 **Disadvantages** of the mode are as follows.

(a) It may be unrepresentative; it takes no account of a high proportion of the data, only representing the most common value.

(b) It does not take every value into account

(c) There can be two or more modes within a set of data.

(d) If the modal class is only very slightly bigger than another class, just a few more items in this other class could mean a substantially different result, suggesting some instability in the measure.

3   THE MEDIAN

KEY TERM

The **median** is the value of the middle item of a distribution once all of the items have been arranged in order of magnitude. The middle item of an odd number of items is calculated as the $\dfrac{(n+1)^{th}}{2}$ item.

3.1 The median of a set of ungrouped data is found by arranging the items in ascending or descending order of value, and selecting the item in the middle of the range. **A list of items in order of value is called an array.**

3.2 EXAMPLE : THE MEDIAN

(a) The median of the following nine values:

8   6   9   12   15   6   3   20   11

is found by taking the middle item (the fifth one) in the array:

3   6   6   8   9   11   12   15   20

The median is 9.

(b) Consider the following array.

8   6   7   2   1   11   3   2   5   2

1   2   2   2   3   5   6   7   8   11

The median is 4 because, with an even number of items, we have to take the arithmetic mean of the two middle ones (in this example, $(3 + 5)/2 = 4$).

Question 3

The following times taken to produce a batch of 100 units of Product X have been noted.

21 mins,	17 mins,	24 mins,	11 mins,	37 mins,	27 mins,
20 mins,	15 mins,	17 mins,	23 mins,	29 mins,	30 mins
24 mins,	18 mins,	17 mins,	21 mins,	24 mins,	20 mins

What is the median time?

Answer

The times can be arranged as follows.

11, 15, 17, 17, 17, 18, 20, 20, 21, 21, 23, 24, 24, 24, 27, 29, 30, 37

There are an even number of items, therefore the median is the arithmetic mean of the two middle items (ie ninth and tenth items) = 21 mins.

Question 4

The following scores are observed for the times taken to complete a task, in minutes.

12, 34, 14, 15, 21, 24, 9, 17, 11, 8

What is the median score?

A 14.00   B 14.10   C 14.50   D 14.60

Answer

The first thing to do is to arrange the scores in order of magnitude.

8, 9, 11, 12, 14, 15, 17, 21, 24, 34

There are ten items, and so the middle item is the $\frac{(10 + 1)^{th}}{2}$ item = $\frac{11}{2}$ = 5½.

The median is therefore the average of the 5th and 6th items = $\frac{14 + 15}{2}$ = $\frac{29}{2}$ = 14.50.

The correct answer is therefore C.

You could have eliminated options B and D straight away. Since there are ten items, and they are all whole numbers, the average of the 5th and 6th items is either going to be a whole number (14.00) or 'something and a half' (14.50).

BPP PUBLISHING

Finding the median of an ungrouped frequency distribution

3.3   The median of an ungrouped frequency distribution is found in a similar way. Consider the following distribution.

Value x	Frequency f	Cumulative frequency
8	3	3
12	7	10
16	12	22
17	8	30
19	5	35
	35	

The median would be the $(35 + 1)/2 = 18$th item. The 18th item has a value of 16, as we can see from the cumulative frequencies in the right hand column of the above table.

Finding the median of a grouped frequency distribution

3.4   **We can establish the median of a grouped frequency distribution from an ogive.**

3.5   **EXAMPLE: THE MEDIAN FROM AN OGIVE**

Construct an ogive of the following frequency distribution and hence establish the median.

Class £	Frequency	Cumulative frequency
≥ 340, < 370	17	17
≥ 370, < 400	9	26
≥ 400, < 430	9	35
≥ 430, < 460	3	38
≥ 460, < 490	2	40
	40	

3.6   **SOLUTION**

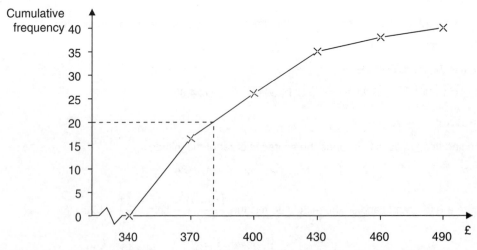

The median is at the $1/2 \times 40 = 20$th item. Reading off from the horizontal axis on the ogive, the value of the median is approximately £380.

3.7   Note that, **because we are assuming that the values are spread evenly within each class, the median calculated is only approximate.**

The advantages and disadvantages of the median

3.8 The **advantages** of the median are as follows.

- It is easy to understand
- It is unaffected by extremely high or low values
- It can be the value of an actual item in the distribution

3.9 The **disadvantages** of the median are as follows.

- It fails to reflect the full range of values
- It is unsuitable for further statistical analysis
- Arranging data into order of size can be tedious

Exam focus point

If you are asked to find the median of a set of ungrouped data, remember to arrange the items in order of value first and then to count the number of items in the array. If you have an even number of items, the median may not be the value of one of the items in the data set. The median of an even number of items is found by calculating the arithmetic mean of the two middle items.

Chapter roundup

- The **arithmetic mean** is the best known type of average and is widely understood. It is used for further statistical analysis.

- The **arithmetic mean of ungrouped data** = sum of items ÷ number of items.

- The **arithmetic mean of grouped data**, $\bar{x} = \dfrac{\Sigma fx}{n}$ or $\dfrac{\Sigma fx}{\Sigma f}$

- The **mode** is the most frequently occurring value.

- The **mode of a grouped frequency distribution** can be calculated from a histogram.

- The **median** is the value of the middle member of an array. The middle item of an odd number of items is calculated as the $\dfrac{(n+1)^{th}}{2}$ item.

- The **median of a grouped frequency distribution** can be established from an ogive.

- The arithmetic mean, mode and median of a grouped frequency distribution can only be estimated approximately.

- Each type of average has a number of advantages and disadvantages that you need to be aware of.

Quick quiz

1 Insert the formulae in the box below into the correct position.

   (a) The arithmetic mean of ungrouped data =

   (b) The arithmetic mean of grouped data =   or

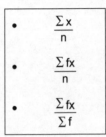

- $\dfrac{\Sigma x}{n}$

- $\dfrac{\Sigma fx}{n}$

- $\dfrac{\Sigma fx}{\Sigma f}$

2 What is the name given to the average which means 'the most frequently occurring value'?

Arithmetic mean
Median
Mode

3 List four advantages of the arithmetic mean.

4 Calculate the mid-points for both discrete and continuous variables in the table below.

Class interval	Mid-point (Discrete data)	Mid-point (Continuous data)
25 < 30		
30 < 35		
35 < 40		
40 < 45		
45 < 50		
50 < 55		
55 < 60		
60 < 65		

5 (a) The mode of a grouped frequency distribution can be found from a(n) histogram/ogive.
   (b) The median of a grouped frequency distribution can be found from a(n) histogram/ogive.

6 List four advantages of the mode.

7 List three disadvantages of the median.

Answers to quick quiz

1 (a) $\dfrac{\Sigma x}{n}$

   (b) $\dfrac{\Sigma fx}{n}$ or $\dfrac{\Sigma fx}{\Sigma f}$

2 Mode

3 • It is easy to calculate
   • It is widely understood
   • It is representative of the whole set of data
   • It is suited to further statistical analysis

4

Class interval	Mid-point (Discrete data)	Mid-point (Continuous data)
25 < 30	27	27.5
30 < 35	32	32.5
35 < 40	37	37.5
40 < 45	42	42.5
45 < 50	47	47.5
50 < 55	52	52.5
55 < 60	57	57.5
60 < 65	62	62.5

5 (a) Histogram
   (b) Ogive

6 • It is easy to find
   • It is not influenced by a few extreme values
   • It can be used for non-numerical data (unlike the mean and the median)
   • It can be the value of an actual item in the distribution

7 • It fails to reflect the full range of values (unrepresentative)
   • It is unsuitable for further statistical analysis
   • Arranging data into order size can be tedious

Now try the following objective test questions

Question bank	Question numbers	Page
Paper-based exam	6	275
Computer-based assessment	6	294

Chapter 7

DISPERSION

Topic list	Syllabus reference	Ability required
1 The range	(ii)	Comprehension and application
2 Quartiles and the semi-interquartile range	(ii)	Comprehension and application
3 The mean deviation	(ii)	Comprehension and application
4 The variance and the standard deviation	(ii)	Comprehension and application
5 The coefficient of variation	(ii)	Comprehension and application
6 Skewness	(ii)	Comprehension and application

Introduction

In Chapter 6 we introduced the first type of statistic that can be used to describe certain aspects of a set of data - **averages**. Averages are a method of determining the '**location**' or **central point** of a distribution, but they give no information about the **dispersion** of values in the distribution.

Measures of dispersion give some idea of the **spread of a variable about its average**. The main measures are as follows.

- The range
- The semi-interquartile range
- The standard deviation
- The variance
- The coefficient of variation

Learning outcomes covered in this chapter

- **Calculate** and **explain** the following summary statistics for ungrouped data: range, standard deviation and variance.

- **Calculate** and **explain** the following summary statistics for grouped data: range, semi-interquartile range (graphical method only), standard deviation and variance.

Syllabus content covered in this chapter

- Summary measures for both grouped and ungrouped data

- Coefficient of variation

1   THE RANGE

KEY TERM

The **range** is the difference between the highest observation and the lowest observation.

1.1 The main properties of the range as a measure of spread are as follows.

- It is easy to find and to understand.
- It is easily affected by one or two extreme values.
- It gives no indication of spread between the extremes.
- It is not suitable for further statistical analysis.

Question 1

Calculate the mean and the range of the following set of data.

4	8	7	3	5	16	24	5

Mean	Range

Answer

Mean	Range
9	21

Workings

Mean, $\bar{x} = \dfrac{72}{8} = 9$

Range = 24 - 3 = 21.

2 QUARTILES AND THE SEMI-INTERQUARTILE RANGE

Quartiles

> **KEY TERMS**
>
> **Quartiles** are one means of identifying the range within which most of the values in the population occur.
>
> - The **lower quartile** (Q_1) is the value below which 25% of the population fall
> - The **upper quartile** (Q_3) is the value above which 25% of the population fall
> - The **median** (Q_2) is the value of the middle member of an array

2.1 If we had 11 data items,

- $Q_1 = 11 \times \frac{1}{4} = 2.75 = 3^{rd}$ item
- $Q_3 = 11 \times \frac{3}{4} = 8.25 = 9^{th}$ item
- $Q_2 = 11 \times \frac{1}{2} = 5.5 = 6^{th}$ item

The semi-interquartile range

2.2 The lower and upper quartiles can be used to calculate a measure of spread called the **semi-interquartile range.**

> **KEY TERM**
>
> The **semi-interquartile range** is half the difference between the lower and upper quartiles and is sometimes called the **quartile deviation**, $\frac{(Q_3 - Q_1)}{2}$

2.3 For example, if the lower and upper quartiles of a frequency distribution were 6 and 11, the semi-interquartile range of the distribution would be $(11 - 6)/2 = 2.5$ units. This shows that the average distance of a quartile from the median is 2.5. The smaller the quartile deviation, the less dispersed is the distribution.

2.4 As with the range, the quartile deviation may be misleading as a measure of spread. If the majority of the data are towards the lower end of the range then the third quartile will be considerably further above the median than the first quartile is below it, and when the two distances from the median are averaged the difference is disguised. Therefore it is often better to quote the actual values of the two quartiles, rather than the quartile deviation.

The inter-quartile range

> **KEY TERM**
>
> The **inter-quartile range** is the difference between the values of the upper and lower quartiles $(Q_3 - Q_1)$ and hence shows the range of values of the middle half of the population.

Question 2

Can you think of some advantages and disadvantages of the semi-interquartile range?

Answer

Advantages

(a) It is easy to understand.
(b) It is unaffected by extreme values.
(c) It can be calculated even if the values of extreme items are not known.

Disadvantages

(a) It does not take all values into account.
(b) Data has to be arranged in order of size.
(c) It is unsuitable for use in further statistical analysis.

2.5 EXAMPLE: USING OGIVES TO FIND THE SEMI-INTERQUARTILE RANGE

Construct an ogive of the following frequency distribution and hence establish the semi-interquartile range.

Class £	Frequency	Cumulative frequency
$\geq 340, < 370$	17	17
$\geq 370, < 400$	9	26
$\geq 400, < 430$	9	35
$\geq 430, < 460$	3	38
$\geq 460, < 490$	2	40
	40	

2.6 SOLUTION

Establish which items are Q_1 and Q_3 (the lower and upper quartiles respectively).

Upper quartile $(Q_3) = \dfrac{3}{4} \times 40 =$ 30th value

Lower quartile $(Q_1) = \dfrac{1}{4} \times 40 =$ 10th value

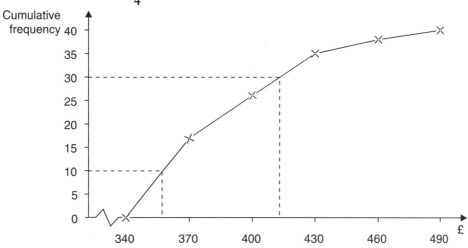

Reading off the values from the ogive, approximate values are as follows.

Q_3 (upper quartile) = £412
Q_1 (lower quartile) = £358

$$\textbf{Semi-interquartile range} = \frac{Q_3 - Q_1}{2}$$

$$= \frac{\pounds(412 - 358)}{2}$$

$$= \frac{\pounds 54}{2}$$

$$= \pounds 27$$

Exam focus point

Remember that the median is equal to Q_2 (the point above which, and below which, 50% of the population fall). In the example in paragraph 2.5 the median would be the $\dfrac{40}{2} = 20^{th}$ item which could be found from reading off the ogive (approximately 385).

---

3 THE MEAN DEVIATION

3.1 Because it only uses the middle 50% of the population, the inter-quartile range is a useful measure of dispersion if there are **extreme values** in the distribution. If there are no extreme values which could potentially distort a measure of dispersion, however, it seems unreasonable to exclude 50% of the data. The mean deviation (the topic of this section), and the standard deviation (the topic of Section 4) are often more useful measures.

KEY TERM

The **mean deviation** is a measure of the average amount by which the values in a distribution differ from the arithmetic mean.

FORMULA TO LEARN

$$\text{Mean deviation} = \frac{\Sigma f|x - \bar{x}|}{n}$$

3.2 (a) $|x - \bar{x}|$ is the difference between each value (x) in the distribution and the arithmetic mean $\bar{x}$ of the distribution. When calculating the mean deviation for grouped data the deviations should be measured to the midpoint of each class: that is, x is the midpoint of the class interval. The vertical bars mean that all differences are taken as positive since the total of all of the differences, if this is not done, will always equal zero. Thus if x = 3 and $\bar{x}$ = 5, then $x - \bar{x}$ = –2 but $|x - \bar{x}|$ = 2.

(b) $f|x - \bar{x}|$ is the value in (a) above, multiplied by the frequency for the class.

(c) $\Sigma f|x - \bar{x}|$ is the sum of the results of all the calculations in (b) above.

(d) n (which equals Σf) is the number of items in the distribution.

3.3 EXAMPLE: THE MEAN DEVIATION

The hours of overtime worked in a particular quarter by the 60 employees of ABC Ltd are as follows.

\ Hours \		Frequency
More than	*Not more than*	
0	10	3
10	20	6
20	30	11
30	40	15
40	50	12
50	60	7
60	70	6
		60

Required

Calculate the mean deviation of the frequency distribution shown above.

3.4 SOLUTION

Midpoint x	f	fx	$\mid x - \bar{x} \mid$	$f\mid x - \bar{x} \mid$
5	3	15	32	96
15	6	90	22	132
25	11	275	12	132
35	15	525	2	30
45	12	540	8	96
55	7	385	18	126
65	6	390	28	168
	$\Sigma f = 60$	$\Sigma fx = 2,220$		780

Arithmetic mean $\bar{x} = \dfrac{\Sigma fx}{\Sigma f} = \dfrac{2,220}{60} = 37$

Mean deviation $= \dfrac{780}{60} = 13$ hours

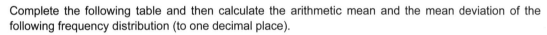

Question 3

Complete the following table and then calculate the arithmetic mean and the mean deviation of the following frequency distribution (to one decimal place).

Value	Frequency of occurrence
5	4
15	6
25	8
35	20
45	6
55	6
	50

x	f	fx	$\mid x - \bar{x} \mid$	$f\mid x - \bar{x} \mid$
5				
15				
25				
35				
45				
55				

Arithmetic mean $\bar{x}$ = [————] = [ ]

Mean deviation = [————] = [ ]

BPP PUBLISHING

Answer

x	f	fx	$|x - \bar{x}|$	$f|x - \bar{x}|$
5	4	20	27.2	108.8
15	6	90	17.2	103.2
25	8	200	7.2	57.6
35	20	700	2.8	56.0
45	6	270	12.8	76.8
55	6	330	22.8	136.8
	50	1,610		539.2

Arithmetic mean $\bar{x} = \dfrac{1,610}{50} = 32.2$

Mean deviation $= \dfrac{539.2}{50} = 10.8$.

3.5 Summary of the **mean deviation.**

(a) It is a measure of dispersion which shows by how much, on average, each item in the distribution differs in value from the arithmetic mean of the distribution.

(b) Unlike quartiles, it uses all values in the distribution to measure the dispersion, but it is not greatly affected by a few extreme values because an average is taken.

(c) It is not, however, suitable for further statistical analysis.

4 THE VARIANCE AND THE STANDARD DEVIATION

KEY TERM

The **variance,** σ^2, is the average of the squared mean deviation for each value in a distribution.

4.1 σ is the Greek letter sigma (in lower case). The variance is therefore called 'sigma squared'.

4.2 **Calculation of the variance for ungrouped data**

Step 1. Difference between value and mean $x - \bar{x}$

Step 2. Square of the difference $(x - \bar{x})^2$

Step 3. Sum of the squares of the difference $\Sigma(x - \bar{x})^2$

Step 4. Average of the sum ($=$ variance $= \sigma^2$) $\dfrac{\Sigma(x - \bar{x})^2}{n}$

The units of the variance are the square of those in the original data because we squared the differences. We therefore need to take the square root to get back to the units of the original data. **The standard deviation = square root of the variance.**

4.3 The standard deviation measures the spread of data around the mean. In general, the larger the standard deviation value in relation to the mean, the more dispersed the data.

4.4 Calculation of the variance for grouped data

Step 1. Difference between value and mean $(x - \bar{x})$

Step 2. Square of the difference $(x - \bar{x})^2$

Step 3. Sum of the squares of the difference $\Sigma f(x - \bar{x})^2$

Step 4. Average of the sum (= variance = σ^2) $\dfrac{\Sigma f(x - \bar{x})^2}{\Sigma f}$

4.5 There are a number of formulae which you may use to calculate the standard deviation; use whichever one you feel comfortable with. The standard deviation formulae provided in your examination are shown as follows.

EXAM FORMULAE

Standard deviation (for **ungrouped data**) $= \sqrt{\dfrac{\Sigma(x - \bar{x})^2}{n}} = \sqrt{\dfrac{\Sigma x^2}{n} - \bar{x}^2}$

Standard deviation (for **grouped data**) $= \sqrt{\dfrac{\Sigma f(x - \bar{x})^2}{\Sigma f}} = \sqrt{\dfrac{\Sigma fx^2}{\Sigma f} - \left(\dfrac{\Sigma fx}{\Sigma f}\right)^2}$

4.6 EXAMPLE: THE VARIANCE AND THE STANDARD DEVIATION

Calculate the variance and the standard deviation of the frequency distribution in Paragraph 2.3

4.7 SOLUTION

Using the formula provided in the examination, the calculation is as follows.

Midpoint x	f	x^2	fx^2
5	3	25	75
15	6	225	1,350
25	11	625	6,875
35	15	1,225	18,375
45	12	2,025	24,300
55	7	3,025	21,175
65	6	4,225	25,350
	60		97,500

Mean $= \dfrac{\Sigma fx}{\Sigma f} = $ (from Paragraph 3.4) $= 37$

Variance $= \dfrac{\Sigma fx^2}{\Sigma f} - \left(\dfrac{\Sigma fx}{\Sigma f}\right)^2 = \dfrac{97,500}{60} - (37)^2 = 256$ hours

Standard deviation $= \sqrt{256} = 16$ hours

Question 4

Calculate the variance and the standard deviation of the frequency distribution in Question 3.

Answer

x	f	x^2	fx^2
5	4	25	100
15	6	225	1,350
25	8	625	5,000
35	20	1,225	24,500
45	6	2,025	12,150
55	6	3,025	18,150
	50		61,250

Mean = 32.2 (from Question 3)

$$\text{Variance} = \frac{61,250}{50} - (32.2)^2 = 188.16$$

Standard deviation = $\sqrt{188.16}$ = 13.72

The main properties of the standard deviation

4.8 The standard deviation's main properties are as follows.

(a) It is based on **all the values in the distribution** and so is more comprehensive than dispersion measures based on quartiles, such as the quartile deviation.

(b) It is suitable for **further statistical analysis**.

(c) It is **more difficult to understand** than some other measures of dispersion.

The importance of the standard deviation lies in its suitability for further statistical analysis (we shall consider this further when we study the normal distribution in Chapter 10).

The variance and the standard deviation of several items together

4.9 You may need to calculate the variance and standard deviation for n items together, given the variance and standard deviation for one item alone.

4.10 EXAMPLE: SEVERAL ITEMS TOGETHER

The daily demand for an item of stock has a mean of 6 units, with a variance of 4 and a standard deviation of 2 units. Demand on any one day is unaffected by demand on previous days or subsequent days.

Required

Calculate the arithmetic mean, the variance and the standard deviation of demand for a five day week.

4.11 SOLUTION

If we let

- Arithmetic mean = $\bar{x}$ = 6
- Variance = σ^2 = 4
- Standard deviation = σ = 2
- Number of days in week = n = 5

The following rules apply to $\bar{x}$, σ^2 and σ when we have several items together.

- **Arithmetic mean** = $n\bar{x} = 5 \times 6 = 30$ units
- **Variance** = $n\sigma^2 = 5 \times 4 = 20$ units
- **Standard deviation** = $\sqrt{n\sigma^2} = \sqrt{20} = 4.47$ units

5 THE COEFFICIENT OF VARIATION

5.1 It is sometimes useful to be able to compare the spreads of two distributions. This comparison can be done using the **coefficient of variation**.

FORMULA TO LEARN

Coefficient of variation (coefficient of relative spread) = $\dfrac{\text{Standard deviation}}{\text{mean}}$

5.2 The bigger the coefficient of variation, the wider the spread. For example, suppose that two sets of data, A and B, have the following means and standard deviations.

	A	B
Mean	120	125
Standard deviation	50	51
Coefficient of variation	0.417	0.408

Although B has a higher standard deviation in absolute terms (51 compared to 50) its relative spread is a bit less than A's since the coefficient of variation is a bit smaller.

Question 5

Calculate the coefficient of variation of the distribution in Questions 3 and 4.

Answer

Coefficient of variation = $\dfrac{\text{standard deviation}}{\text{mean}} = \dfrac{13.72}{32.2} = 0.426$

Question 6

The number of new orders received by five salesmen last week is: 1, 3, 5, 7, 9. The variance of the number of new orders received is:

A   2.40
B   2.83
C   6.67
D   8.00

Answer

x	1	3	5	7	9
$(x-\bar{x})^2$	16	4	0	4	16

$\sum x = 25$

$\therefore \bar{x} = \dfrac{25}{5} = 5$

$\sum(x-\bar{x})^2 = 40$

$$\frac{\sum(x-\bar{x})^2}{n} = \frac{40}{5} = 8$$

The correct answer is therefore D.

---

6 SKEWNESS

6.1 As well as being able to calculate the average and spread of a frequency distribution, you should be aware of the **skewness** of a distribution. **Skewed** means that a distribution is either symmetrical or asymmetrical.

6.2 A **symmetrical frequency distribution** (a normal distribution) can be drawn as follows.

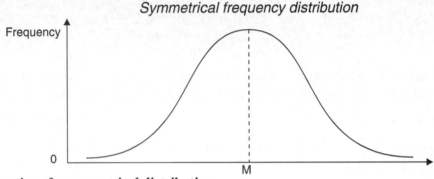

Symmetrical frequency distribution

Properties of a symmetrical distribution

- Its mean, mode and median all have the same value, M
- Its two halves are mirror images of each other

6.3 A **positively skewed** distribution's graph will lean towards the **left hand side**, with a tail stretching out to the right, and can be drawn as follows.

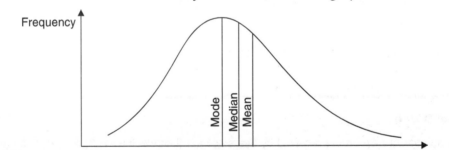

Positively skewed distribution graph

Properties of a positively skewed distribution

- Its mean, mode and median all have different values
- The mode will have a lower value than the median
- Its mean will have a higher value than the median (and than most of the distribution)
- It does not have two halves which are mirror images of each other

6.4 A **negatively skewed distribution's** graph will lean towards the **right hand side**, with a tail stretching out to the left, and can be drawn as follows.

Negatively skewed distribution graph

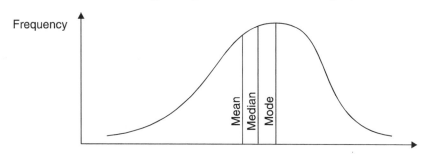

Properties of a negatively skewed distribution

- Its mean, median and mode all have different values
- The mode will be higher than the median
- The mean will have a lower value than the median (and than most of the distribution)

6.5 Since the mean is affected by extreme values, it may not be representative of the items in a very skewed distribution.

Coefficient of skewness

6.6 The **skewness of frequency distribution curves** can be compared using **Pearson's coefficient of skewness**.

$$\text{Coefficient of skewness} = \frac{3\,(\text{mean} - \text{median})}{\text{standard deviation}}$$

Question 7

Use arrows to match the following coefficient values with the correct descriptions.

Coefficient values	Description
0	Maximum negative skewness
+3	Maximum positive skewness
−3	Symmetrical distribution

Answer

Coefficient values   *Description*

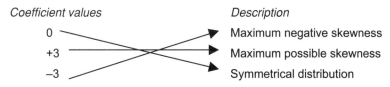

6.7 EXAMPLE: SKEWNESS

In a quality control test, the weights of standard packages were measured to give the following grouped frequency table.

Weights in grams	Number of packages
198 and less than 199	3
199 and less than 200	8
200 and less than 201	93
201 and less than 202	148
202 and less than 203	48

BPP PUBLISHING

Required

(a) Calculate the mean, standard deviation, mode and median of the weights of the packages.

(b) Explain whether or not you think that the distribution is symmetrical.

(c) Calculate the coefficient of skewness and comment on the result.

6.8 SOLUTION

Weight	Mid point				
g	*x*	*f*	*fx*	$x - \bar{x}$	$f(x - \bar{x})^2$
198 and less than 199	198.5	3	595.5	−2.77	23.0187
199 and less than 200	199.5	8	1,596.0	−1.77	25.0632
200 and less than 201	200.5	93	18,646.5	−0.77	55.1397
201 and less than 202	201.5	148	29,822.0	0.23	7.8292
202 and less than 203	202.5	48	9,720.0	1.23	72.6192
		300	60,380.0		183.6700

$$\text{Mean} = \frac{\Sigma fx}{\Sigma f} = \frac{60,380}{300} = 201.27\text{g}$$

$$\text{Standard deviation} = \sqrt{\frac{183.67}{300}} = 0.78\text{g}$$

The distribution appears not to be symmetrical, but negatively skewed.

(a) The mean is in the higher end of the range of values at 201.27 g.

(b) The mode could be estimated as

$$201 + \frac{(148 - 93) \times 1}{(2 \times 148) - 93 - 48} = 201.35\text{g}$$

(c) The **median** (the 150th item) could be estimated as

$$201 + \frac{(150 - 93 - 8 - 3)}{148} = 201.31\text{g}$$

The median has a higher value than the mean, and the mode has a higher value than the median. This suggests that the frequency distribution is negatively skewed.

$$\textbf{Coefficient of skewness} = \frac{3\,(\text{mean} - \text{median})}{\text{standard deviation}}$$

$$= \frac{3(201.27 - 201.31)}{0.78}$$

$$= -0.15$$

The distribution is negatively skewed but the skewness is relatively small.

Chapter roundup

- **Measures of spread** give some idea of the spread of variables about the average.

- The **range** is the difference between the highest and lowest observations.

- The **quartiles** and the **median** divide the population into four groups of equal size.

- The **quartile deviation** is half the difference between the two quartiles.

- The **interquartile range** is the difference between the upper and lower quartiles.

- The **mean deviation** is a measure of the average amount by which the values in a distribution differ from the arithmetic mean.

- The **standard deviation**, which is the square root of the variance, is the most important measure of spread used in statistics. Make sure you understand how to calculate the standard deviation of a set of data.

- The spreads of two distributions can be compared using the **coefficient of variation**.

- **Skewness** is the asymmetry of a frequency distribution curve.

- Measures of spread are valuable in giving a full picture of a frequency distribution. We would nearly always want to be told an average for a distribution, but just one more number, a measure of spread, can be very informative.

Quick quiz

1   What is the range?

2   Fill in the blanks in the statements below using the words in the box.

(a)   .... quartile = Q_1 = value .... which 25% of the population fall.

(b)   .... quartile = Q_3 = value .... which 25% of the population fall.

Upper	Above	Below	Lower

3   (a)   The formula for the semi-interquartile range is ....

(b)   The semi-interquartile range is also known as the ....

4   What are the main properties of the standard deviation?

Answers to quick quiz

1   The difference between the highest and lowest observations.

2   (a)   Lower quartile = Q_1 = value below which 25% of the population fall
(b)   Upper quartile = Q_3 = value above which 25% of the population fall

3   (a) $\dfrac{Q_3 - Q_1}{2}$

(b)   Quartile deviation

4   •   It is based on all values in the distribution
•   It is suitable for further statistical analysis
•   It is more difficult to understand than some other measures of dispersion

Now try the following objective test questions

Question bank	Question numbers	Page
Paper-based exam	7	276
Computer-based assessment	7	295

Chapter 8

INDEX NUMBERS

Topic list		Syllabus reference	Ability required
1	Basic terminology	(ii)	Comprehension and application
2	Simple indices	(ii)	Comprehension and application
3	Index relatives	(ii)	Comprehension and application
4	Time series deflation	(ii)	Comprehension and application
5	Composite index numbers	(ii)	Comprehension and application
6	Weighted index numbers	(ii)	Comprehension and application
7	The Retail Prices Index for the United Kingdom			

Introduction

A number of methods of data presentation looked at in Chapter 5 can be used to identify visually the **trends** in data over a period of time. It may also be useful, however, to identify trends using statistical rather than visual means. This is frequently achieved by constructing a set of **index numbers**.

Index numbers provide a **standardised way of comparing the values**, over time, of prices, wages, volume of output and so on. They are used extensively in business, government and commerce.

Learning outcomes covered in this chapter

- **Calculate** and **explain** a simple index number, a fixed base and chain base series of index numbers

- **Use** index numbers to deflate a series and explain the results

- **Calculate** a simple weighted index number. Candidates will not have to decide whether to use base or current weights

Syllabus content covered in this chapter

- Index numbers

1 BASIC TERMINOLOGY

Price indices and quantity indices

> **KEY TERMS**
>
> An **index** is a measure, over time, of the average changes in the values (prices or quantities) of a group of items. **An index comprises a series of index numbers** and may be a **price index** or a **quantity index**.
>
> - A **price index** measures the change in the money value of a group of items over time.
>
> - A **quantity index** (also called a volume index) measures the change in the non-monetary values of a group of items over time.

1.1 It is possible to prepare an index for a single item, but such an index would probably be unnecessary. **An index is a most useful measure of comparison when there is a group of items.**

Index points

1.2 **The term 'points' refers to the difference between the index values in two years.**

1.3 EXAMPLE: INDEX POINTS

For example, suppose that the index of food prices in 20X1 – 20X6 was as follows.

20X1	180
20X2	200
20X3	230
20X4	250
20X5	300
20X6	336

The index has risen 156 points between 20X1 and 20X6 (336 – 180). This is an increase of $(156/180) \times 100 = 86.7\%$.

Similarly, the index rose 36 points between 20X5 and 20X6 (336 – 300), a rise of 12%.

The base period, or base year

1.4 **Index numbers normally take the value for a base date as 100.** The base period is usually the starting point of the series, though this is not always the case.

2 SIMPLE INDICES

2.1 When one commodity only is under consideration, we have the following formulae.

FORMULAE TO LEARN

- Price index $= 100 \times \dfrac{P_1}{P_0}$

- Quantity index $= 100 \times \dfrac{Q_1}{Q_0}$

where P_1 = the price for the period under consideration
P_0 = the price for the base period
Q_1 = the quantity for the period under consideration
Q_0 = the quantity for the base period

2.2   EXAMPLE: SINGLE-ITEM INDICES

(a)   **Price index number**

If the price of a cup of coffee was 40p in 20X0, 50p in 20X1 and 76p in 20X2, then using 20X0 as a base year the **price index numbers** for 20X1 and 20X2 would be as follows.

20X1 price index $= 100 \times \dfrac{50}{40} = 125$

20X2 price index $= 100 \times \dfrac{76}{40} = 190$

(b)   **Quantity index number**

If the number of cups of coffee sold in 20X0 was 500,000, in 20X1 700,000 and in 20X2 600,000, then using 20X0 as a base year, the **quantity index numbers** for 20X1 and 20X2 would be as follows.

20X1 quantity index $= 100 \times \dfrac{700,000}{500,000} = 140$

20X2 quantity index $= 100 \times \dfrac{600,000}{500,000} = 120$

3   INDEX RELATIVES

KEY TERM

An **index relative** (sometimes just called a **relative**) is the name given to an index number which measures the change in a single distinct commodity.

EXAM FORMULAE

- A **price relative** is calculated as $100 \times P_1/P_0$
- A **quantity relative** is calculated as $100 \times Q_1/Q_0$

3.1 We calculated price and quantity relatives for cups of coffee in paragraph 2.2.

Time series of relatives

3.2 There are two ways in which index relatives can be calculated.

  (a) The **fixed base method**. A base year is selected (index 100), and all subsequent changes are measured against this base. Such an approach should only be used if **the basic nature of the commodity is unchanged over time**.

  (b) The **chain base method**. Changes are calculated with respect to the value of the commodity in the period immediately before. This approach can be used for any set of commodity values but must be used if **the basic nature of the commodity is changing over time**.

3.3 EXAMPLE: FIXED BASE METHOD

The price of a commodity was £2.70 in 20X0, £3.11 in 20X1, £3.42 in 20X2 and £3.83 in 20X3. Construct a **fixed base index** for the years 20X0 to 20X3 using 20X0 as the base year.

3.4 SOLUTION

Fixed base index	20X0	100	
	20X1	115	
	20X2	127	$(3.42/2.70 \times 100)$
	20X3	142	$(3.83/2.70 \times 100)$

3.5 EXAMPLE: CHAIN BASE METHOD

Using the information in Paragraph 3.3 construct a chain base index for the years 20X0 to 20X3 using 20X0 as the base year.

3.6 SOLUTION

Chain base index	20X0	100	
	20X1	115	$(3.11/2.70 \times 100)$
	20X2	110	$(3.42/3.11 \times 100)$
	20X3	112	$(3.83/3.42 \times 100)$

3.7 **The chain base relatives show the rate of change in prices from year to year, whereas the fixed base relatives show changes relative to prices in the base year.**

Changing the base of fixed base relatives

3.8 It is sometimes necessary to change the base of a time series (to **rebase**) of fixed base relatives, perhaps because the **base time point is too far in the past**. The following time series has a base date of 1970 which would probably be considered too out of date.

	1990	*1991*	*1992*	*1993*	*1994*	*1995*
Index (1970 = 100)	451	463	472	490	499	505

To change the base date, divide each relative by the relative corresponding to the new base time point and multiply the result by 100.

Question 1

Rebase the index in Paragraph 3.8 to 1993.

Answer

	1990	1991	1992	1993	1994	1995
Index (1993 = 100)	92*	94	96	100**	102***	103

* $451/490 \times 100$
** $490/490 \times 100$
*** $499/490 \times 100$

Comparing sets of fixed base relatives

3.9   You may be required to compare two sets of time series relatives. For example, an index of the annual number of advertisements placed by an organisation in the press and the index of the number of the organisation's product sold per annum might be compared. If the base years of the two indices differ, however, comparison is extremely difficult (as the illustration below shows).

	20W8	20W9	20X0	20X1	20X2	20X3	20X4
Number of advertisements							
Placed (20X0 = 100)	90	96	100	115	128	140	160
Volumes of sales (20W0 = 100)	340	347	355	420	472	515	572

3.10 From the figures above it is impossible to determine whether sales are increasing at a greater rate than the number of advertisements placed, or vice versa. This difficulty can be overcome by **rebasing** one set of relatives so that the **base dates are the same**. For example, we could rebase the index of volume of sales to 20X0.

	20W8	20W9	20X0	20X1	20X2	20X3	20X4
Number of advertisements							
Placed (20X0 = 100)	90	96	100	115	128	140	160
Volumes of sales (20X0 = 100)	96	98*	100	118	133**	145	161

* $347/355 \times 100$
** $472/355 \times 100$

3.11 The two sets of relatives are now much easier to compare. They show that volume of sales is increasing at a slightly faster rate, in general, than the number of advertisements placed.

4   TIME SERIES DEFLATION

4.1   The real value of a commodity can only be measured in terms of some 'indicator' such as the **rate of inflation** (normally represented by the Retail Prices Index (RPI)). For example the cost of a commodity may have been £10 in 20X0 and £11 in 20X1, representing an increase of 10%. However, if we are told the prices **in general** (as measured by the RPI) increased by 12% between 20X0 and 20X1, we can argue that the **real** cost of the commodity has decreased.

4.2   EXAMPLE: DEFLATION

Mack Johnson works for Pound of Flesh Ltd. Over the last five years he has received an annual salary increase of £500. Despite his employer assuring him that £500 is a reasonable annual salary increase, Mack is unhappy because, although he agrees £500 is a lot of money, he finds it difficult to maintain the standard of living he had when he first joined the company.

Consider the figures below.

Year	(a) Wages £	(b) RPI	(c) Real wages £	(d) Real wages index
1	12,000	250	12,000	100.0
2	12,500	260	12,019	100.2
3	13,000	275	11,818	98.5
4	13,500	295	11,441	95.3
5	14,000	315	11,111	92.6

(a) This column shows Mack's wages over the five-year period.

(b) This column shows the current RPI.

(c) This column shows what Mack's wages are worth taking prices, as represented by the RPI, into account. The wages have been deflated relative to the new base period (year 1). Economists call these deflated wage figures **real wages**. The real wages for years 2 and 4, for example, are calculated as follows.

Year 2: £12,500 × 250/260 = £12,019
Year 4: £13,500 × 250/295 = £11,441

(d) This column is calculated by dividing the entries in column (c) by £12,000:

$$\textbf{Real index} = \frac{\text{current value}}{\text{base value}} \times \frac{\text{base indicator}}{\text{current indicator}}$$

So, for example, the real wage index in year 4 $= \frac{13,500}{12,000} \times \frac{250}{295} \times 100 = 95.3$

4.3 The real wages index shows that the real value of Mack's wages has fallen by 7.4% over the five-year period. In real terms he is now earning £11,111 compared to £12,000 in year 1. He is probably justified, therefore, in being unhappy.

5 COMPOSITE INDEX NUMBERS

5.1 Most practical indices cover more than one item and are hence termed **composite index numbers**.

5.2 Suppose that the cost of living index is calculated from only three commodities: bread, tea and caviar, and that the prices for 20X1 and 20X2 were as follows.

	20X1	20X2
Bread	20p a loaf	40p a loaf
Tea	25p a packet	30p a packet
Caviar	450p a jar	405p a jar

5.3 A simple index could be calculated by adding the prices for single items in 20X2 and dividing by the corresponding sum relating to 20X1 (if 20X1 is the base year). In general, if the sum of the prices in the base year is ΣP_0 and the sum of the prices in the new year is ΣP_1, the index is $100 \times \frac{\Sigma P_1}{\Sigma P_0}$. The index, known as a **simple aggregate price index**, would therefore be calculated as follows.

	P_0	P_1
	20X1	*20X2*
	£	£
Bread	0.20	0.40
Tea	0.25	0.30
Caviar	4.50	4.05
	$\Sigma P_0 = 4.95$	$\Sigma P_1 = 4.75$

Year	$\Sigma P_1 / \Sigma P_0$	Simple aggregate price index
20X1	4.95/4.95 = 1.00	100
20X2	4.75/4.95 = 0.96	96

5.4 The simple aggregate price index has a number of **disadvantages**.

(a) It ignores the **amounts** of bread, tea and caviar consumed (and hence the importance of each item).

(b) It ignores the **units** to which the prices refer. If, for example, we had been given the price of a cup of tea rather than a packet of tea, the index would have been different.

Average relatives indices

5.5 To overcome the problem of different units we consider the changes in prices as **ratios** rather than absolutes so that all price movements, whatever their absolute values, are treated as equally important. Price changes are considered as ratios rather than absolutes by using the **average price relatives index**. Quantity changes are considered as ratios by using the **average quantity relatives index**.

> **FORMULAE TO LEARN**
>
> • **Average price relatives index** $= 100 \times \dfrac{1}{n} \times \Sigma(P_1/P_0)$
>
> • **Average quantity relatives index** $= 100 \times \dfrac{1}{n} \times \Sigma(Q_1/Q_0)$
>
> where n is the number of goods.

5.6 The price relative P_1/P_0 (so called because it gives the new price level of each item relative to the base year price) for a particular commodity will have the same value whatever the unit for which the price is quoted.

5.7 Using the information in Paragraph 5.2, we can construct the **average price relatives index** as follows.

Commodity	P_0	P_1	P_1/P_0
	£	£	
Bread	0.20	0.40	2.00
Tea	0.25	0.30	1.20
Caviar	4.50	4.05	0.90
			4.10

Year	$\dfrac{1}{n}\Sigma(P_1/P_0)$	Average price relatives index
20X1	$^1/_3 \times 3.00 = 1.00$	100
20X2	$^1/_3 \times 4.10 = 1.37$	137

5.8   There has therefore been an average price increase of 37% between 20X1 and 20X2.

5.9   No account has been taken of the **relative importance** of each item in this index. Bread is probably more important than caviar. To overcome both the problem of quantities in different units and the need to attach importance to each item, we can use **weighting** which reflects the **importance of each item**. To decide the weightings of different items in an index, it is necessary to obtain information, perhaps by market research, about the **relative importance** of each item. The next section of this chapter shall look at **weighted index numbers**.

6   WEIGHTED INDEX NUMBERS

6.1   There are two types of index which give different weights to different items.

- Weighted average of relatives indices
- Weighted aggregate indices

The weighted average of relatives index is the one that you need to be able to calculate in your examination.

Weighted average of relatives indices

6.2   **This method of weighting involves calculating index relatives for each of the components and using the weights given to obtain a weighted average of the relatives.**

> **EXAM FORMULAE**
>
> - **Weighted average of price relative index** $= \dfrac{\sum W \times {}^{P_1}/_{P_0}}{\sum W} \times 100$
>
> - **Weighted average of quantity relative index0** $= \dfrac{\sum W \times {}^{Q_1}/_{Q_0}}{\sum W} \times 100$
>
> where W = the weighting factor

6.3   EXAMPLE: WEIGHTED AVERAGE OF RELATIVES INDICES

Use both the information in Paragraph 5.2 and the following details about quantities purchased by each household in a week in 20X1 to determine a weighted average of price relatives index number for 20X2 using 20X1 as the base year.

	Quantity
Bread	12
Tea	5
Caviar	3

6.4 SOLUTION

Price relatives (P_1/P_0)	Bread	40/20 =	2.00
	Tea	30/25 =	1.20
	Caviar	405/450 =	0.90

Weightings (W)	Bread		12.00
	Tea		5.00
	Caviar		3.00
	ΣW =		20.00

Index	Bread	2×12 =	24.00
	Tea	1.2×5 =	6.00
	Caviar	0.9×3 =	2.70
	$\Sigma W \times P_1/P_0$ =		32.70

Index number = $\dfrac{32.7}{20.0} \times 100$ = 163.5

Question 2

The average prices of three commodities and the number of units used annually by a company are given below.

	20X1	20X2	
Commodity	Price per unit (P_0)	Price per unit(P_1)	Quantity
	£	£	Units
X	20	22	20
Y	40	48	2
Z	100	104	10

The price for 20X2 based on 20X1, calculated using the weighted average of relatives method is (to the nearest whole number)

A   107
B   108
C   109
D   110

Answer

Commodity	Price $\dfrac{P_1}{P_0}$	Weight (W)	Relative weight $\left(W \times \dfrac{P_1}{P_0}\right)$
X	$\dfrac{22}{20}$ = 1.1	20	22.0
Y	$\dfrac{48}{40}$ = 1.2	2	2.4
Z	$\dfrac{104}{100}$ = 1.04	10	10.4
		ΣW = 32	34.8

Index = $\dfrac{34.8}{32} \times 100$ = 108.75 = 109

The correct answer is therefore C.

---

7 THE RETAIL PRICES INDEX FOR THE UNITED KINGDOM

7.1 We will conclude our study of index numbers by looking at the construction of the UK Retail Prices Index (RPI). On one particular day of each month, data are collected about prices of the following groups of items.

- Food
- Alcoholic drink
- Tobacco
- Housing
- Fuel and light
- Durable household goods
- Clothing and footwear
- Transport and vehicles
- Miscellaneous goods
- Services
- Meals bought and consumed outside the home

7.2 Each group is sub-divided into sections: for example 'food' will be sub-divided into bread, butter, potatoes and so on. These sections may in turn be sub-divided into more specific items. The groups do not cover every item of expenditure (for example they exclude income tax, pension fund contributions and football pools).

7.3 The weightings given to each group, section and sub-section are based on information provided by the *Family Expenditure Survey* which is based on a survey of over 10,000 households, spread evenly over the year.

Each member of the selected households (aged 16 or over) is asked to keep a detailed record of their expenditure over a period of 14 days, and to provide information about longer-term payments (such as insurance premiums). Information is also obtained about their income.

7.4 The weightings used in the construction of the RPI are not revised every year, but are revised from time to time using information in the Family Expenditure Survey of the previous year.

Chapter roundup

- An **index** is a measure, over time, of the average changes in the value (price or quantity) of a group of items relative to the situation at some period in the past.

- An **index relative** is an index number which measures the change in a single distinct commodity.

- Index relatives can be calculated using the **fixed base method** or the **chain base method**.

- In order to compare two time series of relatives, each series should have the same base period and hence one (or both) may need **rebasing**.

- The **real value** of a commodity can only be measured in terms of some '**indicator**' (such as the RPI).

- **Time series deflation** is a technique used to obtain a set of index relatives that measure the changes in the real value of some commodity with respect to some given indicator.

- **Composite indices** cover more than one item.

- **Weighting** is used to reflect the importance of each item in the index.

- **Weighted means of relatives indices** are found by calculating indices and then applying weights.

- **Index numbers** are a very useful way of summarising a large amount of data in a single series of numbers. They do, however, have a number of **limitations**.

Quick quiz

1   What does a price index measure?

2   What does a quantity index measure?

3   Complete the following equations using the symbols in the box below.

   (a)   **Price index** =   × 100

P_1	P_0
Q_1	Q_0

   (b)   **Quantity index** =   × 100

4   An index relative is the name given to an index number which measures the change in a group of items.

   True   ☐

   False   ☐

5

Fixed base method		Changes are measured against base period
Chain base method	?	Changes are measured against the previous period

6   What is a composite index number?

7   How are problems of quantities different units and the need to attach importance to each item over come?

8   There are two types of index which give different weights to different items.

   - Weighted average of relatives indices
   - Weighted aggregate indices

   What is the general form of a weighted average of quantity relative index number?

Answers to quick quiz

1   The change in the money value of a group of items over time.

2   The change in the non-monetary values of a group of items over time.

3   (a)   Price index $= \dfrac{P_1}{P_0} \times 100$

    (b)   Quantity index $= \dfrac{Q_1}{Q_0} \times 100$

4   False. An index relative is an index number which measures the change in a **single distinct commodity.**

5   Fixed base method ⟶ Changes are measured against the base period

    Chain base method ⟶ Changes are measured against the previous period

6   A composite index number is an index covering more than one item.

7   By using weightings and calculating weighted index numbers.

8    $\dfrac{\Sigma W \times \dfrac{Q_1}{Q_0}}{\Sigma W}$

    Where   W   = the weighing factor

           $\dfrac{Q_1}{Q_0}$ = the index relative

Now try the following objective test questions

Question bank	Question numbers	Page
Paper-based exam	8	278
Computer-based assessment	8	296

Part C
Probability

Chapter 9

INTRODUCTION TO PROBABILITY

Topic list	Syllabus reference	Ability required
1 The concept of probability	(iii)	Application
2 The laws of probability	(iii)	Application
3 Expected values	(iii)	Comprehension and Application
4 Expectation and decision making	(iii)	Comprehension and Application
5 Permutations and combinations	(iii)	Application

Introduction

We are now going to move away from the summary and analysis of data and look at a new topic area, **probability**.

'The likelihood of rain this afternoon is fifty percent' warns the weather report from your radio alarm clock. 'There's no chance of you catching that bus' grunts the helpful soul as you puff up the hill. The headline on your newspaper screams 'Odds of Rainbow Party winning the election rise to one in four'.

'**Likelihood**' and '**chance**' are expressions used in our everyday lives to denote a **level of uncertainty**. **Probability**, a word which often strikes fear into the hearts of students, is simply the mathematical term used when we need to imply a degree of **uncertainty**.

There are a number of ways of analysing. Underlying all of these methods is, however, one concept: **probability**. An understanding of the concept of probability is vital if you are to take account of uncertainty.

This chapter will therefore explain various techniques for assessing probability and look at how it can be applied in business decision making. In Chapter 10, we will build upon the basics learnt in this chapter and look at a particular probability distribution: the **normal distribution**.

Learning outcomes covered in this chapter

- **Calculate** a simple probability
- **Demonstrate** the use of the addition and multiplication rules of probability
- **Calculate** a simple conditional probability
- **Calculate** and **explain** an expected value
- **Demonstrate** the use of expected values to make decisions
- **Explain** the limitations of expected values

Syllabus content covered in this chapter

- The relationship between probability, proportion and percent
- The addition and multiplication rules
- Expected values

1 THE CONCEPT OF PROBABILITY

> **KEY TERM**
>
> **Probability** is a measure of likelihood and can be stated as a percentage, a ratio, or more usually as a number from 0 to 1.

1.1 Consider the following.

- Probability = 0 = impossibility
- Probability = 1 = certainty
- Probability = ½ = a 50% chance of something happening
- Probability = ¼ = a 1 in 4 chance of something happening

1.2 In statistics, **probabilities** are more commonly expressed as **proportions** than as **percentages**. Consider the following possible outcomes.

Possible outcome	Probability as a percentage	Probability as a proportion
A	15.0%	0.150
B	20.0%	0.200
C	32.5%	0.325
D	7.5%	0.075
E	12.5%	0.125
F	12.5%	0.125
	100.0%	1.000

1.3 It is useful to consider how probability can be quantified. A businessman might estimate that if the selling price of a product is raised by 20p, there would be a 90% probability that demand would fall by 30%, but how would he have reached his estimate of 90% probability?

1.4 There are several ways of assessing probabilities.

- They may be measurable with **mathematical certainty**.

  - If a coin is tossed, there is a 0.5 probability that it will come down heads, and a 0.5 probability that it will come down tails.

  - If a die is thrown, there is a one-sixth probability that a 6 will turn up.

- They may be measurable from an analysis of **past experience**.

- Probabilities can be estimated from **research** or **surveys**.

1.5 It is important to note that probability is a measure of the likelihood of an event happening in the long run, or over a large number of times.

1.6 The laws of probability in section 2 will go through in detail how to calculate probability in various situations.

2 THE LAWS OF PROBABILITY

2.1 It is the year 2020 and examiners are extinct. A mighty but completely fair computer churns out examinations that are equally likely to be easy or difficult. There is no link between the number of questions on each paper, which is arrived at on a fair basis by the computer, and the standard of the paper. You are about to take five examinations.

Simple probability

2.2 It is vital that the first examination is easy as it covers a subject which you have tried, but unfortunately failed, to understand. What is the probability that it will be an easy examination?

2.3 Obviously (let us hope), the probability of an easy paper is $\frac{1}{2}$ (or 50% or 0.5). This reveals a very important principle (which holds if each result is equally likely).

> **FORMULA TO LEARN**
>
> **Probability of achieving the desired result**
>
>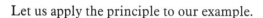
> $$= \frac{\text{Number of ways of achieving desired result}}{\text{Total number of possible outcomes}}$$

Let us apply the principle to our example.

Total number of possible outcomes = 'easy' or 'difficult'	= 2
Total number of ways of achieving the desired result (which is 'easy')	= 1
The probability of an easy examination, or P(easy examination)	= $\frac{1}{2}$

2.4 EXAMPLE: SIMPLE PROBABILITY

Suppose that a coin is tossed in the air. What is the probability that it will come down heads?

2.5 SOLUTION

$$P(\text{heads}) = \frac{\text{Number of ways of achieving desired result (heads)}}{\text{Total number of possible outcomes (heads or tails)}}$$

$$= \quad \frac{1}{2} \text{ or } 50\% \text{ or } 0.5.$$

Complementary outcomes

2.6 You are desperate to pass more of the examinations than your sworn enemy but, unlike you, he is more likely to pass the first examination if it is difficult. (He is very strange!!) What is the probability of the first examination being more suited to your enemy's requirements?

2.7 We know that the probability of certainty is one. The certainty in this scenario is that the examination will be easy or difficult.

P(easy or difficult examination)	=	1
From Paragraph 2.3, P(easy examination)	=	$\frac{1}{2}$
P(not easy examination)	=	P(difficult examination)
	=	1 – P(easy examination)
	=	1 – $\frac{1}{2}$
	=	$\frac{1}{2}$

FORMULA TO LEARN

$P(\overline{A}) = 1 - P(A)$, where $\overline{A}$ is 'not A'.

2.8 EXAMPLE: COMPLEMENTARY OUTCOMES

If there is a 25 per cent chance of the Rainbow Party winning the next general election, use the law of complementary events to calculate the probability of the Rainbow Party *not* winning the next election.

2.9 SOLUTION

P(winning)   = $25\% = \frac{1}{4}$

P(not winning)   = $1 - P(\text{winning}) = 1 - \frac{1}{4} = \frac{3}{4}$

The simple addition or OR law

2.10 The time pressure in the second examination is enormous. The computer will produce a paper which will have between five and nine questions. You know that, easy or difficult, the examination must have six questions at the most for you to have any hope of passing it.

What is the probability of the computer producing an examination with six or fewer questions? In other words, what is the probability of an examination with five *or* six questions?

2.11 Don't panic. Let us start by using the basic principle.

P(5 questions)   = $\dfrac{\text{Total number of ways of achieving a five question examination}}{\text{Total number of possible outcomes } (= 5,6,7,8 \text{ or } 9 \text{ questions})}$

= $\frac{1}{5}$

Likewise P(6 questions) = $\frac{1}{5}$

Either five questions or six questions would be acceptable, so the probability of you passing the examination must be greater than if just five questions or just six questions (but not both) were acceptable. We therefore add the two probabilities together so that the probability of passing the examination has increased.

2.12 So P(5 or 6 questions)   = P(5 questions) + P(6 questions)

= $\frac{1}{5} + \frac{1}{5} = \frac{2}{5}$

EXAM FORMULA

The **simple addition law** or **OR law** is:

P(A or B) = P(A) + P(B)

where A and B are **mutually exclusive outcomes,** which means that the occurrence of one of the outcomes excludes the possibility of any of the others happening.

In the example the outcomes are **mutually exclusive** because it is impossible to have five questions *and* six questions in the same examination.

2.13 EXAMPLE: MUTUALLY EXCLUSIVE OUTCOMES

The delivery of an item of raw material from a supplier may take up to six weeks from the time the order is placed. The probabilities of various delivery times are as follows.

Delivery time	Probability
≤ 1 week	0.10
> 1, ≤ 2 weeks	0.25
> 2, ≤ 3 weeks	0.20
> 3, ≤ 4 weeks	0.20
> 4, ≤ 5 weeks	0.15
> 5, ≤ 6 weeks	0.10
	1.00

Required

Calculate the probability that a delivery will take the following times.

(a) Two weeks or less
(b) More than three weeks

2.14 SOLUTION

(a) P (≤ 1 or > 1, ≤ 2 weeks) = P (≤ 1 week) + P (> 1, ≤ 2 weeks)
$$= 0.10 + 0.25$$
$$= 0.35$$

(b) P (> 3, ≤ 6 weeks) = P (> 3, ≤ 4 weeks) + P (> 4, ≤ 5 weeks) + P (> 5, ≤ 6 weeks)
$$= 0.20 + 0.15 + 0.10$$
$$= 0.45$$

The simple multiplication or AND law

2.15 You still have three examinations to sit: astrophysics, geography of the moon and computer art. Stupidly, you forgot to revise for the astrophysics examination, which will have between 15 and 20 questions. You think that you may scrape through this paper if it is easy *and* if there are only 15 questions.

What is the probability that the paper the computer produces will exactly match your needs? Do not forget that there is no link between the standard of the examination and the number of questions.

2.16 The best way to approach this question is diagrammatically, showing all the possible outcomes.

		Number of questions				
	15	16	17	18	19	20
Type of paper						
Easy (E)	E and 15*	E and 16	E and 17	E and 18	E and 19	E and 20
Difficult (D)	D and 15	D and 16	D and 17	D and 18	D and 19	D and 20

The diagram shows us that, of the twelve possible outcomes, there is only one 'desired result' (which is asterisked). We can therefore calculate the probability as follows.

P(easy paper *and* 15 questions) = $^1/_{12}$.

2.17 The answer can be found more easily as follows.

BPP
PUBLISHING

P(easy paper *and* 15 questions) = P(easy paper) × P(15 questions) = $\frac{1}{2} \times \frac{1}{6} = \frac{1}{12}$.

> ## EXAM FORMULA
>
> The **simple multiplication law** or **AND law** is: P(A and B) = P(A) P(B)
>
> where A and B are **independent** events, which means that the occurrence of one event in no way affects the outcome of the other events.

2.18 The number of questions has no effect on, nor is it affected by whether it is an easy or difficult paper.

2.19 EXAMPLE: INDEPENDENT EVENTS

A die is thrown and a coin is tossed simultaneously. What is the probability of throwing a 5 and getting heads on the coin?

2.20 SOLUTION

The probability of throwing a 5 on a die is $\frac{1}{6}$
The probability of a tossed coin coming up heads is $\frac{1}{2}$
The probability of throwing a 5 and getting heads on a coin is $\frac{1}{2} \times \frac{1}{6} = \frac{1}{12}$

The general rule of addition

2.21 The three examinations you still have to sit are placed face down in a line in front of you at the final examination sitting. There is an easy astrophysics paper, a difficult geography of the moon paper and a difficult computer art paper. Without turning over any of the papers you are told to choose one of them. What is the probability that the first paper that you select is difficult or is the geography of the moon paper?

2.22 Let us think about this carefully.

There are two difficult papers, so P(difficult) = $\frac{2}{3}$

There is one geography of the moon paper, so P(geography of the moon) = $\frac{1}{3}$

2.23 If we use the OR law and add the two probabilities then we will have double counted the difficult geography of the moon paper. It is included in the set of difficult papers and in the set of geography of the moon papers. In other words, we are *not* faced with mutually exclusive outcomes because the occurrence of a geography of the moon paper does not exclude the possibility of the occurrence of a difficult paper. We therefore need to take account of this double counting.

P(difficult paper or geography of the moon paper) = P(difficult paper) + P(geography of the moon paper) – P(difficult paper and geography of the moon paper).

Using the AND law, P(difficult paper or geography of the moon paper) = $\frac{2}{3} + \frac{1}{3} - (\frac{1}{3}) = \frac{2}{3}$.

> ## EXAM FORMULA
>
> The **general rule of addition** is: P(A or B) = P(A) + P(B) – P(A and B)
>
> where the word 'or' is used in an inclusive sense: either A or B or both. A and B are therefore *not* mutually exclusive.

2.24 Since it is *not* impossible to have an examination which is difficult *and* about the geography of the moon, these two events are not mutually exclusive.

Question 1

If one card is drawn from a normal pack of 52 playing cards, what is the probability of getting an ace or a spade?

		Probability	
Ace	*Spade*	*Ace of spades*	*Ace or spade*

Answer

		Probability	
Ace	*Spade*	*Ace of spades*	*Ace or spade*
4/52	13/52	1/52	4/3

Working

P(ace or spade) = 4/52 + 13/52 – 1/52 = 16/52 = 4/13

The general rule of multiplication

2.25 Computer art is your last examination. Understandably you are very tired and you are uncertain whether you will be able to stay awake. You believe that there is a 70% chance of your falling asleep if it becomes too hot and stuffy in the examination hall. It is well known that the air conditioning system serving the examination hall was installed in the last millennium and is therefore extremely unreliable. There is a 1 in 4 chance of it breaking down during the examination, thereby causing the temperature in the hall to rise. What is the likelihood that you will drop off?

2.26 The scenario in Paragraph 2.25 has led us to face what is known as **conditional probability**. We can rephrase the information provided as 'the probability that you will fall asleep, given that it is too hot and stuffy, is equal to 70%' and we can write this as follows.

P(fall asleep/too hot and stuffy) = 70%.

2.27 Whether you fall asleep is **conditional** upon whether the hall becomes too hot and stuffy. The events are not, therefore, independent and so we cannot use the simple multiplication law. So:

P(it becomes too hot and stuffy and you fall asleep)

= P(too hot and stuffy) × P(fall asleep/too hot and stuffy)
= 25% × 70% = 0.25 × 0.7 = 0.175 = $17\frac{1}{2}$%

EXAM FORMULA

The **general rule of multiplication** is: P(A and B) =P(A) × P(B/A) =P(B) × P(A/B)

where A and B are **dependent** (ie not independent) events, the occurrence of the second event being dependent upon the occurrence of the first.

2.28 When A and B are independent events, then P(B/A) = P(B) since, by definition, the occurrence of B (and therefore P(B)) does not depend upon the occurrence of A. Similarly P(A/B) = P(A).

2.29 EXAMPLE: CONDITIONAL PROBABILITY

The board of directors of Shuttem Ltd has warned that there is a 60% probability that a factory will be closed down unless its workforce improves its productivity. The factory's manager has estimated that the probability of success in agreeing a productivity deal with the workforce is only 30%.

Required

Determine the likelihood that the factory will be closed.

2.30 SOLUTION

If outcome A is the shutdown of the factory and outcome B is the failure to improve productivity:

$$\text{P (A and B)} = \text{P(B)} \times \text{P(A/B)}$$
$$= 0.7 \times 0.6$$
$$= 0.42$$

Another method of dealing with some conditional probabilities is by using contingency tables. Their use is best explained by an example.

2.31 EXAMPLE: CONTINGENCY TABLES

A cosmetics company has developed a new anti-dandruff shampoo which is being tested on volunteers. Seventy percent of the volunteers have used the shampoo whereas others have used a normal shampoo, believing it to be the new anti-dandruff shampoo. Two sevenths of those using the new shampoo showed no improvement whereas one third of those using the normal shampoo had less dandruff.

Required

A volunteer shows no improvement. What is the probability that he used the normal shampoo?

2.32 SOLUTION

The problem is solved by drawing a contingency table, showing 'improvement' and 'no improvement', volunteers using normal shampoo and volunteers using the new shampoo.

Let us suppose that there were 1,000 volunteers (we could use any number). We could depict the results of the test on the 1,000 volunteers as follows.

	New shampoo	Normal shampoo	Total
Improvement	***500	****100	600
No improvement	**200	200	400
	*700	***300	1,000

* 70% × 1,000 ** $^2/_7$ × 700

*** Balancing figure **** $^1/_3$ × 300

We can now calculate P(used normal shampoo/showed no improvement)

P(shows no improvement) = 400/1,000

P(used normal shampoo/shows no improvement) = 200/400 = ½

Other probabilities are just as easy to calculate.

P(shows improvement/used new shampoo) = 500/700 = $^5/_7$

P(used new shampoo/shows improvement) = 500/600 = $^5/_6$

Question 2

The independent probabilities that the three sections of a management accounting department will encounter one computer error in a week are respectively 0.1, 0.2 and 0.3. There is never more than one computer error encountered by any one section in a week. Calculate the probability that there will be the following number of errors encountered by the management accounting department next week.

(a)   At least one computer error
(b)   One and only one computer error

Answer

(a)   The probability of at least one computer error is 1 minus the probability of no error. The probability of no error is $0.9 \times 0.8 \times 0.7 = 0.504$.

(Since the probability of an error is 0.1, 0.2 and 0.3 in each section, the probability of no error in each section must be 0.9, 0.8 and 0.7 respectively.)

The probability of at least one error is 1 – 0.504 = 0.496.

(b)   Y = yes, N = no

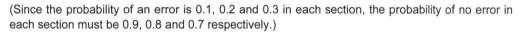

		Section 1	Section 2	Section 3
(i)	Error?	Y	N	N
(ii)	Error?	N	Y	N
(iii)	Error?	N	N	Y

		Probabilities
(i)	0.1 × 0.8 × 0.7 =	0.056
(ii)	0.9 × 0.2 × 0.7 =	0.126
(iii)	0.9 × 0.8 × 0.3 =	0.216
	Total	0.398

The probability of only one error only is 0.398.

Question 3

In a student survey, 60% of the students are male and 75% are CIMA candidates. The probability that a student chosen at random is either female or a CIMA candidate is:

A 0.85   B 0.30   C 0.40   D 1.00

Answer

P(male) = 60% = 0.6
P(female) = 1 – 0.6 = 0.4
P(CIMA candidate) = 75% = 0.75

We need to use the general rule of addition to avoid double counting.

∴ P(female or CIMA candidate) = P(female) + P(CIMA candidate) – P(female *and* CIMA candidate)

$$= 0.4 + 0.75 - (0.4 \times 0.75)$$
$$= 1.15 - 0.3$$
$$= 0.85$$

The correct answer is A.

You should have been able to eliminate options C and D immediately. 0.4 is the probability that the candidate is female and 1.00 is the probability that something will definitely happen - neither of these options are likely to correspond to the probability that the candidate is both female or a CIMA candidate.

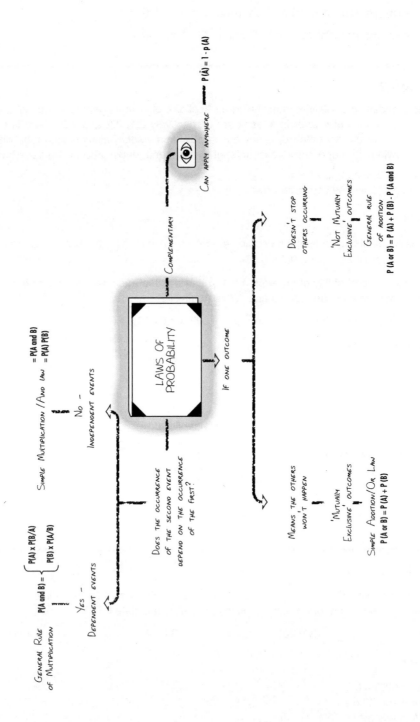

General Rule of Multiplication

$$P(A \text{ and } B) = \begin{cases} P(A) \times P(B/A) \\ P(B) \times P(A/B) \end{cases}$$

Yes -
Dependent events

Does the occurrence of the second event depend on the occurrence of the first?

Simple Multiplication / And Law

$P(A \text{ and } B) = P(A) P(B)$

No -
Independent events

LAWS OF PROBABILITY

Complementary

$P(\bar{A}) = 1 - p(A)$

Can apply anywhere

If one outcome

Doesn't stop others occurring

'Not Mutually Exclusive' outcomes

General rule of addition

$P(A \text{ or } B) = P(A) + P(B) - P(A \text{ and } B)$

Means the others won't happen

'Mutually Exclusive' outcomes

Simple Addition / Or Law

$P(A \text{ or } B) = P(A) + P(B)$

3   EXPECTED VALUES

> **KEY TERM**
>
> An **expected value** (or EV) is a weighted average value, based on probabilities.

3.1   If the probability of an outcome of an event is p, then the expected number of times that this outcome will occur in n events (the expected value) is equal to n × p.

For example, suppose that the probability that a transistor is defective is 0.02. How many defectives would we expect to find in a batch of 4,000 transistors?

$$EV = 4,000 \times 0.02$$
$$= 80 \text{ defectives}$$

3.2   EXAMPLE: EXPECTED VALUES

The daily sales of Product T may be as follows.

Units	Probability
1,000	0.2
2,000	0.3
3,000	0.4
4,000	0.1
	1.0

Required

Calculate the expected daily sales.

3.3   SOLUTION

The EV of daily sales may be calculated by multiplying each possible outcome (volume of daily sales) by the probability that this outcome will occur.

Units	Probability	Expected value Units
1,000	0.2	200
2,000	0.3	600
3,000	0.4	1,200
4,000	0.1	400
	EV of daily sales	2,400

In the long run the expected value should be approximately the actual average, if the event occurs many times over. In the example above, we do not expect sales on any one day to equal 2,400 units, but in the long run, over a large number of days, average sales should equal 2,400 units a day.

Expected values and single events

3.4   The point made in the preceding paragraph is an important one. An **expected value** can be calculated when the **event will only occur once or twice**, but it will not be a true long-run average of what will actually happen, because there is no long run.

3.5 Suppose, for example, that a businessman is trying to decide whether to invest in a project. He estimates that there are three possible outcomes.

Outcome	Profit/(loss) £	Probability
Success	10,000	0.2
Moderate success	2,000	0.7
Failure	(4,000)	0.1

The expected value of profit may be calculated as follows.

Profit/(loss) £	Probability	Expected value £
10,000	0.2	2,000
2,000	0.7	1,400
(4,000)	0.1	(400)
	Expected value of profit	3,000

3.6 In this example, the project is a one-off event, and as far as we are aware, it will not be repeated. The actual profit or loss will be £10,000, £2,000 or £(4,000), and the average value of £3,000 will not actually happen. There is no long-run average of a single event.

3.7 Nevertheless, the expected value can be used to help the manager decide whether or not to invest in the project. Generally the following rules apply.

- A project with a **positive EV** (an expected value which is a profit) should be **accepted**
- A project with a **negative EV** (an expected value which is a loss) should be **rejected**

3.8 Provided that we understand the limitations of using expected values for single events, they can offer a helpful guide for management decisions, and suggest to managers whether any particular decision is worth the risk of taking (subject, of course, to reasonable accuracy in the estimates of the probabilities themselves).

Question 4

A company manufactures and sells product D. The selling price of the product is £6 per unit, and estimates of demand and variable costs of sales are as follows.

Probability	Demand Units	Probability	Variable cost per unit £
0.3	5,000	0.1	3.00
0.6	6,000	0.3	3.50
0.1	8,000	0.5	4.00
		0.1	4.50

The unit variable costs do not depend on the volume of sales.

Fixed costs will be £10,000.

Required

Calculate the expected profit.

Answer

The EV of demand is as follows.

Demand Units	Probability	Expected value Units
5,000	0.3	1,500
6,000	0.6	3,600
8,000	0.1	800
	EV of demand	5,900

The EV of the variable cost per unit is as follows.

Variable costs £	Probability	Expected value £
3.00	0.1	0.30
3.50	0.3	1.05
4.00	0.5	2.00
4.50	0.1	0.45
	EV of unit variable costs	3.80

		£
Sales	5,900 units × £6.00	35,400
Less variable costs	5,900 units × £3.80	22,420
Contribution		12,980
Less fixed costs		10,000
Expected profit		2,980

3.9 The expected value is summarised in equation form as follows.

$$E(x) = \Sigma x P(x)$$

This is read as 'the expected value of "x" is equal to the sum of the products of each value of x and the corresponding probability of that value of x occurring'.

4 EXPECTATION AND DECISION MAKING

4.1 The concepts of probability and expected value are vital in **business decision making**. The expected values for single events can offer a helpful guide for management decisions.

* A project with a positive EV should be accepted
* A project with a negative EV should be rejected

4.2 Another decision rule involving expected values that you are likely to come across is the choice of an option or alternative which has the **highest EV of profit** (or the **lowest EV of cost**).

4.3 Choosing the option with the highest EV of profit is a decision rule that has both merits and drawbacks, as the following simple example will show.

4.4 EXAMPLE: THE EXPECTED VALUE CRITERION

Suppose that there are two mutually exclusive projects with the following possible profits.

Project A		*Project B*	
Probability	*Profit* £	*Probability*	*Profit/(loss)* £
0.8	5,000	0.1	(2,000)
0.2	6,000	0.2	5,000
		0.6	7,000
		0.1	8,000

Required

Determine which project should be chosen.

4.5 SOLUTION

The EV of profit for each project is as follows. £

(a) Project A (0.8 × 5,000) + (0.2 × 6,000) = 5,200
(b) Project B (0.1 × (2,000)) + (0.2 × 5,000) + (0.6 × 7,000) + (0.1 × 8,000) = 5,800

153 BPP

Project B has a higher EV of profit. This means that on the balance of probabilities, it could offer a better return than A, and so is arguably a better choice.

On the other hand, the minimum return from project A would be £5,000 whereas with B there is a 0.1 chance of a loss of £2,000. So project A might be a safer choice.

Payoff tables

4.6 Decisions have to be taken about a wide variety of matters (capital investment, controls on production, project scheduling and so on) and under a wide variety of conditions from **virtual certainty** to **complete uncertainty**.

4.7 There are, however, certain common factors in many business decisions.

(a) When a decision has to be made, there will be a range of possible **actions**.

(b) Each action will have certain **consequences**, or **payoffs** (for example, profits or losses).

(c) The payoff from any given action will depend on the **circumstances** (for example, high demand or low demand), which may or may not be known when the decision is taken. Frequently each circumstance will be assigned a probability of occurrence. The circumstances are *not* dependent on the action taken.

4.8 For a decision with these elements, a **payoff table** can be prepared. This is simply a table with **rows for circumstances** and **columns for actions** (or vice versa), and the payoffs in the cells of the table.

4.9 A payoff table may look something like this.

Payoff table for decision on level of advertising expenditure:
payoffs in £'000 of profit after advertising expenditure

		Actions: expenditure		
		High	*Medium*	*Low*
Circumstances:	Boom	+50	+30	+15
the state of the	Stable	+20	+25	+5
economy	Recession	0	−10	−35

Sometimes the circumstances will be another person's action, for example a competitor's level of advertising expenditure. Note that payoff tables can also show costs or losses instead of profits, in which case we would hope for low figures. **A payoff table showing profits may be called a profit table**.

4.10 EXAMPLE: PAYOFF TABLE

A cinema has to decide how many programmes to print for a premiere of a film. From previous experience of similar events, it is expected that the probability of sales will be as follows.

Number of programmes demanded	*Probability of demand*
250	0.1
500	0.2
750	0.4
1,000	0.1
1,250	0.2

The best print quotation received is £2,000 plus 20 pence per copy. Advertising revenue from advertisements placed in the programme totals £2,500. Programmes are sold for £2 each. Unsold programmes are worthless.

Required

(a) Construct a payoff table.

(b) Find the most profitable number of programmes to have printed.

4.11 SOLUTION

(a) *Actions: print levels*

			250	500	750	1,000	1,250
	250	(p = 0.1)	950	900	850	800	750
Circumstances:	500	(p = 0.2)	950	1,400	1,350	1,300	1,250
demand levels	750	(p = 0.4)	950	1,400	1,850	1,800	1,750
	1,000	(p = 0.1)	950	1,400	1,850	2,300	2,250
	1,250	(p = 0.2)	950	1,400	1,850	2,300	2,750

These figures are calculated as the profit under each set of circumstances. For example, if the cinema produces 1,000 programmes and 1,000 are demanded, the profit is calculated as follows.

Total revenue	= advertising revenue + sale of programmes
	= £2,500 + £(1,000 × 2)
	= £4,500

Total costs	= £2,000 + £(0.20 × 1,000)
	= £2,000 + £200
	= £2,200

Profit = total revenue – total costs = £4,500 – £2,200 = £2,300

Similarly, if the cinema produces 750 programmes, but only 500 are demanded, the profit is calculated as follows.

Total revenue	= £2,500 + £(500 × 2)
	= £2,500 + £1,000 = £3,500

Total costs	= £2,000 + £(0.20 × 500)
	= £2,000 + £100
	= £2,100

Profit = total revenue – total costs = £3,500 – £2,100 = £1,400

Note that whatever the print level, the maximum profit that can be earned is determined by the demand. This means that when 250 programmes are printed, the profit is £950 when demand is 250. Profit is also £950 when demand is 500, 750, 1,000 or 1,250.

(b) The expected profits from each of the possible print levels are as follows.
Print 250

Expected profit = £((950 × 0.1) + (950 × 0.2) + (950 × 0.4) + (950 × 0.1) + (950 × 0.2)) = £950

Print 500

Expected profit = £((900 × 0.1) + (1,400 × (0.2 + 0.4 + 0.1 + 0.2))) = £1,350

Print 750

Expected profit = £((850 × 0.1) + (1,350 × 0.2) + (1,850 × 0.7)) = £1,650

Print 1,000

Expected profit = £((800 × 0.1) + (1,300 × 0.2) + (1,800 × 0.4) + (2,300 × 0.3)) = £1,750

Print 1,250

Expected profit = £((750 × 0.1) + (1,250 × 0.2) + (1,750 × 0.4) + (2,250 × 0.1) +
(2,750 × 0.2)) = £1,800

1,250 programmes should therefore be printed in order to **maximise expected profit**.

EXAM FORMULA

E (X) = Expected value = Probability × Pay off

Question 5

In a restaurant there is a 30% chance of five apple pies being ordered a day and a 70% chance of ten being ordered. Each apple pie sells for £2. It costs £1 to make an apple pie. Using a payoff table, decide how many apple pies the restaurant should prepare each day, bearing in mind that unsold apple pies must be thrown away at the end of each day.

Answer

		Prepared	
		5	10
Demand	5 (0.3)	5	0
	10 (0.7)	5	10

Prepare 5, profit = (£5 × 0.3) + (£5 × 0.7) = £5
Prepare 10, profit = (£0 × 0.3) + (£10 × 0.7) = £7

Ten pies should be prepared.

Limitations of expected values

4.12 Evaluating decisions by using expected values have a number of limitations.

(a) The **probabilities** used when calculating expected values are likely to be estimates. They may therefore be **unreliable** or **inaccurate**.

(b) Expected values are **long-term averages** and may not be suitable for use in situations involving **one-off decisions**. They may therefore be useful as a **guide** to decision making.

(c) Expected values do not consider the **attitudes to risk of** the people involved in the decision-making process. They do not, therefore, take into account all of the factors involved in the decision.

(d) The time value of money may not be taken into account: £100 now is worth more than £100 in ten years' time. We shall study the time value of money in Section D of this Study Text.

5   PERMUTATIONS AND COMBINATIONS

Permutations

5.1 The theory of permutations and combinations is an important tool in probability theory.

KEY TERM

A **permutation** is an arrangement of items in which the order matters.

5.2 EXAMPLE: SIMPLE PERMUTATIONS

If you have three pieces of fruit, an apple, a banana and a pear, you can eat them in a number of different orders, or **permutations**. The permutations for eating these fruit are as follows.

Order in which fruit is eaten

Permutation	1st	2nd	3rd
1	apple	pear	banana
2	apple	banana	pear
3	pear	apple	banana
4	pear	banana	apple
5	banana	apple	pear
6	banana	pear	apple

Permutation 1 shows that the apple is eaten first, followed by the pear and then the banana. Permutation 5 shows that the banana is eaten first, followed by the apple and then the pear. For three pieces of fruit there are therefore six different permutations or orders in which they may be eaten. Note how each different permutation (1 - 6) has the fruits in a **unique arrangement**.

5.3 Statisticians will often need to work out the number of ways that an event can occur in order to calculate probabilities. Listing each permutation or order can be very time consuming and possibly inaccurate. Formulae may be used in order to calculate the number of permutations or orders.

5.4 In general, the number of permutations of n objects is written as n! (n factorial).

$$n! = n(n-1)(n-2)(n-3)......$$

5.5 In our fruit example, 3 pieces of fruit may be arranged in 3! ways.

$$3! = 3 \times 2 \times 1 = 6 \text{ arrangements}$$

Note that this is the same answer as the one which was obtained by writing out all of the different arrangements or permutations in paragraph 5.2.

Permutations of groups

5.6 It is possible that we may wish to calculate the number of permutations of eating only two of the fruits from the apple, banana and pear. The ways in which these fruits may be arranged are as follows.

Permutation	1st	2nd
1	apple	pear
2	pear	apple
3	apple	banana
4	banana	apple
5	pear	banana
6	banana	pear

There are therefore six permutations of eating two pieces of fruit from a possible three pieces of fruit, where **order matters**.

BPP PUBLISHING

FORMULA TO LEARN

The number of **permutations** of n items, selecting x at a time is denoted by the term $_nP_x$ and the formula is as follows.

$$_nP_x = \frac{n!}{(n-x)!}$$

5.7   In the fruit example above, there are three pieces of fruit (n = 3) and we wish to select two pieces of fruit (x = 2). Using the formula we can calculate the number of permutations.

$$_3P_2 = \frac{3!}{(3-2)!} = \frac{3!}{1!} = \frac{3 \times 2 \times 1}{1} = 6 \text{ permutations}$$

5.8   A **permutation** is therefore an arrangement of items in which the **order matters**. An arrangement of items where the **order does not matter** is known as a **combination**.

Combinations

KEY TERM

A **combination** is an arrangement of items where the order does not matter.

5.9   **EXAMPLE: SIMPLE COMBINATIONS**

Let us consider the apple, banana and pear example in paragraph 5.2. Where we have three pieces of fruit, how many ways can we select the fruit where order does not matter? The answer is only 1, since the arrangement apple, pear, banana is the same as apple, banana, pear which is the same as banana, apple, pear and so on. In fact the different permutations listed (1-6) are all the same combination of fruit.

FORMULA TO LEARN

The number of **combinations** of n items, x at a time is denoted by the term ^nC_x and the formula is as follows.

$$^nC_x = \frac{n!}{x!(n-x)!}$$

where   n = total number of items
               x = the number of items per arrangement

5.10   If we use the formula to calculate the number of ways of combining three fruit out of three fruit, we get the following answer.

Let n = 3 and let x = 3

$$^3C_3 = \frac{3!}{3!(3-3)!} = \frac{3!}{3!0!} = \frac{3 \times 2 \times 1}{3 \times 2 \times 1 \times 1} = 1$$

Note that **0! = 1** (always).

5.11 In paragraph 5.6 we considered the permutations of eating two pieces of fruit. The combinations of eating two pieces of fruit out of three pieces of fruit may be calculated by using the formula in the above example. We wish to calculated $^3C_2$.

$$^3C_2 = \frac{3!}{(3-2)!2!} = \frac{3!}{1!2!} = \frac{3 \times 2 \times 1}{1 \times 2 \times 1} = 3$$

5.12 We can list the three combinations of selecting the pieces of fruit out of a possible three pieces. Remember that order does not matter, so the permutations 1 and 2 in paragraph 3.6 are the same combination of fruit. **Combinations do not worry about the order of things** and therefore apple 1st, pear 2nd is the same combination as pear 1st, apple 2nd.

Combination of fruit eaten

apple	pear
apple	banana
pear	banana

The number of combinations is three which is the same as the answer which was calculated by using the formula in paragraph 5.11.

5.13 EXAMPLE: COMBINATIONS OF ONE OR TWO ITEMS

A hardware storekeeper sells paint which he mixes himself in pairs to get the right colours. If we assume that by mixing two of the basic paints he always gets a colour different to any of the other mixtures and different to any of the basic colours, how many different shades can he obtain by stocking n basic paints? (*Note.* Any one basic paint itself counts as one shade.)

5.14 SOLUTION

The total number of mixtures (combinations) of two paints will be:

$$^nC_2 = \frac{n!}{(n-2)!2!} = \frac{n \times (n-1)}{2 \times 1} = \frac{n^2 - n}{2}$$

If we add to this the number of paints stocked, n, (which are themselves different shades) we get a total of

$$\frac{n^2 - n}{2} + n$$

Question 6

A class of 15 students is about to sit a statistics examination. They will subsequently be listed in descending order by reference to the marks scored. Assume that there are no tied positions with two or more students having the same mark.

Required

Calculate the following.

(a) The number of different possible orderings for the whole class

(b) The number of different possible results for the top three places

(c) The number of different possible ways of having three people taking the top three places (irrespective of order)

BPP
PUBLISHING

Answer

(a) The number of different possible orderings of the whole class is

$$_{15}P_{15} = \frac{15!}{(15-15)!} = \frac{15!}{0!} = 15! = 1,307,674,368,000$$

(b) The number of different possible results for the top three places is given by the number of permutations of three out of 15.

$$_{15}P_{3} = \frac{15!}{(15-3)!} = \frac{15!}{12!} = 15 \times 14 \times 13 = 2,730$$

(c) The number of ways of having three people taking the top three places is given by the number of combinations of three out of 15.

$$^{15}C_{3} = \frac{15!}{(15-3)!3!} = \frac{15 \times 14 \times 13}{3 \times 2 \times 1} = 455$$

Exam focus point

Do not underestimate the importance of probability in the **Business Mathematics** examination – this topic accounts for 20% of the syllabus.

Chapter roundup

- **Mutually exclusive outcomes** are outcomes where the occurrence of one of the outcomes excludes the possibility of any of the others happening.

- **Independent events** are events where the outcome of one event in no way affects the outcome of the other events.

- **Dependent** or **conditional** events are events where the outcome of one event depends on the outcome of the others.

- The **addition laws** for two events, A and B, are as follows.

    P(A or B) = P(A) + P(B) when A and B have mutually exclusive outcomes.

    P(A or B) = P(A) + P(B) – P(A and B) when A and B are independent events.

- **Contingency tables** can be useful for dealing with **conditional probability**.

- The **multiplication laws** for two events, A and B, are as follows.

    P(A and B) = 0 when A and B have mutually exclusive outcomes.

    P(A and B) = P(A) P(B) when A and B are independent events.

    P(A and B) = P(A) P(B/A) = P(B) P(A/B) when A and B are dependent/conditional events.

- An **expected value (EV)** is a weighted average, based on probabilities. The expected value for a single event can offer a helpful guide for management decisions: **a project with a positive EV should be accepted** and a **project with a negative EV should be rejected**.

- **Probability and expectation should be seen as an aid to decision making**.

    ○ Probabilities based on past experience have some degree of reliability.

    ○ Subjective estimates of probabilities may be open to question.

    ○ The use of the EV approach in one-off decisions may not be valid, although an EV based on repeated events may be more reliable.

    ○ Probability and expectation take no account of the decision maker's attitude to risk.

- A **combination** is a set of items, selected from a larger collection of items, regardless of the order in which they are selected.

- A **permutation** is a set of items, selected from a larger group of items, in which the order of selection or arrangement is significant.

Quick quiz

1   Complete the following equations

(a)   P ($\overline{X}$) = 1 – ....

(b)   **Simple addition/OR law**

P(A or B or C) = ...

where A, B and C are ....

(c)   **Simple multiplication/AND law**

P(A and B) = ...

where A and B are ....

(d)   **General rule of addition**

P(A or B) = ...

where A and B are ....

(e)   **General rule of multiplication**

P(A and B) = ...

where A and B are ....

2

1	Mutually exclusive outcomes
2	Independent events
3	Conditional events

A   The occurrence of one of the outcomes excludes the possibility of any of the others happening

| 1 | 2 | 3 |

B   Events where the outcome of one event depends on the outcome of the others

| 1 | 2 | 3 |

C   Events where the outcome of one event in no way affects the outcome of the other events

| 1 | 2 | 3 |

3   What is an expected value?

4   Expected values can be used to help managers decide whether or not to invest in a project. Generally, a project with a .... NPV should be rejected, and one with a .... NPV should be ....

5   • A **combination** is an arrangement of items in which the order does/does not matter.
    • A **permutation** is an arrangement of items in which the order does/does not matter.

Answers to quick quiz

1   (a) $1 - P(X)$
    (b) $P(A) + P(B) + P(C)$ Mutually exclusive outcomes
    (c) $P(A) \times P(B)$ Independent events
    (d) $P(A) + P(B) - P(A \text{ and } B)$ Not mutually exclusive outcomes
    (e) $P(A) \times P(B/A) = P(B) \times P(A/B)$ Dependent events

2   A = 1
    B = 3
    C = 2

3   A weighted average value based on probabilities.

4   Generally, a project with a negative NPV should be rejected, and one with a positive NPV should be accepted.

5   • Combination - order does not matter
    • Permutation - order does matter

Now try the following objective test questions

Question bank	Question numbers	Page
Paper-based exam	9	279
Computer-based assessment	9	297

Chapter 10

THE NORMAL DISTRIBUTION

Topic list		Syllabus reference	Ability required
1	Probability distributions	(iii)	Application
2	The normal distribution	(iii)	Application
3	The standard deviation and the normal distribution	(iii)	Application
4	Using the normal distribution to calculate probabilities	(iii)	Application

Introduction

In Chapter 9 we looked at the calculation and interpretation of probability and uncertainty. This chapter begins by examining **probability distributions**. Probability distributions analyse the proportion of times a particular value occurs in a set of items. The importance of probability distributions is that they extend the areas to which probability can be applied and they provide a method of arriving at the probability of an event without having to go through all the probability rules examined in the previous chapter. We will then turn our attention to a particular probability distribution: the **normal distribution**.

Learning outcomes covered in this chapter

- **Demonstrate** the use of the normal distribution and the CIMA tables

- **Demonstrate** the application of the normal distribution to calculate probabilities

Syllabus content covered in this chapter

- Normal distribution

1 PROBABILITY DISTRIBUTIONS

1.1 If we convert the frequencies in the following frequency distribution table into proportions, we get a **probability distribution**.

BPP PUBLISHING

Marks out of 10 (statistics test)	Number of students (frequency distribution)	Proportion or probability (probability distribution)
0	0	0.00
1	0	0.00
2	1	0.02★
3	2	0.04
4	4	0.08
5	10	0.20
6	15	0.30
7	10	0.20
8	6	0.12
9	2	0.04
10	0	0.00
	50	1.00

★ $^1/_{50} = 0.02$

KEY TERM

A **probability distribution** is an analysis of the proportion of times each particular value occurs in a set of items.

1.2 A graph of the probability distribution would be the same as the graph of the frequency distribution, but with the **vertical axis marked in proportions** rather than in numbers.

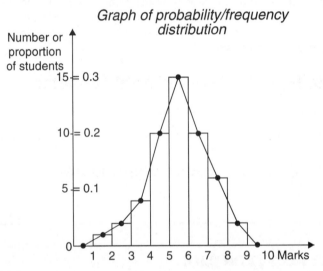

Graph of probability/frequency distribution

1.3 (a) The area under the curve in the frequency distribution represents the total number of students whose marks have been recorded, 50 people.

(b) **The area under the curve in a probability distribution is 100%, or 1** (the total of all the probabilities).

1.4 There are a number of different probability distributions but the only one that you need to know about for the *Business Mathematics* examination is: the **normal distribution**.

2 THE NORMAL DISTRIBUTION

2.1 The normal distribution is an important probability distribution which is often applied to **continuous variables**. In other words, in calculating P(x), x can be any value, and does not have to be a whole number.

2.2 The normal distribution can also apply to **discrete variables** which can take **many possible values**. For example, the volume of sales, in units, of a product might be any whole number in the range 100 – 5,000 units. There are so many possibilities within this range that the variable is for all practical purposes **continuous**.

2.3 The normal distribution can be drawn as a graph, and it would be a **bell-shaped curve**.

Normal distribution

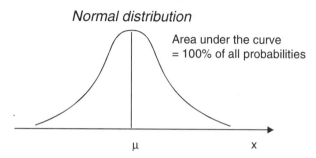

2.4 **Properties of the normal distribution** are as follows.

- It is symmetrical.
- The mean of the distribution is known as μ (pronounced mew).
- The area to the left of μ is the mirror image of the area to the right of μ.
- The area under the curve totals exactly 1.

2.5 The normal distribution is important because in the practical application of statistics, it has been found that **many probability distributions are close enough to a normal distribution** to be treated as one without any significant loss of accuracy.

3 THE STANDARD DEVIATION AND THE NORMAL DISTRIBUTION

3.1 For any normal distribution, the **dispersion** around the mean (μ) of the frequency of occurrences can be measured exactly in terms of the **standard deviation** (σ) (a concept we covered in Chapter 7).

3.2 The entire frequency curve represents all the possible outcomes and their frequencies of occurrence. Since the normal curve is **symmetrical, 50% of occurrences have a value greater than the mean value** (μ), and **50% of occurrences have a value less than the mean value** (μ).

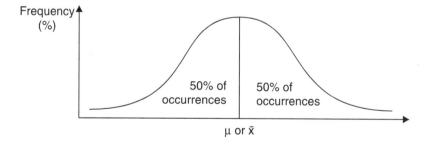

3.3 **About 68% of frequencies have a value within one standard deviation either side of the mean.** Thus if a normal distribution has a **mean of 80** and a **standard deviation of 3**, 68% ($2 \times 34\%$) of the total frequencies would occur **within the range ± one standard deviation from the mean**. Since the curve is symmetrical, 34% of the values must fall in the range 77 – 80 and 34% in the range 80 – 83.

ie mean ± one standard deviation ($=3$)

$=$ 80 ± 3

$=$ $80 + 3 = 83$

or $80 - 3 = 77$

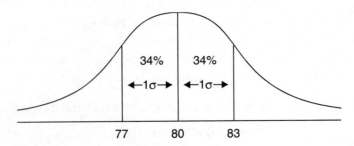

3.4   **95% of the frequencies in a normal distribution occur in the range ± 1.96 standard deviations from the mean.**

In our example, when μ = 80, and σ = 3, 95% of the frequencies in the distribution would occur in the range

    mean ± 1.96 standard deviations
    80 ± 1.96 (3)
=   80 ± 5.88 (the range 74.12 to 85.88)

47½% would be in the range 74.12 to 80 and 47½% would be in the range 80 to 85.88.

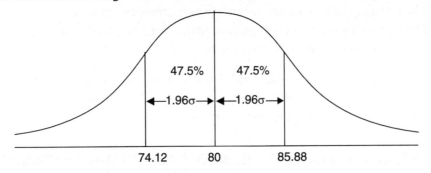

3.5   **99% of the frequencies occur in the range ± 2.58 standard deviations from the mean.**

In our example, 99% of frequencies in a normal distribution with μ = 80 and σ = 3 would lie in the range

    mean ± 2.58 standard deviations
    80 ± 2.58 (3)
=   80 ± 7.74
=   72.26 to 87.74.

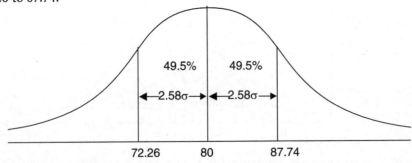

49½% would be in the range 72.26 – 80 and 49½% would be in the range 80 – 87.74

Normal distribution tables

3.6 Although there is an infinite number of normal distributions, depending on values of the mean μ and the standard deviation σ, **the relative dispersion of frequencies around the mean, measured as proportions of the total population, is exactly the same for all normal distributions.** In other words, whatever the normal distribution, 47.5% of outcomes will always be in the range between the mean and 1.96 standard deviations below the mean, 49.5% of outcomes will always be in the range between the mean and 2.58 standard deviations below the mean and so on.

3.7 A normal distribution table, shown at the end of this Study Text, gives the proportion of the total between the mean and a point above or below the mean for any multiple of the standard deviation.

EXAM FORMULA

Distances above or below the mean are expressed in numbers of **standard deviations, z.**

$$z = \frac{x - \mu}{\sigma}$$

where
z = the number of standard deviations above or below the mean (z score)
x = the value of the variable under consideration
μ = the mean
σ = the standard deviation.

3.8 EXAMPLE: NORMAL DISTRIBUTION TABLES

Calculate the following z scores and identify the corresponding proportions using normal distribution tables.

(a) x = 100, μ = 200, σ = 50
(b) x = 1,000, μ = 1,200, σ = 200
(c) x = 25, μ = 30, σ = 6

3.9 SOLUTION

(a) $z = \dfrac{x - \mu}{\sigma}$

$= \dfrac{100 - 200}{50}$

$= 2$

A z score of 2 corresponds to a proportion of 0.4772 or 47.72%.

(b) $z = \dfrac{x - \mu}{\sigma}$

$= \dfrac{1,000 - 1,200}{200}$

$= 1$

A z score of 1 corresponds to a proportion of 0.3413 or 34.13%.

(c) $z = \dfrac{x - \mu}{\sigma}$

$= \dfrac{25 - 30}{6}$

$= 0.8333$

0.8333 corresponds to a proportion of 0.2967 or 29.67%

3.10 If a z score of 1.96 is calculated, what does this mean?

1.96 corresponds to an area of 0.4750 or 47.5%

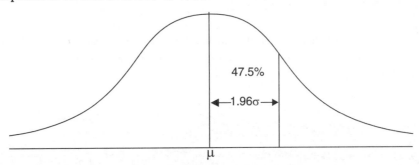

Since the normal distribution is symmetrical 1.96σ below the mean will also correspond to an area of 47.5%.

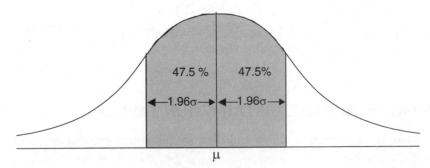

The total shaded area = 47.5% × 2 = 95%

95% of the area under a probability curve therefore lies between mean, μ and 1.96σ above and below the mean. Do you recognise this figure?

3.11 In paragraph 3.4 we said that 95% of the frequencies in a normal distribution lie in the range ± 1.96 standard deviations from the mean but we did not say what this figure was based on. It was of course based on the corresponding value in the normal distribution tables (when z = 1.96) as shown in the paragraph above.

3.12 We also said that 99% of the frequencies occur in the range ± 2.58 standard deviation from the mean.

Why did we say that?

Well, a z score of 2.58 corresponds to an area of 0.4949 (or 49.5%). Remember, the normal distribution is symmetrical.

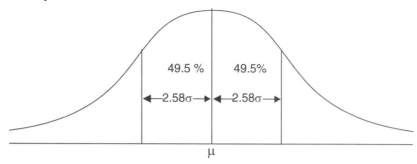

$49.5\% \times 2 = 99\%$

If   mean, $\mu + 2.58\sigma$ =   49.5% and
mean, $\mu - 2.58\sigma$ =   49.5%
Range = mean $\pm 2.58\sigma$ =   99.0%

Therefore, 99% of frequencies occur in the range mean (μ) $\pm$ 2.58 standard deviations (σ), as proved by using normal distribution tables.

Question 1

Prove that approximately 68% of frequencies have a value within one standard deviation either side of the mean, μ.

Answer

One standard deviation corresponds to z = 1

If z = 1, we can look this value up in normal distribution tables to get a value (area) of 0.3413. One standard deviation above the mean can be shown on a graph as follows.

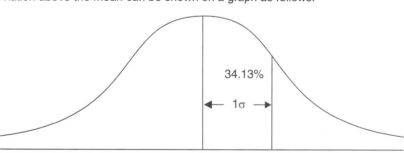

The normal distribution is symmetrical, and we must therefore show the area corresponding to one standard deviation below the mean on the graph also.

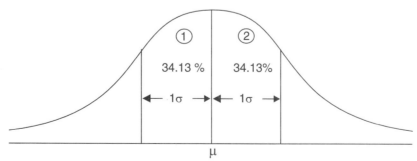

① The area one standard deviation *below* the mean

② The area one standard deviation *above* the mean

Area one standard deviation above *and* below the mean

= ① + ②

= 34.13% + 34.13%

= 68.26% ≏ 68%

4 USING THE NORMAL DISTRIBUTION TO CALCULATE PROBABILITIES

4.1 We have already mentioned that the normal distribution is a type of **probability distribution**. The normal distribution can therefore be used to calculate probabilities. Let's look at some examples to demonstrate how the normal distribution can be used to calculate probabilities.

4.2 A frequency distribution is normal, with a mean of 100 and a standard deviation of 10.

Required

Calculate the proportion of the total frequencies which will be:

(a) above 80
(b) above 90
(c) above 100
(d) above 115
(e) below 85
(f) below 95
(g) below 108
(h) in the range 80 - 110
(i) in the range 90 - 95

4.3 EXAMPLE: USING THE NORMAL DISTRIBUTION TO CALCULATE THE PROPORTION OF FREQUENCIES ABOVE A CERTAIN VALUE

If the value (x) is below the mean (μ), the total proportion is **0.5 plus proportion between the value and the mean (area (a))**.

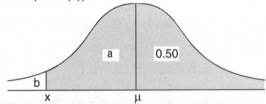

(a) Using the information in paragraph 4.2, the proportion of the total frequencies which will be above 80 is calculated as follows.

$$\frac{80 - 100}{10} = 2 \text{ standard deviations } \textbf{below} \text{ the mean.}$$

From the tables, where z = 2 the proportion is 0.4772.

The proportion of frequencies above 80 is 0.5 + 0.4772 = 0.9772.

(b) Using the information in paragraph 4.2, the proportion of the total frequencies which will be above 90 is calculated as follows.

$$\frac{90 - 100}{10} = 1 \text{ standard deviation } \textbf{below} \text{ the mean.}$$

From the tables, when z = 1, the proportion is 0.3413.

The proportion of frequencies above 90 is 0.5 + 0.3413 = 0.8413.

(c) 100 is the mean. The proportion above this is 0.5. (The normal curve is symmetrical and 50% of occurrences have a value greater than the mean, and 50% of occurrences have a value less than the mean.)

If the value is **above** the mean, the proportion (b) is **0.5 – proportion between the value and the mean (area (a))**.

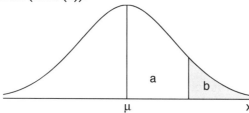

(d) Using the information in paragraph 4.2, the proportion of the total frequencies which will be above 115 is calculated as follows.

$$\frac{115-100}{10} = 1.5 \text{ standard deviations } \textbf{above} \text{ the mean.}$$

From the tables, where z = 1.5, the proportion is 0.4332.

The proportion of frequencies above 115 is therefore 0.5 – 0.4332 = 0.0668.

4.4 EXAMPLE: USING THE NORMAL DISTRIBUTION TO CALCULATE THE PROPORTION OF FREQUENCIES BELOW A CERTAIN VALUE

If the value is below the mean, the proportion (b) is 0.5 – proportion between the value and the mean (area (a)).

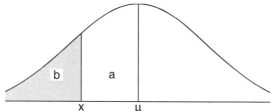

(e) Using the information in paragraph 4.2 the proportion of the total frequencies which will be below 85 is calculated as follows.

$$\frac{85-100}{10} = 1.5 \text{ standard deviations } \textbf{below} \text{ the mean.}$$

The proportion of frequencies below 85 is therefore the same as the proportion above 115, 0.0668.

(f) Using the information in paragraph 4.2 the proportion of the total frequencies which will be below 95 is calculated as follows.

$$\frac{95-100}{10} = 0.5 \text{ standard deviations } \textbf{below} \text{ the mean.}$$

When z = 0.5, the proportion from the tables is 0.1915. The proportion of frequencies below 95 is therefore 0.5 – 0.1915 = 0.3085.

If the value is **above** the mean, the proportion required (b) is **0.5 plus the proportion between the value and the mean (area (a))**.

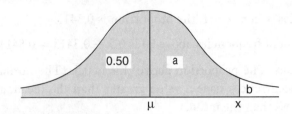

(g) Using the information in paragraph 4.2 the proportion of the total frequencies which will be below 108 is calculated as follows.

$$\frac{108-100}{10} = 0.8 \text{ standard deviations } \textbf{above} \text{ the mean.}$$

From the tables for $z = 0.8$ the proportion is 0.2881.

The proportion of frequencies below 108 is $0.5 + 0.2881 = 0.7881$.

4.5 EXAMPLE: USING THE NORMAL DISTRIBUTION TO CALCULATE THE PROPORTION OF FREQUENCIES WITHIN A CERTAIN RANGE

(h) Using the information in paragraph 4.2 the proportion of the total frequencies which will be in the range 80-110 is calculated as follows. The range 80 to 110 may be divided into two parts:

(i)   80 to 100 (the mean);
(ii) 100 to 110.

The proportion in the range 80 to 100 is (2 standard deviations) 0.4772

The proportion in the range 100 to 110 is (1 standard deviation) 0.3413

The proportion in the total range 80 to 110 is $0.4772 + 0.3413 = 0.8185$.

(i) The range 90 to 95 may be analysed as:

(i)   the proportion above 90 and below the mean
(ii) minus the proportion above 95 and below the mean

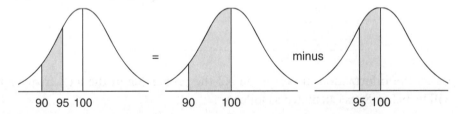

Proportion above 90 and below the mean (1 standard deviation)	0.3413
Proportion above 95 and below the mean (0.5 standard deviations)	0.1915
Proportion between 90 and 95	0.1498

Question 2

The salaries of employees in an industry are normally distributed, with a mean of £14,000 and a standard deviation of £2,700.

Required

(a) Calculate the proportion of employees who earn less than £12,000.
(b) Calculate the proportion of employees who earn between £11,000 and £19,000.

Answer

(a)

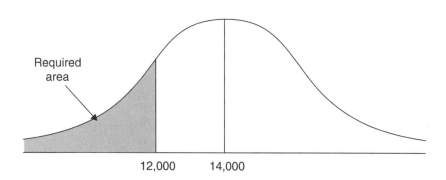

$$z = \frac{12{,}000 - 14{,}000}{2{,}700}$$

$$= -0.74$$

From normal distribution tables, the proportion of salaries between £12,000 and £14,000 is 0.2704 (from tables). The proportion of salaries less than £12,000 is therefore 0.5 − 0.2704 = 0.2296.

(b)

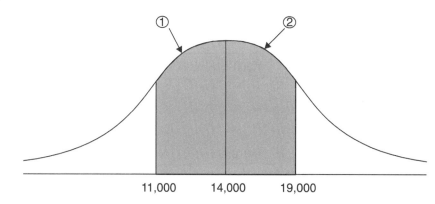

① $z = \dfrac{11{,}000 - 14{,}000}{2{,}700}$

$= 1.11$

② $z = \dfrac{19{,}000 - 14{,}000}{2{,}700}$

$= 1.85$

The proportion with earnings between £11,000 and £14,000 is 0.3665 (from tables where z = 1.11).

The proportion with earnings between £14,000 and £19,000 is 0.4678 (from tables where z = 1.85).

The required proportion is therefore 0.3665 + 0.4678 = 0.8343.

4.6 Note that **the normal distribution is, in fact, a way of calculating probabilities**. In the previous question, for example, the **probability** that an employee earns less than £12,000 (part (a)) is 0.2296 (or 22.96%) and the probability that an employee earns between £11,000 and £19,000 is 0.8343 (or 83.43%).

Question 3

The distribution of sales is normal, with a mean of 1,500 items per week, and a variance of 500 items. The probability that sales are less than 1,300 items in any one week is (delete as appropriate):

15.54%	65.54%
84.46%	34.46%

Answer

~~15.54%~~	~~65.54%~~
~~84.46%~~	34.46%

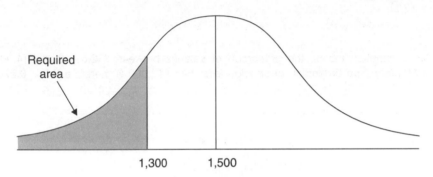

$$z = \frac{x - \mu}{\sigma}$$

$$= \frac{1,300 - 1,500}{500}$$

$$= 0.4$$

A z score of 0.4 corresponds to a probability of 0.1554 (ie probability that sales are between 1,300 and 1,500). The probability that sales are less than 1,300 = 0.5 − 0.1554 = 0.3446 or 34.46%.

Question 4

Use the information in Question 3 to answer this question.

There is a probability of 30.85% that sales will be above how many items per week?

A   1,550
B   1,650
C   1,750
D   1,850

Answer

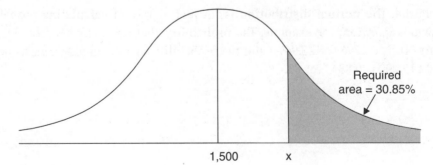

The probability that sales are between 1,500 and x items per week is found as follows. The shaded area = 30.85% (probability sales are greater than x). The probability that sales are between 1,500 and x = 50% - 30.85% = 19.15% = 0.1915. 0.1915 corresponds to a z score of 0.5.

$$\therefore \quad z \quad = \quad \frac{x - \mu}{\sigma}$$

$$\therefore \quad 0.5 \quad = \quad \frac{x - 1,500}{500}$$

$$\therefore \quad x \quad = \quad (0.5 \times 500) + 1,500$$

$$= \quad 1,750 \text{ items}$$

The correct answer is therefore C.

Exam focus point

Make sure that you always draw a sketch of a normal distribution to identify the areas that you are concerned with when using the normal distribution to calculate probabilities. You should also make sure that you are confident with reading normal distribution tables – marks are allocated in the examination for correctly reading values from the tables.

Chapter roundup

- If we convert the frequencies in a frequency distribution table into proportions, we get a **probability distribution.**

- The **normal distribution** is a probability distribution which usually applies to **continuous variables,** such as distance and time.

- Properties of the normal distribution

  ○ It is symmetrical
  ○ It has a mean, μ
  ○ The area under the curve totals exactly 1
  ○ The area to the left of μ = area to right of μ
  ○ It is a bell shaped curve

- The distance of a point above or below the mean of a normal distribution is expressed in numbers of **standard deviations**, z.

  $$z \quad = \quad \frac{x - \mu}{\sigma}$$

  Where

  z = the number of standard deviations above or below the mean
  x = the value of the variable under consideration
  μ = the mean
  σ = the standard deviation

- Sketching a graph of a normal distribution curve often helps in normal distribution problems.

- A given range in a normal distribution = mean ± z standard deviations.

  ○ 68% of outcomes are ± 1 standard deviation from the mean (Range = Mean ± 1 standard deviation)

  ○ 95% of outcomes are ± 1.96 standard deviations from the mean (Range = Mean ± 1.96 standard deviations)

  ○ 99% of outcomes are ± 2.58 standard deviations from the mean (Range = Mean ± 2.58 standard deviations)

- The normal distribution can be used to calculate probabilities.

Quick quiz

1   The normal distribution is a type of .... distribution.

2   The area under the curve of a normal distribution = ... which represents ....% of all probabilities.

3   The mean of a normal distribution = σ

    True   ☐

    False   ☐

4   X% of the frequencies in a normal distribution occur in the range ± y standard deviations from due mean. Match the following x values with the correct y values.

    (a)   If x = 68%, y = ?
    (b)   If x = 95%, y = ?
    (c)   If x = 99%, y = ?

5   Use the following symbols to create a formula for calculating the 'z score'.

x	μ	z	σ

6   What proportions/percentages do the following z scores represent?

    (a)   1.45
    (b)   2.93
    (c)   0.955

7   What are the corresponding z scores for the following proportions/percentages?

    (a)   0.4382
    (b)   0.4750
    (c)   0.4747

Answers to quick quiz

1   Probability

2   1, 100%

3   False. The mean of a normal distribution = μ

4   (a)   1.00
    (b)   1.96
    (c)   2.58

5   $z = \dfrac{x - \mu}{\sigma}$

6   (a)   0.4265   =   42.65%
    (b)   0.4983   =   49.83%
    (c)   0.3302   =   33.02% (Take average of 0.95 and 0.96 = (0.3289 + 0.3315) ÷ 2 = 0.3302.)

7   (a)   1.54
    (b)   1.96
    (c)   1.955

Now try the following objective test questions

Question bank	Question numbers	Page
Paper-based exam	10	279
Computer-based assessment	10	298

Part D
Financial mathematics

Chapter 11

INTEREST

Topic list		Syllabus reference	Ability required
1	Simple interest	(iv)	Application
2	Compound interest	(iv)	Application
3	Regular savings and sinking funds	(iv)	Application
4	Loans and mortgages	(iv)	Application
5	Annual Percentage Rate (APR) of interest	(iv)	Application

Introduction

The previous chapters introduced a variety of quantitative methods relevant to business analysis. This chapter and the next extend the use of mathematics and look at aspects of financial analysis typically undertaken in a business organisation.

In general, financial mathematics deals with problems of **investing money**, or **capital**. If a company (or an individual investor) puts some capital into an investment, a financial return will be expected.

The two major techniques of financial mathematics are **compounding** and **discounting**. This chapter will describe compounding and the next will introduce discounting.

Learning outcomes covered in this chapter

- **Calculate** future values of an investment using both simple and compound interest
- **Calculate** an Annual Percentage Rate of interest given a quarterly or monthly rate
- **Calculate** loan/mortgage repayments and the value of an outstanding loan/mortgage
- **Calculate** the future value of regular savings (sinking funds) or find the savings given the future value, if necessary, using the sum of a geometric progression

Syllabus content covered in this chapter

- Simple and compound interest
- Loans and mortgages
- Sinking funds and savings funds

1 SIMPLE INTEREST

> **KEY TERM**
>
> - **Interest** is the amount of money which an investment earns over time.
> - **Simple interest** is interest which is earned in equal amounts every year (or month) and which is a given proportion of the original investment (the principal).

BPP PUBLISHING

Part D: Financial mathematics

1.1 If a sum of money is invested for a period of time, then the amount of simple interest which accrues is equal to the number of periods × the interest rate × the amount invested. We can write this as a formula.

> **FORMULA TO LEARN**
>
> The formula for **simple interest** is as follows.
>
> S = X + nrX
>
> where X = the original sum invested
>
> r = the interest rate (expressed as a proportion, so 10% = 0.1)
>
> n = the number of periods (normally years)
>
> S = the sum invested after n periods, consisting of the original capital (X) plus interest earned.

1.2 EXAMPLE: SIMPLE INTEREST

How much will an investor have after five years if he invests £1,000 at 10% simple interest per annum?

1.3 SOLUTION

Using the formula S = X + nrX

where X = £1,000
       r = 10%
       n = 5

$\therefore$ S = £1,000 + (5 × 0.1 × £1,000) = £1,500

1.4 If, for example, the sum of money is invested for 3 months and the interest rate is a rate per annum, then n = $^3/_{12}$ = $^1/_4$. If the investment period is 197 days and the rate is an annual rate, then n = $^{197}/_{365}$.

2 COMPOUND INTEREST

Compounding

2.1 Interest is normally calculated by means of **compounding**.

If a sum of money, the principal, is invested at a fixed rate of interest such that the interest is added to the principal and no withdrawals are made, then the amount invested will grow by an increasing number of pounds in each successive time period, because **interest earned in earlier periods will itself earn interest in later periods**.

2.2 EXAMPLE: COMPOUND INTEREST

Suppose that £2,000 is invested at 10% interest. After one year, the original principal plus interest will amount to £2,200.

	£
Original investment	2,000
Interest in the first year (10%)	200
Total investment at the end of one year	2,200

(a) After two years the total investment will be £2,420.

	£
Investment at end of one year	2,200
Interest in the second year (10%)	220
Total investment at the end of two years	2,420

The second year interest of £220 represents 10% of the original investment, and 10% of the interest earned in the first year.

(b) Similarly, after three years, the total investment will be £2,662.

	£
Investment at the end of two years	2,420
Interest in the third year (10%)	242
Total investment at the end of three years	2,662

2.3 Instead of performing the calculations in Paragraph 2.2, we could have used the following formula.

EXAM FORMULA

The basic formula for **compound interest** is $S = X(1 + r)^n$

where X = the original sum invested
 r = the interest rate, expressed as a proportion (so 5% = 0.05)
 n = the number of periods
 S = the sum invested after n periods

2.4 Using the formula for compound interest, $S = X(1 + r)^n$

where X = £2,000
 r = 10% = 0.1
 n = 3

S = £2,000 × 1.10^3
 = £2,000 × 1.331
 = £2,662.

The interest earned over three years is £662, which is the same answer that was calculated in the example above.

Question 1

Simon invests £5,000 now. To what value would this sum have grown after the following periods using the given interest rates? State your answer to two decimal places.

Value now	Investment period	Interest rate	Final value
£	Years	%	£
5,000	3	20	
5,000	4	15	
5,000	3	6	

Answer

Value now	Investment period	Interest rate	Final value
£	Years	%	£
5,000	3	20	8,640.00 [(1)]
5,000	4	15	8,745.03 [(2)]
5,000	3	6	5,955.08 [(3)]

Workings

(1) £5,000 × 1.20^3 = £8,640.00
(2) £5,000 × 1.15^4 = £8,745.03
(3) £5,000 × 1.06^3 = £5,955.08

Question 2

At what annual rate of compound interest will £2,000 grow to £2,721 after four years?

A 7% B 8% C 9% D 10%

Answer

Using the formula for compound interest, $S = X(1 + r)^n$, we know that X = £2,000, S = £2,721 and n = 4. We need to find r. It is essential that you are able to rearrange equations confidently when faced with this type of multiple choice question - there is not a lot of room for guessing!

$$2,721 = 2,000 \times (1 + r)^4$$
$$(1 + r)^4 = 2,721/2,000 = 1.3605$$
$$1 + r = \sqrt[4]{1.3605} = 1.08$$
$$r = 0.08 = 8\%$$

The correct answer is B.

Inflation

2.5 The same compounding formula can be used to **predict future prices** after allowing for **inflation**. For example, if we wish to predict the salary of an employee in five years time, given that he earns £8,000 now and wage inflation is expected to be 10% per annum, the compound interest formula would be applied as follows.

$$\begin{aligned} S &= X(1 + r)^n \\ &= £8,000 \times 1.10^5 \\ &= £12,884.08 \end{aligned}$$

say, £12,900.

Withdrawals of capital or interest

2.6 If an investor takes money out of an investment, it will cease to earn interest. Thus, if an investor puts £3,000 into a bank deposit account which pays interest at 8% per annum, and makes no withdrawals except at the end of year 2, when he takes out £1,000, what would be the balance in his account after four years?

	£
Original investment	3,000.00
Interest in year 1 (8%)	240.00
Investment at end of year 1	3,240.00
Interest in year 2 (8%)	259.20
Investment at end of year 2	3,499.20
Less withdrawal	1,000.00
Net investment at start of year 3	2,499.20
Interest in year 3 (8%)	199.94
Investment at end of year 3	2,699.14
Interest in year 4 (8%)	215.93
Investment at end of year 4	2,915.07

2.7 A quicker approach would be as follows.

	£
£3,000 invested for 2 years at 8% would increase in value to £3,000 × 1.08² =	3,499.20
Less withdrawal	1,000.00
	2,499.20

£2,499.20 invested for a further two years at 8% would increase in value to

£2,499.20 × 1.08² = £2,915.07

Reverse compounding

2.8 The basic principle of compounding can be applied in a number of different situations.

Reducing balance depreciation

2.9 The basic compound interest formula can be used to deal with one method of **depreciation** (as you should already know, depreciation is an accounting technique whereby the cost of a capital asset is spread over a number of different accounting periods as a charge against profit in each of the periods).

2.10 The reducing balance method of depreciation is a kind of **reverse compounding** in which **the value of the asset goes down at a certain rate**. The **rate of 'interest'** is therefore **negative**.

2.11 EXAMPLE: REDUCING BALANCE DEPRECIATION

An item of equipment is bought for £1,000 and is to be depreciated at a fixed rate of 40% per annum. What will be its value at the end of four years?

2.12 SOLUTION

A depreciation rate of 40% equates to a **negative rate of interest,** therefore r = –40% = –0.4. We are told that X = £1,000 and that n = 4. Using the formula for compound interest we can calculate the value of S, the value of the equipment at the end of four years.

$$S = X(1 + r)^n = 1,000(1 + (-0.4))^4 = £129.60.$$

Falling prices

2.13 As well as rising at a compound rate, perhaps because of inflation, costs can also **fall at a compound rate**.

2.14 EXAMPLE: FALLING PRICES

Suppose that the cost of product X is currently £10.80. It is estimated that over the next five years its cost will **fall by 10% pa compound**. The cost of product X at the end of five years is therefore calculated as follows, using the formula for compound interest, $S = X(1 + r)^n$.

$X = £10.80$
$r = -10\% = -0.1$
$n = 5$
$\therefore S = £10.80 \times (1 + (-0.1))^5 = £6.38$

Changes in the rate of interest

2.15 It is possible that the rate of interest will change during the period of an investment. When this happens, the compounding formula must be amended slightly.

FORMULA TO LEARN

The formula for **compound interest** when there are changes in the rate of interest is as follows.

$$S = X(1 + r_1)^y (1 + r_2)^{n-y}$$

where
r_1 = the initial rate of interest
y = the number of years in which the interest rate r_1 applies
r_2 = the next rate of interest
$n - y$ = the (balancing) number of years in which the interest rate r_2 applies.

Question 3

(a) If £8,000 is invested now, to earn 10% interest for three years and 8% thereafter, what would be the size of the total investment at the end of five years?

(b) An investor puts £10,000 into an investment for ten years. The annual rate of interest earned is 15% for the first four years, 12% for the next four years and 9% for the final two years. How much will the investment be worth at the end of ten years?

(c) An item of equipment costs £6,000 now. The annual rates of inflation over the next four years are expected to be 16%, 20%, 15% and 10%. How much would the equipment cost after four years?

Answer

(a) $£8,000 \times 1.10^3 \times 1.08^2 = £12,419.83$
(b) $£10,000 \times 1.15^4 \times 1.12^4 \times 1.09^2 = £32,697.64$
(c) $£6,000 \times 1.16 \times 1.20 \times 1.15 \times 1.10 = £10,565.28$

3 REGULAR SAVINGS AND SINKING FUNDS

3.1 An investor may decide to add to his investment from time to time, and you may be asked to calculate the **final value** (or **terminal value**) of an investment to which equal annual amounts will be added. An example might be an individual or a company making annual payments into a pension fund: we may wish to know the value of the fund after n years.

3.2 EXAMPLE: REGULAR SAVINGS

A person invests £400 now, and a further £400 each year for three more years. How much would the total investment be worth after four years, if interest is earned at the rate of 10% per annum?

3.3 SOLUTION

In problems such as this, we call **now 'Year 0'**, the time **one year from now 'Year 1'** and so on. It is also a good idea to draw a time line in order to establish exactly when payments are made.

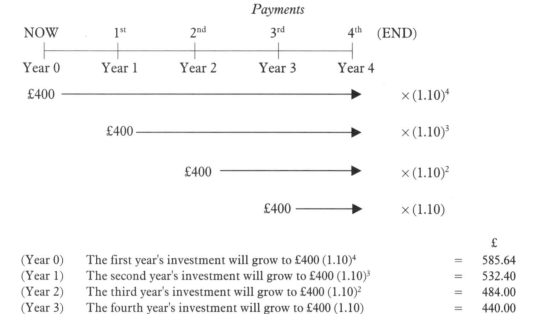

		£
(Year 0)	The first year's investment will grow to £400 $(1.10)^4$	= 585.64
(Year 1)	The second year's investment will grow to £400 $(1.10)^3$	= 532.40
(Year 2)	The third year's investment will grow to £400 $(1.10)^2$	= 484.00
(Year 3)	The fourth year's investment will grow to £400 (1.10)	= 440.00
		2,042.04

3.4 The solution can be written as $(400 \times 1.1) + (400 \times 1.1^2) + (400 \times 1.1^3) + (400 \times 1.1^4)$ with the values placed in reverse order for convenience. This is a **geometric progression** with A (the first term) = (400×1.1), R = 1.1 and n = 4. (Look back to Chapter 1 if you need reminding about geometric progressions.)

FORMULA TO LEARN

The sum of a **geometric progression**, $S = \dfrac{A(R^n - 1)}{R - 1}$

where   A = the first term
         R = the common ratio
         n = the number of terms

In our example:

A = 400×1.1
R = 1.1
n = 4

If $S = \dfrac{A(R^n - 1)}{R - 1}$

BPP PUBLISHING

$$S = \frac{400 \times 1.1(1.1^4 - 1)}{1.1 - 1}$$

$$= £2,042.04$$

3.5 EXAMPLE: INVESTMENTS AT THE ENDS OF YEARS

(a) If, in the previous example, the investments had been made at the end of each of the first, second, third and fourth years, so that the last £400 invested had no time to earn interest. We can show this situation on the following time line.

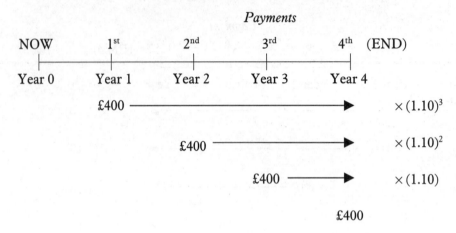

Payments

(Year 0)   No payment
(Year 1)   The first year's investment will grow to $£400 \times (1.10)^3$
(Year 2)   The second year's investment will grow to $£400 \times (1.10)^2$
(Year 3)   The third year's investment will grow to $£400 \times (1.10)$
(Year 4)   The fourth year's investment remains at £400

The value of the fund at the end of the four years is as follows.

$$400 + (400 \times 1.1) + (400 \times 1.1^2) + (400 \times 1.1^3)$$

This is a **geometric progression** with

A = £400
R = 1.1
n = 4

If $S = \dfrac{A(R^n - 1)}{R - 1}$

$$S = \frac{400(1.1^4 - 1)}{1.1 - 1}$$

$$= £1,856.40$$

(b) If our investor made investments as in (a) above, but also put in a £2,500 lump sum one year from now, the value of the fund after four years would be

$$£1,856.40 + £2,500 \times 1.1^3$$
$$= \quad £1,856.40 + £3,327.50 = £5,183.90$$

That is, **we can compound parts of investments separately, and add up the results.**

Question 4

A man invests £1,000 now, and a further £1,000 each year for five more years. How much would the total investment be worth after six years, if interest is earned at the rate of 8% per annum?

Answer

This is a geometric progression with A (the first term) = £1,000 × 1.08, R = 1.08 and n=6.

If $S = \dfrac{A(R^n - 1)}{R - 1}$

$S = \dfrac{1,000 \times 1.08\,(1.08^6 - 1)}{1.08 - 1}$

$= £7,922.80$

Sinking funds

> **KEY TERM**
>
> A **sinking fund** is an investment into which equal annual instalments are paid in order to earn interest, so that by the end of a given number of years, the investment is large enough to pay off a known commitment at that time.

3.6 Repayments against a repayment mortgage can of course be seen as payments into a sinking fund. The total of the constant annual payments (which are usually paid in equal monthly instalments) plus the interest they earn over the term of the mortgage must be sufficient to pay off the initial loan plus accrued interest. We shall be looking at mortgages later on in this chapter.

3.7 Another common known future commitment is the need to **replace an asset at the end of its life**. To ensure that the money is available to buy a replacement a company might decide to invest cash in a sinking fund during the course of the life of the existing asset.

3.8 EXAMPLE: SINKING FUNDS

A company has just bought an asset with a life of four years. At the end of four years, a replacement asset will cost £12,000, and the company has decided to provide for this future commitment by setting up a sinking fund into which equal annual investments will be made, starting at year 1 (one year from now). The fund will earn interest at 12%.

Required

Calculate the annual investment.

3.9 SOLUTION

Let us start by drawing a time line where £A = equal annual investments.

Part D: Financial mathematics

Payments

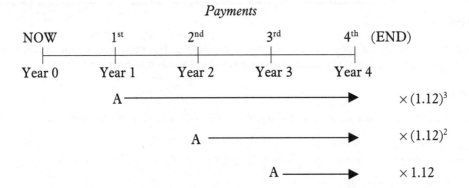

(Year 0)   No payment
(Year 1)   The first year's investment will grow to $£A \times (1.12)^3$
(Year 2)   The second year's investment will grow to $£A \times (1.12)^2$
(Year 3)   The third year's investment will grow to $£A \times (1.12)$
(Year 4)   The fourth year's investment will remain at £A.

The value of the fund at the end of four years is as follows.

$$A + A(1.12) + A(1.12^2) + A(1.12^3)$$

This is a geometric progression with

$$A = A$$
$$R = 1.12$$
$$n = 4$$

The value of the sinking fund at the end of year 4 is £12,000 (given in the question) therefore

$$£12,000 \quad = \quad \frac{A(1.12^4 - 1)}{1.12 - 1}$$

$$£12,000 \quad = \quad 4.779328A$$

$$\therefore A \quad = \quad \frac{£12,000}{4.779328}$$

$$\quad = \quad £2,510.81$$

Therefore, four investments, each of £2,510.81 should therefore be enough to allow the company to replace the asset.

Question 5

A farmer has just bought a combine harvester which has a life of ten years. At the end of ten years a replacement combine harvester will cost £100,000 and the farmer would like to provide for this future commitment by setting up a sinking fund into which equal annual investments will be made, starting *now*. The fund will earn interest at 10% per annum.

Answer

The value of the fund at the end of ten years is a geometric progression with:

$$A = £A \times 1.1$$
$$R = 1.1$$
$$n = 10$$

Therefore the value of the sinking fund at the end of ten years is £100,000.

$$\therefore \quad \text{£100,000} = \frac{A \times 1.1(1.1^{10} - 1)}{1.1 - 1}$$

$$A = \frac{\text{£100,000} \times 0.1}{1.1(1.1^{10} - 1)}$$

$$= \frac{\text{£10,000}}{1.75311670611}$$

$$= \text{£5,704.12}$$

4 LOANS AND MORTGAGES

Loans

4.1 Most people will be familiar with the repayment of loans. The repayment of loans is best illustrated by means of an example.

4.2 EXAMPLE: LOANS

Timothy Lakeside borrows £50,000 now at an interest rate of 8 percent per annum. The loan has to be repaid through five equal instalments *after* each of the next five years. What is the annual repayment?

4.3 SOLUTION

Let us start by calculating the final value of the loan (at the end of year 5).

Using the formula $S = X(1 + r)^n$

where
$$X = \text{£50,000}$$
$$r = 8\% = 0.08$$
$$n = 5$$
$$S = \text{the sum invested after 5 years}$$
$$\therefore \quad S = \text{£50,000}(1 + 0.08)^5$$
$$= \text{£73,466.40}$$

The value of the initial loan after 5 years (£73,466.40) must equal the sum of the repayments.

A time line will clarify when each of the repayments are made. Let £A = the annual repayments which start a year from now, ie at year 1.

Repayments

	NOW	1st	2nd	3rd	4th	5th (END)	
	Year 0	Year 1	Year 2	Year 3	Year 4	Year 5	
		£A ────────────────────────────→					$\times (1.08)^4$
			£A ─────────────────────→				$\times (1.08)^3$
				£A ──────────────→			$\times (1.08)^2$
					£A ──────→		$\times (1.08)$
						£A	

(Year 0)   No payment
(Year 1)   The first year's investment will grow to £A $\times (1.08)^4$
(Year 2)   The second year's investment will grow to £A $\times (1.08)^3$
(Year 3)   The third year's investment will grow to £A $\times (1.08)^2$
(Year 4)   The fourth year's investment will grow to £A $\times (1.08)$
(Year 5)   The fourth year's investment remains at £A.

The value of the repayments at the end of five years is as follows.

$$A + (A \times 1.08) + (A \times 1.08^2) + (A \times 1.08^3) + (A \times 1.08^4)$$

This is a geometric progression with

A = A
R = 1.08
n = 5

The sum of this geometric progression, $S = \dfrac{A(R^n - 1)}{R - 1} = £73,466.40$ since the sum of repayments must **equal** the final value of the loan (ie £73,466.40).

$$S = £73,466.40 = \frac{A(1.08^5 - 1)}{1.08 - 1}$$

£73,466.40   = A $\times$ 5.86660096

A $= \dfrac{£73,466.40}{5.86660096}$

= £12,522.82

The annual repayments are therefore £12,522.82.

Question 6

John Johnstone borrows £50,000 now at an interest rate of 7% per annum. The loan has to be repaid through ten equal instalments after each of the next ten years. What is the annual repayment?

Answer

The final value of the loan (at the end of year 10) is

$$S = £50,000 (1 + 0.07)^{10}$$
$$= £98,357.57$$

The value of the initial loan after 10 years (£98,357.57) must equal the sum of the repayments.

The sum of the repayments is a geometric progression with

A = A
R = 1.07
n = 10

The sum of the repayments = £98,357.57

$$S = £98,357.57 = \frac{A(R^n - 1)}{R - 1}$$

$$= \frac{A(1.07^{10} - 1)}{1.07 - 1}$$

$$= 13.816448A$$

$$\therefore \qquad A \; = \; \frac{£98,357.57}{13.816448}$$

$$= \quad £7,118.88 \text{ per annum}$$

Sinking funds and loans compared

4.4 (a) **Sinking funds**. The sum of the **regular savings**, £A per period at r% over n periods *must* equal the sinking fund required at the end of n periods.

(b) **Loan repayments**. The sum of the **regular repayments** of £A per period at r% over n periods *must* equal the final value of the loan at the end of n periods.

The final value of a loan can therefore be seen to be equivalent to a sinking fund.

Mortgages

4.5 As you are probably aware, when a mortgage is taken out on a property over a number of years, there are several ways in which the loan can be repaid. One such way is the **repayment mortgage** which has the following features.

- A certain amount, S, is borrowed to be paid back over n years.
- Interest, at a rate r, is added to the loan retrospectively at the end of each year.
- A constant amount A is paid back each year.

Income tax relief affects repayments but, for simplicity, we will ignore it here.

4.6 Let us consider the repayments.

(a) At the end of one year A has been repaid.

(b) At the end of two years the initial repayment of A has earned interest and so has a value of $A(1 + r)$ and another A has been repaid. The value of the amount repaid is therefore $A(1 + r) + A$.

(c) At the end of three years, the initial repayment will have a value of $A(1 + r)^2$, the second repayment a value of $A(1 + r)$ and a third repayment of A will have been made. The value of the amount repaid is therefore $A(1 + r)^2 + (1 + r) + A$.

(d) At the end of n years the value of the repayments is therefore $A(1 + r)^{n-1} + A(1 + r)^{n-2} + ... + A(1 + r)^2 + A(1 + r) + A$.

This is a **geometric progression** with 'A' = A, 'R' = $(1 + r)$ and 'n' = n and hence the **sum of the repayments** $= \dfrac{A[(1+r)^n - 1]}{r} = \dfrac{A(R^n - 1)}{R - 1}$

4.7 During the time the repayments have been made, the initial loan has accrued interest and hence has a value of $S(1 + r)^n$.

The repayments must, at the end of n years, repay the initial loan plus the accrued interest and hence, after n years.

Therefore the **sum of the repayments** must equal the **final value of the mortgage**.

Sum of repayments = final value of mortgage

$$\frac{A(R^n - 1)}{R - 1} = SR^n$$

$$\therefore A = \frac{SR^n \times (R-1)}{(R^n - 1)}$$

4.8 EXAMPLE: MORTGAGES

(a) Sam has taken out a £30,000 mortgage over 25 years. Interest is to be charged at 12%. Calculate the monthly repayment.

(b) After nine years, the interest rate changes to 10%. What is the new monthly repayment?

4.9 SOLUTION

(a) **Final value of mortgage** $= £30,000 \times (1.12)^{25}$
$$= £510,002$$

Sum of repayments, S, where A = annual repayment
$$R = 1.12$$
$$n = 25$$

$$\therefore S = \frac{A(1.12^{25} - 1)}{1.12 - 1}$$

$$= 133.334A$$

Sum of repayments = final value of mortgage

$$133.334A = £510,002$$

$$A = \frac{£510,002}{133.334}$$

$$A = £3,825$$

If annual repayment = £3,825

Monthly repayment $= \dfrac{£3,825}{12}$

$$\doteqdot £318.75$$

(b) After 9 years, the **value of the loan** $= £30,000 \times (1.12)^9$
$$= £83,192$$

After 9 years, the **sum of the repayments** $= \dfrac{A(R^n - 1)}{R - 1}$

where A = £3,825
$$R = 1.12$$
$$n = 9$$

$$\therefore \text{Sum of repayments} = \frac{3,825(1.12^9 - 1)}{1.12 - 1}$$

$$= £56,517$$

	£
Value of loan at year 9	83,192
Sum of repayments at year 9	56,517
Loan outstanding at year 9	26,675

A new interest rate of 10% is to be charged on the outstanding loan of £26,675 for 16 years (25 – 9).

Final value of loan $= £26,675 \times (1.1)^{16}$

$\qquad\qquad\qquad\quad = £122,571$

Sum of repayments $= \dfrac{A(R^n - 1)}{R - 1}$

where $R = 1.1$

$\qquad\; n = 16$

$\qquad\; A =$ annual repayment

$\therefore$ Sum of repayments $= \dfrac{A(1.1^{16} - 1)}{1.1 - 1}$

$\qquad\qquad\qquad\qquad = 35.94973A$

Final value of loan = sum of repayments

$\qquad £122,571 \; = \; 35.94973A$

$\qquad\quad \therefore A \;\; = \; \dfrac{£122,571}{35.94973}$

$\qquad\qquad A \;\; = \; £3,410$

$\therefore$ monthly repayment $= \dfrac{£3,410}{12}$

$\qquad\qquad\qquad\qquad = £284$

4.10   The final value of a loan/mortgage can be likened to a sinking fund also, since the final value must equate to the sum of the periodic repayments (compare this with a sinking fund where the sum of the regular savings must equal the fund required at some point in the future).

Question 7

Nicky Eastlacker has taken out a £200,000 mortgage over 25 years. Interest is to be charged at 9%. Calculate the monthly repayment.

Answer

Final value of mortgage $= £200,000 \times (1.09)^{25}$

$\qquad\qquad\qquad\qquad\;\; = £1,724,616$

Sum of repayments, S $= \dfrac{A(R^n - 1)}{R - 1}$

Where $A =$ Annual repayment

$\qquad\quad R = 1.09$

$\qquad\quad n = 25$

$\therefore £1,724,616 \;\; = \dfrac{A(1.09^{25} - 1)}{1.09 - 1}$

$\therefore A = £20,361.25$ per annum

If annual repayment $= £20,361.25$

Monthly repayment $= \dfrac{£20,361.25}{12}$

$\qquad\qquad\qquad\;\; = £1,696.77$

5   ANNUAL PERCENTAGE RATE (APR) OF INTEREST

Effective annual rate of interest

5.1   In the previous examples, interest has been calculated **annually**, but this isn't always the case. Interest may be compounded **daily, weekly, monthly** or **quarterly**.

The **equivalent annual** rate of interest, when interest is compounded at shorter intervals, is known as an **effective annual rate of interest**.

> ### FORMULA TO LEARN
>
> **Effective Annual Rate of Interest** $= [(1+r)^{\frac{12}{n}} - 1]$ or $[(1+r)^{\frac{365}{y}} - 1]$
>
> where   r is the rate of interest for each time period
> n is the number of months in the time period
> y is the number of days in the time period.

5.2   EXAMPLE: THE EFFECTIVE ANNUAL RATE OF INTEREST

Calculate the effective annual rate of interest of:

(a)   1.5% per month, compound
(b)   4.5% per quarter, compound
(c)   9% per half year, compound

5.3   SOLUTION

(a) $(1.015)^{12} - 1$ $= 0.1956 = 19.56\%$
(b) $(1.045)^{4} - 1$ $= 0.1925 = 19.25\%$
(c) $(1.09)^{2} - 1$ $= 0.1881 = 18.81\%$

Nominal rates of interest and the annual percentage rate

5.4   **Most interest rates are expressed as per annum figures** even when the interest is compounded over periods of less than one year. In such cases, the given interest rate is called a **nominal rate**. We can, however, work out the **effective rate**. It is this effective rate (shortened to one decimal place) which is quoted in advertisements as the **annual percentage rate (APR)**, sometimes called the **compound annual rate (CAR)**.

> ### Exam focus point
>
> Students often become seriously confused about the various rates of interest.
>
> - The **NOMINAL RATE** is the interest rate expressed as a per annum figure, eg 12% pa nominal even though interest may be compounded over periods of less than one year.
>
> - Adjusted nominal rate = **EQUIVALENT ANNUAL RATE**
>
> - Equivalent annual rate (the rate per day or per month adjusted to give an annual rate) = **EFFECTIVE ANNUAL RATE**
>
> - Effective annual rate = **ANNUAL PERCENTAGE RATE (APR) = COMPOUND ANNUAL RATE (CAR)**

5.5 EXAMPLE: NOMINAL AND EFFECTIVE RATES OF INTEREST

A building society may offer investors 10% per annum interest payable half-yearly. If the 10% is a nominal rate of interest, the building society would in fact pay 5% every six months, compounded so that the effective annual rate of interest would be

$[(1.05)^2 - 1] = 0.1025 = 10.25\%$ per annum.

5.6 Similarly, if a bank offers depositors a nominal 12% per annum, with interest payable quarterly, the effective rate of interest would be 3% compound every three months, which is

$[(1.03)^4 - 1] = 0.1255 = 12.55\%$ per annum.

Question 8

A bank adds interest monthly to investors' accounts even though interest rates are expressed in annual terms. The current rate of interest is 12%. Fred deposits £2,000 on 1 July. How much interest will have been earned by 31 December (to the nearest £)?

A £123.00   B £60.00   C £240.00   D £120.00

Answer

The nominal rate is 12% pa payable monthly.

$\therefore$ The effective rate $= \dfrac{12\%}{12 \text{ months}} = 1\%$ compound monthly.

$\therefore$ In the six months from July to December, the interest earned = (£2,000 $\times$ (1.01)^6) − £2,000 = £123.04.

The correct answer is A.

Exam focus point

You will probably find it useful to draw a time line to identify the time periods and interest rates involved when answering questions on financial mathematics. Don't be afraid to include a quick sketch of a time line in an examination – it should help to clarify exactly when investments are made in saving funds or repayments are made on a loan. It will also show the examiner that you know what you are doing!

Chapter roundup

- **Simple interest** is interest which is earned in equal amounts every year (or month) and which is a given proportion of the principal. The simple interest formula is $S = X + nrX$.

- **Compounding** means that, as interest is earned, it is added to the original investment and starts to earn interest itself. The basic formula for compound interest is $S = X(1 + r)^n$.

- If the **rate of interest changes during the period** of an investment, the compounding formula must be amended slightly to $S = X(1+r_1)^y(1 + r_2)^{n-y}$

- The **final value** (or **terminal value**), S, of an investment to which equal annual amounts will be added is found using the formula $S, = A(R^n - 1)/(R - 1)$ (the formula for a geometric progression).

- The basic compound interest formula can be used to calculate the net book value of an asset depreciated using the reducing balance method of depreciation by using a negative rate of 'interest' (**reverse compounding**).

- A **sinking fund** is an investment into which equal annual instalments are paid in order to earn interest, so that by the end of a given number of years, the investment is large enough to pay off a known commitment at that time. Commitments include the replacement of an asset and the repayment of a mortgage

$$S = A\frac{(R^n - 1)}{R - 1}$$

  where S = the required value of the fund at the end of n years
  A = the annual payment into the fund
  R = the common ratio

  Note that this is the same formula as that of a geometric progression.

- The **annual repayment (A)** under a repayment mortgage can be calculated as

$$\frac{SR^n \times (R - 1)}{(R^n - 1)}$$

  Note that this is a rearrangement of the formula for that of a geometric progression.

- An **effective annual rate of interest** is the corresponding annual rate when interest is compounded at intervals shorter than a year.

- A **nominal rate** of interest is an interest rate expressed as a per annum figure although the interest is compounded over a period of less than one year. The corresponding effective rate of interest shortened to one decimal place is the **annual percentage rate (APR)**.

Quick quiz

1   The formula for simple interest is ....

    Where   X   = ...
            r   = ...
            n   = ...
            S   = ...

2   The basic formula for compound interest is ....

    Where   X   = ...
            r   = ...
            n   = ...
            S   = ...

3   A depreciation rate of 20% equates to an interest rate of

A $\pm\,20\%$
B -20%
C $+0.2$
D -0.2

4   If Smita Smitten invests £250 *now* and a further £250 each year for five more years at an interest rate of 20%, which of the following are true if the final investment is calculated using the formula for the sum of a geometric progression?

	A =	n =
A	£250 × 1.2	5
B	£250 × 1.2	4
C	£250	5
D	£250	4

5   A shopkeeper wishes to refurbish his store in five years' time. At the end of five years, the refurbishment will cost £50,000, and the storekeeper has decided to provide for this future refurbishment by setting up a sinking fund into which equal annual investments will be made, starting one year from now. The fund will earn interest at 10%. Using the formula for the sum of a geometric progression, calculate the annual investment.

6   What is the formula used for calculating the sum of the repayments of a mortgage?

7   The effective annual rate of interest is the same as the annual percentage rate which is the same as the compound annual rate.

True   ☐

False   ☐

8   What is the formula used to calculate the APR?

Answers to quick quiz

1    $S = X + nrX$

Where   X = the original sum invested
         r = the rate of interest (as a proportion)
         n = the number of periods
         S = the sum invested after n periods

2    $S = X(1 + r)^n$

Where   X = the original sum invested
         r = the rate of interest (as a proportion)
         n = the number of periods
         S = the sum invested after n periods

3   D   A depreciation rate of 20% equates to a negative rate of interest of –20% where r = –0.2.

4   A $S = \dfrac{A(R^n - 1)}{R - 1}$

Where   A = the first term
             = £250 × 1.2 (as investment is made *now*)
         n = 5 years (the number of periods)

5 Using $S = \dfrac{A(R^n - 1)}{R - 1}$

      Where S = final value of fund = £50,000
               A = annual investment = ?
               R = common ratio = 1.1
               n = number of periods = 5

$£50,000 = \dfrac{A(1.1^5 - 1)}{1.1 - 1}$

$\therefore A = \dfrac{£50,000 \times (1.1 - 1)}{(1.1^5 - 1)}$

$= £8,189.87$

6   $S = \dfrac{A(R^n - 1)}{R - 1}$ (the sum of a geometric progression formula)

7   True.   Effective annual rate = APR = CAR

8   $APR = [(1 + r^{12/n}) - 1]$ or $[(1 + r)^{365/y} - 1]$

    where r = the rate of interest for each time period
             n = the number of months in the time period
             y = the number of days in the time period

Now try the following objective test questions

Question bank	Question numbers	Page
Paper-based exam	11	280
Computer-based assessment	11	300

Chapter 12

DISCOUNTING

Topic list	Syllabus reference	Ability required
1 The concept of discounting	(iv)	Application
2 The net present value (NPV) method	(iv)	Application
3 The internal rate of return (IRR) method	(iv)	Application and comprehension
4 Annuities and perpetuities	(iv)	Application
5 Linking compounding and discounting	(iv)	Application

Introduction

Discounting is the reverse of compounding, the topic of the previous chapter. Its major application in business is in the **evaluation of investments**, to decide whether they offer a satisfactory return to the investor. We will be looking at two methods of using discounting to appraise investments, the **net present value (NPV) method** and the **internal rate of return (IRR) method**.

Learning outcomes covered in this chapter

- **Calculate** the present value of a future cash sum using both a formula and CIMA tables
- **Calculate** the present value of an annuity using both a formula and CIMA tables
- **Calculate** the present value of a perpetuity
- **Calculate** loan/mortgage repayments and the value of an outstanding loan/mortgage
- **Calculate** the NPV of a project and use this to decide whether a project should be undertaken, or choose between mutually exclusive projects
- **Calculate** and **explain** the use of the IRR of a project

Syllabus content covered in this chapter

- Discounting to find the present value
- Annuities and perpetuities
- Loans and mortgages
- Sinking funds and saving funds
- Simple investment appraisal

1   THE CONCEPT OF DISCOUNTING

The basic principles of discounting

1.1   The **basic principle of compounding** is that if we invest £X now for n years at r% interest per annum, we should obtain £X $(1 + r)^n$ in n years time.

1.2 Thus if we invest £10,000 now for four years at 10% interest per annum, we will have a total investment worth £10,000 × 1.10⁴ = £14,641 at the end of four years (that is, at year 4 if it is now year 0).

KEY TERM

The basic principle of **discounting** is that if we wish to have £V in n years' time, we need to invest a certain sum *now* (year 0) at an interest rate of r% in order to obtain the required sum of money in the future.

1.3 For example, if we wish to have £14,641 in four years' time, how much money would we need to invest now at 10% interest per annum? This is the reverse of the situation described in Paragraph 1.2.

Using our corresponding formula, $S = X(1 + r)^n$

where X = the original sum invested
  r = 10%
  n = 4
  S = £14,641

£14,641 $= X(1 + 0.1)^4$

£14,641 $= X \times 1.4641$

∴X $= \dfrac{£14,641}{1.4641} = £10,000$

1.4 £10,000 now, with the capacity to earn a return of 10% per annum, is the equivalent in value of £14,641 after four years. We can therefore say that **£10,000 is the present value of £14,641 at year 4, at an interest rate of 10%.**

Present value

KEY TERM

The term '**present value**' simply means the amount of money which must be invested now for n years at an interest rate of r%, to earn a given future sum of money at the time it will be due.

The formula for discounting

> **FORMULA TO LEARN**
>
> The **discounting formula** is
>
> $$X = S \times \frac{1}{(1+r)^n}$$
>
>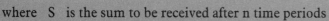
>
> where   S is the sum to be received after n time periods
>   X is the present value (PV) of that sum
>   r is the rate of return, expressed as a proportion
>   n is the number of time periods (usually years).
>
> The rate r is sometimes called a cost of capital.
>
> **Note that this equation is just a rearrangement of the compounding formula.**

1.5   EXAMPLE: DISCOUNTING

(a)   Calculate the present value of £60,000 at year 6, if a return of 15% per annum is obtainable.

(b)   Calculate the present value of £100,000 at year 5, if a return of 6% per annum is obtainable.

(c)   How much would a person need to invest now at 12% to earn £4,000 at year 2 and £4,000 at year 3?

1.6   SOLUTION

The discounting formula, $X = S \times \dfrac{1}{(1+r)^n}$ is required.

(a)   S   = £60,000
  n   = 6
  r   = 0.15

  PV $= 60,000 \times \dfrac{1}{1.15^6}$

    $= 60,000 \times 0.432$
    $= £25,920$

(b)   S   = £100,000
  n   = 5
  r   = 0.06

  PV $= 100,000 \times \dfrac{1}{1.06^5}$

    $= 100,000 \times 0.747$
    $= £74,700$

(c)   S   = £4,000
  n   = 2 or 3
  r   = 0.12

BPP PUBLISHING

$$PV = (4{,}000 \times \frac{1}{1.12^2}) + (4{,}000 \times \frac{1}{1.12^3})$$

$$= 4{,}000 \times (0.797 + 0.712)$$
$$= £6{,}036$$

This calculation can be checked as follows.

	£
Year 0	6,036.00
Interest for the first year (12%)	724.32
	6,760.32
Interest for the second year (12%)	811.24
	7,571.56
Less withdrawal	(4,000.00)
	3,571.56
Interest for the third year (12%)	428.59
	4,000.15
Less withdrawal	(4,000.00)
Rounding error	0.15

Question 1

The present value at 7% interest of £16,000 at year 12 is £ ☐

Answer

┌─────────┐
│ £7,104 │
└─────────┘

Working

Using the discounting formula, $X = S \times \dfrac{1}{(1+r)^n}$

where S = £16,000
       n = 12
       r = 0.07
       X = PV

$$PV = £16{,}000 \times \frac{1}{1.07^{12}} = £7{,}104$$

Capital expenditure appraisal

1.7 **Discounted cash flow techniques can be used to evaluate capital expenditure proposals (investments).**

KEY TERM

Discounted cash flow (DCF) involves the application of discounting arithmetic to the estimated future cash flows (receipts and expenditures) from a project in order to decide whether the project is expected to earn a satisfactory rate of return.

There are two methods of using DCF techniques.

- The net present value (NPV) method
- The internal rate of return (IRR) method

2 THE NET PRESENT VALUE (NPV) METHOD

> **KEY TERM**
>
> The **net present value (NPV) method** works out the present values of all items of income and expenditure related to an investment at a given rate of return, and then works out a net total. If it is positive, the investment is considered to be acceptable. If it is negative, the investment is considered to be unacceptable.

2.1 EXAMPLE: THE NET PRESENT VALUE OF A PROJECT

Dog Ltd is considering whether to spend £5,000 on an item of equipment. The 'cash profits', the excess of income over cash expenditure, from the project would be £3,000 in the first year and £4,000 in the second year.

The company will not invest in any project unless it offers a return in excess of 15% per annum.

Required

Assess whether the investment is worthwhile, or 'viable'.

2.2 SOLUTION

In this example, an outlay of £5,000 now promises a return of £3,000 **during** the first year and £4,000 **during** the second year. It is a convention in DCF, however, that cash flows spread over a year are assumed to occur **at the end of the year,** so that the cash flows of the project are as follows.

	£
Year 0 (now)	(5,000)
Year 1 (at the end of the year)	3,000
Year 2 (at the end of the year)	4,000

2.3 The NPV method takes the following approach.

(a) The project offers £3,000 at year 1 and £4,000 at year 2, for an outlay of £5,000 now.

(b) The company might invest elsewhere to earn a return of 15% per annum.

(c) If the company did invest at exactly 15% per annum, how much would it need to invest now, at 15%, to earn £3,000 at the end of year 1 plus £4,000 at the end of year 2?

(d) Is it cheaper to invest £5,000 in the project, or to invest elsewhere at 15%, in order to obtain these future cash flows?

2.4 If the company did invest elsewhere at 15% per annum, the amount required to earn £3,000 in year 1 and £4,000 in year 2 would be as follows.

Year	Cash flow £	Discount factor 15%	Present value £
1	3,000	$\dfrac{1}{1.15} = 0.870$	2,610
2	4,000	$\dfrac{1}{(1.15)^2} = 0.756$	3,024
			5,634

2.5 The choice is to invest £5,000 in the project, or £5,634 elsewhere at 15%, in order to obtain these future cash flows. We can therefore reach the following conclusion.

- It is cheaper to invest in the project, by £634.
- The project offers a return of over 15% per annum.

2.6 The net present value is the difference between the present value of cash inflows from the project (£5,634) and the present value of future cash outflows (in this example, £5,000 × $1/1.15^0 = £5,000$).

2.7 An NPV statement could be drawn up as follows.

Year	Cash flow £	Discount factor 15%	Present value £
0	(5,000)	1.000	(5,000)
1	3,000	$\dfrac{1}{1.15} = 0.870$	2,610
2	4,000	$\dfrac{1}{(1.15)^2} = 0.756$	3,024
		Net present value	+634

The project has a positive net present value, so it is acceptable.

Question 2

A company is wondering whether to spend £18,000 on an item of equipment, in order to obtain cash profits as follows.

Year	£
1	6,000
2	8,000
3	5,000
4	1,000

The company requires a return of 10% per annum.

Required

Use the NPV method to assess whether the project is viable.

Answer

	Cash flow £	Discount factor 10%	Present value £
0	(18,000)	1.000	(18,000)
1	6,000	$\dfrac{1}{1.10} = 0.909$	5,454
2	8,000	$\dfrac{1}{1.10^2} = 0.826$	6,608
3	5,000	$\dfrac{1}{1.10^3} = 0.751$	3,755
4	1,000	$\dfrac{1}{1.10^4} = 0.683$	683
		Net present value	(1,500)

The NPV is negative. We can therefore draw the following conclusions.

(a) It is cheaper to invest elsewhere at 10% than to invest in the project.
(b) The project would earn a return of less than 10%.
(c) The project is not viable (since the PV of the costs is greater than the PV of the benefits).

Discount tables

2.8 Assuming that money earns, say, 10% per annum:

(a) the PV (present value) of £1 at year 1 is $£1 \times \dfrac{1}{1.10}$ = £1 × 0.909;

(b) similarly, the PV of £1 at year 2 is $£1 \times \dfrac{1}{(1.10)^2}$ = £1 × 0.826;

(c) the PV of £1 at year 3 is $£1 \times \dfrac{1}{(1.10)^3}$ = £1 × 0.751.

Discount tables show the value of $1/(1 + r)^n$ for different values of r and n. The 10% discount factors of 0.909, 0.826 and 0.751 are shown in the discount tables at the end of this Study Text in the column for 10%. (You will be given discount tables in your examination.)

Project comparison

2.9 **The NPV method can also be used to compare two or more investment options**. For example, suppose that Daisy Ltd can choose between the investment outlined in Question 2 above *or* a second investment, which also costs £28,000 but which would earn £6,500 in the first year, £7,500 in the second, £8,500 in the third, £9,500 in the fourth and £10,500 in the fifth. Which one should Daisy Ltd choose?

2.10 **The decision rule is to choose the option with the highest NPV.** We therefore need to calculate the NPV of the second option.

Year	Cash flow £	Discount factor 11%	Present value £
0	(28,000)	1.000	(28,000)
1	6,500	0.901	5,857
2	7,500	0.812	6,090
3	8,500	0.731	6,214
4	9,500	0.659	6,261
5	10,500	0.593	6,227
		NPV =	2,649

Daisy Ltd should therefore invest in the second option since it has the higher NPV.

Expected values and discounting

2.11 Future cash flows cannot be predicted with complete accuracy. To take account of this uncertainty an **expected net present value** can be calculated which is a **weighted average net present value based on the probabilities of different sets of circumstances occurring**. Let us have a look at an example.

2.12 EXAMPLE: EXPECTED NET PRESENT VALUE

An organisation with a cost of capital of 5% is contemplating investing £340,000 in a project which has a 25% chance of being a big success and producing cash inflows of £210,000 after one and two years. There is, however, a 75% change of the project not being quite so successful, in which case the cash inflows will be £162,000 after one year and £174,000 after two years.

Required

Calculate an NPV and hence advise the organisation.

2.13 SOLUTION

Year	Discount factor 5%	Success Cash flow £'000	PV £'000	Failure Cash flow £'000	PV £'000
0	1.000	(340)	(340.00)	(340)	(340.000)
1	0.952	210	199.92	162	154.224
2	0.907	210	190.47	174	157.818
			50.39		(27.958)

NPV = (25% × 50.39) + (75% × –27.958) = –8.371

The NPV is – £8,371 and hence the organisation should not invest in the project.

Limitations of using the NPV method

2.14 There are a number of problems associated with using the NPV method in practice.

(a) **The future discount factors** (or interest rates) which are used in calculating NPVs can only be **estimated** and are not known with certainty. Discount rates that are estimated for time periods far into the future are therefore less likely to be accurate, thereby leading to less accurate NPV values.

(b) Similarly, NPV calculations make use of estimated **future cash flows**. As with future discount factors, cash flows which are estimated for cash flows several years into the future cannot really be predicted with any real certainty.

(c) When using the NPV method it is common to assume that all cash flows occur **at the end of the year**. However, this assumption is also likely to give rise to less accurate NPV values.

2.15 There are a number of computer programs available these days which enable a range of NPVs to be calculated for a number of different circumstances (best-case and worst-case situations and so on). Such programs allow some of the limitations mentioned above to be alleviated.

3 THE INTERNAL RATE OF RETURN (IRR) METHOD

3.1 The **internal rate of return (IRR) method** of evaluating investments is an alternative to the NPV method. The NPV method of discounted cash flow determines whether an investment earns a **positive or a negative NPV when discounted at a given rate of interest**. If the NPV is zero (that is, the present values of costs and benefits are equal) the return from the project would be exactly the rate used for discounting.

KEY TERM

The **IRR method of discounted cash flow** is a method which determines the rate of interest (the internal rate of return) at which the NPV is 0. The internal rate of return is therefore the rate of return on an investment.

3.2   The IRR method will indicate that a project is viable **if the IRR exceeds the minimum acceptable rate of return**. Thus if the company expects a minimum return of, say, 15%, a project would be viable if its IRR is more than 15%.

3.3   EXAMPLE: THE IRR METHOD OVER ONE YEAR

If £500 is invested today and generates £600 in one year's time, the internal rate of return (r) can be calculated as follows.

PV of cost   =   PV of benefits

$$500 = \frac{600}{(1+r)}$$

$$500(1+r) = 600$$

$$1+r = \frac{600}{500} = 1.2$$

$$r = 0.2 = 20\%$$

3.4   The arithmetic for calculating the IRR is more complicated for investments and cash flows extending over a period of time longer than one year. A technique known as the **interpolation method** can be used to calculate an approximate IRR.

3.5   EXAMPLE: INTERPOLATION

A project costing £800 in year 0 is expected to earn £400 in year 1, £300 in year 2 and £200 in year 3.

Required

Calculate the internal rate of return.

3.6   SOLUTION

The IRR is calculated by first of all finding the NPV at each of two interest rates. Ideally, one interest rate should give a small positive NPV and the other a small negative NPV. The IRR would then be somewhere between these two interest rates: above the rate where the NPV is positive, but below the rate where the NPV is negative.

A very rough guideline for estimating at what interest rate the NPV might be close to zero, is to take

$$\frac{2}{3} \times \left(\frac{\text{profit}}{\text{cost of the project}}\right)$$

In our example, the total profit over three years is £(400 + 300 + 200 − 800) = £100. An approximate IRR is therefore calculated as:

$$\frac{2}{3} \times \frac{100}{800} = 0.08 \text{ approx.}$$

A starting point is to try 8%.

(a) Try 8%

Year	Cash flow	Discount factor	Present value
	£	8%	£
0	(800)	1.000	(800.0)
1	400	0.926	370.4
2	300	0.857	257.1
3	200	0.794	158.8
		NPV	(13.7)

The NPV is negative, therefore the project fails to earn 8% and the IRR must be less than 8%.

(b) Try 6%

Year	Cash flow	Discount factor	Present value
	£	6%	£
0	(800)	1.000	(800.0)
1	400	0.943	377.2
2	300	0.890	267.0
3	200	0.840	168.0
		NPV	12.2

The NPV is positive, therefore the project earns more than 6% and less than 8%.

The **IRR is now calculated by interpolation**. The result will not be exact, but it will be a close approximation. Interpolation assumes that the NPV falls in a straight line from +12.2 at 6% to −13.7 at 8%.

Graph to show IRR calculation by interpolation

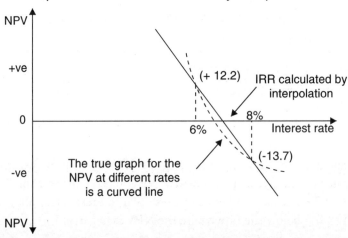

FORMULA TO LEARN

The IRR, where the NPV is zero, can be calculated as follows.

$$\text{IRR} = a\% + \left[\frac{A}{A-B} \times (b-a)\right]\% \text{ where}$$

    a is one interest rate
    b is the other interest rate
    A is the NPV at rate a
    B is the NPV at rate b

(c) Thus, in our example, $\text{IRR} = 6\% + \left[\dfrac{12.2}{(12.2+13.7)} \times (8-6)\right]\%$

$$= 6\% + 0.942\%$$
$$= 6.942\% \text{ approx}$$

(d) The answer is only an **approximation** because the NPV falls in a slightly curved line and not a straight line between +12.2 and –13.7. Provided that NPVs close to zero are used, the linear assumption used in the interpolation method is nevertheless fairly accurate.

(e) Note that the formula will still work if A and B are both positive, or both negative, and even if a and b are a long way from the true IRR, but the results will be less accurate.

Question 3

The net present value of an investment at 15% is £50,000 and at 20% is - £10,000. The internal rate of return of this investment (to the nearest whole number) is:

A   16%
B   17%
C   18%
D   19%

Answer

$$\text{IRR} = a\% + [\frac{A}{A-B} \times (b-a)]\%$$

Where   a   =   one interest rate = 15%
        b   =   other interest rate = 20%
        A   =   NPV at rate a = £50,000
        B   =   NPV at rate b = –£10,000

$$\text{IRR} = 15\% + [\frac{£50,000}{£50,000-(-10,000)} \times (20-15)]\%$$

$$= 15\% + 4.17\%$$
$$= 19.17\%$$
$$= 19\%$$

The correct answer is therefore D.

Exam focus point

The IRR of a project can be estimated by plotting NPVs and their corresponding discount rates **accurately** on a graph. When all of the points are joined together, the approximate IRR value can be read off the graph at the point at which the line plotted crosses the x-axis.

4   ANNUITIES AND PERPETUITIES

KEY TERM

An **annuity** is a constant sum of money received or paid each year for a given number of years.

4.1 Many individuals nowadays may invest in **annuities** which can be purchased either through a single payment or a number of payments. For example, individuals planning for their retirement might make regular payments into a pension fund over a number of years. Over the years, the pension fund should (hopefully) grow and the final value of the fund can be used to buy an annuity. (There may also be a lump sum payment of up to 25% of the final fund value but don't worry about these details as they are not part of your *Business Mathematics* syllabus.)

4.2 An **annuity** might run until the recipient's death, or it might run for a guaranteed term of n years.

The formula for the present value of an annuity

4.3 The syllabus for *Business Mathematics* states that you need to be able to calculate the present value of an annuity using both a formula and CIMA Tables. Let's have a look at the formula you need to be able to use when calculating the PV of an annuity.

EXAM FORMULA

The **present value of an annuity** of *£1* per annum receivable or payable for n years commencing in one year, discounted at r% per annum:

$$PV = \frac{1}{r}\left(1 - \frac{1}{(1+r)^n}\right)$$

Note that it is the PV of an annuity of *£1* and so you need to multiply it by the actual value of the annuity.

4.4 EXAMPLE: THE ANNUITY FORMULA

What is the present value of £4,000 per annum for years 1 to 4, at a discount rate of 10% per annum?

4.5 SOLUTION

Using the annuity formula with r = 0.1 and n = 4.

$$PV = 4,000 \times \left(\frac{1}{0.1}\left(1 - \frac{1}{(1+0.1)^4}\right)\right)$$

$$= 4,000 \times 3.170 = £12,680$$

Calculating a required annuity

4.6 If PV of £1 $= \frac{1}{r}\left(1 - \frac{1}{(1+r)^n}\right)$, then PV of £a $= a\left(\frac{1}{r}\left(1 - \frac{1}{(1+r)^n}\right)\right)$

$$\therefore a = \frac{PV \text{ of } £a}{\left(\frac{1}{r}\left(1 - \frac{1}{(1+r)^n}\right)\right)}$$

This enables us to calculate the annuity required to yield a given rate of return (r) on a given investment (P).

4.7 EXAMPLE: REQUIRED ANNUITY

The present value of a ten-year annuity receivable which begins in one year's time at 7% per annum compound is £3,000. What is the annual amount of the annuity?

4.8 SOLUTION

PV of £a = £3,000

$$r = 0.07$$

$$t = 10$$

$$a = \frac{3,000}{\left(\frac{1}{0.07} \left(1 - \frac{1}{(1.07)^{10}} \right) \right)}$$

$$= \frac{£3,000}{7.024} = 427.11$$

Question 4

(a) It is important to practise using the annuity factor formula. Calculate annuity factors in the following cases.

    (i)   n = 4, r = 10%

    (ii)   n = 3, r = 9.5%

    (iii) For twenty years at a rate of 25%

(b) What is the present value of £4,000 per annum for four years, **years 2 to 5**, at a discount rate of 10% per annum? Use the annuity formula.

Answer

(a)   (i) $\frac{1}{0.1} \left(1 - \frac{1}{(1+0.1)^4} \right) = 3.170$

    (ii) $\frac{1}{0.095} \left(1 - \frac{1}{(1+0.095)^3} \right) = 2.509$

    (iii) $\frac{1}{0.25} \left(1 - \frac{1}{(1+0.25)^{20}} \right) = 3.954$

(b) The formula will give the value of £4,000 at 10% per annum, not as a year 0 present value, but as a value at the year preceding the first annuity cash flow, that is, at year (2 - 1) = year 1. We must therefore discount our solution in paragraph 4.5 further, from a year 1 to a year 0 value.

$$PV = £12,680 \times \frac{1}{1.10} = £11,527.27$$

Question 5

In the formula

$$PV = \frac{1}{r}\left(1 - \frac{1}{(1+r)^n}\right)$$

r = 0.04

n = 10

What is the PV?

A   6.41
B   7.32
C   8.11
D   9.22

Answer

$$PV = \frac{1}{0.04}\left(1 - \frac{1}{(1+0.04)^{10}}\right)$$

$$= 8.11$$

The correct answer is therefore C.

Annuity tables

4.9   To calculate the present value of a constant annual cash flow, or annuity, we can multiply the annual cash flows by the sum of the discount factors for the relevant years. These total factors are known as **cumulative present value factors** or **annuity factors**. As with 'present value factors of £1 in year n', there are tables for annuity factors, which are shown at the end of this text. (For example, the cumulative present value factor of £1 per annum for five years at 11% per annum is in the column for 11% and the year 5 row, and is 3.696).

The use of annuity tables to calculate a required annuity

4.10   Just as the formula can be used to calculate an annuity, so too can the tables. Since the present value of an annuity is PV = a × annuity factor from the tables, we have

> **FORMULA TO LEARN**
>
> **Annuity** (a) = $\dfrac{\text{Present value of an annuity}}{\text{Annuity factor}}$

4.11 EXAMPLE: ANNUITY TABLES

A bank grants a loan of £3,000 at 7% per annum. The borrower is to repay the loan in ten annual instalments. How much must she pay each year?

4.12 SOLUTION

Since the bank pays out the loan money *now*, the present value (PV) of the loan is £3,000. The annual repayment on the loan can be thought of as an annuity. We can therefore use the annuity formula

$$\text{Annuity} = \frac{PV}{\text{annuity factor}}$$

in order to calculate the loan repayments. The annuity factor is found by looking in the cumulative present value tables under n = 10 and r = 7%. The corresponding factor = 7.024.

Therefore, annuity $= \dfrac{£3,000}{7.024}$

$\qquad\qquad\qquad = £427.11$

The loan repayments are therefore £427.11 per annum.

Perpetuities

KEY TERMS

- A **perpetuity** is an annuity which lasts for ever, instead of stopping after n years.

- The **present value of a perpetuity** is PV = a/r where r is the cost of capital as a proportion.

EXAM FORMULA

The present value of £1 per annum, payable or receivable in perpetuity, commencing in one year, discounted at r% per annum

$$PV = \frac{1}{r}$$

4.13 EXAMPLE: A PERPETUITY

How much should be invested *now* (to the nearest £) to receive £35,000 per annum in perpetuity if the annual rate of interest is 9%?

4.14 SOLUTION

$PV = \dfrac{a}{r}$

where a = £35,000
    r = 9%

$\therefore PV \quad = \dfrac{£35,000}{0.09}$

$\qquad\quad = £388,889$

4.15 EXAMPLE: A PERPETUITY

Mostly Ltd is considering a project which would cost £50,000 now and yield £9,000 per annum every year in perpetuity, starting a year from now. The cost of capital is 15%.

Required

Assess whether the project is viable.

4.16 SOLUTION

Year	Cash flow £	Discount factor 15%	Present value £
0	(50,000)	1.0	(50,000)
1 - ∞	9,000	1/0.15	60,000
		NPV	10,000

The project is viable because it has a positive net present value when discounted at 15%.

The timing of cash flows

4.17 Note that both annuity tables and the formulae assume that the first payment or receipt is a year from now. Always check examination questions for when the first payment falls.

For example, if there are five equal payments starting now, and the interest rate is 8%, we should use a factor of 1 (for today's payment) + 3.312 (for the other four payments) = 4.312.

Question 6

Hilarious Jokes Ltd has arranged a fifteen year lease, at an annual rent of £9,000. The first rental payment is to be paid immediately, and the others are to be paid at the end of each year.

What is the present value of the lease at 9%?

 A £79,074   B £72,549   C £81,549   D £70,074

Answer

The correct way to answer this question is to use the cumulative present value tables for r = 9% and n = 14 because the first payment is to be paid immediately (and not in one year's time). A common trap in a question like this would be to look up r = 9% and n = 15 in the tables. If you did this, get out of the habit now, before you sit your exam!

From the cumulative present value tables, when r = 9% and n = 14, the annuity factor is 7.786.

The first payment is made now, and so has a PV of £9,000 (£9,000 × 1.00). Payments 2-15 have a PV of £9,000 × 7.786 = £70,074.

∴ The total PV   = £9,000 (1st payment) + £70,074 (Payments 2-15)
                           = £79,074.

The correct answer is A.

(Alternatively, the annuity factor can be increased by 1 to take account of the fact that the first payment is *now*.

∴ annuity factor = 7.786 + 1 = 8.786

∴ PV = annuity × annuity factor
          = £9,000 × 8.786 = £79,074)

Question 7

How much should be invested now (to the nearest £) to receive £20,000 per annum in perpetuity if the annual rate of interest is 20%?

 A   £4,000
 B   £24,000
 C   £93,500
 D   £100,000

Answer

$$PV = \frac{a}{r}$$

Where a = annuity = £20,000
       r = cost of capital as a proportion = 0.2

$$PV = \frac{£20,000}{0.2}$$

$$= £100,000$$

The correct answer is therefore D.

---

5 LINKING COMPOUNDING AND DISCOUNTING

Sinking funds

5.1 In the previous chapter we introduced you to **sinking funds**. You will remember that a sinking fund is an investment into which equal annual instalments (an **annuity**) are paid in order to earn interest, so that by the end of a given period, the investment is large enough to pay off a known commitment at that time (**final value**).

5.2 EXAMPLE: A SINKING FUND (1)

Jamie wants to buy a Porsche 911. This will cost him £45,000 in two years' time. He has decided to set aside an equal amount each quarter until he has the amount he needs. Assuming he can earn interest in his building society account at 5% pa how much does he need to set aside each year? Assume the first amount is set aside one period from now.

(a) Calculate the amounts using the annuity formula.
(b) Calculate the amounts using annuity tables.

5.3 SOLUTION

If Jamie needs £45,000 in two years' time, the present value that he needs is

$$PV = \frac{£45,000}{(1+0.05)^2}$$

$$= £40,816$$

(a) **Using the annuity formula**

The annuity factor $= \frac{1}{r}\left(1 - \frac{1}{(1+r)^n}\right)$

where r = 0.05
       n = 2

Annuity factor $= \frac{1}{0.05}\left(1 - \frac{1}{(1+0.05)^2}\right)$

$$= 1.8594$$

The amount to save each quarter is an annuity. We can therefore use the formula

$$\text{Annuity} = \frac{\text{PV}}{\text{Annuity factor}}$$

$$= \frac{£40,816}{1.8594}$$

$$= £21,951$$

Therefore Jamie must set aside £21,951 per annum.

(b) **Using annuity tables**

When n = 2 and r = 5%, the annuity factor (from cumulative present value tables) is 1.859.

$$\text{Annuity} = \frac{\text{PV}}{\text{Annuity factor}}$$

$$= \frac{£40,816}{1.859}$$

$$= £21,956$$

The difference of £5 (£21,956 – £21,951) is due to rounding.

5.4 EXAMPLE: A SINKING FUND (2)

At this point it is worth considering the value of the fund that would have built up if we had saved £21,956 pa for two years at an interest rate of 5%, with the first payment at the end of year 1.

5.5 SOLUTION

The situation we are looking at here can be shown on the following time line.

Saving

NOW	1st	2nd	(END)
0	1	2	

£21,956 $\longrightarrow$ × (1.05)

£21,956 × 1

The value of the fund at the end of year 2 is

$$21,956 + 21,956(1.05)$$

This is a geometric progression with

A = £21,956
R = 1.05
n = 2

If $S = \dfrac{A(R^n - 1)}{R - 1}$

$$= \frac{21,956(1.05^2 - 1)}{1.05 - 1}$$

$$= £45,000 \text{ (to the nearest £100)}$$

Therefore, if we were to save £21,956 for two years at 5% per annum we would achieve a final value of £45,000. Can you see how compounding and discounting really are the reverse of each other? In our first example, we calculated that Jamie needed to save £21,956 pa for two years at a cost of capital of 5%. In the second example, we demonstrated that using the equation for the sum of a geometric progression, saving £21,956 pa for two years would result in a sinking fund of £45,000.

5.6 Work through these two examples again if you are not totally clear: it is vitally important that you understand how compounding and discounting are linked.

Mortgages

5.7 We also considered mortgages in Chapter 11. You will remember that the final value of a mortgage must be equal to the sum of the repayments. If the repayments are regular, they can be treated as an annuity, in which case the annuity formula may be used in mortgage calculations.

5.8 When an individual takes out a mortgage, the present value of the mortgage is the amount of the loan taken out. Most mortgages will be taken out at a given rate of interest for a fixed term.

$$\text{Annuity} = \frac{\text{Present value of annuity (original vaue of mortgage)}}{\text{Annuity factor (from formula or tables)}}$$

The annuity is the regular repayment value.

Let's have a look at an example.

5.9 EXAMPLE: MORTGAGES

Tim has taken out a £30,000 mortgage over 25 years. Interest is to be charged at 12%. Calculate the monthly repayment.

5.10 SOLUTION

Present value of mortgage $= £30,000$

Annuity factor $= \dfrac{1}{0.12}\left(1 - \dfrac{1}{(1+0.12)^{25}}\right)$

$= 7.843$

Annuity (annual repayments) $= \dfrac{\text{PV}}{\text{annuity factor}}$

$= \dfrac{£30,000}{7.843}$

$= £3,825$

Monthly repayment $= £3,825 \div 12 = £318.75$

Did you recognise any of these figures? Look back at Paragraph 4.8 in the previous chapter. We have used the same information but used the annuity formula method rather than the sum of a geometric progression.

5.11 EXAMPLE: INTEREST RATE CHANGES

After nine years, the interest rate on Tim's mortgage changes to 10%. What is the new monthly repayment?

5.12 SOLUTION

In the solution in Paragraph 4.9 in Chapter 11, it was established that the value of the mortgage after 9 years was £26,675.

After 9 years, our annuity factor changes to

Annuity factor
$$= \frac{1}{0.1}\left(1 - \frac{1}{(1+0.1)^{16}}\right)$$

$$= 7.8237$$

Annuity (annual repayments)
$$= \frac{PV}{\text{annuity factor}}$$

$$= \frac{£26,675}{7.8237}$$

$$= £3,410$$

∴ The monthly repayments $= £3,410 \div 12 = £284$

This is the same as the answer that we calculated in Chapter 11, Paragraph 4.9 when we used the sum of a geometric progression formula.

5.13 Sinking funds are an example of **saving** whilst mortgages are an example of **borrowing**.

Borrowing versus saving

5.14 The chief advantage of borrowing money via a loan or mortgage is that the asset the money is used to purchase can be **owned now** (and therefore be put to use to earn money) rather than waiting. On the other hand, borrowing money **takes some control away from the business's managers** and **makes a business venture more risky**. Because an obligation is owed to the lender the managers may have **less freedom** to do what they like with their assets. If the business is not successful the debt will still be owed, and if the lender demands that it is repaid immediately the business might collapse.

5.15 The advantages of saving up are that **no interest has to be paid** and the business **does not have to surrender any control to a third party**. The savings will **earn** interest. However the money will not be available for other, potentially more profitable, uses. Also, the business cannot be **sure** in advance that it will be able to generate the cash needed over the timescale envisaged.

Exam focus point

Note that both annuity tables and the formulae used in this chapter assume that the first payment or receipt is **a year from now**. Always check examination questions for when the first payment falls. For example, if there are five equal payments starting **now**, and the interest rate is 8% we should use a factor of 1 (for today's payment) + 3.312 (for the other four payments) = 4.312.

Chapter roundup

- **Discounting** is the reverse of compounding. The discounting formula is $X = S \times 1/(1+r)^n$.

- The concept of present value can be thought of in two ways.

    ° It is the value today of an amount to be received some time in the future.

    ° It is the amount which would have to be invested today to produce a given amount at some future date.

- The **discounting formula** is $X = S \times \dfrac{1}{(1+r)^n}$ which is a rearrangement of the compounding formula.

- **Discounted cash flow techniques** can be used to evaluate capital expenditure projects. There are two methods: the **NPV method** and the **IRR method**.

- The **NPV method** works out the present values of all items of income and expenditure related to an investment at a given rate of return, and then works out a net total. If it is **positive**, the investment is considered to be **acceptable**. If it is **negative**, the investment is considered to be **unacceptable**.

- The **IRR method** is to determine the rate of interest (the IRR) at which the NPV is 0. Interpolation, using the following formula, is often necessary. **The project is viable if the IRR exceeds the minimum acceptable return**.

    $$IRR = a\% + \left[\frac{A}{A-B} \times (b-a) \right]\%$$

- An **annuity** is a constant sum of money each year for a given number of years. The present value of an annuity can be calculated using the following formula.

    $$PV = \frac{1}{r}\left(1 - \frac{1}{(1+r)^t} \right)$$

    Alternatively, the present value of an annuity can be calculated by using annuity factors found in annuity tables.

    $$Annuity = \frac{PV\ of\ annuity}{Annuity\ factor}$$

- A **perpetuity** is an annuity which lasts forever, instead of stopping after n years. The present value of a perpetuity = a/r.

- Compounding and discounting are directly linked to each other. Make sure that you understand clearly the relationship between them.

Quick quiz

1   What does the term present value mean?

2   The discounting formula is $X = S \times \dfrac{1}{(1+r)^n}$

    Where

    $$S\ =$$
    $$X\ =$$
    $$r\ =$$
    $$n\ =$$

    (a)   the rate of return (as a proportion)
    (b)   the sum to be received after n time periods

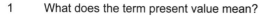

BPP
PUBLISHING

     (c)   the PV of that sum

     (d)   the number of time periods

3   What are the two usual methods of capital expenditure appraisal using DCF techniques?

4   What is the formula used to calculate the IRR and what do the symbols used represent?

5   An annuity is a sum of money received every year.

     True   ☐

     False   ☐

6   What is a perpetuity?

7   What is the formula for the present value of a perpetuity?

8   If Fred were to save £7,000 per annum, and we used the formula for the sum of a geometric progression to calculate the value of the fund that would have built up over ten years at an interest rate of 20%, what is the value of A to be used in the formula if:

     (a)   the first payment is now

     (b)   the first payment is in one year's time

9   What is the main advantage of borrowing as opposed to saving?

Answers to quick quiz

1   The amount of money which must be invested now for n years at an interest rate of r% to give a future sum of money at the time it will be due.

2   S = (b)
         X = (c)
         r = (a)
         n = (d)

3   The net present value (NPV) method
         The Internal rate of return (IRR) method

4     $IRR = a\% + \left[\dfrac{A}{A - B} \times (b - a) \right]\%$

     Where   a = one interest rate
                b = another interest rate
                A = the NPV at rate a
                B = the NPV at rate b

5   False.   It is a **constant** sum of money **received** or **paid** each year for a **given number** of years.

6   An annuity which lasts forever.

7     $PV = a/r$

8   (a)   A = £7,000 × 1.2
         (b)   A = £7,000

9   The money is available **now** to buy the required asset as opposed to at the end of the savings period.

Now try the following objective test questions

Question bank	Question numbers	Page
Paper-based exam	12, 13	281-282
Computer-based assessment	12	300

Part E
Forecasting

Chapter 13

TIME SERIES ANALYSIS

Topic list	Syllabus reference	Ability required
1 The components of time series	(v)	Application and comprehension
2 Finding the trend	(v)	Application
3 Finding the seasonal variations	(v)	Application and comprehension
4 Forecasting and time series analysis	(v)	Application and comprehension

Introduction

At last we come to the final topic in the Study Text: **forecasting**. In this chapter we will be looking at a technique called **time series analysis**. With this forecasting method we look at **past data** about the variable which we want to forecast (such as sales levels) to see if there are **any patterns**. We then assume that these patterns will continue into the future. We are then able to forecast what we believe will be the value of a variable at some particular point of time in the future.

Learning outcomes covered in this chapter

- **Prepare** a time series graph and identify trends and patterns

- **Identify** the components of a time series model

- **Calculate** the trend using a graph or moving averages and be able to forecast the trend

- **Calculate** the seasonal variations for both additive and multiplicative models

- **Calculate** a forecast of the actual value using either the additive or the multiplicative model

- **Explain** the difference between the additive and multiplicative models, and where each is appropriate

- **Calculate** the seasonally-adjusted values in a time series

- **Explain** the reliability of any forecasts made

Syllabus content covered in this chapter

- Time series analysis - graphical analysis

- Calculation of trend using graph and moving averages

- Seasonal variations - additive and multiplicative

- Forecasting

1   THE COMPONENTS OF TIME SERIES

BPP
PUBLISHING

KEY TERM

A **time series** is a series of figures or values recorded over time. The graph of a time series is called a **historigram** (see Section 6 of Chapter 5).

1.1 The following are examples of time series.

- Output at a factory each day for the last month
- Monthly sales over the last two years
- Total annual costs for the last ten years
- The Retail Prices Index each month for the last ten years
- The number of people employed by a company each year for the last 20 years

1.2 The main features of a time series are as follows.

- A trend
- Seasonal variations or fluctuations
- Cycles, or cyclical variations
- Non-recurring, random variations

The trend

KEY TERM

The **trend** is the underlying long-term movement over time in the values of the data recorded.

1.3 EXAMPLE: PREPARING TIME SERIES GRAPHS AND IDENTIFYING TRENDS

	Output per labour hour Units	Cost per unit £	Number of employees
20X4	30	1.00	100
20X5	24	1.08	103
20X6	26	1.20	96
20X7	22	1.15	102
20X8	21	1.18	103
20X9	17	1.25	98
	(A)	(B)	(C)

(a) In time series (A) there is a **downward trend** in the output per labour hour. Output per labour hour did not fall every year, because it went up between 20X5 and 20X6, but the long-term movement is clearly a downward one.

Graph showing trend of output per labour hour in years 20X4-X9

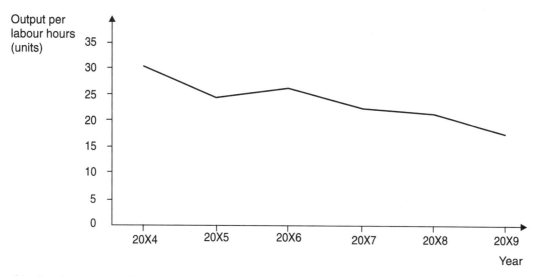

(b) In time series (B) there is an **upward trend** in the cost per unit. Although unit costs went down in 20X7 from a higher level in 20X6, the basic movement over time is one of rising costs.

Graph showing trend of costs per unit in years 20X4-X9

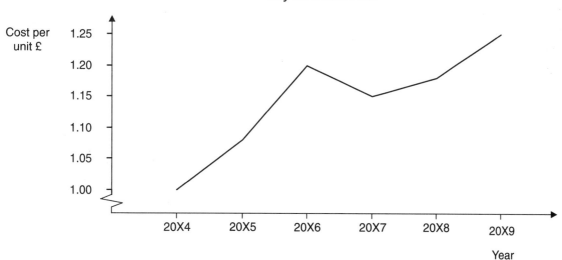

(c) In time series (C) there is no clear movement up or down, and the number of employees remained fairly constant around 100. The trend is therefore a **static, or level one.**

BPP PUBLISHING

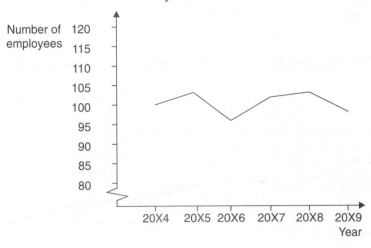

Graph showing trend of number of employees in year 20X4-X9

Seasonal variations

KEY TERM

Seasonal variations are short-term fluctuations in recorded values, due to different circumstances which affect results at different times of the year, on different days of the week, at different times of day, or whatever.

1.4 Examples of seasonable variations are as follows.

(a) Sales of ice cream will be higher in summer than in winter, and sales of overcoats will be higher in autumn than in spring.

(b) Shops might expect higher sales shortly before Christmas, or in their winter and summer sales.

(c) Sales might be higher on Friday and Saturday than on Monday.

(d) The telephone network may be heavily used at certain times of the day (such as mid-morning and mid-afternoon) and much less used at other times (such as in the middle of the night).

1.5 EXAMPLE: A TREND AND SEASONAL VARIATIONS

The number of customers served by a company of travel agents over the past four years is shown in the following **historigram** (time series graph).

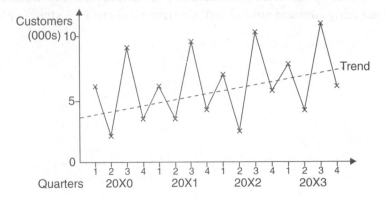

In this example, there would appear to be large seasonal fluctuations in demand, but there is also a basic upward trend.

Cyclical variations

1.6 **Cyclical variations** are medium-term changes in results caused by circumstances which repeat in cycles. In business, cyclical variations are commonly associated with **economic cycles, successive booms** and **slumps** in the economy. Economic cycles may last a few years. **Cyclical variations are longer term than seasonal variations**.

Summarising the components

1.7 The components of a time series can be summarised by the following equation.

$$Y = T + S + C + I$$

where Y = the actual time series
       T = the trend series
       S = the seasonal component
       C = the cyclical component
       I = the random or irregular component

1.8 Though you should be aware of the cyclical component, you will not be expected to carry out any calculation connected with isolating it. The mathematical model which we will use, the **additive model**, therefore excludes any reference to C.

EXAM FORMULA

Additive model: Series = Trend + Seasonal + Random

$$Y = T + S + I$$

2   FINDING THE TREND

2.1 **The main problem we are concerned with in time series analysis is how to identify the trend and seasonal variations.**

2.2 There are three main methods of finding a trend.

(a) A **line of best fit** (the **trend line**) can be drawn by eye on a graph. (We will cover this in Section 4 of this chapter.)

(b) A statistical technique known as **linear regression by the least squares method** can be used. (We will cover this in Chapter 14.)

(c) A technique known as **moving averages** can be used.

Finding the trend by moving averages

> **KEY TERMS**
>
> - A **moving average** is an average of the results of a fixed number of periods.
>
> - The **moving averages method** is a technique used to find the trend. This method attempts to remove seasonal variations from actual data by a process of averaging.

2.3 EXAMPLE: MOVING AVERAGES OF AN ODD NUMBER OF RESULTS

Year	Sales
	Units
20X0	390
20X1	380
20X2	460
20X3	450
20X4	470
20X5	440
20X6	500

Required

Take a moving average of the annual sales over a period of three years.

2.4 SOLUTION

(a) Average sales in the three year period 20X0 – 20X2 were

$$\left(\frac{390 + 380 + 460}{3}\right) = \frac{1,230}{3} = 410$$

This average relates to the middle year of the period, 20X1.

(b) Similarly, average sales in the three year period 20X1 – 20X3 were

$$\left(\frac{380 + 460 + 450}{3}\right) = \frac{1,290}{3} = 430$$

This average relates to the middle year of the period, 20X2.

(c) The average sales can also be found for the periods 20X2 - 20X4, 20X3 - 20X5 and 20X4 - 20X6, to give the following.

Year	Sales	Moving total of 3 years' sales	Moving average of 3 years' sales (÷ 3)
20X0	390		
20X1	380	1,230	410
20X2	460	1,290	430
20X3	450	1,380	460
20X4	470	1,360	453
20X5	440	1,410	470
20X6	500		

Note the following points.

(i) The moving average series has five figures relating to the years from 20X1 to 20X5. The original series had seven figures for the years from 20X0 to 20X6.

(ii)   There is an upward trend in sales, which is more noticeable from the series of moving averages than from the original series of actual sales each year.

2.5   The above example averaged over a three-year period. Over what period should a moving average be taken? The answer to this question is that **the moving average which is most appropriate will depend on the circumstances and the nature of the time series**. Note the following points.

(a)   A moving average which takes an average of the results in many time periods will represent results over a longer term than a moving average of two or three periods.

(b)   On the other hand, with a moving average of results in many time periods, the last figure in the series will be out of date by several periods. In our example, the most recent average related to 20X5. With a moving average of five years' results, the final figure in the series would relate to 20X4.

(c)   When there is a known cycle over which seasonal variations occur, such as all the days in the week or all the seasons in the year, the most suitable moving average would be one which covers one full cycle.

Question 1

Using the following data, complete the following table in order to determine the three-month moving average for the period January–June.

Month	No of new houses finished	Moving total 3 months new houses finished	Moving average of 3 months new houses finished
January	500		
February	450		
March	700		
April	900		
May	1,250		
June	1,000		

Answer

Month	No of new houses finished	Moving total 3 months new houses finished	Moving average of 3 months new houses finished (÷ 3)
January	500		
February	450	1,650	550
March	700	2,050	683.33
April	900	2,850	950
May	1,250	3,150	1,050
June	1,000		

Moving averages of an even number of results

2.6   In the previous example, moving averages were taken of the results in an **odd number of time periods,** and the average then related to the **mid-point of the overall period.** If a moving average were taken of results in an **even number of time periods,** the basic technique would be the same, but **the mid-point of the overall period would not relate to a single period.** For example, suppose an average were taken of the following four results.

Spring	120	
Summer	90	average 115
Autumn	180	
Winter	70	

The average would relate to the mid-point of the period, between summer and autumn. The trend line average figures need to relate to a particular time period; otherwise, seasonal variations cannot be calculated. To overcome this difficulty, we take a **moving average of the moving average.** An example will illustrate this technique.

2.7 EXAMPLE: MOVING AVERAGES OVER AN EVEN NUMBER OF PERIODS

Calculate a moving average trend line of the following results.

Year	Quarter	Volume of sales '000 units
20X5	1	600
	2	840
	3	420
	4	720
20X6	1	640
	2	860
	3	420
	4	740
20X7	1	670
	2	900
	3	430
	4	760

2.8 SOLUTION

A moving average of four will be used, since the volume of sales would appear to depend on the season of the year, and each year has four quarterly results.

The moving average of four does not relate to any specific period of time; therefore a second moving average of two will be calculated on the first moving average trend line.

Year	Quarter	Actual volume of sales '000 units (A)	Moving total of 4 quarters' sales '000 units (B)	Moving average of 4 quarters' sales '000 units (B ÷ 4)	Mid-point of 2 moving averages Trend line '000 units (C)
20X5	1	600			
	2	840			
	3	420	2,580	645.0	650.00
	4	720	2,620	655.0	657.50
20X6	1	640	2,640	660.0	660.00
	2	860	2,640	660.0	662.50
	3	420	2,660	665.0	668.75
	4	740	2,690	672.5	677.50
20X7	1	670	2,730	682.5	683.75
	2	900	2,740	685.0	687.50
	3	430	2,760	690.0	
	4	760			

By taking a **mid point** (a moving average of two) **of the original moving averages, we can relate the results to specific quarters** (from the third quarter of 20X5 to the second quarter of 20X7).

3 FINDING THE SEASONAL VARIATIONS

3.1 Once a trend has been established, by whatever method, we can find the **seasonal variations**.

3.2 How do we go about finding the seasonal component?

Step 1. The additive model for time series analysis is $Y = T + S + I$.

Step 2. If we deduct the trend from the additive model, we get $Y - T = S + I$.

Step 3. If we assume that I, the random, or irregular component of the time series is relatively small and therefore negligible, then $S = Y - T$.

Therefore, the seasonal component, $S = Y - T$ (the de-trended series).

3.3 EXAMPLE: THE TREND AND SEASONAL VARIATIONS

Output at a factory appears to vary with the day of the week. Output over the last three weeks has been as follows.

	Week 1 '000 units	*Week 2* '000 units	*Week 3* '000 units
Monday	80	82	84
Tuesday	104	110	116
Wednesday	94	97	100
Thursday	120	125	130
Friday	62	64	66

Required

Find the seasonal variation for each of the 15 days, and the average seasonal variation for each day of the week using the moving averages method.

3.4 SOLUTION

Actual results fluctuate up and down according to the day of the week and so a **moving average of five** will be used. **The difference between the actual result on any one day (Y) and the trend figure for that day (T) will be the seasonal variation (S) for the day.** The seasonal variations for the 15 days are as follows.

		Actual (Y)	*Moving total of five days'* *output*	*Trend* (T)	*Seasonal* *variation* (Y–T)
Week 1	Monday	80			
	Tuesday	104			
	Wednesday	94	460	92.0	+2.0
	Thursday	120	462	92.4	+27.6
	Friday	62	468	93.6	–31.6
Week 2	Monday	82	471	94.2	–12.2
	Tuesday	110	476	95.2	+14.8
	Wednesday	97	478	95.6	+1.4
	Thursday	125	480	96.0	+29.0
	Friday	64	486	97.2	–33.2

		Actual (Y)	Moving total of five days' output	Trend (T)	Seasonal variation (Y–T)
Week 3	Monday	84	489	97.8	–13.8
	Tuesday	116	494	98.8	+17.2
	Wednesday	100	496	99.2	+0.8
	Thursday	130			
	Friday	66			

You will notice that the variation between the actual results on any one particular day and the trend line average is not the same from week to week. This is because **Y – T** contains **not only seasonal variations but random variations,** but **an average of these variations can be taken.**

	Monday	*Tuesday*	*Wednesday*	*Thursday*	*Friday*
Week 1			+2.0	+27.6	–31.6
Week 2	–12.2	+14.8	+1.4	+29.0	–33.2
Week 3	–13.8	+17.2	+0.8		
Average	–13.0	+16.0	+1.4	+28.3	–32.4

Variations around the basic trend line should cancel each other out, and add up to 0. At the moment they do not. **The average seasonal estimates must therefore be corrected so that they add up to zero** and so we spread the total of the daily variations (0.30) across the five days (0.3 ÷ 5) so that the final total of the daily variations goes to zero.

	Monday	*Tuesday*	*Wednesday*	*Thursday*	*Friday*	*Total*
Estimated average daily variation	–13.00	+16.00	+1.40	+28.30	–32.40	0.30
Adjustment to reduce total variation to 0	–0.06	–0.06	–0.06	–0.06	–0.06	–0.30
Final estimate of average daily variation	–13.06	+15.94	+1.34	+28.24	–32.46	0.00

These might be rounded up or down as follows.

Monday –13; Tuesday +16; Wednesday +1; Thursday +28; Friday –32; Total 0.

Question 2

Calculate a four-quarter moving average trend centred on actual quarters and then find seasonal variations from the following.

	Spring	Sales in £'000 *Summer*	*Autumn*	*Winter*
20X7	200	120	160	280
20X8	220	140	140	300
20X9	200	120	180	320

Answer

		Sales (Y)	4-quarter total	8-quarter total	Moving average (T)	Seasonal variation (Y-T)
20X7	Spring	200				
	Summer	120				
			760			
	Autumn	160		1,540	192.5	−32.5
			780			
	Winter	280		1,580	197.5	+82.5
			800			
20X8	Spring	220		1,580	197.5	+22.5
			780			
	Summer	140		1,580	197.5	−57.5
			800			
	Autumn	140		1,580	197.5	−57.5
			780			
	Winter	300		1,540	192.5	+107.5
			760			
20X9	Spring	200		1,560	195.0	+5.0
			800			
	Summer	120		1,620	202.5	−82.5
			820			
	Autumn	180				
	Winter	320				

We can now average the seasonal variations.

	Spring	Summer	Autumn	Winter	Total
20X7			−32.5	+82.5	
20X8	+22.5	−57.5	−57.5	+107.5	
20X9	+5.0	−82.5			
	+27.5	−140.0	−90.0	+190.0	
Average variations (in £'000)	+13.75	−70.00	−45.00	+95.00	−6.25
Adjustment so sum is zero	+1.5625	+1.5625	+1.5625	+1.5625	+6.25
Adjusted average variations	+15.3125	−68.4375	−43.4375	+96.5625	0

These might be rounded up or down to:

Spring £15,000, Summer −£68,000, Autumn −£43,000, Winter £96,000

Seasonal variations using the multiplicative model

3.5 The method of estimating the seasonal variations in the additive model is to use the differences between the trend and actual data. **The additive model assumes that the components of the series are independent of each other,** an increasing trend not affecting the seasonal variations for example.

The alternative is to use the **multiplicative model** whereby **each actual figure is expressed as a proportion of the trend**. Sometimes this method is called the **proportional model**.

EXAM FORMULA

Multiplicative model: Series = Trend × Seasonal × Random

Y = T × S × I

3.6 The additive model example above (in Paragraph 3.3) can be reworked on this alternative basis. The trend is calculated in exactly the same way as before but we need a different approach for the seasonal variations.

The multiplicative model is Y = T × S × I and, just as we calculated S = Y – T for the additive model we can calculate **S = Y/T for the multiplicative model.**

		Actual (Y)	Trend (T)	Seasonal variation (Y/T)
Week 1	Monday	80		
	Tuesday	104		
	Wednesday	94	92.0	1.022
	Thursday	120	92.4	1.299
	Friday	62	93.6	0.662
Week 2	Monday	82	94.2	0.870
	Tuesday	110	95.2	1.155
	Wednesday	97	95.6	1.015
	Thursday	125	96.0	1.302
	Friday	64	97.2	0.658
Week 3	Monday	84	97.8	0.859
	Tuesday	116	98.8	1.174
	Wednesday	100	99.2	1.008
	Thursday	130		
	Friday	66		

3.7 The summary of the seasonal variations expressed in **proportional terms** is as follows.

	Monday	Tuesday	Wednesday	Thursday	Friday
Week 1			1.022	1.299	0.662
Week 2	0.870	1.155	1.015	1.302	0.658
Week 3	0.859	1.174	1.008		
Total	1.729	2.329	3.045	2.601	1.320
Average	0.8645	1.1645	1.0150	1.3005	0.6600

Instead of summing to zero, as with the absolute approach, these should sum (in this case) to 5 (an average of 1).

They actually sum to 5.0045 so 0.0009 has to be deducted from each one. This is too small to make a difference to the figures above, so we should deduct 0.002 and 0.0025 to each of two seasonal variations. We could arbitrarily decrease Monday's variation to 0.8625 and Tuesday's to 1.162.

3.8 **The multiplicative model is better than the additive model for forecasting when the trend is increasing or decreasing over time.** In such circumstances, seasonal variations are likely to be increasing or decreasing too. The additive model simply adds absolute and unchanging seasonal variations to the trend figures whereas the multiplicative model, by multiplying increasing or decreasing trend values by a constant seasonal variation factor, takes account of changing seasonal variations.

3.9 We can summarise the steps to be carried out when calculating the seasonal variation as follows.

Step 1. Calculate the moving total for an appropriate period.

Step 2. Calculate the moving average (the trend) for the period. (Calculate the mid-point of two moving averages if there are an even number of periods.)

Step 3. Calculate the seasonal variation. For an additive model, this is Y – T. For a multiplicative model, this is Y/T.

Step 4. Calculate an average of the seasonal variations.

Step 5. Adjust the average seasonal variations so that they add up to **zero** for an **additive model**. When using the **multiplicative model**, the average seasonal variations should add up to an **average of 1**.

Question 3

Find the average seasonal variations for the sales data in Question 2 using the multiplicative model.

Answer

	Spring	Summer	Autumn	Winter	Total
20X7			0.83*	1.42	
20X8	1.11	0.71	0.71	1.56	
20X9	1.03	0.59			
	2.14	1.30	1.54	2.98	

	Spring	Summer	Autumn	Winter	Total
Average variations	1.070	0.650	0.770	1.490	3.980
Adjustment to sum to 4	+ 0.005	+ 0.005	+ 0.005	+ 0.005	0.020
Adjusted average variations	1.075	0.655	0.775	1.495	4.000

*Seasonal variation $\dfrac{Y}{T} = \dfrac{160}{192.5} = 0.83$

Seasonally-adjusted data

KEY TERM

Seasonally-adjusted data (deseasonalised) are data which have had any seasonal variations taken out, so leaving a figure which might indicate the trend. Seasonally-adjusted data should indicate whether the overall trend is rising, falling or stationary.

3.10 EXAMPLE: SEASONALLY-ADJUSTED DATA

Actual sales figures for four quarters, together with appropriate seasonal adjustment factors derived from previous data, are as follows.

		Seasonal adjustments	
Quarter	Actual sales £'000	Additive model £'000	Multiplicative model
1	150	+3	1.02
2	160	+4	1.05
3	164	–2	0.98
4	170	–5	0.95

Required

Deseasonalise these data.

3.11 SOLUTION

We are reversing the normal process of applying seasonal variations to trend figures.

The rules for deseasonalising data are as follows.

- **Additive model** - subtract positive seasonal variations from and add negative seasonal variations to actual results.

- **Multiplicative model** - divide the actual results by the seasonal variation factors.

		Deseasonalised sales	
	Actual	*Additive*	*Multiplicative*
Quarter	*sales*	*model*	*model*
	£'000	£'000	£'000
1	150	147	147
2	160	156	152
3	164	166	167
4	170	175	179

4   FORECASTING AND TIME SERIES ANALYSIS

Making a forecast

4.1   Time series analysis data can be used to make forecasts as follows.

Step 1.   **Plot a trend line**: use the line of best fit method or the moving averages method.

Step 2.   **Extrapolate the trend line**. This means extending the trend line outside the range of known data and forecasting future results from historical data.

Step 3.   **Adjust forecast trends** by the applicable average seasonal variation to obtain the actual forecast.

    (a)   **Additive model** - add positive variations to and subtract negative variations from the forecast trends.

    (b)   **Multiplicative model** - multiply the forecast trends by the seasonal variation.

4.2   EXAMPLE: FORECASTING

Use the trend values and the estimates of seasonal variations calculated in Paragraph 3.4 to forecast sales in week 4.

4.3   SOLUTION

We begin by plotting the trend values on a graph and extrapolating the trend line.

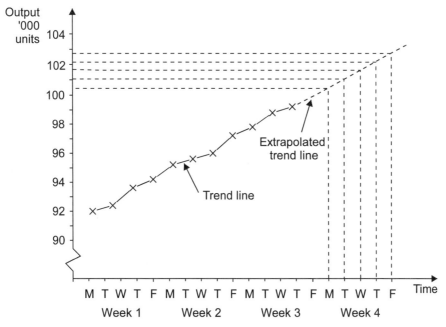

From the extrapolated trend line we can take the following readings and adjust them by the seasonal variations.

Week 4	Trend line readings	Seasonal variations	Forecast
Monday	100.5	−13	87.5
Tuesday	101.5	+16	117.1
Wednesday	101.7	+1	102.7
Thursday	102.2	+28	130.2
Friday	102.8	−32	70.8

4.4   If we had been using the multiplicative model the forecast for Tuesday, for example, would be $101.1 \times 1.1645 = 117.7$ (from Paragraph 3.7).

4.5   You may be asked to forecast sales of a particular product in a given year by using an equation which calculates the trend.

4.6   EXAMPLE: FORECASTING USING AN EQUATION TO CALCULATE THE TREND

In a time series analysis, the trend equation for product Z is given by

$\text{TREND} = 0.0002 \star \text{YEAR}^2 + 0.1 \star \text{YEAR} + 40.1$

Due to the cyclical factor, it is estimated that the forecast sales for 1997 is estimated at 1.92 times trend. Calculate the forecast sales for 1997.

4.7   SOLUTION

YEAR	$= 1997$
TREND	$= (0.0002 \times 1997^2) + (0.1 \times 1997) + 40.1$
	$= 1{,}037$
FORECAST	$= 1{,}037 \times 1.92$
	$= 1{,}992$

Part E: Forecasting

Question 4

Unemployment numbers actually recorded in a town for the first quarter of 20X9 were 4,700. The underlying trend at this point was 4,400 people and the seasonal factor is 0.85. Using the multiplicative model for seasonal adjustment, the seasonally-adjusted figure (in whole numbers) for the quarter is

A 5,529   B 5,176   C 3,995   D 3,740

Answer

The correct answer is A.

If you remembered the ruling that you need to **divide** by the seasonal variation factor to obtain seasonally-adjusted figures (using the multiplicative model), then you should have been able to eliminate options C and D. This might have been what you did if you weren't sure whether you divided the **actual results** or the **trend** by the seasonal variation factor.

$$\text{Seasonally adjusted data} = \frac{\text{Actual results}}{\text{Seasonal factor}} = \frac{4,700}{0.85} = 5,529$$

Residuals

> **KEY TERM**
>
> A **residual** is the difference between the results which would have been predicted (for a past period for which we already have data) by the trend line adjusted for the average seasonal variation and the actual results.

4.8   **The residual is therefore the difference which is not explained by the trend line and the average seasonal variation**. The residual gives some indication of how much actual results were affected by other factors. Large residuals suggest that any forecast is likely to be unreliable.

4.9   In the example in Paragraph 3.4, the 'prediction' for Wednesday of week 2 would have been 95.6 + 1 = 96.6. As the actual value was 97, the residual was only 97 − 96.6 = 0.4.

The reliability of time series analysis forecasts

4.10   All forecasts are subject to error, but the likely errors vary from case to case.

  (a)   The further into the future the forecast is for, the more unreliable it is likely to be.

  (b)   The less data available on which to base the forecast, the less reliable the forecast.

  (c)   The pattern of trend and seasonal variations cannot be guaranteed to continue in the future.

  (d)   There is always the danger of random variations upsetting the pattern of trend and seasonal variation.

  (e)   The extrapolation of the trend line is done by judgement and can introduce error.

Exam focus point

Do not underestimate the importance of forecasting in the **Business Mathematics** examination - the topic of forecasting represents 25% of the syllabus.

The following information is to be used for questions 5 and 6 below

In a time series analysis, the multiplicative model is used to forecast sales and the following seasonal variations apply.

Quarter	1	2	3	4
Seasonal variation	0.8	1.9	0.75	?

The actual sales value for the last two quarters of 20X1 were:

Quarter 3: £250,000
Quarter 4: £260,000

Question 5

The seasonal variation for the fourth quarter is:

A   0.55
B   −3.45
C   1.00
D   1.45

Answer

The correct answer is A.

As this is a multiplicative model, the seasonal variations should sum (in this case) to 4 (an average of 1) as there are four quarters.

Let x = seasonal variation in quarter 4.

$0.8 + 1.9 + 0.75 + x = 4$

$$\therefore 3.45 + x = 4$$
$$x = 4 - 3.45$$
$$x = 0.55$$

Question 6

The trend line for sales:

A   remained constant between quarter 3 and quarter 4
B   increased between quarter 3 and quarter 4
C   decreased between quarter 3 and quarter 4
D   cannot be determined from the information given

Answer

The correct answer is B.

For a multiplicative model, the seasonal component is as follows.

$S = Y/T$

$\therefore T = Y/S$

BPP PUBLISHING

	Quarter	
	3	*4*
Seasonal component (S)	0.75	0.55
Actual series (Y)	£250,000	£260,000
Trend (T) (= Y/S)	£333,333	£472,727

The trend line for sales has therefore increased between quarter 3 and quarter 4.

Chapter roundup

- A **time series** is a series of figures or values recorded over time. A graph of a time series is called a **historigram**.

- There are four components of a time series: **trend**, **seasonal variations**, **cyclical variations** and **random variations**.

- The **trend** is the underlying long-term movement over time in the values of the data recorded. **Seasonal variations** are short-term fluctuations due to different circumstances which affect results at different points in time. **Cyclical variations** are medium-term changes in results caused by circumstances which repeat in cycles.

- One method of finding the trend is by the use of **moving averages**.

- Remember that when finding the moving average of an **even number of results**, a second moving average has to be calculated so that trend values can relate to specific actual figures.

- **Seasonal variations are the difference between actual and trend figures**. An average of the seasonal variations for each time period within the cycle must be determined and then adjusted so that the total of the seasonal variations sums to zero.

- Seasonal variations can be estimated using the **additive model (Y = T + S + I, with seasonal variations = Y – T)** or the **proportional (multiplicative) model (Y = T × S × I, with seasonal variations = Y/T)**.

- **Forecasts** can be made by **extrapolating the trend** and **adjusting for seasonal variations**. Remember, however, that all forecasts are subject to error.

Quick quiz

1   What are the four main components of a time series?

2   **Additive model**

Y = T + S + I

where   Y =
 T =
 S =
 I =

3   What is the formula for the multiplicative model?

4   If the trend is increasing or decreasing over time, it is better to use the additive model for forecasting.

True   ☐

False   ☐

5   List three methods for finding trend lines.

6   **Results**   **Method**

Odd number of time periods   Calculate 1 moving average

 ?

Even number of time periods   Calculate 2 moving averages

7 A = Y – T
   B = Y/T

Seasonal variation

Multiplicative model =
Additive model =

8 When calculating seasonal variations, adjust the average seasonal variations so that they add up to zero for a(n) additive/multiplicative model. When using the additive/multiplicative model, the average seasonal variations should add up to an average of 1.

9 When deseasonalising data, the following rules apply to the additive model.

   I   Add positive seasonal variations
   II   Subtract positive seasonal variations
   III Add negative seasonal variations
   IV   Subtract negative seasonal variations

   A   I and II
   B   II and III
   C   II and IV
   D   I only

10 Time series analysis data can be used to make forecasts by **extrapolating** the trend line. What does extrapolation mean?

11 Cyclical variation is the term used for the difference which is not explained by the trend line and the average seasonal variation.

   True   ☐

   False   ☐

12 List the factors that might explain why time series analysis forecasts may not be 100% reliable.

BPP
PUBLISHING

Answers to quick quiz

1   • Trend
    • Seasonal variation (fluctuation)
    • Cyclical variations
    • Random variations

2   Y   = the actual time series
    T   = the trend series
    S   = the seasonal component
    I   = the random/irregular component

3   $Y = T \times S \times I$

4   False

5   • Line of best fit
    • Linear regression
    • Moving averages

6   Odd number of time periods = calculate 1 moving average
    Even number of time periods = calculate 2 moving averages.

7   Multiplicative model   = B = Y/T
    Additive model   = A = Y – T

8   When calculating seasonal variations, adjust the average seasonal variations so that they add up to **zero** for an **additive model**. When using the **multiplicative model**, the average seasonal variations should add up to an average of **1**.

9   B

10 Extending the trend line outside the range of known data and forecasting future results from historical data.

11 False. The residual is the term used to explain the difference which is not explained by the trend line and the average seasonal variation.

12 (a) The further into the future a forecast is made, the more unreliable it is likely to be.
    (b) The less data available for forecasting, the less reliable the forecast.
    (c) The trend and seasonal variation patterns identified may not continue in the future.
    (d) Random variations may upset the pattern of trend and seasonal variation.
    (e) The extrapolation of the trend line is done by judgement and may not be accurate.

Now try the following objective test questions

Question bank	Question numbers	Page
Paper-based exam	14	283
Computer-based assessment	13	302

Chapter 14

CORRELATION AND REGRESSION

Topic list	Syllabus reference	Ability required
1 Correlation	(v)	Application
2 The correlation coefficient and the coefficient of determination	(v)	Application and comprehension
3 Spearman's rank correlation coefficient	(v)	Application
4 Lines of best fit	(v)	Application
5 The scattergraph method	(v)	Application
6 Least squares method of linear regression analysis	(v)	Application
7 The reliability of regression analysis forecasts	(v)	Comprehension

Introduction

We looked at one mathematical forecasting technique in Chapter 13 and now we are going to look at the second in this, the final chapter. The first three sections deal with **correlation**, which is concerned with assessing the strength of the relationship between two variables.

We then turn our attention to forecasting. We will see how, if we assume that there is a **linear relationship** between two variables (such as selling costs and sales volume) we can determine the equation of a straight line to represent the relationship between the variables and use that equation to make **forecasts** or **predictions**. The equation can be derived and the predictions made using one of two methods, the **scattergraph method** or **linear regression analysis**, both of which are covered in this chapter.

Learning outcomes covered in this chapter

- **Calculate** the correlation coefficient between two variables and **explain** the value

- **Calculate** the rank correlation coefficient between two sets of data and **explain** the value

- **Explain** the meaning of $100r^2$ (the coefficient of determination)

- **Demonstrate** the use of regression analysis between two variables to find the line of best fit and **explain** its meaning

- **Calculate** a forecast of the value of the dependent variable, given the value of the independent variable

- **Calculate** the trend using linear regression, and be able to **forecast** the trend

Syllabus content covered in this chapter

- Correlation

- Simple linear regression

1 CORRELATION

1.1 Examples of variables which might be correlated are as follows.

- A person's height and weight
- The distance of a journey and the time it takes to make it

1.2 One way of showing the correlation between two related variables is on a **scattergraph** or **scatter diagram**, plotting a number of pairs of data on the graph. For example, a scattergraph showing monthly selling costs against the volume of sales for a 12-month period might be as follows.

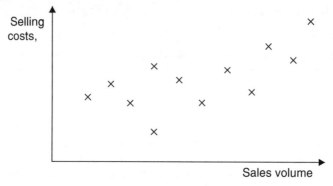

This scattergraph suggests that there is some correlation between selling costs and sales volume, so that as sales volume rises, selling costs tend to rise as well.

Degrees of correlation

1.3 Two variables can be one of the following.

- Perfectly correlated
- Partly correlated
- Uncorrelated

These differing degrees of correlation can be illustrated by scatter diagrams.

Perfect correlation

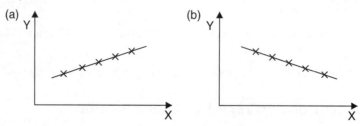

All the pairs of values lie on a straight line. An exact **linear relationship** exists between the two variables.

Partial correlation

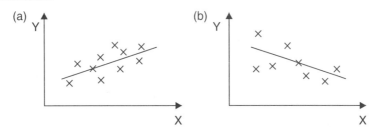

In (a), although there is no exact relationship, low values of X tend to be associated with low values of Y, and high values of X with high values of Y.

In (b) again, there is no exact relationship, but low values of X tend to be associated with high values of Y and vice versa.

No correlation

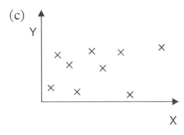

The values of these two variables are not correlated with each other.

Positive and negative correlation

1.4   Correlation, whether perfect or partial, can be **positive** or **negative**.

KEY TERMS

- **Positive correlation** means that low values of one variable are associated with low values of the other, and high values of one variable are associated with high values of the other.

- **Negative correlation** means that low values of one variable are associated with high values of the other, and high values of one variable with low values of the other.

---

2   THE CORRELATION COEFFICIENT AND THE COEFFICIENT OF DETERMINATION

The correlation coefficient

2.1   The degree of correlation between two variables can be measured, and we can decide, using actual results in the form of pairs of data, whether two variables are perfectly or partially correlated, and if they are partially correlated, whether there is a **high** or **low degree of partial correlation.**

2.2   This degree of correlation is measured by the **Pearsonian correlation coefficient** (the coefficient of correlation), r (also called the 'product moment correlation coefficient').

EXAM FORMULA

Correlation coefficient, $r = \dfrac{n\Sigma XY - \Sigma X \Sigma Y}{\sqrt{[n\Sigma X^2 - (\Sigma X)^2][n\Sigma Y^2 - (\Sigma Y)^2]}}$

where X and Y represent pairs of data for two variables X and Y

n = the number of pairs of data used in the analysis

2.3 The correlation coefficient, r must always fall between –1 and +1. If you get a value outside this range you have made a mistake.

- **r = +1** means that the variables are **perfectly positively correlated**
- **r = –1** means that the variables are **perfectly negatively correlated**
- **r = 0** means that the variables are **uncorrelated**

2.4 EXAMPLE: THE CORRELATION COEFFICIENT

The cost of output at a factory is thought to depend on the number of units produced. Data have been collected for the number of units produced each month in the last six months, and the associated costs, as follows.

Month	Output '000s of units X	Cost £'000 Y
1	2	9
2	3	11
3	1	7
4	4	13
5	3	11
6	5	15

Required

Assess whether there is there any correlation between output and cost.

2.5 SOLUTION

$r = \dfrac{n\Sigma XY - \Sigma X \Sigma Y}{\sqrt{[n\Sigma X^2 - (\Sigma X)^2][n\Sigma Y^2 - (\Sigma Y)^2]}}$

We need to find the values for the following.

(a) ΣXY Multiply each value of X by its corresponding Y value, so that there are six values for XY. Add up the six values to get the total.

(b) ΣX Add up the six values of X to get a total. $(\Sigma X)^2$ will be the square of this total.

(c) ΣY Add up the six values of Y to get a total. $(\Sigma Y)^2$ will be the square of this total.

(d) ΣX^2 Find the square of each value of X, so that there are six values for X^2. Add up these values to get a total.

(e) ΣY^2 Find the square of each value of Y, so that there are six values for Y^2. Add up these values to get a total.

Workings

X	Y	XY	X²	Y²
2	9	18	4	81
3	11	33	9	121
1	7	7	1	49
4	13	52	16	169
3	11	33	9	121
5	15	75	25	225
$\Sigma X = 18$	$\Sigma Y = 66$	$\Sigma XY = 218$	$\Sigma X^2 = 64$	$\Sigma Y^2 = 766$

$(\Sigma X)^2 = 18^2 = 324 \qquad (\Sigma Y)^2 = 66^2 = 4{,}356$

$n = 6$

$$r = \frac{(6 \times 218) - (18 \times 66)}{\sqrt{(6 \times 64 - 324) \times (6 \times 766 - 4{,}356)}}$$

$$= \frac{1{,}308 - 1{,}188}{\sqrt{(384 - 324) \times (4{,}596 - 4{,}356)}}$$

$$= \frac{120}{\sqrt{60 \times 240}} = \frac{120}{\sqrt{14{,}400}} = \frac{120}{120} = 1$$

2.6 There is **perfect positive correlation** between the volume of output at the factory and costs which means that there is a perfect linear relationship between output and costs.

Correlation in a time series

2.7 Correlation exists in a time series if there is a relationship between the period of time and the recorded value for that period of time. The correlation coefficient is calculated with time as the X variable although it is convenient to use simplified values for X instead of year numbers.

For example, instead of having a series of years 20X1 to 20X5, we could have values for X from 0 (20X1) to 4 (20X5).

Note that whatever starting value you use for X (be it 0, 1, 2 ... 721, ... 953), the value of r will always be the same.

Question 1

Sales of product A between 20X7 and 20Y1 were as follows.

Year	Units sold ('000s)
20X7	20
20X8	18
20X9	15
20Y0	14
20Y1	11

Required

Determine whether there is a trend in sales. In other words, decide whether there is any correlation between the year and the number of units sold.

Answer

Workings

Let 20X7 to 20Y1 be years 0 to 4.

BPP PUBLISHING

X	Y	XY	X^2	Y^2
0	20	0	0	400
1	18	18	1	324
2	15	30	4	225
3	14	42	9	196
4	11	44	16	121
$\Sigma X = \underline{\underline{10}}$	$\Sigma Y = \underline{\underline{78}}$	$\Sigma XY = \underline{\underline{134}}$	$\Sigma X^2 = \underline{\underline{30}}$	$\Sigma Y^2 = \underline{\underline{1,266}}$

$(\Sigma X)^2 = 100 \qquad (\Sigma Y)^2 = 6,084$

$n \quad = \quad 5$

$$r = \frac{(5 \times 134) - (10 \times 78)}{\sqrt{(5 \times 30 - 100) \times (5 \times 1,266 - 6,084)}}$$

$$= \frac{670 - 780}{\sqrt{(150 - 100) \times (6,330 - 6,084)}} = \frac{-110}{\sqrt{50 \times 246}}$$

$$= \frac{-110}{\sqrt{12,300}} = \frac{-110}{110.90537} = -0.992$$

There is **partial negative correlation** between the year of sale and units sold. The value of r is close to –1, therefore a **high degree of correlation exists**, although it is not quite perfect correlation. This means that there is a **clear downward trend** in sales.

The coefficient of determination, r^2

2.8 Unless the correlation coefficient r is exactly or very nearly +1, –1 or 0, its meaning or significance is a little unclear. For example, if the correlation coefficient for two variables is +0.8, this would tell us that the variables are positively correlated, but the correlation is not perfect. It would not really tell us much else. A more meaningful analysis is available from **the square of the correlation coefficient, r**, which is called the **coefficient of determination, r^2**

> ### KEY TERM
>
> The **coefficient of determination, r^2** (alternatively R^2) measures the proportion of the total variation in the value of one variable that can be explained by variations in the value of the other variable.

2.9 In Question 1 above, r = –0.992, therefore r^2 = 0.984. This means that over 98% of variations in sales can be explained by the passage of time, leaving 0.016 (less than 2%) of variations to be explained by other factors.

2.10 Similarly, if the correlation coefficient between a company's output volume and maintenance costs was 0.9, r^2 would be 0.81, meaning that 81% of variations in maintenance costs could be explained by variations in output volume, leaving only 19% of variations to be explained by other factors (such as the age of the equipment).

2.11 Note, however, that if r^2 = 0.81, we would say that 81% of **the variations in y can be explained by variations in x**. We do not necessarily conclude that 81% of variations in y are *caused* by the variations in x. We must beware of reading too much significance into our statistical analysis.

Correlation and causation

2.12 If two variables are well correlated, either positively or negatively, this may be due to **pure chance** or there may be a **reason** for it. The larger the number of pairs of data collected, the less likely it is that the correlation is due to chance, though that possibility should never be ignored entirely.

2.13 If there is a reason, it may not be causal. For example, monthly net income is well correlated with monthly credit to a person's bank account, for the logical (rather than causal) reason that for most people the one equals the other.

2.14 Even if there is a causal explanation for a correlation, it does not follow that variations in the value of one variable cause variations in the value of the other. For example, sales of ice cream and of sunglasses are well correlated, not because of a direct causal link but because the weather influences both variables.

3 SPEARMAN'S RANK CORRELATION COEFFICIENT

3.1 In the examples considered above, the data were given in terms of the values of the relevant variables, such as the number of hours. Sometimes however, they are given in terms of **order** or **rank** rather than actual values. When this occurs, a correlation coefficient known as **Spearman's rank correlation coefficient**, **R** should be calculated using the following formula.

> **EXAM FORMULA**
>
> **Coefficient of rank correlation,** $R = 1 - \left[\dfrac{6\Sigma d^2}{n(n^2 - 1)} \right]$
>
> where n = number of pairs of data
> d = the difference between the rankings in each set of data.

The coefficient of rank correlation can be interpreted in exactly the same way as the ordinary correlation coefficient. Its value can range from –1 to +1.

3.2 EXAMPLE: THE RANK CORRELATION COEFFICIENT

The examination placings of seven students were as follows.

Student	Statistics placing	Economics placing
A	2	1
B	1	3
C	4	7
D	6	5
E	5	6
F	3	2
G	7	4

Required

Judge whether the placings of the students in statistics correlate with their placings in economics.

3.3 SOLUTION

Correlation must be measured by **Spearman's coefficient** because we are given the **placings** of students, and not their actual marks.

$$R = 1 - \frac{6\Sigma d^2}{n(n^2 - 1)}$$

where d is the difference between the rank in statistics and the rank in economics for each student.

Student	Rank Statistics	Rank Economics	d	d^2
A	2	1	1	1
B	1	3	2	4
C	4	7	3	9
D	6	5	1	1
E	5	6	1	1
F	3	2	1	1
G	7	4	3	9
			$\Sigma d^2 =$	26

$$R = 1 - \frac{6 \times 26}{7 \times (49 - 1)} = 1 - \frac{156}{336} = 0.536$$

The correlation is **positive**, 0.536, but the correlation is **not strong**.

Tied ranks

3.4 If in a problem some of the items **tie for a particular ranking**, these must be given an **average place** before the coefficient of rank correlation is calculated. Here is an example.

Position of students in examination			Express as
A	1 =	average of 1 and 2	1.5
B	1 =		1.5
C	3		3
D	4		4
E	5 =		6
F	5 =	average of 5, 6 and 7	6
G	5 =		6
H	8		8

Question 2

Five artists were placed in order of merit by two different judges as follows.

Artist	Judge P Rank	Judge Q Rank
A	1	4 =
B	2 =	1
C	4	3
D	5	2
E	2 =	4 =

Required

Assess how the two sets of rankings are correlated.

Answer

	Judge P Rank	Judge Q Rank	d	d^2
A	1.0	4.5	3.5	12.25
B	2.5	1.0	1.5	2.25
C	4.0	3.0	1.0	1.00
D	5.0	2.0	3.0	9.00
E	2.5	4.5	2.0	4.00
				28.50

$$R = 1 - \frac{6 \times 28.5}{5 \times (25 - 1)} = -0.425$$

There is a **slight negative correlation** between the rankings.

4 LINES OF BEST FIT

4.1 **Correlation enables us to determine the strength of any relationship between two variables but it does not offer us any method of forecasting values for one variable, Y, given values of another variable, X.**

4.2 If we assume that there is a **linear relationship** between the two variables, however, and we determine the **equation of a straight line (Y = a + bX)** which is a good fit for the available data plotted on a scattergraph, we can use the equation for forecasting: we can substitute values for X into the equation and derive values for Y.

4.3 There are a number of techniques for estimating the equation of a line of best fit. We will be looking at the **scattergraph method** and **simple linear regression analysis**. Both provide a technique for estimating values for a and b in the equation

   Y = a + bX

where   X and Y are the related variables and
       a and b are estimated using pairs of data for X and Y.

5 THE SCATTERGRAPH METHOD

KEY TERM

The **scattergraph method** is to plot pairs of data for two related variables on a graph, to produce a scattergraph, and then to **use judgement** to draw what seems to be a line of best fit through the data.

5.1 EXAMPLE: THE SCATTERGRAPH METHOD

Suppose we have the following pairs of data about output and costs.

Month	Output '000 units	Costs £'000
1	20	82
2	16	70
3	24	90
4	22	85
5	18	73

(a) These pairs of data can be plotted on a **scattergraph** (the **horizontal** axis representing the **independent** variable and the **vertical** axis the **dependent**) and a line of best fit might be judged as the one shown below. It is drawn to pass through the middle of the data points, thereby having as many data points below the line as above it.

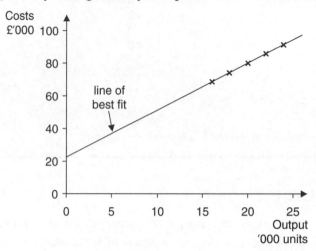

(b) **A formula for the line of best fit** can be found. In our example, suppose that we read the following data from the graph.

   (i)   When $X = 0$, $Y = 22,000$. This must be the value of a in the formula $Y = a + bX$.

   (ii) When $X = 20,000$, $Y = 81,000$. Since $Y = a + bX$, and $a = 22,000$, this gives us a value for b of

$$\frac{81,000 - 22,000}{20,000} = 2.95$$

(c) In this example the estimated equation from the scattergraph is $Y = 22,000 + 2.95X$.

Forecasting and scattergraphs

5.2   If the company to which the data in Paragraph 5.1 relates wanted to predict costs at a certain level of output (say 13,000 units), the value of 13,000 could be substituted into the equation $Y = 22,000 + 2.95X$ and an estimate of costs made.

   If $X = 13$, $Y = 22,000 + (2.95 \times 13,000)$

   $\therefore Y = £60,350$

5.3   Of course, predictions can be made directly from the scattergraph on the following page.

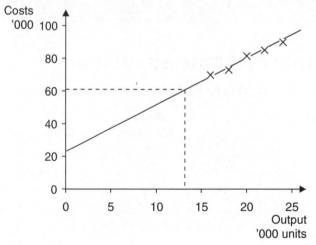

The prediction of the cost of producing 13,000 units from the scattergraph is £61,000.

6 LEAST SQUARES METHOD OF LINEAR REGRESSION ANALYSIS

EXAM FORMULA

The **least squares method of linear regression analysis** involves using the following formulae for a and b in $Y = a + bX$.

$$b = \frac{n\Sigma XY - \Sigma X\Sigma Y}{n\Sigma X^2 - (\Sigma X)^2}$$

$$a = \overline{Y} - b\overline{X}$$

where n   is the number of pairs of data
      $\overline{X}$ is the average X value of all the pairs of data
      $\overline{Y}$ is the average Y value of all the pairs of data

6.1 There are some points to note about these formulae.

(a) The line of best fit that is derived represents the **regression of Y upon X**.

A different line of best fit could be obtained by interchange in X and Y in the formulae. This would then represent the regression of X upon Y ($X = a + bY$) and it would have a slightly different slope. For examination purposes, always use the regression of Y upon X, where X is the independent variable, and Y is the dependent variable whose value we wish to forecast for given values of X. In a time series, X will represent time.

(b) Since $a = \overline{Y} - b\overline{X}$, it follows that the line of best fit must *always* pass through the point $(\overline{X}, \overline{Y})$.

6.2 EXAMPLE: THE LEAST SQUARES METHOD

(a) Given that there is a fairly high degree of correlation between the output and the costs detailed in Paragraph 5.1 (so that a linear relationship can be assumed), calculate an equation to determine the expected level of costs, for any given volume of output, using the least squares method.

(b) Prepare a budget for total costs if output is 22,000 units.

(c) Confirm that the degree of correlation between output and costs is high by calculating the correlation coefficient.

6.3 SOLUTION

(a) *Workings*

X	Y	XY	X^2	Y^2
20	82	1,640	400	6,724
16	70	1,120	256	4,900
24	90	2,160	576	8,100
22	85	1,870	484	7,225
18	73	1,314	324	5,329
$\Sigma X = 100$	$\Sigma Y = 400$	$\Sigma XY = 8,104$	$\Sigma X^2 = 2,040$	$\Sigma Y^2 = 32,278$

$$n = 5 \text{ (There are five pairs of data for x and y values)}$$

$$b = \frac{n\Sigma XY - \Sigma X \Sigma Y}{n\Sigma X^2 - (\Sigma X)^2} = \frac{(5 \times 8{,}104) - (100 \times 400)}{(5 \times 2{,}040) - 100^2}$$

$$= \frac{40{,}520 - 40{,}000}{10{,}200 - 10{,}000} = \frac{520}{200} = 2.6$$

$$a = \overline{Y} - b\overline{X} = \frac{400}{5} - 2.6 \times \left(\frac{100}{5}\right) = 28$$

$$Y = 28 + 2.6X$$

where Y = total cost, in thousands of pounds
       X = output, in thousands of units.

Compare this equation to that determined in Paragraph 5.1.

Note that the fixed costs are £28,000 (when X = 0 costs are £28,000) and the variable cost per unit is £2.60.

(b) If the output is 22,000 units, we would expect costs to be

$$28 + 2.6 \times 22 = 85.2 = £85{,}200.$$

(c) $r = \dfrac{520}{\sqrt{200 \times (5 \times 32{,}278 - 400^2)}} = \dfrac{520}{\sqrt{200 \times 1{,}390}} = \dfrac{520}{527.3} = +0.99$

Regression lines and time series

6.4 The same technique can be applied to calculate a **regression line** (a **trend line**) for a time series. This is particularly useful for purposes of forecasting. As with correlation, years can be numbered from 0 upwards.

Question 3

Using the data in Question 1, calculate the trend line of sales and forecast sales in 20Y2 and 20Y3.

Answer

Using workings from Question 1:

$$b = \frac{(5 \times 134) - (10 \times 78)}{(5 \times 30) - (10)^2} = \frac{670 - 780}{150 - 100} = -2.2$$

$$a = \overline{Y} - b\overline{X} = \frac{78}{5} - \frac{(-2.2 \times 10)}{5} = 20$$

∴ Y = 20 – 2.2X where X = 0 in 20X7, X = 1 in 20X8 and so on.

Using the trend line, predicted sales in 20Y2 (year 5) would be:

20 – (2.2 × 5) = 9 ie 9,000 units

and predicted sales in 20Y3 (year 6) would be:

20 – (2.2 × 6) = 6.8 ie 6,800 units.

6.5 In some instances you may have to adjust your regression line forecasts by **seasonal variations**.

Question 4

Suppose that a trend line, found using linear regression analysis, is Y = 300 – 4.7X where X is time (in quarters) and Y = sales level in thousands of units. Given that X = 0 represents 20X0 quarter 1 and that the seasonal variations are as set out below.

	Q_1	Q_2	Q_3	Q_4
Seasonal variations ('000 units)	–20	–8	+4	+15

The forecast sales level for 20X5 quarter 4 is ⬚ units

Answer

| 206,900 | units

Working

X = 0 corresponds to 20X0 quarter 1

∴ X = 23 corresponds to 20X5 quarter 4

Trend sales level = 300 – (4.7 × 23) = 191.9 ie 191,900 units

Seasonally-adjusted sales level = 191.9 + 15 = 206.9 ie 206,900 units

Question 5

Over a 36-month period, sales have been found to have an underlying linear trend of Y = 14.224 + 7.898X, where Y is the number of items sold and X represents the month. Monthly deviations from trend have been calculated and month 37 is expected to be 1.28 times the trend value.

The forecast number of items to be sold in month 37 is approximately

A 389   B 390   C 391   D 392

Answer

This is typical of multiple choice questions that you must work through fully if you are to get the right answer.

Y = 14.224 + 7.898X

If X = 37, trend in sales for month 37 = 14.224 + (7.898 × 37)

= 306.45

∴ Seasonally-adjusted trend value = 306.45 × 1.28

= 392.256

∴ The correct answer is 392, option D.

7   THE RELIABILITY OF REGRESSION ANALYSIS FORECASTS

7.1   As with all forecasting techniques, the results from regression analysis will not be wholly reliable. There are a number of factors which affect the reliability of forecasts made using regression analysis.

(a) **It assumes a linear relationship exists between the two variables** (since linear regression analysis produces an equation in the linear format) whereas a non-linear relationship might exist.

(b) It **assumes that the value of one variable, Y, can be predicted or estimated from the value of one other variable, X**. In reality the value of Y might depend on several other variables, not just X.

(c) When it is used for forecasting, **it assumes that what has happened in the past will provide a reliable guide to the future**.

(d) When calculating a line of best fit, there will be a range of values for X. In the example in Paragraph 6.2 and 6.3, the line $Y = 28 + 2.6X$ was predicted from data with output values ranging from $X = 16$ to $X = 24$. Depending on the degree of correlation between X and Y, we might safely use the estimated line of best fit to predict values for Y in the future, provided that the value of X remains within the range 16 to 24. We would be on less safe ground if we used the formula to predict a value for Y when $X = 10$, or 30, or any other value outside the range 16 to 24, because we would have to **assume that the trend line applies outside the range of X values used to establish the line in the first place**.

   (i) **Interpolation** means using a line of best fit to predict a value within the two extreme points of the observed range.

   (ii) **Extrapolation** means using a line of best fit to predict a value outside the two extreme points.

   When linear regression analysis is used for forecasting a time series (when the X values represent time) it **assumes that the trend line can be extrapolated into the future**. This might not necessarily be a good assumption to make.

(e) As with any forecasting process, **the amount of data available is very important**. Even if correlation is high, if we have fewer than about ten pairs of values, we must regard any forecast as being somewhat unreliable. (It is likely to provide more reliable forecasts than the scattergraph method, however, since it uses all of the available data.)

(f) **The reliability of a forecast will depend on the reliability of the data collected to determine the regression analysis equation**. If the data is not collected accurately or if data used is false, forecasts are unlikely to be acceptable.

7.2   A check on the reliability of the estimated line $Y = 28 + 2.6X$ can be made, however, by calculating the coefficient of correlation. From Paragraph 6.3, we know that $r = 0.99$. This is a high positive correlation, and $r^2 = 0.9801$, indicating that 98.01% of the variation in cost can be explained by the variation in volume. This would suggest that a **fairly large degree of reliance** can probably be placed on estimates .

7.3   If there is a **perfect linear relationship** between X and Y ($r = \pm 1$) then we can predict Y from any given value of X with **great confidence**.

7.4   If correlation is high (for example $r = 0.9$) the actual values will all lie quite close to the regression line and so predictions should not be far out. If correlation is below about 0.7, predictions will only give a very rough guide as to the likely value of Y.

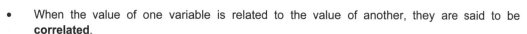

Chapter roundup

- When the value of one variable is related to the value of another, they are said to be **correlated**.

- Two variables might be **perfectly correlated**, **partly correlated** or **uncorrelated**. Correlation can be **positive** or **negative**.

- The **degree of correlation** between two variables is measured by the **Pearsonian** (product moment) **correlation coefficient, r**. The nearer r is to +1 or -1, the stronger the relationship.

- The **coefficient of determination, r^2**, measures the proportion of the total variation in the value of one variable that can be explained by the variation in the value of the other variable.

- **Spearman's rank correlation coefficient** is used when data is given in terms of order or rank rather than actual values.

- The **scattergraph method** involves the use of judgement to draw what seems to be a line of best fit through plotted data.

- **Linear regression analysis** (the **least squares method**) is one technique for estimating a line of best fit.

- Once an equation for a line of best fit has been determined, forecasts can be made.

- Like all forecasting techniques, the results obtained will not be wholly reliable. There are a number of factors which affect the reliability of forecasts made using regression analysis.

Quick quiz

1   .... means that low values of one variable are associated with low values of the other, and high values of one variable are associated with high values of the other.

2   .... means that low values of one variable are associated with high values of the other, and high values of one variable with low values of the other.

3
- Perfect positive correlation, r = ...
- Perfect negative correlation, r = ...
- No correlation, r = ...

The correlation coefficient, r, must always fall within the range .... to ....

4   If the correlation coefficient of a set of data is 0.95, what is the coefficient of determination and how is it interpreted?

5   Complete the following formula.

Coefficient of rank correlation, $R = 1 - \left[\dfrac{6\Sigma}{n(\quad)} \right]$

Where   n = ...
          d = ...

6   When should Spearman's rank correlation coefficient be used?

7   (a)   The equation of a straight line is given as Y = a + bX. Give two methods used for estimating the above equation.

   (b)   If Y = a + bX, it is best to use the regression of Y upon X where X is the dependent variable and Y is the independent variable.

   True ☐

   False ☐

8   List five factors affecting the reliability of regression analysis forecasts.

Answers to quick quiz

1   Positive correlation

2   Negative correlation

3   • r = +1
    • r = −1
    • r = 0

   The correlation coefficient, r, must always fall within the range −1 to +1.

4   Correlation coefficient = r = 0.95

   Coefficient of determination = r^2 = 0.95^2 = 0.9025 or 90.25%

   This tells us that over 90% of the variations in the dependent variable (Y) can be explained by variations in the independent variable, X.

5   $$R = 1 - \left[\frac{6\Sigma d^2}{n(n^2 - 1)} \right]$$

   where   n = number of pairs of data
           d = difference between the rankings in each set of data

6   When values of the relevant variables are given in terms of order or rank.

7   (a) • Scattergraph method (line of best fit)
        • Simple linear regression analysis

   (b) False. When using the regression of Y upon X, X is the independent variable and Y is the dependent variable (the value of Y will depend upon the value of X).

8   (a) It assumes a linear relationship exists between the two variables.

   (b) It assumes that the value of one variable, Y, can be predicted or estimated from the value of another variable, X.

   (c) It assumes that what happened in the past will provide a reliable guide to the future.

   (d) It assumes that the trend line can be extrapolated into the future.

   (e) The amount of data available.

Now try the following objective test questions

Question bank	Question numbers	Page
Paper-based exam	15, 16	284-285
Computer-based assessment	14	303

Appendix: Mathematical tables

LOGARITHMS

	0	1	2	3	4	5	6	7	8	9	1	2	3	4	5	6	7	8	9
10	0000	0043	0086	0128	0170						4	9	13	17	21	26	30	34	38
						0212	0253	0294	0334	0374	4	8	12	16	20	24	28	32	37
11	0414	0453	0492	0531	0569						4	8	12	15	19	23	27	31	35
						0607	0645	0682	0719	0755	4	7	11	15	19	22	26	30	33
12	0792	0828	0864	0899	0934	0969					3	7	11	14	18	21	25	28	32
							1004	1038	1072	1106	3	7	10	14	17	20	24	27	31
13	1139	1173	1206	1239	1271						3	7	10	13	16	20	23	26	30
						1303	1335	1367	1399	1430	3	7	10	12	16	19	22	25	29
14	1461	1492	1523	1553							3	6	9	12	15	18	21	24	28
					1584	1614	1644	1673	1703	1732	3	6	9	12	15	17	20	23	26
15	1761	1790	1818	1847	1875	1903					3	6	9	11	14	17	20	23	26
							1931	1959	1987	2014	3	5	8	11	14	16	19	22	25
16	2041	2068	2095	2122	2148						3	5	8	11	14	16	19	22	24
						2175	2201	2227	2253	2279	3	5	8	10	13	15	18	21	23
17	2304	2330	2355	2380	2405	2430					3	5	8	10	13	15	18	20	23
							2455	2480	2504	2529	2	5	7	10	12	15	17	19	22
18	2553	2577	2601	2625	2648						2	5	7	9	12	14	16	19	21
						2672	2695	2718	2742	2765	2	5	7	9	11	14	16	18	21
19	2788	2810	2833	2856	2878						2	4	7	9	11	13	16	18	20
						2900	2923	2945	2967	2989	2	4	6	8	11	13	15	17	19
20	3010	3032	3054	3075	3096	3118	3139	3160	3181	3201	2	4	6	8	11	13	15	17	19
21	3222	3243	3263	3284	3304	3324	3345	3365	3385	3404	2	4	6	8	10	12	14	16	18
22	3424	3444	3464	3483	3502	3522	3541	3560	3579	3598	2	4	6	8	10	12	14	15	17
23	3617	3636	3655	3674	3692	3711	3729	3747	3766	3784	2	4	6	7	9	11	13	15	17
24	3802	3820	3838	3856	3874	3892	3909	3927	3945	3962	2	4	5	7	9	11	12	14	16
25	3979	3997	4014	4031	4048	4065	4082	4099	4116	4133	2	3	5	7	9	10	12	14	15
26	4150	4166	4183	4200	4216	4232	4249	4265	4281	4298	2	3	5	7	8	10	11	13	15
27	4314	4330	4346	4362	4378	4393	4409	4425	4440	4456	2	3	5	6	8	9	11	13	14
28	4472	4487	4502	4518	4533	4548	4564	4579	4594	4609	2	3	5	6	8	9	11	12	14
29	4624	4639	4654	4669	4683	4698	4713	4728	4742	4757	1	3	4	6	7	9	10	12	13
30	4771	4786	4800	4814	4829	4843	4857	4871	4886	4900	1	3	4	6	7	9	10	11	13
31	4914	4928	4942	4955	4969	4983	4997	5011	5024	5038	1	3	4	6	7	8	10	11	12
32	5051	5065	5079	5092	5105	5119	5132	5145	5159	5172	1	3	4	5	7	8	9	11	12
33	5185	5198	5211	5224	5237	5250	5263	5276	5289	5302	1	3	4	5	6	8	9	10	12
34	5315	5328	5340	5353	5366	5378	5391	5403	5416	5428	1	3	4	5	6	8	9	10	11
35	5441	5453	5465	5478	5490	5502	5514	5527	5539	5551	1	2	4	5	6	7	9	10	11
36	5563	5575	5587	5599	5611	5623	5635	5647	5658	5670	1	2	4	5	6	7	8	10	11
37	5682	5694	5705	5717	5729	5740	5752	5763	5775	5786	1	2	3	5	6	7	8	9	10
38	5798	5809	5821	5832	5843	5855	5866	5877	5888	5899	1	2	3	5	6	7	8	9	10
39	5911	5922	5933	5944	5955	5966	5977	5988	5999	6010	1	2	3	4	5	7	8	9	10
40	6021	6031	6042	6053	6064	6075	6085	6096	6107	6117	1	2	3	4	5	6	8	9	10
41	6128	6138	6149	6160	6170	6180	6191	6201	6212	6222	1	2	3	4	5	6	7	8	9
42	6232	6243	6253	6263	6274	6284	6294	6304	6314	6325	1	2	3	4	5	6	7	8	9
43	6335	6345	6355	6365	6375	6385	6395	6405	6415	6425	1	2	3	4	5	6	7	8	9
44	6435	6444	6454	6464	6474	6484	6493	6503	6513	6522	1	2	3	4	5	6	7	8	9
45	6532	6542	6551	6561	6571	6580	6590	6599	6609	6618	1	2	3	4	5	6	7	8	9
46	6628	6637	6646	6656	6665	6675	6684	6693	6702	6712	1	2	3	4	5	6	7	7	8
47	6721	6730	6739	6749	6758	6767	6776	6785	6794	6803	1	2	3	4	5	5	6	7	8
48	6812	6821	6830	6839	6848	6857	6866	6875	6884	6893	1	2	3	4	4	5	6	7	8
49	6902	6911	6920	6928	6937	6946	6955	6964	6972	6981	1	2	3	4	4	5	6	7	8

LOGARITHMS

	0	1	2	3	4	5	6	7	8	9	1	2	3	4	5	6	7	8	9
50	6990	6998	7007	7016	7024	7033	7042	7050	7059	7067	1	2	3	3	4	5	6	7	8
51	7076	7084	7093	7101	7110	7118	7126	7135	7143	7152	1	2	3	3	4	5	6	7	8
52	7160	7168	7177	7185	7193	7202	7210	7218	7226	7235	1	2	2	3	4	5	6	7	7
53	7243	7251	7259	7267	7275	7284	7292	7300	7308	7316	1	2	2	3	4	5	6	6	7
54	7324	7332	7340	7348	7356	7364	7372	7380	7388	7396	1	2	2	3	4	5	6	6	7
55	7404	7412	7419	7427	7435	7443	7451	7459	7466	7474	1	2	2	3	4	5	5	6	7
56	7482	7490	7497	7505	7513	7520	7528	7536	7543	7551	1	2	2	3	4	5	5	6	7
57	7559	7566	7574	7582	7589	7597	7604	7612	7619	7627	1	2	2	3	4	5	5	6	7
58	7634	7642	7649	7657	7664	7672	7679	7686	7694	7701	1	1	2	3	4	4	5	6	7
59	7709	7716	7723	7731	7738	7745	7752	7760	7767	7774	1	1	2	3	4	4	5	6	7
60	7782	7789	7796	7803	7810	7818	7825	7832	7839	7846	1	1	2	3	4	4	5	6	6
61	7853	7860	7868	7875	7882	7889	7896	7903	7910	7917	1	1	2	3	4	4	5	6	6
62	7924	7931	7938	7945	7952	7959	7966	7973	7980	7987	1	1	2	3	3	4	5	6	6
63	7993	8000	8007	8014	8021	8028	8035	8041	8048	8055	1	1	2	3	3	4	5	5	6
64	8062	8069	8075	8082	8089	8096	8102	8109	8116	8122	1	1	2	3	3	4	5	5	6
65	8129	8136	8142	8149	8156	8162	8169	8176	8182	8189	1	1	2	3	3	4	5	5	6
66	8195	8202	8209	8215	8222	8228	8235	8241	8248	8254	1	1	2	3	3	4	5	5	6
67	8261	8267	8274	8280	8287	8293	8299	8306	8312	8319	1	1	2	3	3	4	5	5	6
68	8325	8331	8338	8344	8351	8357	8363	8370	8376	8382	1	1	2	3	3	4	4	5	6
69	8388	8395	8401	8407	8414	8420	8426	8432	8439	8445	1	1	2	2	3	4	4	5	6
70	8451	8457	8463	8470	8476	8482	8488	8494	8500	8506	1	1	2	2	3	4	4	5	6
71	8513	8519	8525	8531	8537	8543	8549	8555	8561	8567	1	1	2	2	3	4	4	5	5
72	8573	8579	8585	8591	8597	8603	8609	8615	8621	8627	1	1	2	2	3	4	4	5	5
73	8633	8639	8645	8651	8657	8663	8669	8675	8681	8686	1	1	2	2	3	4	4	5	5
74	8692	8698	8704	8710	8716	8722	8727	8733	8739	8745	1	1	2	2	3	4	4	5	5
75	8751	8756	8762	8768	8774	8779	8785	8791	8797	8802	1	1	2	2	3	3	4	5	5
76	8808	8814	8820	8825	8831	8837	8842	8848	8854	8859	1	1	2	2	3	3	4	5	5
77	8865	8871	8876	8882	8887	8893	8899	8904	8910	8915	1	1	2	2	3	3	4	4	5
78	8921	8927	8932	8938	8943	8949	8954	8960	8965	8971	1	1	2	2	3	3	4	4	5
79	8976	8982	8987	8993	8998	9004	9009	9015	9020	9025	1	1	2	2	3	3	4	4	5
80	9031	9036	9042	9047	9053	9058	9063	9069	9074	9079	1	1	2	2	3	3	4	4	5
81	9085	9090	9096	9101	9106	9112	9117	9122	9128	9133	1	1	2	2	3	3	4	4	5
82	9138	9143	9149	9154	9159	9165	9170	9175	9180	9186	1	1	2	2	3	3	4	4	5
83	9191	9196	9201	9206	9212	9217	9222	9227	9232	9238	1	1	2	2	3	3	4	4	5
84	9243	9248	9253	9258	9263	9269	9274	9279	9284	9289	1	1	2	2	3	3	4	4	5
85	9294	9299	9304	9309	9315	9320	9325	9330	9335	9340	1	1	2	2	3	3	4	4	5
86	9345	9350	9355	9360	9365	9370	9375	9380	9385	9390	1	1	2	2	3	3	4	4	5
87	9395	9400	9405	9410	9415	9420	9425	9430	9435	9440	0	1	1	2	2	3	3	4	4
88	9445	9450	9455	9460	9465	9469	9474	9479	9484	9489	0	1	1	2	2	3	3	4	4
89	9494	9499	9504	9509	9513	9518	9523	9528	9533	9538	0	1	1	2	2	3	3	4	4
90	9542	9547	9552	9557	9562	9566	9571	9576	9581	9586	0	1	1	2	2	3	3	4	4
91	9590	9595	9600	9605	9609	9614	9619	9624	9628	9633	0	1	1	2	2	3	3	4	4
92	9638	9643	9647	9652	9657	9661	9666	9671	9675	9680	0	1	1	2	2	3	3	4	4
93	9685	9689	9694	9699	9703	9708	9713	9717	9722	9727	0	1	1	2	2	3	3	4	4
94	9731	9736	9741	9745	9750	9754	9759	9763	9768	9773	0	1	1	2	2	3	3	4	4
95	9777	9782	9786	9791	9795	9800	9805	9809	9814	9818	0	1	1	2	2	3	3	4	4
96	9823	9827	9832	9836	9841	9845	9850	9854	9859	9863	0	1	1	2	2	3	3	4	4
97	9868	9872	9877	9881	9886	9890	9894	9899	9903	9908	0	1	1	2	2	3	3	4	4
98	9912	9917	9921	9926	9930	9934	9939	9943	9948	9952	0	1	1	2	2	3	3	4	4
99	9956	9961	9965	9969	9974	9978	9983	9987	9991	9996	0	1	1	2	2	3	3	3	4

TABLES

AREA UNDER THE NORMAL CURVE

This table gives the area under the normal curve between the mean and the point Z standard deviations above the mean. The corresponding area for deviations below the mean can be found by symmetry.

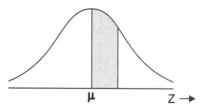

$Z=\dfrac{(x-\mu)}{\sigma}$	0.00	0.01	0.02	0.03	0.04	0.05	0.06	0.07	0.08	0.09
0.0	.0000	.0040	.0080	.0120	.0160	.0199	.0239	.0279	.0319	.0359
0.1	.0398	.0438	.0478	.0517	.0557	.0596	.0636	.0675	.0714	.0753
0.2	.0793	.0832	.0871	.0910	.0948	.0987	.1026	.1064	.1103	.1141
0.3	.1179	.1217	.1255	.1293	.1331	.1368	.1406	.1443	.1480	.1517
0.4	.1554	.1591	.1628	.1664	.1700	.1736	.1772	.1808	.1844	.1879
0.5	.1915	.1950	.1985	.2019	.2054	.2088	.2123	.2157	.2190	.2224
0.6	.2257	.2291	.2324	.2357	.2389	.2422	.2454	.2486	.2517	.2549
0.7	.2580	.2611	.2642	.2673	.2704	.2734	.2764	.2794	.2823	.2852
0.8	.2881	.2910	.2939	.2967	.2995	.3023	.3051	.3078	.3106	.3133
0.9	.3159	.3186	.3212	.3238	.3264	.3289	.3315	.3340	.3365	.3389
1.0	.3413	.3438	.3461	.3485	.3508	.3531	.3554	.3577	.3599	.3621
1.1	.3643	.3665	.3686	.3708	.3729	.3749	.3770	.3790	.3810	.3830
1.2	.3849	.3869	.3888	.3907	.3925	.3944	.3962	.3980	.3997	.4015
1.3	.4032	.4049	.4066	.4082	.4099	.4115	.4131	.4147	.4162	.4177
1.4	.4192	.4207	.4222	.4236	.4251	.4265	.4279	.4292	.4306	.4319
1.5	.4332	.4345	.4357	.4370	.4382	.4394	.4406	.4418	.4429	.4441
1.6	.4452	.4463	.4474	.4484	.4495	.4505	.4515	.4525	.4535	.4545
1.7	.4554	.4564	.4573	.4582	.4591	.4599	.4608	.4616	.4625	.4633
1.8	.4641	.4649	.4656	.4664	.4671	.4678	.4686	.4693	.4699	.4706
1.9	.4713	.4719	.4726	.4732	.4738	.4744	.4750	.4756	.4761	.4767
2.0	.4772	.4778	.4783	.4788	.4793	.4798	.4803	.4808	.4812	.4817
2.1	.4821	.4826	.4830	.4834	.4838	.4842	.4846	.4850	.4854	.4857
2.2	.4861	.4864	.4868	.4871	.4875	.4878	.4881	.4884	.4887	.4890
2.3	.4893	.4896	.4898	.4901	.4904	.4906	.4909	.4911	.4913	.4916
2.4	.4918	.4920	.4922	.4925	.4927	.4929	.4931	.4932	.4934	.4936
2.5	.4938	.4940	.4941	.4943	.4945	.4946	.4948	.4949	.4951	.4952
2.6	.4953	.4955	.4956	.4957	.4959	.4960	.4961	.4962	.4963	.4964
2.7	.4965	.4966	.4967	.4968	.4969	.4970	.4971	.4972	.4973	.4974
2.8	.4974	.4975	.4976	.4977	.4977	.4978	.4979	.4979	.4980	.4981
2.9	.4981	.4982	.4982	.4983	.4984	.4984	.4985	.4985	.4986	.4986
3.0	.49865	.4987	.4987	.4988	.4988	.4989	.4989	.4989	.4990	.4990
3.1	.49903	.4991	.4991	.4991	.4992	.4992	.4992	.4992	.4993	.4993
3.2	.49931	.4993	.4994	.4994	.4994	.4994	.4994	.4995	.4995	.4995
3.3	.49952	.4995	.4995	.4996	.4996	.4996	.4996	.4996	.4996	.4997
3.4	.49966	.4997	.4997	.4997	.4997	.4997	.4997	.4997	.4997	.4998
3.5	.49977									

PRESENT VALUE TABLE

Present value of £1 ie $(1+r)^{-n}$ where r = interest rate, n = number of periods until payment or receipt.

Periods					Interest rates (r)					
(n)	1%	2%	3%	4%	5%	6%	7%	8%	9%	10%
1	0.990	0.980	0.971	0.962	0.952	0.943	0.935	0.926	0.917	0.909
2	0.980	0.961	0.943	0.925	0.907	0.890	0.873	0.857	0.842	0.826
3	0.971	0.942	0.915	0.889	0.864	0.840	0.816	0.794	0.772	0.751
4	0.961	0.924	0.888	0.855	0.823	0.792	0.763	0.735	0.708	0.683
5	0.951	0.906	0.863	0.822	0.784	0.747	0.713	0.681	0.650	0.621
6	0.942	0.888	0.837	0.790	0.746	0.705	0.666	0.630	0.596	0.564
7	0.933	0.871	0.813	0.760	0.711	0.665	0.623	0.583	0.547	0.513
8	0.923	0.853	0.789	0.731	0.677	0.627	0.582	0.540	0.502	0.467
9	0.914	0.837	0.766	0.703	0.645	0.592	0.544	0.500	0.460	0.424
10	0.905	0.820	0.744	0.676	0.614	0.558	0.508	0.463	0.422	0.386
11	0.896	0.804	0.722	0.650	0.585	0.527	0.475	0.429	0.388	0.350
12	0.887	0.788	0.701	0.625	0.557	0.497	0.444	0.397	0.356	0.319
13	0.879	0.773	0.681	0.601	0.530	0.469	0.415	0.368	0.326	0.290
14	0.870	0.758	0.661	0.577	0.505	0.442	0.388	0.340	0.299	0.263
15	0.861	0.743	0.642	0.555	0.481	0.417	0.362	0.315	0.275	0.239
16	0.853	0.728	0.623	0.534	0.458	0.394	0.339	0.292	0.252	0.218
17	0.844	0.714	0.605	0.513	0.436	0.371	0.317	0.270	0.231	0.198
18	0.836	0.700	0.587	0.494	0.416	0.350	0.296	0.250	0.212	0.180
19	0.828	0.686	0.570	0.475	0.396	0.331	0.277	0.232	0.194	0.164
20	0.820	0.673	0.554	0.456	0.377	0.312	0.258	0.215	0.178	0.149

Periods					Interest rates (r)					
(n)	11%	12%	13%	14%	15%	16%	17%	18%	19%	20%
1	0.901	0.893	0.885	0.877	0.870	0.862	0.855	0.847	0.840	0.833
2	0.812	0.797	0.783	0.769	0.756	0.743	0.731	0.718	0.706	0.694
3	0.731	0.712	0.693	0.675	0.658	0.641	0.624	0.609	0.593	0.579
4	0.659	0.636	0.613	0.592	0.572	0.552	0.534	0.516	0.499	0.482
5	0.593	0.567	0.543	0.519	0.497	0.476	0.456	0.437	0.419	0.402
6	0.535	0.507	0.480	0.456	0.432	0.410	0.390	0.370	0.352	0.335
7	0.482	0.452	0.425	0.400	0.376	0.354	0.333	0.314	0.296	0.279
8	0.434	0.404	0.376	0.351	0.327	0.305	0.285	0.266	0.249	0.233
9	0.391	0.361	0.333	0.308	0.284	0.263	0.243	0.225	0.209	0.194
10	0.352	0.322	0.295	0.270	0.247	0.227	0.208	0.191	0.176	0.162
11	0.317	0.287	0.261	0.237	0.215	0.195	0.178	0.162	0.148	0.135
12	0.286	0.257	0.231	0.208	0.187	0.168	0.152	0.137	0.124	0.112
13	0.258	0.229	0.204	0.182	0.163	0.145	0.130	0.116	0.104	0.093
14	0.232	0.205	0.181	0.160	0.141	0.125	0.111	0.099	0.088	0.078
15	0.209	0.183	0.160	0.140	0.123	0.108	0.095	0.084	0.074	0.065
16	0.188	0.163	0.141	0.123	0.107	0.093	0.081	0.071	0.062	0.054
17	0.170	0.146	0.125	0.108	0.093	0.080	0.069	0.060	0.052	0.045
18	0.153	0.130	0.111	0.095	0.081	0.069	0.059	0.051	0.044	0.038
19	0.138	0.116	0.098	0.083	0.070	0.060	0.051	0.043	0.037	0.031
20	0.124	0.104	0.087	0.073	0.061	0.051	0.043	0.037	0.031	0.026

CUMULATIVE PRESENT VALUE TABLE

This table shows the present value of £1 per annum, receivable or payable at the end of each year for n years $\frac{1-(1+r)^{-n}}{r}$.

Periods						Interest rates (r)				
(n)	**1%**	**2%**	**3%**	**4%**	**5%**	**6%**	**7%**	**8%**	**9%**	**10%**
1	0.990	0.980	0.971	0.962	0.952	0.943	0.935	0.926	0.917	0.909
2	1.970	1.942	1.913	1.886	1.859	1.833	1.808	1.783	1.759	1.736
3	2.941	2.884	2.829	2.775	2.723	2.673	2.624	2.577	2.531	2.487
4	3.902	3.808	3.717	3.630	3.546	3.465	3.387	3.312	3.240	3.170
5	4.853	4.713	4.580	4.452	4.329	4.212	4.100	3.993	3.890	3.791
6	5.795	5.601	5.417	5.242	5.076	4.917	4.767	4.623	4.486	4.355
7	6.728	6.472	6.230	6.002	5.786	5.582	5.389	5.206	5.033	4.868
8	7.652	7.325	7.020	6.733	6.463	6.210	5.971	5.747	5.535	5.335
9	8.566	8.162	7.786	7.435	7.108	6.802	6.515	6.247	5.995	5.759
10	9.471	8.983	8.530	8.111	7.722	7.360	7.024	6.710	6.418	6.145
11	10.368	9.787	9.253	8.760	8.306	7.887	7.499	7.139	6.805	6.495
12	11.255	10.575	9.954	9.385	8.863	8.384	7.943	7.536	7.161	6.814
13	12.134	11.348	10.635	9.986	9.394	8.853	8.358	7.904	7.487	7.103
14	13.004	12.106	11.296	10.563	9.899	9.295	8.745	8.244	7.786	7.367
15	13.865	12.849	11.938	11.118	10.380	9.712	9.108	8.559	8.061	7.606
16	14.718	13.578	12.561	11.652	10.838	10.106	9.447	8.851	8.313	7.824
17	15.562	14.292	13.166	12.166	11.274	10.477	9.763	9.122	8.544	8.022
18	16.398	14.992	13.754	12.659	11.690	10.828	10.059	9.372	8.756	8.201
19	17.226	15.679	14.324	13.134	12.085	11.158	10.336	9.604	8.950	8.365
20	18.046	16.351	14.878	13.590	12.462	11.470	10.594	9.818	9.129	8.514

Periods									Interest rates (r)	
(n)	**11%**	**12%**	**13%**	**14%**	**15%**	**16%**	**17%**	**18%**	**19%**	**20%**
1	0.901	0.893	0.885	0.877	0.870	0.862	0.855	0.847	0.840	0.833
2	1.713	1.690	1.668	1.647	1.626	1.605	1.585	1.566	1.547	1.528
3	2.444	2.402	2.361	2.322	2.283	2.246	2.210	2.174	2.140	2.106
4	3.102	3.037	2.974	2.914	2.855	2.798	2.743	2.690	2.639	2.589
5	3.696	3.605	3.517	3.433	3.352	3.274	3.199	3.127	3.058	2.991
6	4.231	4.111	3.998	3.889	3.784	3.685	3.589	3.498	3.410	3.326
7	4.712	4.564	4.423	4.288	4.160	4.039	3.922	3.812	3.706	3.605
8	5.146	4.968	4.799	4.639	4.487	4.344	4.207	4.078	3.954	3.837
9	5.537	5.328	5.132	4.946	4.772	4.607	4.451	4.303	4.163	4.031
10	5.889	5.650	5.426	5.216	5.019	4.833	4.659	4.494	4.339	4.192
11	6.207	5.938	5.687	5.453	5.234	5.029	4.836	4.656	4.486	4.327
12	6.492	6.194	5.918	5.660	5.421	5.197	4.988	4.793	4.611	4.439
13	6.750	6.424	6.122	5.842	5.583	5.342	5.118	4.910	4.715	4.533
14	6.982	6.628	6.302	6.002	5.724	5.468	5.229	5.008	4.802	4.611
15	7.191	6.811	6.462	6.142	5.847	5.575	5.324	5.092	4.876	4.675
16	7.379	6.974	6.604	6.265	5.954	5.668	5.405	5.162	4.938	4.730
17	7.549	7.120	6.729	6.373	6.047	5.749	5.475	5.222	4.990	4.775
18	7.702	7.250	6.840	6.467	6.128	5.818	5.534	5.273	5.033	4.812
19	7.839	7.366	6.938	6.550	6.198	5.877	5.584	5.316	5.070	4.843
20	7.963	7.469	7.025	6.623	6.259	5.929	5.628	5.353	5.101	4.870

Appendix: mathematical tables

Probability

A∪B = A **or** B. A∩B = A **and** B (overlap). P(B/A) = probability of B, **given** A.

Rules of addition

If A and B are *mutually exclusive*: $\qquad$ P(A∪B) = P(A) + P(B)
If A and B are **not** mutually exclusive: $\qquad$ P(A∪B) = P(A) + P(B) − P(A∩B)

Rules of multiplication

If A and B are *independent*: $\qquad$ P(A∩B) = P(A) * P(B)
If A and B are **not** independent: $\qquad$ P(A∩B) = P(A) * P(B/A)

E(X) = expected value = probability * payoff

Quadratic equations

If $aX^2 + bX + c = 0$ is the general quadratic equation, then the two solutions (roots) are given

by $X = \dfrac{-b \pm \sqrt{b^2 - 4ac}}{2a}$

Descriptive statistics

Arithmetic mean

$\bar{x} = \dfrac{\sum x}{n}$ or $\bar{x} = \dfrac{\sum fx}{\sum f}$

Standard deviation

$\sqrt{\dfrac{\sum (x - \bar{x})^2}{n}}$

$SD = \sqrt{\dfrac{\sum fx^2}{\sum f} - \bar{x}^2}$ (frequency distribution)

Index numbers

Price relative = $100 * P_1/P_0$ $\qquad$ Quantity relative = $100 * Q_1/Q_0$

Price: $\qquad \sum W * P_1/P_0 / \sum W * 100$ where W denotes weights

Quantity: $\qquad \sum W * Q_1/Q_0 / \sum W * 100$ where W denotes weights

Time series

Additive model: Series = Trend + Seasonal + Random

Multiplicative model: Series = Trend * Seasonal * Random

Linear regression and correlation

The linear regression equation of Y on X is given by:

Y $\quad$ = a + bX *or*

$Y - \bar{Y}$ = b(X − $\bar{X}$), where

b $\quad = \dfrac{\text{Covariance (XY)}}{\text{Variance (X)}} = \dfrac{n\sum XY - (\sum X)(\sum Y)}{n\sum X^2 - (\sum X)^2}$

and a = $\bar{Y} - b\bar{X}$,

or solve $\qquad \Sigma Y = na + b\Sigma X$

$\qquad\qquad \Sigma XY = a\Sigma X + b\Sigma X^2$

Coefficient of correlation (r)

$$r = \frac{\text{Covariance (XY)}}{\sqrt{\text{VAR(X).VAR(Y)}}}$$

$$= \frac{n\sum XY - (\sum X)(\sum Y)}{\sqrt{\left\{n\sum X^2 - (\sum X)^2\right\}\left\{n\sum Y^2 - (\sum Y)^2\right\}}}$$

$$R(\text{rank}) = 1 - \left[6\sum d^2/n(n^2-1)\right]$$

Financial mathematics

Compound Interest (Values and Sums)

Future Value of S_1 of a sum X, invested for n periods, compounded at r% interest:

$$S = X[1+r]^n$$

Annuity

Present value of an annuity of £1 per annum receivable or payable, for n years, commencing in one year, discounted at r% per annum:

$$PV = \frac{1}{r}\left[1 - \frac{1}{[1+r]^n}\right]$$

Perpetuity

Present value of £1 per annum, payable or receivable in perpetuity, commencing in one year discounted at r% per annum

$$PV = \frac{1}{r}$$

Question bank
(paper-based
exam)

1   LONG WINTER

(a) What is 23% of £5,000?   **2 Marks**

(b) What is £18 as a percentage of £45?   **2 Marks**

(c) Deirdre Fowler now earns £25,000 per annum after an annual increase of 2.5%. What was her annual salary to the nearest £ before the increase?   **4 Marks**

(d) If purchases at Watkins Ltd are £200,000 in 20X0 and there was a percentage decrease of 5% in 20X1, what are purchases in 20X1?   **3 Marks**

(e) An accountant charges £X per hour to which value added tax of 17.5% is added. If her final hourly charge is £235, what is the value of X?   **4 Marks**

                                                                          Total Marks = 15

2   SOLVE

(a) Solve the following simultaneous equations.

$x - y = -9$
$9x - 13y = -97$

x =   y =   **4 Marks**

(b) The sum of the squares of two positive numbers (x and y) is 890, and the difference between the two numbers is 4. Find a quadratic equation in terms of either x or y.

                                                                          4 Marks

(c) A rectangle has a perimeter of 44 metres and an area of 112 square metres. Find a quadratic equation in terms of either length 'a' or breadth 'b'.

                                                                          4 Marks

(d) Solve the following quadratic equation.

$-3x^2 + 6x + 24 = 0$

x =   or   **4 Marks**

                                                                          Total Marks = 16

3   RODEO ROUND-UP LTD

(a) Rodeo Round-up Ltd is a company of circus performers which tours the country. Box office takings for the recent month have been as follows.

Venue	Box office receipts £	Box office receipts to nearest £100
Clapham	3,480	A
West Riding	5,278	-
Weston-Super-Mare	1,356	-
Badminton	2,542	-
Huntingdon	3,174	B
Epsom	2,603	-
Ascot	1,539	-
Wincanton	4,562	-
Reading	4,328	-
	28,862	C

Required:

(i) Round the box office receipts to the nearest £100 and state the values of A, B and C.

A = 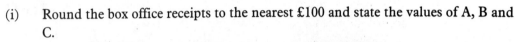 B = C = **3 Marks**

(ii) Calculate the maximum possible error in the total of the rounded data.

2 Marks

(iii) Calculate the maximum possible percentage error in the total of the rounded data.

2 Marks

(b) In the formula X = P – QR/S, the variables are estimated as follows, subject to the possible errors stated below.

Variable	Estimate	Maximum error (±%)
P	560	5
Q	400	1
R	25	1
S	20	4

Required:

(i) State the maximum and minimum possible values of P

Maximum =

Minimum = **2 Marks**

(ii) Calculate the maximum possible value of QR/S, giving your answer to two decimal places.

4 Marks

(iii) Calculate the maximum possible value of X, giving your answer correct to two decimal places.

4 Marks

Total Marks = 17

4   SAMPLING

(a) Sampling methods are frequently used for the collection of data. Five commonly used types of samples are (A) simple random, (B) stratified random, (C) systematic, (D) cluster and (E) quota. State which of these sample types is being described in the following situations.

(i) One school in an area is selected at random and then all pupils in that school are surveyed.

Type of sample is ▮▮▮▮▮▮   **2 Marks**

(ii) The local authority has a list of all pupils in the area and the sample is selected in such a way that all pupils have an equal probability of selection.

Type of sample is ▮▮▮▮▮▮   **2 Marks**

(iii) An interviewer surveys pupils emerging from every school in the area, attempting to question them randomly but in line with specified numbers of boys and girls in the various age groups.

Type of sample is ▮▮▮▮▮▮   **2 Marks**

(iv) The local authority has a list of all pupils in the selected area, categorised according to their gender and age. The sample selected is chosen randomly from the various categories, in proportion to their sizes.

Type of sample is ▮▮▮▮▮▮   **2 Marks**

(v) The local authority has a list of all pupils in the selected area. The first pupil is selected randomly from the list and then every 100th pupil thereafter is selected for the survey.

Type of sample is ▮▮▮▮▮▮   **2 Marks**

(b) Suggest, using no more than 30 words in each case, a suitable sampling frame for each of the following situations in which statistical data will be collected.

(i) An investigation into the reactions of workers in a large factory to new proposals for shift working.

2 Marks

(ii) A survey about the relevance and quality of the teaching received by students at a college for their professional examinations.

2 Marks

(iii) An enquiry into the use of home computers by the inhabitants of a large city.

2 Marks

Total Marks = 16

273

BPP
PUBLISHING

5   PARROTS LTD

The distribution of average weekly wages paid to direct labour employees at the factory of Parrots Ltd is as follows.

Weekly average wage £	Number of employees	Frequency density	Cumulative frequency
51 and < 61	13	A	
61 and < 66	12	B	
66 and < 71	16	C	
71 and < 76	21		E
76 and < 81	25		F
81 and < 86	20		
86 and < 91	14		
91 and< 101	9	D	G

Required:

(a) Using a standard interval size of £5, calculate the frequency densities corresponding to the letters A, B, C and D.

A =

B =

C =

D =   **4 Marks**

(b) Illustrate the data given above by means of a histogram.

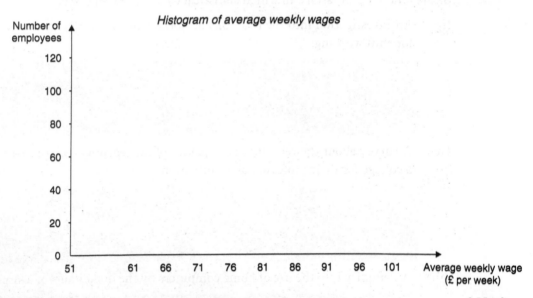

(c) Calculate cumulative frequencies corresponding to the letters E, F and G as shown in the table above.

E =

F =

G =   **3 Marks**

... the data given above by means of an ogive.

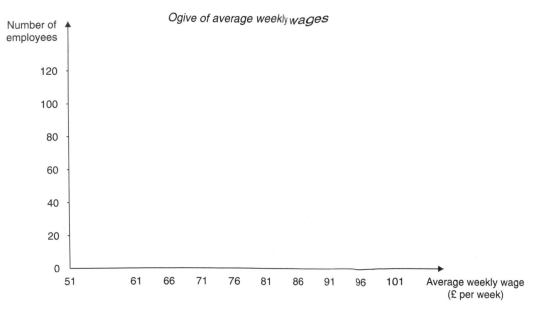

4 Marks
Total Marks = 15

6   **JOURNEY TIMES**

(a)   Give one advantage and one disadvantage of the mean, the median and the mode. In each case you may use up to 20 words.

Mean

Advantage

1 Mark

Disadvantage

1 Mark

Median

Advantage

1 Mark

Disadvantage

1 Mark

Mode

Advantage

1 Mark

Disadvantage

1 Mark

(b) Journey times to work of employees of a company were as follows.

	Time Minutes		No of employees
	less than	10	14
10 but	" "	20	26
20 "	" "	30	64
30 "	" "	40	46
40 "	" "	50	28
50 "	" "	60	16
60 "	" "	80	8
80 "	" "	100	4

Required:

(i) Calculate the mean journey time, giving your answer correct to two correct decimal places.

⬛⬛⬛⬛⬛ minutes   **4 Marks**

(ii) If the median is known to be 30 minutes and the mode 27 minutes, interpret the values of the mean, median and mode using no more than 30 words in each case.

Mean

⬛⬛⬛⬛⬛⬛⬛⬛⬛⬛⬛

                                                                    2 Marks

Median

⬛⬛⬛⬛⬛⬛⬛⬛⬛⬛⬛

                                                                    2 Marks

Mode

⬛⬛⬛⬛⬛⬛⬛⬛⬛⬛⬛

                                                                    2 Marks

(iii) In no more than 20 words explain why the three averages take different values with the mode being smallest and the mean being largest.

⬛⬛⬛⬛⬛⬛⬛⬛⬛⬛⬛

                                                                    1 Mark

                                                        Total Marks = 17

7   JELLY BEANS

The director of a medium-sized company has decided to analyse the salaries that are paid to staff. The frequency distribution of salaries that are currently being paid is as follows.

	Number of staff (frequency)	Cumulative frequency
Under 10	16	
10 to under 20	30	
20 to under 30	34	A
30 to under 40	22	
40 to under 50	10	
50 to under 70	5	
70 and over	3	B

Records from five years ago include the following statistics about salaries that were paid *then*.

Median salary = £17,000   Quartile deviation = £6,200

(a) Calculate the cumulative frequencies represented by the values A and B shown in the table above.

A =    **1 Mark**

B =   **1 Mark**

(b) Plot the ogive of the distribution on the axis provided below.

Ogive of current salaries paid to members of staff

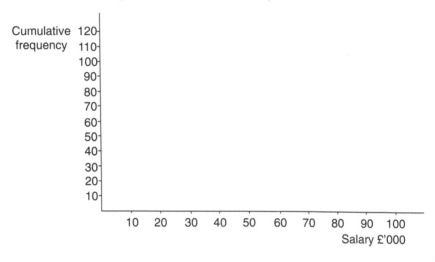

3 Marks

(c) Use your graph to estimate the following values.

Median =   **2 Marks**

Upper quartile =   **1 Mark**

Lower quartile =   **1 Mark**

Semi-interquartile range =   **1 Mark**

(d) Using no more than 30 words, interpret the value estimated for the median and compare it to the median value five years ago.

3 Marks

(e) Using no more than 30 words, interpret the value estimated for the semi-interquartile range and compare it to the semi-interquartile value five years ago.

3 Marks

Total marks = 16

8 STUART LTD

Stuart Ltd wishes to construct a price index for three commodities, A, B and C.

	20X0	*Prices relative to 20X0 (%)*	
	Quantities	*20X1*	*20X2*
A	5,000	100	110
B	6,000	108	115
C	3,000	90	100

Required:

(a) Calculate the weighted average of price relative index for 20X1 with base 20X0 using 20X0 quantities as weights. Give your answer to one decimal place.

4 Marks

(b) Calculate the weighted average of price relative index for 20X2 with base 20X0 using 20X0 quantities as weights. Give your answer to one decimal place.

4 Marks

(c) If the price index for 20X3 were 112, interpret this value using no more than 20 words.

2 Marks

(d) If you were to change from a base weighted price index to one with current weights, what change (if any) would you generally expect to observe in the value of the index?

(Give your answer in no more than 15 words)

2 Marks

(e) In no more than 40 words explain the answer you have given in (d).

3 Marks

(f) In no more than 20 words each, give one advantage and one disadvantage of using base year weights.

Advantage

1 Mark

Disadvantage

1 Mark

Total Marks = 17

9 ACE

Calculate the following probabilities, giving all answers correct to 3 significant figures.

(a) Drawing two aces from a pack of 52 playing cards in two successive draws (with and without replacement).

With replacement   **1 Mark**

Without replacement   **1 Mark**

(b) Drawing the ace of hearts and the ace of spades in that order (assuming replacement).

2 Marks

(c) It is assumed that home, car and television ownership are independent. Selecting from a list of respondents to a questionnaire used in a sample survey it was found that 50% owned their own homes, 60% owned a car and 90% had a television set. The probability that a respondent who owned:

(i) his home and a car =   **1 Mark**

(ii) all three of the above assets =   **1 Mark**

(iii) none of the above assets =   **2 Marks**

(d) Suppose that 50% of respondents owned their own homes and 60% owned a car. In addition, it was found that the percentage of home owners who owned a car was 80%.

(i) Find the percentage of car owners amongst those respondents who do not own their own home.

4 Marks

(ii) If a car owner is selected at random, find the probability that he/she is also a home owner.

4 Marks

Total Marks = 16

10 BATTERIES

A company produces batteries whose lifetimes are normally distributed with a mean of 100 hours. It is known that 96% of the batteries last at least 40 hours. Throughout this question all answers should be given correct to one decimal place.

(a) If $P(z > a) = 0.96$, use normal distribution tables to find the value of 'a'.

a =   **3 Marks**

(b) Estimate the standard deviation lifetime.

4 Marks

(c) Calculate the percentage of batteries that will last less than 57 hours.

3 Marks

(d) The company is liable to replace any battery which lasts for less than 40 hours. The company wishes to reduce the percentage of defective batteries from the current level of 4% to 2%.

    (i) Use normal tables to find the value 'b' such that $P(z < b) = 2\%$.

3 Marks

    (ii) The company can use a chemical procedure which changes the values of the mean and standard deviation. If the standard deviation is set at 35 hours, find the mean lifetime which will reduce the percentage of defectives to 2%.

4 Marks

Total Marks = 17

11   HOUND CAMPING LTD

(a) The treasurer of Hound Camping Ltd needed to invest some surplus cash. He decided to make the following investments. Calculate the interest earned on each of the following investments (correct to the nearest £).

    (i) £8,000 was placed in a bank deposit account for three years. The expected annual rate of interest is 11%, calculated yearly.

2 Marks

    (ii) £15,000 was placed in a savings account for five years, with interest added yearly at 14%.

2 Marks

    (iii) £6,000 was placed in an account for four years where the annual interest rate is expected to be 10% for the first two years and 15% in years 3 and 4, with interest added at the end of each year.

3 Marks

(b) The treasurer is also considering three further investments A, B and C. In each case calculate the effective annual rate of interest to 2 decimal places.

    (i) Investment A would last for three years, and pay interest at a nominal rate of 10.5%. Compound interest would be added every half year.

3 Marks

    (ii) Investment B would last for five years, with a nominal interest rate of 12%, payable monthly.

3 Marks

    (iii) Investment C would last for four years, with a nominal interest rate of 12%, payable quarterly.

3 Marks

Total Marks = 17

DAISY HOOF LTD

Daisy Hoof Ltd is considering a project to purchase some equipment which would generate the following cash flows.

Year	Cash flow £
0	(50,000)
1	18,000
2	25,000
3	15,000
4	10,000

The estimated trade-in value of the equipment, which is £2,000, has not been included in the cash flows above.

The company has a cost of capital of 16%.

Required:

(a) Complete the following table by filling in the values represented by letters. Calculate present values to the nearest £.

Year	Net cash flow £	Discount factor 16%	Present value £
0	..	B	
1	..	..	D
2	..	..	E
3	..	C	
4	A	..	
		Net Present Value =	F

A = _____   **1 Mark**

B = _____   **1 Mark**

C = _____   **1 Mark**

D = _____   **1 Mark**

E = _____   **1 Mark**

F = _____   **2 Marks**

(b) The company wishes to calculate the internal rate of return of the project and in order to do this the net present value at a different rates of interest must be calculated. Calculate the net present value to the nearest £ using a discount rate of 18%.

4 Marks

(c) Estimate the internal rate of return to one decimal place using the formula

$$IRR = R_1 + [\frac{NPV_1}{NPV_1 - NPV_2} \times (R_2 - R_1)]\%$$

IRR = _____   **3 Marks**

(d) In no more than 20 words, define the internal rate of return.

2 Marks

Total Marks = 16

13   **SAVINGS VS. BORROWING (Pilot paper - amended)**

A retailer is facing increasing competition from new shops that are opening in his area. He thinks that if he does not modernise his premises, he will lose sales. A local builder has estimated that the cost of modernising the shop will be £40,000 if the work is started now. The retailer is not sure whether to borrow the money and modernise the premises now, or to save up and have the work carried out when he has sufficient funds in the future. Current forecasts show that if he delays the work for three years, the cost of the modernisation is likely to rise by 4% per annum.

Investigations have revealed that, if he borrows, he will have to pay interest at the rate of 3% per quarter, but if he saves the money himself he will only earn 2% per quarter.

Required:

(a) The retailer borrows £40,000 at 3% per quarter, and repays £X at the end of each quarter for three years.

   (i)   Use tables to find the present value of the repayments as a function of X.

   3 Marks

   (ii) Find the value of X to the nearest £.

   2 Marks

(b) If the retailer decides to save money at 2% per quarter so that he has sufficient funds to carry out the work in three years' time, complete the following shaded boxes.

   (i)   The cost of modernisation in three years' time correct to 2 decimal places.

   2 Marks

   (ii) If twelve instalments of £Y are invested, the first being paid immediately, use tables to find the present value of the instalments as a function of Y.

   3 Marks

   (iii) Use tables to find the value of Y to the nearest £10.

   3 Marks

(c) (i)   On the basis of the results that you have calculated above, what would you advise the retailer to do? (Tick as appropriate).

   Modernise now

   Save and modernise later

   2 Marks

(..) In no more than *20* words, state one reservation that you have about the course of action you have recommended in (c)(i) above.

2 Marks

Total Marks = 17

14 HOPWOOD TRENDS LTD

The accountant at Hopwood Trends Ltd has carried out a time series analysis of quarterly sales, calculating the moving average trend and average seasonal variations using the additive method. She has only partially completed this analysis. The calculations carried out so far are shown in the following table.

Year	Quarter	Sales	Moving total of 4 quarters' sales	Moving average of 4 quarters' sales	Trend	Seasonal variation
20X2	1	200				
	2	110				
			870	217.5		
	3	320			219	+101
			884	221.0		
	4	240			222	+18
			892	223.0		
20X3	1	214			225	−11
			906	226.5		
	2	118			229	−111
			926	231.5		
	3	334			232	+102
			932	233.0		
	4	260			234	+26
			938	234.5		
20X4	1	220			235	−15
			A	C		
	2	124			E	F
			B	D		
	3	340				
	4	278				

(a) Complete the table by finding the missing values indicated by the letters. All answers should be correct to the nearest whole number except for C and D which should be correct to one decimal place.

A =   **1 Mark**

B =   **1 Mark**

C =   **1 Mark**

D =   **1 Mark**

E =   **2 Marks**

F =   **1 Mark**

(b) Complete the following table to calculate the seasonal components. I a. represented by letters, giving your answers to one decimal place throughout.

Year	Quarter 1	2	3	4	Total
20X2			..	..	
20X3	..	..	..	..	
20X4	..	..			
Average seasonal variation	..	..	..	..	G
Adjustment	H	..	..	..	..
Adjusted seasonal variation	I	J	K	L	

G =   **1 Mark**

H =   **1 Mark**

I =   **1 Mark**

J =   **1 Mark**

K =   **1 Mark**

L =   **1 Mark**

(c) Seasonally adjust the sales for the fourth quarter of 20X4.

2 Marks

(d) If the predicted trend for the first quarter in 20X5 is 245, forecast the actual sales.

2 Marks

Total Marks = 17

15 SMALL COMPANY

A small company has recorded the following data on volumes and costs of production for the last ten months.

X = Production ('000 units)	10	4	6	9	10	8	5	7	11	12
Y = Costs (£'000)	15	11	12	19	22	20	16	13	24	20

	Production	Costs	
Sums	$\Sigma X = 82$	$\Sigma Y = 172$	$\Sigma XY = 1,492$
Sums of squares	$\Sigma X^2 = 736$	$\Sigma Y^2 = 3,136$	

Required:

(a) If the regression equation of costs (Y) on production (X) = Y = a + bX, calculate the following.

(i) Calculate the value of b to 4 decimal places.

4 Marks

(ii) Calculate the value of a to 2 decimal places.

2 Marks

(b) If the regression equation based on the data given above was calculated to be Y = 7 + 1.5X with a product moment correlation coefficient of 0.8, answer the following questions.

(i) What would the fixed costs of the factory be?

2 Marks

(ii)   Plot the regression line Y = 7 + 1.5X on the axes provided.

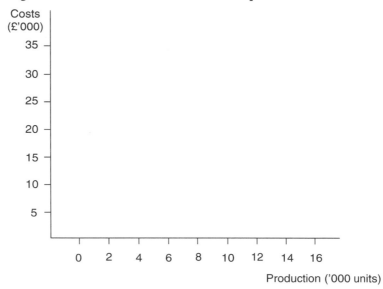

3 Marks

(iii)   Predict the total production costs for next month if an output volume of 10,000 units is forecast.

2 Marks

(iv)   Give two reasons (using no more than 20 words each) why the predicted production costs that you have calculated in (iii) above are likely to be reliable.

Reason 1

2 Marks

Reason 2

2 Marks

Total Marks = 17

16   JAM ROLY POLY (Pilot paper - amended)

A company is building a model in order to forecast total costs based on the level of output. The following data is available for last year.

Month	Output '000 units (X)	Costs £000 (Y)
January	16	170
February	20	240
March	23	260
April	25	300
May	25	280
June	19	230
July	16	200
August	12	160
September	19	240
October	25	290
November	28	350
December	12	200

Required:

(a) Plot a scattergraph of costs on output using the axes provided below.

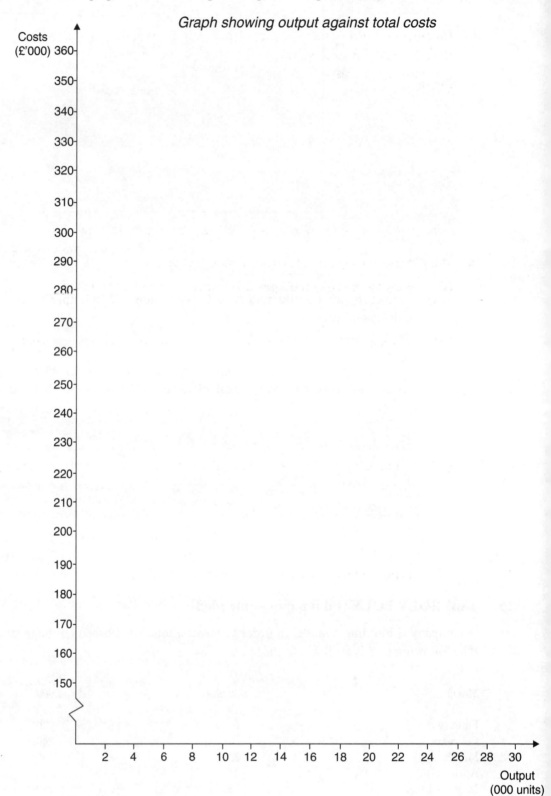

Graph showing output against total costs

4 Marks

(b) If $\Sigma X = 240$

$\Sigma Y = 2,920$

$\Sigma X^2 = 5,110$

$\Sigma Y^2 = 745,200$

$\Sigma XY = 61,500$

Calculate the correlation coefficient between output and costs, stating your answer correct to 3 decimal places.

4 Marks

(c) Comment on two features of the relationship between output and costs. Use no more than 20 words for each feature.

Feature 1

1 Mark

Feature 2

1 Mark

(d) If the regression equation of costs on output were $Y = 43 + 10X$ for the above data

(i) Forecast the costs if output were expected to be 40,000 units

2 Marks

(ii) Using no more than 20 words, give a reason why your forecast might not be very reliable.

1 Mark

(iii) Using no more than 30 words, interpret the value 43 in the regression equation.

2 Marks

(iv) Using no more than 30 words, interpret the value 10 in the regression equation.

2 Marks

Total Marks = 17

BPP PUBLISHING

Question bank
(computer-based
assessment)

1 (a) The expression $\dfrac{(x^2)^3}{x^6}$ equals

   A   0
   B   1
   C   x
   D x^2

   (b) The term $1/_x$ can also be written as

   A   –x
   B x^{-1}
   C x^2
   D   x –1

   (c) Lynn and Laura share out a certain sum of money in the ratio 4 : 5, and Laura ends up with £6.

   (i)   How much was shared out in the first place?

   (ii) How much would have been shared out if Laura had got £6 and the ratio had been 5 : 4 instead of 4 : 5?

2 (a) In the formula $Q = \sqrt{\dfrac{2C_oD}{C_h}}$, if C_o = £40, D = 48,000

   and Q = 200, then C_h is closest in value to

   A   £3.43
   B   £11.77
   C   £96.00
   D   £138.56

   (b) If demand D = 30 – 3P, how is price (P) expressed in terms of D?

   A   P = 10 – D
   B   P = D/27
   C   P = 10 + D/3
   D   P = 10 – D/3

   (c) If x^3 = 4.913, then x =

   (d) If 34x – 7.6 = (17x – 3.8) × (x + 12.5), then x =

3 (a) If A is measured to within ±10%, B to within ±20% and C to within ±20%, then $\dfrac{AB}{C}$

   will be subject to a **maximum error** closest to

   A   65%
   B   10%
   C   –10%
   D   –40%

   (b) What is 628.0273 to:

(i)	five significant figures	
(ii)	four significant figures	

4 (a) A company which makes rechargeable batteries selects some of the batteries for examination. The procedure used chooses two random numbers, say n and m. Starting at the nth battery, every battery at an interval of m is then chosen for examination.

This type of sampling is known as:

A   Stratified
B   Systematic
C   Random
D   Multistage

(b)   Which of the following statements are true?

I   In quota sampling, investors are told to interview all the people they meet up to a certain quota.

II   In cluster sampling, there is very little potential for bias.

III   A sampling frame is a numbered list of all items in a sample.

IV   If a sample is selected using random sampling, it will be free from bias.

A   I only
B   I and IV
C   I, II and IV
D   I, II, III and IV

(c)   A survey is being carried out to find out the number of goals scored by the ten most popular football clubs in Britain in their past ten matches to see if there is much variation between the teams. What sort of data is being collected in such a survey?

A   Quantitative   Continuous
B   Quantitative   Discrete
C   Qualitative   Continuous
D   Qualitative   Discrete

(d)   Identify the sampling methods that require a sampling frame by putting a tick (✓) in the relevant box.

Sampling method	Sampling frame required (✓)
Random	
Stratified	
Quota	
Systematic	

5   (a)   In a histogram, one class is two thirds the width of the other classes.

If the score in that class is 20, the correct height to plot on the histogram is

A   13.33
B   21.00
C   30.00
D   33.33

(b)   A histogram uses a set of bars to represent a grouped frequency table. To be correctly presented, the histogram must show the relationship of the rectangles to the frequencies by reference to the

A   Diagonal of each bar
B   Area of each bar
C   Width of each bar
D   Height of each bar

(c) The graph below is an ogive showing the value of invoices selected in a sample.

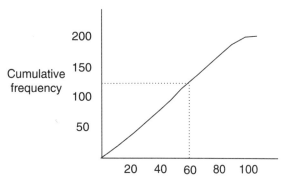

Which of the following statements is true?

A   There are 100 sales with values of £60

B   There are more than 100 sales with values of £60 or more

C   There are 100 sales with values of less than £60

D   There are more than 100 sales with values of £60 or more and there are 100 sales with values of less than £60

(d) Expenditure for Virgo Properties Ltd is made up as follows.

	20X0	20X1	20X2
	£'000	£'000	£'000
Commission	3,579	2,961	2,192
Directors' expenses	857	893	917
Interest	62	59	70

Using the above data, complete the following graphs.

(i) *Component bar chart*

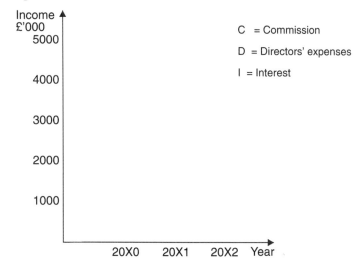

(ii)   *Percentage component bar chart*

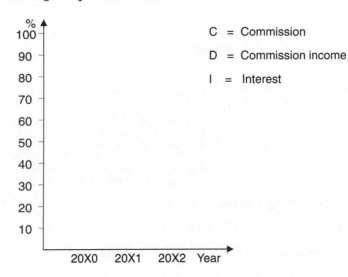

6   (a)   Over a period, a firm made purchases of £800, £1,000, £1,100 and £1,200 on items, the unit cost of which were £5.00, £6.25, £5.50 and £6.00 respectively.

To the nearest penny, the average price paid per item was

A   £5.69
B   £5.70
C   £5.71
D   £5.72

(b)   The following scores are observed for the times taken to complete a task, in minutes

24, 68, 28, 30, 42, 48, 18, 34, 22, 16

The median score is

A   26
B   28
C   29
D   32

(c)   The arithmetic mean of nineteen numbers is 10. When a twentieth number, x, is added the overall mean becomes 17. What is the value of x

A   15
B   20
C   25
D   30

(d)   The sales of colour televisions on each of 40 days was as follows.

Daily sales	Frequency f	Midpoint x	fx
$> 0 \leq 3$	8		
$> 3 \leq 6$	16		
$> 6 \leq 9$	12		
$> 9 \leq 12$	4		
	40		

Fill in the gaps in the table above.

The variables in the table are discrete/continuous.

The arithmetic mean of the data = ...

7   (a) What is the value of the quartile deviation of the following set of numbers?

32	72	40	44	45	36	70

    A   48
    B   44
    C   34
    D   17

    (b) A statistician wishes to compare the dispersion of four frequency distributions. Data for the distributions are as follows:

Distribution	Mean	Standard deviation
1	£140	£33
2	£25,104	£6,290
3	77 kg	27 kg
4	154 miles	32 miles

    The relative dispersion of the distributions is to be measured using the coefficient of variation., Which frequency distribution has the largest coefficient of variation?

    A   Distribution 1
    B   Distribution 2
    C   Distribution 3
    D   Distribution 4

    (c) What is the variance of the five numbers, 4, 6, 8, 12, 15?

    A   8.9
    B   9.0
    C   16
    D   80

    (d) Calculate the mean and range of the following set of data.

10	7	9	11	11	8	9	7

Mean	Range

    (e) The weights of three items X, Y and Z vary independently and have the following means and standard deviations.

	Mean weight kg	Standard deviation kg
X	10	2
Y	14	2
Z	6	1

    The three items are sold together in a single packet.

    Complete the following table.

	Value	Units
Mean of X + Y + Z		
Variance of X + Y + Z		
Standard deviation of X + Y + Z		

8   (a) An index of machine prices has year 1 as the base year, with an index number of 100. By the end of year 9 the index had risen to 180 and by the end of year 14 it had risen by another 18 points.

What was the percentage increase in machine prices between years 9 and 14?

A   2%
B   9%
C   10%
D   18%

(b) The price of a kilogram of raw material was £80 in year 1 and £120 in year 2. Using year 1 as a base year, the price index number for year 2 is

A   67
B   140
C   150
D   167

(c) A company used 20,000 litres of a raw material in year 1. In year 5 the usage of the same raw material amounted to 25,000 litres. Using year 1 as a base year, the quantity index number for year 5 is

A   105
B   120
C   125
D   180

(d) The mean weekly take-home pay of the employees of Staples Ltd and a price index for the 11 years from 20X0 to 20Y0 are as follows.

Year	Weekly wage	Price index (20X0 = 100)
	£	
20X0	150	100
20X1	161	103
20X2	168	106
20X3	179	108
20X4	185	109
20X5	191	112
20X6	197	114
20X7	203	116
20X8	207	118
20X9	213	121
20Y0	231	123

Complete the following table in order to construct a time series of real wages for 20X0 to 20Y0 using a price index with 20X6 as the base year.

Year	Index	Real wage
		£
20X0		
20X1		
20X2		
20X3		
20X4		
20X5		
20X6		
20X7		
20X8		
20X9		
20Y0		

9   (a) An analysis of 480 working days in a factory shows that on 360 days there were no machine breakdowns. Assuming that this pattern will continue, what is the probability that there will be a machine breakdown on a particular day?

   A   0%
   B   25%
   C   35%
   D   75%

(b) A distributor has recorded the following demand for a stock item over the last 200 days.

Daily demand	Number of days
Units	
50	27
51	35
52	38
53	42
54	57

   If these data are representative of the normal pattern of sales, what is the probability of a daily demand of 53 units?

   A   17.5%
   B   19.5%
   C   21.0%
   D   28.5%

(c) A production director is responsible for overseeing the operations of three factories – North, South and West. He visits one factory per week. He visits the West factory as often as he visits the North factory, but he visits the South factory twice as often as he visits the West factory.

   What is the probability that in any one week he will visit the North factory?

   A   0.17
   B   0.20
   C   0.25
   D   0.33

(d) A company is deciding whether to invest in a project. There are three possible outcomes of the investment:

Outcome	Profit/(Loss) £'000
Optimistic	19.2
Most likely	12.5
Pessimistic	(6.7)

There is a 30% chance of the optimistic outcome, and a 60% chance of the most likely outcome arising. The expected value of profit from the project is

A   £7,500
B   £12,590
C   £13,930
D   £25,000

(e) Next year, sales may rise, fall or remain the same as this year, with the following respective probabilities: 0.61, 0.17 and 0.22.

The probability of sales remaining the same or rising is

A   0.13
B   0.17
C   0.70
D   0.83

(f) A salesman has three small areas to cover, areas x, y and z. He never sells more than one item per day and the probabilities of making a sale when he visits each area are as follows.

Area	Probability
x	0.40
y	0.35
z	0.25

He visits only one area each day. He visits area x twice as often as he visits areas y and z.

Calculate the EV of probability of a sale in each of the areas x, y and z and the probabilities of visiting each of the areas.

Probability of visiting area x =

Probability of visiting area y =

Probability of visiting area z =

EV of probability of a sale in area x =

EV of probability of a sale in area y =

EV of probability of a sale in area z =

Select your answers from the list below.

0.0625
0.0825
0.20
0.25
0.25
0.50

10   (a) The weights of elephants are normally distributed. The mean weight is 5,200 kg and the probability of an elephant weighing over 6,000 kg is 0.0314. What is the standard deviation of the weights of elephants?

A	186 kg
B	215 kg
C	372 kg
D	430 kg

(b) A normal distribution has a mean of 60 and a standard deviation of 3.8.

The probability of a score of 56 or less is

A	85%
B	50%
C	35%
D	15%

(c) A normal distribution has a mean of 75 and a variance of 25.

The lower quartile of this distribution is therefore

A	58.25
B	71.65
C	78.35
D	91.75

(d) In a normal distribution with a standard deviation of 90, 28.23% of the population lies between the mean and 900. The mean is

A	860
B	850
C	840
D	830

(e) A normal distribution has a mean of 200 and a variance of 1,600.

Approximately 20% of the population is above which of the following values?

A	234
B	240
C	251
D	278

(f) Consider the following normal distribution.

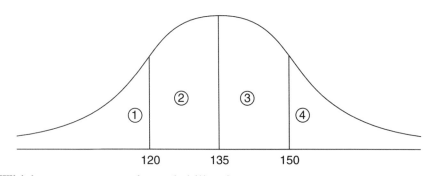

Which area represents the probability that:

(a) $x < 120$

(b) x is between 120 and 150

(c) $x > 150$

(d) $x > 120$

11 (a) How much will an investor have after eight years if he invests £2,000 at 12% per annum simple interest?

       A   £1,920
       B   £3,680
       C   £3,920
       D   £4,952

(b) In four years, an investment of £900 has grown to £1,548. What has been the monthly rate of simple interest?

       A   1.1%
       B   1.5%
       C   15%
       D   18%

(c) A one-year investment yields a return of 20%. The cash returned from the investment, including principal and interest is £3,000. The interest is

       A   £300
       B   £400
       C   £500
       D   £600

(d) It is estimated that a particular cost will decline by 8% per annum on a compound basis.

If the cost is now £12000, by the end of year 3 the cost will be approximately

       A   £8,597
       B   £9,120
       C   £9,344
       D   £10,157

(e) House prices rise at 3% per calendar month. The annual rate of increase correct to one decimal place is

       A   42.6%
       B   36.0%
       C   14.26%
       D   12.36%

(f) (i) The effective annual rate of interest of 15% nominal per annum compounded quarterly is [   ] %

    (ii) The effective annual rate of interest of 24% nominal per annum compounded monthly is [   ] %

12 (a) A firm has arranged a ten-year lease, at an annual rent of £12,000. The first rental payment has to be paid immediately, and the others are to be paid at the end of each year.

What is the present value of the lease at 12%?

       A   £63,936
       B   £67,800
       C   £75,936
       D   £79,800

(b) A mortgage of £60,000 is to be repaid by 15 equal year-end payments. If interest is charged at 9% the value of the annual payment (using tables) correct to the nearest £10 is

A   £2,050
B   £4,000
C   £6,830
D   £7,440

(c) The NPV of an investment is £460 when the discount rate is 10% and £320 when it is 24%. Estimate the internal rate of return to two decimal places

A   17.00%
B   18.20%
C   56.00%
D   It is not possible to estimate the IRR unless one of the NPVs is negative

(d) Over a period of 12 months, the present value of the payments made on a credit card is £21,000 at a discount rate of 3% per month. What is the equivalent constant monthly amount, to the nearest £?

A   £1,750
B   £2,110
C   £8,743
D   £14,721

(e) Which of the following mutually exclusive projects would you advise your client to undertake if only one could be undertaken, given *only* the following information.

	IRR %	NPV £
Project A	15.6	1,600
Project B	16.7	1,400
Project C	17.6	1,200
Project D	18.5	1,000

A   Project A
B   Project B
C   Project C
D   Project D

(f) Daisy Ltd is considering whether to make an investment costing £28,000 which would earn £8,000 cash per annum for five years. The company expects to make a return of at least 11% per annum.

Complete the following table and state whether the project is viable or not.

Year	Cash flow £	Discount factor 11%	Present value £
0			
1			
2			
3			
4			
5			
		NPV	

Project viable   Yes

                  No

13   (a)   Based on the last 7 periods, the underlying trend of sales is $y = 690.24 - 2.75x$. If the 8th period has a seasonal factor of -25.25, assuming an additive forecasting model, then the forecast for that period, in whole units is

          A   643
          B   646
          C   668
          D   671

    (b)   Which of the following are necessary if forecasts obtained from a time series analysis are to be reliable?

          I   There must be no seasonal variation
          II   The trend must be increasing
          III   The model used must fit the past data
          IV   There must be no unforeseen events

          A   I and III only
          B   I and IV only
          C   II and III only
          D   III and IV only

    (c)   The results of an additive time series model analysing production are shown below.

	Weekly production '000 units
Week 1	−4
Week 2	+5
Week 3	+9
Week 4	−6

       Which of the following statements is/are true in relation to the data shown in the table above?

          I   Production is on average 9,000 units above the trend in week 3.
          II   Production is an average 4% below the trend in week 1.
          III   Production is an average 5% above the trend in week 2.
          IV   Production in week 4 is typically 6% below the trend.

          A   I only
          B   I and II only
          C   I and III only
          D   II and IV only

    (d)   A time series was analysed using a multiplicative model. The seasonal variations given by actual value ÷ trend, are adjusted so that they total 4.

	Quarter			
	1	*2*	*3*	*4*
Unadjusted average	1.09	0.93	1.17	0.78

       The correct adjusted average is

          A   Quarter 1 adjusted average = 1.0975
          B   Quarter 2 adjusted average = 0.96
          C   Quarter 3 adjusted average = 1.1400
          D   Quarter 4 adjusted average = 0.7725

    (e)   In a time series analysis, the multiplicative model is used to forecast sales and the following seasonal variations apply.

Quarter	*1*	*2*	*3*	*4*
Seasonal variation	0.45	1.22	1.31	?

The seasonal variation for quarter 4 is

A   0.02
B   1.02
C   1.98
D   2.98

(f)   In 20X8, seasonal variations and trend values in quarters 1-4 are as follows.

Quarter	Seasonal variation	Trend
1	0.6	4,500
2	0.4	4,800
3	1.2	5,200
4	1.0	5,300

Match the sales values forecast with the correct quarters shown below.

Quarter	Sales forecast
1	6,591
2	7,489
3	2,364
4	3,358

14   (a) If n = 4

$\Sigma X = 10$
$\Sigma Y = 22$
$\Sigma X^2 = 30$
$\Sigma XY = 57$
$\Sigma Y^2 = 134$

The product moment correlation coefficient is

A   −0.25
B   −0.06
C   +0.06
D   +0.25

(b) Seven novels were reviewed by two different book critics, and the novels were ranked as follows.

	Critic 1 Rank	Critic 2 Rank
Captain Corelli's guitar	2	1
Debbie Jones's diary	1	3
The songs of a bird	4	7
Cold love in a warm climate	6	5
Raging wars and peacefulness	5	6
Charlotte Black	3	2
The name of the tulip	7	4

The rank correlation coefficient is

A   −0.464
B   −0.536
C   +0.464
D   +0.536

BPP PUBLISHING

(c) In calculating the regression equation linking two variables, the standard formulae for the regression coefficients are given in terms of X and Y. Which of the following is **not** true?

I   X must be the variable which will be forecast
II It does not matter which variable is which
III Y must be the dependent variable
IV Y must be the variable shown on the vertical axis of a scattergram

A   I and II
B   I, II and III
C   I, II and IV
D   I, III and IV

(d) If $\Sigma X = 21$
$\Sigma Y = 184$
$\Sigma X^2 = 91$
$\Sigma XY = 587$
$n = 7$

Which of the following values for a and b are correct in the formula $Y = a + bx$?

	a	b
A	−22.5	−1.25
B	−22.5	+1.25
C	+22.5	−1.25
D	+22.5	+1.25

(e) The regression equation $Y = 5 + 4X$ has been calculated from 6 pairs of values, with X ranging from 1 to 10. The correlation coefficient is 0.9. It is estimated that $Y = 85$ when $X = 20$. Which of the following are true?

I   The estimate is not reliable because the sample is small
II The estimate is reliable
III The estimate is not reliable because the correlation is low
IV The estimate is not reliable because X is outside the range of the data

A   I and II only
B   I and III only
C   I and IV only
D   II and IV only

(f) When the value of one variable is related to the value of another, they are said to be **correlated**. Correlation therefore means an inter-relationship or correspondence.

If the following points were plotted on a graph, what sort of correlation would they display? (Tick as appropriate)

(2, 3)	?	Perfect positive correlation Perfect negative correlation Uncorrelated
(2, 3) (3, 1.5) (4, 0)	?	Perfect positive correlation Perfect negative correlation Uncorrelated
(2, 3) (4, 0) (4, 6)	?	Perfect positive correlation Perfect negative correlation Uncorrelated

Answer bank (paper-based exam)

1   LONG WINTER

(a)   £1,150

(b)   40%

(c)   £24,390

(d)   £190,000

(e)   £200

Workings

(a)   23% of £5,000 = 0.23 × £5,000 = £1,150

(b)   £18 as a percentage of £45 = $\dfrac{18}{45} \times 100\% = \dfrac{1}{2.5} \times 100\% = 40\%$

(c)

Deirdre's salary *before* increase (original)	100%
Salary increase	2.5%
Deirdre's salary after increase (final)	102.5%

102.5%   = £25,000 (final salary)

$1\% \quad = \dfrac{£25,000}{102.5}$

= £243.90 (to 2 dp)

∴ 100% (original salary *before* increase)   =   £243.90 × 100

=   £24,390 (to nearest £)

(d)

Purchases – 20X0 (original)	100%
Percentage decrease	-5%
Purchases – 20X1 (final)	95%

If   100%   = £200,000

1%   = £2,000

∴   95%   = £2,000 × 95

= £190,000

(e)   Initial fee, X   = 100%

VAT   = 17.5%

Final fee   = 117.5% = £235

$1\% \quad = \dfrac{£235}{117.5}$

$100\% \quad = \dfrac{£235}{117.5} \times 100$

= £200

2   **SOLVE**

(a)   x = ⬛ –5 ⬛   y = ⬛ 4 ⬛

(b)

⬛ $x^2 - 4x - 437 = 0$ ⬛

or

⬛ $y^2 + 4y - 437 = 0$ ⬛

(c)

⬛ $-b^2 + 22b - 112 = 0$ ⬛

or

⬛ $-a^2 + 22a - 112 = 0$ ⬛

(d)   x = ⬛ –2 ⬛   or   ⬛ +4 ⬛

Workings

(a) $x - y$ $= -9$ (1)
         $9x - 13y$ $= -97$ (2)
         $9x - 9y$ $= -81$ (3) (1) × 9
              $4y$ $= 16$ (3) – (2)
               y $= 4$

Substituting in (1) we get

         $x - 4$ $= -9$
            x $= -9 + 4$
            x $= -5$

(b)   Let the two positive numbers be x and y.

      $x^2 + y^2$ $= 890$ (1)
      $x - y$ $= 4$ (2)
      y $= x - 4$ (3) (from (2)).

      Substituting in (1) we get $x^2 + (x - 4)^2 = 890$
                                    $x^2 + (x^2 - 8x + 16) = 890$
                                    $2x^2 - 8x - 874 = 0$
                                    $x^2 - 4x - 437 = 0$

      Alternatively $x = y + 4$ (3)

      and hence $(y + 4)^2 + y^2 = 890$

      $y^2 + 8y + 16 + y^2$ $= 890$
      $2y^2 + 8y - 874$ $= 0$
      $y^2 + 4y - 437$ $= 0$

(c)   Let the length and breadth of the rectangle be a and b.

      $2a + 2b = 44$
      $a + b$ $= 22$ (1)
      ab $= 112$ (2)

      From (1) we get $a = 22 - b$

      Substituting in (2) we get
      $b(22 - b) = 112$
      $-b^2 + 22b - 112 = 0$

By symmetry the same equation:

$-a^2 + 22a - 112 = 0$

can be solved for 'a'.

(d) $-3x^2 + 6x + 24 = 0$

This can be solved using:

$$x = \frac{-b \pm \sqrt{b^2 - 4ac}}{2a}$$

Where $a = -3, b = 6, c = 24$

$$\begin{aligned} x &= [-6 \pm \sqrt{(6^2 + 4 \times 3 \times 24)}]/(2 \times -3) \\ &= [-6 \pm \sqrt{324}]/(-6) \\ &= [-6 \pm 18]/(-6) \\ &= -2 \text{ or } +4. \end{aligned}$$

3 RODEO ROUND-UP LTD

(a) (i)   A = 3,500   B = 3,200   C = 28,900

(ii)   ± £450

(iii)   ±1.56%

(b) (i)   Maximum = £532

Minimum = £588

(ii)   £531.20

(iii)   £116.80

Workings

(a) (i)

Venue	Box office receipts to nearest £100 £
Clapham	3,500
West Riding	5,300
Weston-Super-Mare	1,400
Badminton	2,500
Huntingdon	3,200
Epsom	2,600
Ascot	1,500
Wincanton	4,600
Reading	4,300
	28,900

(ii)   The maximum error in the rounding for each venue is ± £50. There are nine venues.

so the maximum absolute error is $9 \times \pm £50 = \pm £450$

(iii)   The maximum relative error is $\dfrac{\pm £450}{£28,900} \times 100\% = \pm 1.56\%$

(b) (i)   Maximum value $= 100\% + 5\% = 105\%$
$= 105\% \times £560 = £588$

$$\text{Minimum value} = 100\% - 5\% = 95\%$$
$$= 95\% \times £560 = £532$$

(ii) The **maximum value of** $\frac{QR}{S}$ is given by taking the maximum value of Q and R and the minimum value of S

Maximum Q	$= 400 \times 1.01$	$= 404$
Maximum R	$= 25 \times 1.01$	$= 25.25$
Minimum S	$= 20 \times 0.96$	$= 19.2$

$\therefore$ **Maximum value of** $\frac{QR}{S} = \frac{404 \times 25.25}{19.2} = £531.30$ (to 2 decimal places)

(iii) The **maximum value of X** is given by taking the maximum value of P and subtracting the minimum value of $\frac{QR}{S}$.

Maximum value of $P = 560 \times 1.05 = 588$

Minimum value of $\frac{QR}{S} = \frac{(400 \times 0.99) \times (25 \times 0.99)}{(20 \times 1.04)}$

$$= \frac{396 \times 24.75}{20.8}$$

$$= 471.20 \text{ (to 2 decimal places)}$$

$\therefore$ **Maximum value of X** $= 588 - 471.20$
$$= 116.80 \text{ (to 2 decimal places)}$$

4   SAMPLING

(a) (i)   D

(ii)   A

(iii)   E

(iv)   B

(v)   C

(b) (i)

A list of all the workers who will be affected by the new proposals.

(ii)

A list of all students attending courses which prepare them for their professional examinations.

(iii)

The electoral register could be used to select households.

5 PARROTS LTD

(a) A = 6.5

B = 12

C = 16

D = 4.5

Workings

The first and last intervals have widths of £10, ie twice the standard width. Their frequencies must therefore be halved in order to calculate the frequency density. In all other cases, the frequency density is the same as the frequency (or number of employees).

Weekly average wage £	Number of employees	Frequency density
51 and <61	13	6.5
61 and <66	12	12
66 and <71	16	16
71 and <76	21	21
76 and <81	25	25
81 and <86	20	20
86 and <91	14	14
91 and <101	9	4.5

(b)

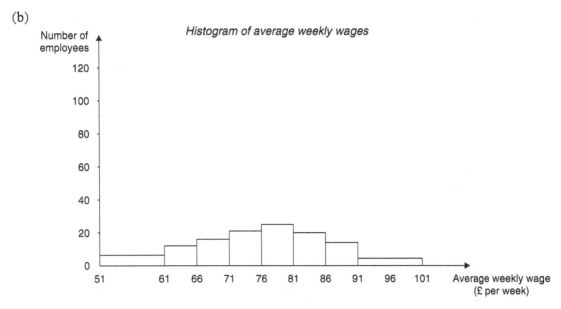

(c) E = 62

F = 87

G = 130

Workings

Average weekly wage £	Number of employees	Cumulative frequency
51 and <61	13	13
61 and <66	12	25
66 and <71	16	41
71 and <76	21	62
76 and <81	25	87
81 and <86	20	107
86 and <91	14	121
91 and <101	9	130

(d)

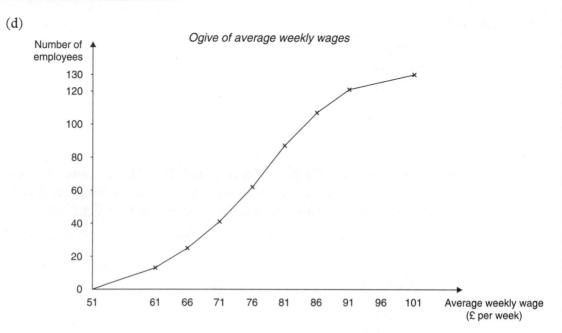

Ogive of average weekly wages

6 JOURNEY TIMES

(a) Mean

Advantage

Widely understood

Disadvantage

Distorted by extreme high or low values

Median

Advantage

Not distorted by extreme values

Disadvantage

Does not take account of all the data

Mode

Advantage

An easily understood average

Disadvantage

It may not be unique

Workings

The mean

The mean has the following advantages.

(1) It is widely understood.

(2) It uses every value in its computation.

(3) It gives a unique value.

It does, however, have two major disadvantages.

(1) It may give an impossible value (eg 2.2 children).

(2) It may be distorted by extremely high or low values.

The median

The median has the advantage that it is not distorted by extreme values but there is a disadvantage to the median. It does not take every value into account.

The mode

Advantages of the mode are as follows.

(1)　It is an actual value.
(2)　The most common value is an easily understood average.

It has the following disadvantages.

(1)　It may not be unique.
(2)　It ignores dispersion about the modal value.
(3)　It does not take every value into account.

(b)　(i)　32.67 minutes

Workings

Times	Midpoint x	Frequency f	fx
0 – 10	5	14	70
10 – 20	15	26	390
20 – 30	25	64	1,600
30 – 40	35	46	1,610
40 – 50	45	28	1,260
50 – 60	55	16	880
60 – 80	70	8	560
80 – 100	90	4	360
		206	6,730

$$\text{Mean } \bar{x} = \frac{\Sigma fx}{\Sigma f} = \frac{6,730}{206} = 32.67 \text{ minutes}$$

(ii)　**Mean**

The mean of 32.67 minutes is the total journey time of the 206 employees divided by the number of employees (206).

Median

Half of the employees take less than 30 minutes to get to work.

Mode

The most common journey time is 27 minutes.

(iii)

The data is positively skewed.

7 JELLY BEANS

(a)　A = 80

　　　B = 120

Workings

£'000	Number of staff (frequency)	Cumulative frequency
Under 10	16	16
10 to under 20	30	46
20 to under 30	34	80
30 to under 40	22	102
40 to under 50	10	112
50 to under 70	5	117
70 and over	3	120
	120	

(b)

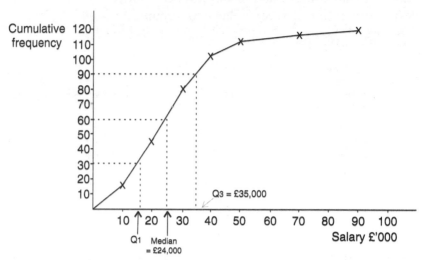

Ogive of current salaries paid to members of staff

Workings

For a grouped frequency distribution such as this, the cumulative frequencies are plotted against the upper limits of the classes.

For the open-ended interval '70 and over' the upper limit is taken to be 90.

(c) Median = £25,000

Upper quartile = £35,000

Lower quartile = £15,000

Semi-interquartile range = £10,000

Workings

Median = $\dfrac{120}{2}$ = 60th item.

From the ogive above, the 60th item can be estimated to be £25,000 (to nearest £5,000)

The semi-interquartile range = $\dfrac{Q_3 - Q_1}{2}$

Where Q_3 is the **upper quartile** (above which 25% of the population fall)
Q_1 is the **lower quartile** (below which 25% of the population fall)

We can estimate Q_3 and Q_1 from the ogive.

$Q_3 = 120 \times \dfrac{3}{4}$ = 90th item = £35,000 (from graph)

$Q_1 = 120 \times \dfrac{1}{4} = 30^{th}$ item $= £15,000$ (from graph)

Semi-interquartile range $= \dfrac{Q_3 - Q_1}{2} = \dfrac{£35,000 - £15,000}{2}$

$$= \dfrac{£20,000}{2} = £10,000$$

(d)

Half of all employees earn less than the median wage of £25,000. This average has increased over the five years.

(e)

The middle 50% of the workforce earn within £10,000 either side of the median. This measure of variability has increased over the five years.

8 STUART LTD

(a) 101.3

Workings

Weighted average of price relative index $= \dfrac{\Sigma W \times {P_1}/{P_0}}{\Sigma W}$

where P_1 = price in 20X1
P_0 = price in 20X0

Price relatives

	Price relative P_1/P_0
A	100/100 = 1.00
B	108/100 = 1.08
C	90/100 = 0.90

Weightings (W)

	Q_0
A	5,000
B	6,000
C	3,000
	14,000

Index

	$W \times P_1/P_0$	
A	$1.00 \times 5,000 =$	5,000
B	$1.08 \times 6,000 =$	6,480
C	$0.90 \times 3,000 =$	2,700
		14,180

Index $= \dfrac{14,180}{14,000} \times 100 = 101.3$ (to 1 decimal place)

(b) 110.0

Workings

Weighted average of price relative index $= \dfrac{\Sigma W \times {P_1}/{P_0}}{\Sigma W}$

Price relatives

	Price relative P_1/P_0
A	$110/100 = 1.1$
B	$115/100 = 1.15$
C	$100/100 = 1.0$

Weightings (W) = 14,000 (as calculated in (a))

Index

	$W \times P_1/P_0$	
A	$1.1 \times 5,000 =$	5,500
B	$1.15 \times 6,000 =$	6,900
C	$1.00 \times 3,000 =$	3,000
		15,400

$$\text{Index} = \frac{15,400}{14,000} \times 100 = 110.0$$

(c)

Prices have risen by 12% on average during the three-year period 20X0-20X3.

(d)

The index would probably be lower.

(e)

When prices rise the quantity of goods purchased will tend to fall. The current-weighted index will reflect this.

In this example, commodity B has increased in price by 15% from 20X0 to 20X2 and it follows that the quantities purchased will probably have fallen (in relation to commodities A and C). A base-weighted index will use the same weighting of 6,000 whereas a current-weighted index would use lower (more up-to-date) weightings.

(f)

Advantage

Weights only need to be calculated once every few years.

Disadvantage

Such weights can become out-of-date very quickly, especially when consumer spending habits change frequently.

There are several other advantages. For example, base weights are only obtained once and are therefore far cheaper than current weights. In addition, base weights remain fixed from one year to the next so that price comparisons can be made over several years (instead of from one year to the next).

9   ACE

(a) With replacement   1/169

Without replacement   1/221

(b)   1/2,704

(c) (i) 0.3

   (ii) 0.27

   (iii) 0.02

(d) (i) 40%

   (ii) 66.67%

Workings

(a) **Assuming replacement**

P(Ace) = 4/52 = 1/13

P(Ace on second draw) = 1/13

P(Ace followed by Ace with replacement) = $(1/13) \times (1/13) = 1/169$

Without replacement

P(Ace) = 1/13

P(Ace on second draw) = 3/51 = 1/17

P(Ace followed by Ace without replacement) = $(1/13) \times (1/17) = 1/221$

(b) P(Drawing ace of Hearts) = 1/52

P(Drawing ace of Spades) = 1/52 (if replacement is assumed)

P(Ace of hearts followed by ace of Spades) = $(1/52) \times (1/52) = 1/2,704$

(c) P(Own Home) = P(H) = 0.5

P(Own Car) = P(C)   = 0.6

P(Own TV) = P(TV)   = 0.9

   (i) P(Home and Car) = P(Home) $\times$ P(Car)

                = 0.3

   (ii) P(all three owned) = P(Home) $\times$ P(car) $\times$ P(TV)

                = 0.27

   (iii) P(None owned) = $(1 - P(H)) (1 - P(C)) (1 - P(TV))$

                = $0.5 \times 0.4 \times 0.1$

                = 0.02

(d) Out of every 100 respondents, 50 own their own homes and 50 do not. This gives the bottom row of the contingency table shown below. Similarly the total column is determined by the 60% of respondents who own cars. Of the 50 home owners, 40 people (80% $\times$ 50) also own cars. The table can now be completed as follows.

	Home owner	*Not home owner*	*Total*
Car	40	20	60
No car	10	30	40
Total	50	50	100

   (i) Of the 50 respondents who do not own homes, only 20 own cars = $\frac{20}{50} \times 100\%$ = 40%

   (ii) Of the 60 who own cars, only 40 are home owners = $\frac{40}{60} \times 100\%$ = 66.7%

10 BATTERIES

(a) −1.75

(b) 34.3 hours

(c) 10.6%

(d) (i) −2.05

(ii) 111.8

Workings

(a)

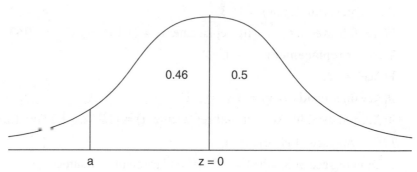

The normal distribution graph above shows the point a above which 96% of the population lies.

Normal distribution tables show that, a z value of 1.75 corresponds to a probability of 0.46. Since a is less than 0, its value is −1.75.

(b)

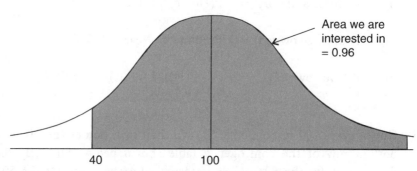

Using $z = \dfrac{x - \mu}{\sigma}$

where $z = 1.75$
  $x = 40$
  $\mu = 100$

  $1.75 = \dfrac{40 - 100}{\sigma}$

  $\mu = \dfrac{40 - 100}{1.75}$

  $= 34.3$ hours (to 1 decimal place)

(c)

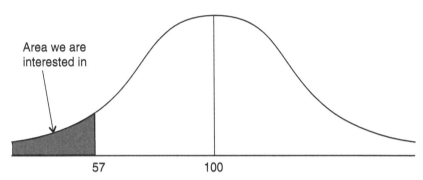

Using $z = \dfrac{x - \mu}{\sigma}$

$z = \dfrac{57 - 100}{34.3}$

$z = 1.25$

When $z = 1.25$, the proportion of batteries lasting between 57 and 100 hours is 0.3944 (from normal distribution tables). The area that we are interested in is the area to the left of 57 hours (shaded area on the graph) = 0.5 – 0.3944 = 0.1056 = 10.6% (to 1 decimal place).

(d) (i)

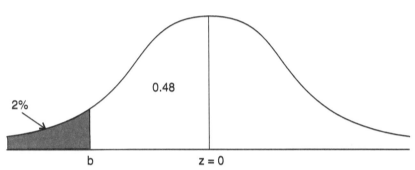

The area between b and 0 = 48% (0.48), and so from normal distribution tables, the value of b shown in the graph above is –2.05.

(ii)

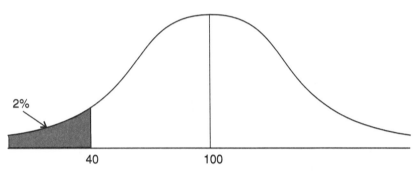

We want 2% of batteries to last for less than 40 hours. From normal distribution tables, this corresponds to a z value of –2.05.

If $z = \dfrac{x - \mu}{\sigma}$

$-2.05 = \dfrac{40 - \mu}{35}$

$(-2.05 \times 35) = 40 - \mu$

$-71.75 = 40 - \mu$

$$\mu = 40 + 71.75$$
$$= 111.75$$
$$= 111.8 \text{ (to 1 decimal place)}$$

11 HOUND CAMPING LTD

(a) (i) £2,941

 (ii) £13,881

 (iii) £3,601

Workings

(i) Value after 3 years $= £8,000 \times 1.11^3 = £10,941$ (to the nearest £)

 $\therefore$ Interest $= £10,941 - £8,000$
 $= £2,941$

(ii) Value after 5 years $= £15,000 \times 1.14^5 = £28,881$ (to the nearest £)

 $\therefore$ Interest $= £28,881 - £15,000$
 $= £13,881$

(iii) Value after 4 years $= £6,000 \times 1.1^2 \times 1.15^2 = £9,601$ (to the nearest £)

 $\therefore$ Interest $= £9,601 - £6,000$
 $= £3,601$

(b) (i) 10.78%

 (ii) 12.68%

 (iii) 12.55%

Workings

(i) Rate of interest $= 5.25\%$ every six months

 $\therefore$ Six monthly ratio $= 1.0525$

 $\therefore$ Annual ratio $= 1.0525^2$
 $= 1.1078$

 $\therefore$ Effective annual rate $= 10.78\%$ (to 2 decimal places)

(ii) Rate of interest $= 1\%$ every month

 $\therefore$ Monthly ratio $= 1.01$

 $\therefore$ Annual ratio $= 1.01^{12}$
 $= 1.1268$

 $\therefore$ Effective annual rate $= 12.68\%$ (to 2 decimal places)

(iii) Rate of interest $= 3\%$ per quarter

 $\therefore$ Quarterly ratio $= 1.03$

 $\therefore$ Annual ratio $= 1.03^4$
 $= 1.1255$

 $\therefore$ Effective annual rate $= 12.55\%$ (to 2 decimal places)

12 DAISY HOOF LTD

(a) A = £12,000

B = 1

C = 0.641

D = £15,516

E = £18,575

F = £330

Workings

Year	Cash flow £	Discount factor 16%	Present value £
0	(50,000)	1.000	(50,000)
1	18,000	0.862	15,516
2	25,000	0.743	18,575
3	15,000	0.641	9,615
4	12,000	0.552	6,624
		NPV	330

(b) −£1,477

Workings

Year	Cash flow £	Discount factor 18%	Present value £
0	(50,000)	1.000	(50,000)
1	18,000	0.847	15,246
2	25,000	0.718	17,950
3	15,000	0.609	9,135
4	12,000	0.516	6,192
		NPV	(1,477)

(c) 16.4%

Workings

Estimated IRR $= 16\% + \left[\frac{330}{330+1,477} \times (18-16)\right]\% = 16.4\%$ (to 1 decimal place).

(d)

The Internal Rate of Return is the discount rate at which the net present value is zero.

13 SAVINGS VS. BORROWING

(a) (i) 9.954X

(ii) £4,018

Workings

The bank pays out the loan *now* so the present value of the loan is £40,000.

The annuity is the amount that needs to be paid at the end of each quarter.

The annuity factor can be found in the cumulative present value tables; the cost of capital is 3%, and the number of time periods we are concerned with is found as follows.

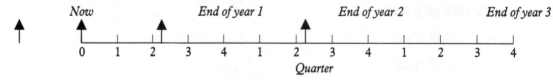

Number of time periods = 12 quarters

Annuity factor = 9.954

Present value of repayments = 9.954X

and x = $\dfrac{£40,000}{9.954}$

= £4,018.49

Therefore, the equal amounts that must be repaid at the end of each quarter = £4,018 (to the nearest £).

(b) (i)   £44,994.56

(ii)   10.787Y

(iii) £3,290

Workings

(i)   In three years' time, the amount of money required to modernise the premises will be:

£40,000 × $(1.04)^3$ = £44,994.56

(ii)   The instalments consist of a payment Y now plus an annuity of 11 payments at 2% per time period. The annuity factor at 2% for 11 periods is 9.787 and hence the present value is Y + 9.787Y = 10.787Y.

(iii) The present value of £44,994.56 at time 12 discounted at 2% = £44,994.56 × 0.788.

∴ 10.787Y = £44,994.56 × 0.788

$$Y = \dfrac{£35,455}{10.787}$$

= £3,290 (to the nearest £10)

(c) (i)   Save and modernise later   ✓

It costs less to save now and modernise later, therefore the retailer should be advised to do this.

(ii)

Sales may be lost through the failure to modernise immediately.

The biggest reservation is that the retailer faces increased competition now and no allowance has been made in the calculations for any immediate loss of sales. Another reservation would be that the future cost of modernising and the future return on investment can not really be known with certainty at present.

14 HOPWOOD TRENDS LTD

(a) A = 944

    B = 962

    C = 236.0

    D = 240.5

    E = 238

    F = –114

Workings

Year	Quarter	Sales	Moving total of 4 quarters' sales	Moving average of 4 quarters' sales	Mid point of moving averages (÷8)	Seasonal variation
20X2	1	200				
	2	110				
			870	217.5		
	3	320			219	+101
			884	221.0		
	4	240			222	+18
			892	223.0		
20X3	1	214			225	-11
			906	226.5		
	2	118			229	-111
			926	231.5		
	3	334			232	+102
			932	233.0		
	4	260			234	+26
			938	234.5		
20X4	1	220			235	-15
			944	236.0		
	2	124			238	-114
			962	240.5		
	3	340				
	4	278				

A = 260 + 220 + 124 + 340 = 944

B = 220 + 124 + 340 + 278 = 962

C = 944 ÷ 4 = 236.0

D = 962 ÷ 4 = 240.5

E = (236.0 + 240.5) ÷ 2 = 476.5 ÷ 2 = 238.25

F = 124 – 238 = –114

(b) G = –2

    H = +0.5

    I = –12.5

    J = –112.0

    K = +102.0

    L = +22.5

Workings

Year	Quarter	1	2	3	4	Total
20X2				+101	+18	
20X3		−11	−111	+102	+26	
20X4		−15	−114			
Average seasonal variation		−13.0	−112.5	+101.5	+22.0	−2
Adjustment		+0.5	+0.5	+0.5	+0.5	+2
Adjusted seasonal variation		−12.5	−112.0	+102.0	+22.5	0

The seasonal variations from the table in (a) are the initial entries in the table shown above. The seasonal variations are averaged by adding them together and dividing by two. The total of the averages gives the value of G, which should ideally be zero. (In this case it is −2.) We adjust the average seasonal variations by subtracting G/4 ($^{-2}/_4$ = −0.5) from each average which in this case means adding H = 0.5 in order to obtain the adjusted seasonal variations I to L.

(c) 255.5

Workings

The additive model is A = T + S and we seasonally adjust the data in order to estimate the trend, T.

$$T = A - S$$
$$= 278 - 22.5$$
$$= 255.5$$

(d) 232.5

Workings

The additive model is A = T + S. Forecast sales are calculated by adding the adjusted seasonal variation (S) to the predicted trend (T).

Forecast sales = 245 − 12.5
= 232.5

15 SMALL COMPANY

(a) (i) 1.2830

(ii) 6.68

Workings

The regression line is Y = a + bX, where

$$b = \frac{n\Sigma XY - \Sigma X\Sigma Y}{n\Sigma X^2 - (\Sigma X)^2}$$

$$a = \overline{Y} - b\overline{X}$$

$$b = \frac{10 \times 1,492 - 82 \times 172}{10 \times 736 - 82^2} = 1.2830$$

$$a = 17.2 - 1.283 \times 8.2 = 6.68$$

Thus Y = 6.68 + 1.283X (£'000).

(b) (i)   £7,000

When production is zero, X = 0 and Y = 7.

∴ Fixed costs = £7,000

(ii)

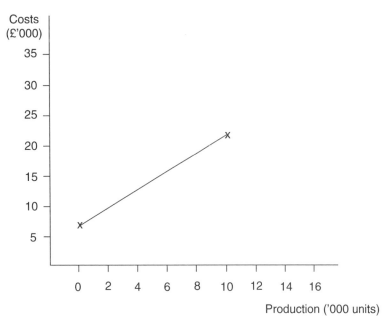

Workings

When X = 0, Y = 7
When X = 10, Y = 7 + 15 = 22

(iii)   £22,000

When production is 10,000, then X = 10 and Y = 22 and total production costs are therefore £22,000.

(iv)

Reason 1

The value X = 10 is within the range of data.

Reason 2

The correlation coefficient indicates that the data are highly correlated.

16   JAM ROLY POLY

(a)

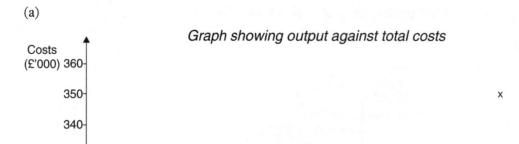

Graph showing output against total costs

(b)   0.946

Workings

The correlation coefficient, r, is calculated using the following formula.

$$r = \frac{n\sum XY - \sum X \sum Y}{\sqrt{[n\sum X^2 - (\sum X)^2][n\sum Y^2 - (\sum Y)^2]}}$$

$$= \frac{37,200}{\sqrt{(12 \times 5,110 - 240^2)(12 \times 745,200 - 2,920^2)}}$$

$$= \frac{37,200}{\sqrt{3,720 \times 416,000}}$$

$$= \frac{37,200}{39,338.531}$$

$$= 0.946$$

(c)

Feature 1

Costs increase as output is increased.

Feature 2

There is a very strong linear relationship between output and costs.

(d) (i)   £443,000

Workings

If output = 40,000 units

Then   X = 40

 Y = (43 + 10) × 40

 = 443

Therefore, forecast costs = £443,000

(ii)

X = 40 is a long way outside the range of the data used to predict the regression equation.

(iii)

£43,000 represents fixed costs.

(iv)

Costs increase by £10 for each additional unit produced.

If the value of X increases by 1, then the value of Y increases by (10 × 1) = 10. Therefore for each additional 1,000 units produced, costs will increase by £10,000. This is equivalent to an extra £10 per unit (£10,000 ÷ 1,000 units).

Answer bank (computer-based assessment)

1   (a)   B $\dfrac{(x^2)^3}{x^6} = x^{(2 \times 3) - 6} = x^{6-6} = x^0 = 1$ (always)

You should have been able to eliminate option A straightaway since you should have been able to see that the correct answer is x or x to the power of something. Remember, x^0 **always** equals 1.

Options C and D are incorrect because $\dfrac{x^6}{x^6}$ **does not** equal x or x^2.

   (b)   B   The term x^{-1} equals 1/x by definition.

   (c)   (i)

£10.80

Workings

Laura's share = £6 = 5 parts
Therefore one part is worth £6 ÷ 5 = £1.20
Total of 9 parts shared out originally
Therefore total was 9 × £1.20 = £10.80

       (ii)

£13.50

Workings

Laura's share = £6 = 4 parts
Therefore one part is worth £6 ÷ 4 = £1.50
Therefore original total was 9 × £1.50 = £13.50

2   (a)   C $Q = \sqrt{\dfrac{2C_oD}{C_h}}$

$200 = \sqrt{\dfrac{2 \times 40 \times 48{,}000}{C_h}}$

Square both sides

$200^2 = \dfrac{2 \times 40 \times 48{,}000}{C_h}$

$C_h = \dfrac{2 \times 40 \times 48{,}000}{200^2}$

$C_h = £96$

If you selected one of the other options, then work through the solution again remembering that if you do anything to one side of an equation, you must make sure you do the same to the other side of the equation as well.

   (b)   D   If   D =   30 − 3P

       D − 30 =   −3P

          3P =   30 − D

            P = $\dfrac{30}{3} - \dfrac{D}{3}$

            P =   10 − D/3

Option A is incorrect since you have divided the 30 by 3 but not the D.

Option B is incorrect because you have (incorrectly) calculated that D = 30 – 3P is D = 27P. This would only be the case if there were brackets as such (D = (30 – 3)P).

Option C is incorrect because you have forgotten to change the sign of the D from positive to negative when you took it to the other side of the equation.

(c) x = | 1.7 |

x^3 = 4.913

x   = 1.7   (take the cube root of each side).

(d) x = | –10.5 |

34x – 7.6 = (17x – 3.8) × (x + 12.5)

This one is easy if you realise that $17 \times 2 = 34$ and $3.8 \times 2 = 7.6$, so 2(17x – 3.8) = 34x – 7.6

We can then divide each side by 17x – 3.8 to get

2 = x + 12.5

– 10.5 = x (subtract 12.5 from each side).

3   (a) A   To ensure that the error is at a maximum, the **numerator** needs to be as **large** as possible and the denominator as **small** as possible.

Say A = B = C = 10
A could be measured from 9 to 11
B could be measured from 8 to 12
C could be measured from 8 to 12
Maximising A and B and minimising C gives

$$\frac{AB}{C} = \frac{11 \times 12}{8} = 16.5$$

Using the actual values of A = B = C = 10.

$$\frac{AB}{C} = \frac{10 \times 10}{10} = 10$$

$\therefore$ Error = $\frac{16.5 - 10}{10} \times 100\% = 65\%$

Option B is incorrect since you have calculated your error by **maximising** A, B and C.

$$\frac{AB}{C} = \frac{11 \times 12}{12} = 11 \therefore \text{Error} = \frac{11 - 10}{10} \times 100\% = 10\%$$

Option C is incorrect since it is calculated by minimising A, B and C.

$$\frac{AB}{C} = \frac{9 \times 8}{8} = 9 \therefore \text{Error} = \frac{9 - 10}{10} \times 100\% = -10\%$$

Option D is incorrect since it is calculated by minimising A and B and maximising C.

$$\frac{AB}{C} = \frac{9 \times 8}{12} = 6 \therefore \text{Error} = \frac{6 - 10}{10} \times 100\% = -40\%$$

(b)

628.03
628.0

4   (a)   B   **Systematic sampling** is a sampling method which works by selecting every n^{th} item (or m^{th} in this case) after a random start.

     (b)   B   A **sampling frame** is a numbered list of all items in a **population** (not a **sample**). Therefore Statement III is not true.

            Cluster sampling involves selecting one definable subsection of the population which therefore makes the potential for **bias** considerable. Therefore Statement II is not true.

            Statements I and IV are true and the correct answer is therefore B.

     (c)   B   The number of goals scored is an example of **quantitative data** as they can be measured. Since the number of goals scored cannot take on any value, they can only score 1, 2, 3 or any **whole** number of goals (they cannot score 2½ goals) the data are said to be **discrete**.

            You should have been able to eliminate option C and D immediately since qualitative data are data that cannot be measured but which reflect some quality of what is being observed.

     (d)

Sampling method	Sampling frame required (✓)
Random	✓
Stratified	✓
Quota	
Systematic	✓

5   (a)   C   Height of histogram $= \dfrac{20}{2/3} = 30$

            If you selected option A, you multiplied 20 by 2/3 instead of dividing it by 2/3.

            Option B is incorrect because it represents the score in the class under consideration.

            Option D represents the score in the class (20) plus 2/3 of 20 = 20 + 13.33 = 33.33.

     (b)   B   A histogram is a chart that looks like a bar chart except that the bars are joined together. On a histogram, frequencies are presented by the **area** covered by the bars.

     (c)   D   An ogive represents a cumulative frequency distribution which shows the cumulative number of items with a value less than or equal to, or alternatively greater than or equal to, a certain amount. This is a 'less than' ogive.

BPP PUBLISHING

(d) (i)   *Component bar chart*

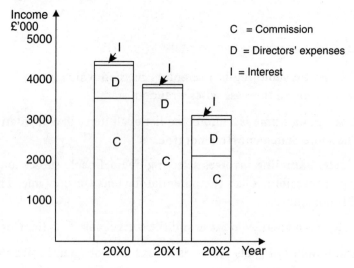

(ii)   *Percentage component bar chart*

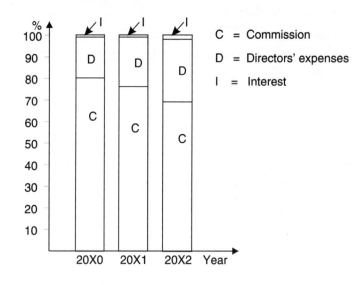

Workings

	20X0			20X1			20X2	
	£'000	%		£'000	%		£'000	%
	3,579	80		2,961	76		2,192	69
	857	19		893	23		917	29
	62	1		59	1		70	2
	4,498	100		3,913	100		3,179	100

6   (a) A

x	fx		f
£	£		
£5.00	800	800 ÷ 5.00	160
£6.25	1,000	1,000 ÷ 6.25	160
£5.50	1,100	1,100 ÷ 5.50	200
£6.00	1,200	1,200 ÷ 6.00	200
	4,100		720

$$\therefore \ \bar{x} \ = \ \frac{\Sigma fx}{\Sigma f} \ = \ \frac{4,100}{720} \ = £5.69$$

(b) C   In order of magnitude, scores are

16	18	22	24	28	30	34	42	48	68

Position of median is $\frac{10+1}{2}$ = 5½ and therefore the median is the average of the 5th and 6th items, ie of 28 and 30. The median is therefore 29.

(c) D   **Arithmetic mean** $= \frac{\Sigma x}{n}$

$\therefore 10 = \frac{\Sigma x}{19}$

$\Sigma x \ = 10 \times 19$
$\qquad = 190$

Let x = twentieth number

$190 + x \ = \ 20 \times 11$
$190 + x \ = \ 220$
$\qquad\quad x \ = \ 220 - 190$
$\qquad\qquad = \ 30$

(d)

Daily sales	Frequency f	Midpoint x	fx
> 0 ≤ 3	8	2	16
> 3 ≤ 6	16	5	80
> 6 ≤ 9	12	8	96
> 9 ≤ 12	4	11	44
	40		236

The variables in the table are **discrete**. The arithmetic mean of the data =

$\frac{\Sigma fx}{\Sigma f} \ = \frac{236}{40} = 5.9$ televisions per day

7   (a) D   Firstly arrange the set in ascending order, as follows.

32	36	40	44	45	70	72

Number of data items = 7

Lower quartile $= 25\% \times 7 = 1.75 = 2^{nd}$ item $= 36$
Upper quartile $= 75\% \times 7 = 5.25 = 6^{th}$ item $= 70$

Quartile deviation $\quad = \dfrac{\text{Upper quartile - lower quartile}}{2}$

$\qquad\qquad\qquad\qquad = \dfrac{70-36}{2} = \dfrac{34}{2}$

$\qquad\qquad\qquad\qquad = 17$

Option A is incorrect because it represents the arithmetic mean to the nearest whole number.

Option B represents the median.

Option C represents the inter-quartile range and you have forgotten to divide by 2 in order to determine the semi-interquartile range.

(b) C   The formula for the coefficient of variation is $\dfrac{\text{Standard deviation}}{\text{Mean}}$

Distribution	Coefficient of variation
1	0.24
2	0.25
3	0.35 ←——— largest
4	0.21

Option C is therefore correct.

If you chose any of the other options you did not calculate the coefficient of variation using the correct formula.

(c) C   The arithmetic mean of the five numbers, $\bar{x}$, is equal to $\dfrac{4+6+8+12+15}{5} = \dfrac{45}{5}$

= 9

We can now calculate the variance:

x	$x - \bar{x}$	$(x - \bar{x})^2$
4	–5	25
6	–3	9
8	–1	1
12	3	9
15	6	36
	$\Sigma(x - \bar{x})^2 =$	$\dfrac{80}{}$

$$\text{Variance} = \frac{\Sigma(x - \bar{x})^2}{n} = \frac{80}{5} = 16$$

The correct answer is therefore C.

If you selected option A, you calculated the standard deviation.

If you selected option B you calculated the arithmetic mean.

If you selected option D, you forgot to divide $\Sigma(x - \bar{x})^2$ by n (or 5).

(d)

Mean	Range
9	4

Workings

Mean, $\bar{x} = \dfrac{72}{8} = 9$

Range = 11 – 7 = 4

(e)

	Value	Units
Mean of X + Y + Z	30	kg
Variance of X + Y + Z	9	kg
Standard deviation of X + Y + Z	3	kg

Workings

Mean of X + Y + Z = (10 + 14 + 6)kg = 30kg

Variance of X + Y + Z = ($2^2 + 2^2 + 1^2$) = 9kg

Standard deviation of X + Y + Z = $\sqrt{9}$ = 3kg

8 (a) C   To find the percentage increase since year 9, we must take the increase as a percentage of the year 9 value. The increase in the index of 18 points between year 9 and year 14 is therefore a percentage increase of $(18/180 \times 100\%) = 10\%$.

The correct answer is therefore C.

If you selected option D you interpreted the increase of 18 points as an increase of 18% which is incorrect.

   (b) C   Year 2 price index $= \dfrac{120}{80} \times 100 = 150$

Option C is therefore correct.

If you selected option A, you have confused the numerator with the denominator and calculated $\dfrac{80}{120}$ instead of $\dfrac{120}{80}$.

If you selected option B, you simply took the price difference of £40 (£120 − £80 = £40) and added this to 100.

If you selected option D, you added $\dfrac{80}{120} \times 100\% = 67\%$ to 100 which equals 167 which is incorrect.

   (c) C   Year 5 quantity index $= \dfrac{25,000}{20,000} \times 100$

$= 125$

If you selected option A, you took the difference in litres $(25,000 − 20,000 = 5,000)$ and interpreted this as a five point increase, ie $100 + 5 = 105$.

If you selected option D you calculated $\dfrac{20,000}{25,000} \times 100 = 80$ and added this to 100 which is not the correct method to use.

   (d)

Year	Index	Real wage
		£
20X0	88	170
20X1	90	179
20X2	93	181
20X3	95	188
20X4	96	193
20X5	98	195
20X6	100	197
20X7	102	199
20X8	104	199
20X9	106	201
20Y0	108	214

The index number for each year with 20X6 as the base year will be the original index number divided by 1.14, and the real wages for each year will be (money wages × 100)/index number for the year.

9 (a) B   The data tells us that there was a machine breakdown on 120 days $(480 − 360)$ out of a total of 480.

P(machine breakdown) = 120/480 × 100%
= 25%

You should have been able to eliminate option A immediately since a probability of 0% = impossibility.

If you selected option C, you calculated the probability of a machine breakdown as 120 out of a possible 365 days instead of 480 days.

If you selected option D, you incorrectly calculated the probability that there was **not** a machine breakdown on any particular day.

(b) C   A demand of 53 units occurred on 42 days out of a total of 200.

P(demand = 53 units) = 42/200 × 100%
= 21%

If you selected option A, you calculated the probability that daily demand was 51 units instead of 53.

If you selected option B, you calculated the probability that daily demand was 52 units instead of 53.

If you selected option D, you calculated the probability that daily demand was 54 units instead of 53.

(c) C

Factory	Ratio of visits
North	1
South	2
West	$\frac{1}{4}$

Pr(visiting North factory) = ¼ = 0.25

If you didn't select the correct option, make sure that you are clear about how the correct answer has been arrived at. Remember to look at the **ratio** of visits since no actual numbers of visits are given.

(d) B   Since the probabilities must total 100%, the probability of the pessimistic outcome = 100% – 60% – 30% = 10%.

Outcome	Profit/(Loss) £	Probability	Expected value £
Optimistic	19,200	0.3	5,760
Most likely	12,500	0.6	7,500
Pessimistic	(6,700)	0.1	(670)
		1.0	12,590

If you selected option A, you calculated the expected value of the most likely outcome instead of the entire project.

If you selected option C, you forgot to treat the 6,700 as a loss, ie as a negative value.

If you selected option D, you forgot to take into account the probabilities of the various outcomes arising.

(e) D   Probability of A or B occurring = P(A) + P(B) provided A and B cannot both be true.

Pr(sales remain same or rise) = P(same) + P(rise)
= 0.61 + 0.22
= 0.83

You must make sure that you understand the laws of probability so that you can apply them correctly to objective test questions such as this.

(f)

Probability of visiting area x =	0.50
Probability of visiting area y =	0.25
Probability of visiting area z =	0.25
EV of probability of a sale in area x =	0.20
EV of probability of a sale in area y =	0.0875
EV of probability of a sale in area z =	0.0625

Workings

The probabilities of visiting each area are obtained from the ratios in which he visits them.

Area	Ratio		Probability
x	2	2/4 =	0.50
y	1	1/4 =	0.25
z	$\frac{1}{4}$	1/4 =	0.25
			1.00

The expected value (EV) of probability of a sale = P(sale) × P(visiting area).

Area	P(sale)	P(visiting area)	EV of probability of a sale
x	0.40	0.50	0.20
y	0.35	0.25	0.0875
z	0.25	0.25	0.0625

10   D

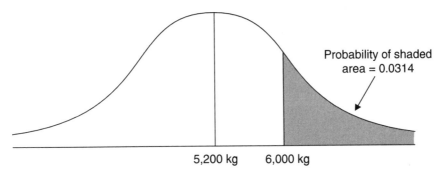

Probability of shaded area = 0.0314

5,200 kg   6,000 kg

Pr(elephants weigh between 5,200 kg and 6,000 kg) = 0.5 − 0.0314
                                                   = 0.4686

From normal distribution tables, 0.4686 corresponds to a z value of 1.86.

$$\text{If} \quad z = \frac{x - \mu}{\sigma}$$

$$1.86 = \frac{6,000 - 5,200}{\sigma}$$

$$\sigma = \frac{6,000 - 5,200}{1.86}$$

$$= 430 \text{ kg}$$

The correct answer is therefore D.

Make sure that you draw a sketch of the area that you are interested in when answering an objective test question such as this. It will help to clarify exactly what you are trying to do.

BPP
PUBLISHING

(b) D

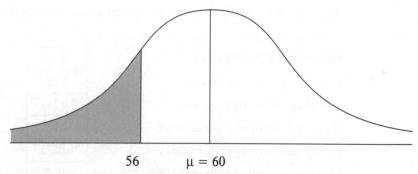

56   μ = 60

We are interested in the shaded area of the graph above, which we can calculate using normal distribution tables.

$$z = \frac{x - \mu}{\sigma}$$

$$= \frac{56 - 60}{3.8}$$

$$= 1.05$$

A z value of 1.05 corresponds to a probability of 0.3531.

The shaded area has a corresponding probability of 0.5 − 0.3531 = 0.1469 or 0.15 or 15%.

Option A is incorrect because it represents the probability of getting a score of 56 or more.

Option B represents the probability of getting a score of 60 or less, ie 50% (the mean represents the point below which 50% of the population lie and above which 50% of the population lie).

If you selected option C, you forgot to deduct your answer from 0.5.

(c) B   25% of normal frequencies will occur between the mean and the lower quartile. From normal distribution tables, 25% of frequencies lie between the mean and a position 0.67 standard deviations below the mean.

$$\sigma = \sqrt{\text{variance}} = \sqrt{25} = 5$$

The lower quartile is 0.67 × 5 = 3.35 below the mean.

∴ lower quartile = 75 − 3.35 = 71.65

If you had forgotten to take the square root of the variance in order to obtain the standard deviation, you would have calculated the lower quartile as being 0.67 × 25 = 16.75 below the mean, ie 75 − 16.75 = 58.25. Option A is incorrect for this reason.

You should have been able to eliminate options C and D straightaway since 78.35 and 91.75 are **above** the mean. The lower quartile of any distribution will be **below** the mean. Option C represents the upper quartile (75 + 3.35).

(d) D   28.23% of the population lies between 900 and the mean. Therefore 0.2823 corresponds to a z value of 0.78 (from normal distribution tables).

If $$z = \frac{x - \mu}{\sigma}$$

$$0.78 = \frac{900 - \mu}{90}$$

$$0.78 \times 90 = 900 - \mu$$

$$70.2 = 900 - \mu$$

$$\mu = 900 - 70.2$$
$$= 829.8 \text{ or } 830$$

Draw a sketch of the area we are concerned with in this question if you had difficulty understanding the answer.

(e)   A

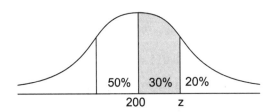

We need to find the point z standard deviations above the mean such that 20% of the frequencies are above it and 30% (50% – 20%) of the frequencies lie between the point z and the mean.

From normal distribution tables, it can be seen that 30% of frequencies lie between the mean and the point 0.84 standard deviations from the mean.

If $z = \dfrac{x - \mu}{\sigma}$

$\quad 0.84 = \dfrac{x - 200}{\sqrt{1,600}} = \dfrac{x - 200}{40}$

$\quad 33.6 = x - 200$

$\qquad x = 200 + 33.6$

$\qquad\quad = 233.6 \text{ or } 234 \text{ (to the nearest whole number)}$

If you selected option B, you incorrectly added one standard deviation to the mean instead of 0.84 standard deviations.

If you selected option C you have added 1.28 standard deviations to the mean instead of 0.84 standard deviations.

If you selected option D, you have found $200 + (1.96 \times 40)$ which accounts for 47.5% of the area from 200 to point z.

(f)   (a)   ①

    (b)   ② + ③

    (c)   ④

    (d)   ② + ③ + ④ = ②   + 0.5

11   (a)   C $S = X + nrX$

$\qquad\qquad = £2,000 + (8 \times 0.12 \times £2,000)$

$\qquad\qquad = £2,000 + £1,920$

$\qquad\qquad = £3,920$

If you selected option A, you calculated the interest element only and forgot to add on the original capital value.

If you selected option B, you used $n = 7$ instead of $n = 8$.

If you selected option D, you used the compound interest formula instead of the simple interest formula.

(b) B   If

$$S = X + nrX$$
$$S - X = nrX \text{ (note } S - X = \text{interest element)}$$
$$£1,548 - £900 = nrX$$
$$4 \text{ years} = 4 \times 12 = 48 \text{ months} = n$$

$$\therefore \quad £648 = 48 \, r \times £900$$

$$\therefore \quad r = \frac{£648}{48 \times £900}$$

$$r = 0.015 \text{ or } 1.5\%$$

If you selected option C, you misinterpreted 0.015 as 15% instead of 1.5%.

If you selected option D, you calculated the annual rate of interest instead of the monthly rate.

(c) C   £3,000 = 120% of the original investment

$$\therefore \text{ Original investment} = \frac{100}{120} \times £3,000$$

$$= £2,500$$

$$\therefore \text{ Interest} = £3,000 \quad £2,500$$
$$= £500$$

Make sure that you always tackle this type of question by establishing what the original investment was first.

If you selected option D, you simply calculated 20% of £3,000 which is incorrect.

(d) C   If a cost declines by 8% per annum on a compound basis, then at the end of the first year it will be worth 0.92 the original value.

Now	= £12,000
End of year 1	= £12,000 × 0.92
End of year 2	= £12,000 × 0.92²
End of year 32	= £12,000 × 0.92³

Now = £12,000

End of year 1 = £12,000 $\times$ 0.92

End of year 2 = £12,000 $\times$ 0.92^2

End of year 32 = £12,000 $\times$ 0.92^3

$\therefore$ At the end of year 3, £12,000 will be worth

£12,000 $\times$ (0.92)^3 = £9,344

If you selected option A, you calculated the value after four years, not three.

If you selected option B, you have assumed that the cost will decline by 8% × 3 = 24% over 3 years therefore leaving a value of £12,000 − (£12,000 × 24%) = £12,000 − £2,880 = £9,120.

If you selected option D, you calculated the value after two years, not three.

(e) A   If house prices rise at 3% per calendar month, this is equivalent to

$(1.03)^{12}$ = 1.426 or 42.6% per annum

If you selected option B, you forgot to take the effect of compounding into account, ie 3% × 12 = 36%.

If you selected option C, you incorrectly translated 1.426 into 14.26% instead of 42.6% per annum.

If you selected option D, you forget to raise 1.03 to the power of 12, instead you multiplied it by 12.

(f) (i) $\boxed{15.87}$ %

Working

15% per annum (nominal rate) is 3.75% per quarter. The effective annual rate of interest is

$[1.0375^4 - 1] = 0.1587 = 15.87\%$

(ii) $\boxed{26.82}$ %

Working

24% per annum (nominal rate) is 2% per month. The effective annual rate of interest is

$[1.02^{12} - 1] = 0.2682 = 26.82\%$

12   (a)   C   Present value of the lease for years 1 – 9 $= £12,000 \times 5.328$
Present value of the lease for years 0 - 9 $= £12,000 \times (1 + 5.328)$

$= £12,000 \times 6.328$
$= £75,936$

If you selected option A, you calculated the PV of the lease for years 1-9 only. If the first payment is made now, you must remember to add 1 to the 5.328.

Option B represents the PV of the lease for years 1-10 (the first payment being made in a one year's time), ie £12,000 × 5.650 = £67,800.

Option D is incorrect because it represents the PV of the lease for years 1-10 plus an additional payment now (ie £12,000 × (1 + 5.650) = £79,800.

(b)   D   Let A = annual repayments

These repayments, A are an annuity for 15 years at 9%.

Annuity (A) $= \dfrac{\text{PV of mortgage}}{\text{Annuity factor}}$

PV of mortgage $= £60,000$

Annuity factor $= 8.061$ (9%, 15 years from CDF tables)

∴ Annuity $= \dfrac{£60,000}{8.061}$

$= £7,440$ (to the nearest £10)

If you selected option A you have confused mortgages with sinking funds and have calculated the PV of the mortgage as if it occurred at time 15 instead of time 0.

If you selected option B you have forgotten to take account of the interest rates (ie 9% for 15 years). You have simply divided £60,000 by 15.

If you selected option C, you have not taken into account the fact that the repayments happen at the year end and that the first repayment is in one year's time and not now.

(c)   C   The IRR can be calculated using the following formula.

$\text{IRR} = a\% + [\dfrac{A}{A - B} \times (b - a)]\%$

BPP
PUBLISHING

where a = 10%
          b = 24%
          A = £460
          B = £320

$$\text{IRR} = 10\% + [\frac{£460}{£460 - £320} \times (24 - 10)]\%$$

$$= 10\% + 46\%$$
$$= 56\%$$

If you selected option A, you have calculated the arithmetic mean of 10% and 24% instead of using the IRR formula.

If you selected option B you have used an NPV of –£320 instead of +£320 in your calculation.

If you selected option D, you must realise that it is possible to use either two positive or two negative NPVs as well as a positive and negative NPV. Using the former method, however, the results will be less accurate.

(d) B   The payments made on a credit card are an annuity of £x per month.

From cumulative present value tables (3%, 12 periods) the annuity factor is 9.954.

$$\text{If Annuity} = \frac{\text{PV of annuity}}{\text{Annuity factor}}$$

$$\text{Annuity} = \frac{£21,000}{9.954}$$

$$= £2,110$$

If you selected option A, you have simply divided £21,000 by 12 without any reference to discounting.

If you selected option C, you have misread the cumulative present value tables (and used the annuity factor for 12% and 3 periods instead of 12 periods and 3%).

If you selected option D, you have calculated the present value of £21,000 in 12 time periods at a discount rate of 3% instead of finding the monthly annuity whose present value over 12 months at 3% gives £21,000.

(e) A   Project A has the highest NPV. When comparing projects it is the NPV of each project which should be calculated and compared. The correct answer is therefore A.

Mutually exclusive projects should not be selected by comparing the IRRs – Option D is therefore incorrect, even though it has the highest IRR, it does not have the highest NPV.

Projects B and C do not have the highest NPVs either and so options B and C are incorrect.

(f)

Year	Cash flow	Discount factor	Present value
	£	11%	£
0	(28,000)	1.000	(28,000)
1	8,000	0.901	7,208
2	8,000	0.812	6,496
3	8,000	0.731	5,848
4	8,000	0.659	5,272
5	8,000	0.593	4,744
		NPV	1,568

Project viable Yes ☑

No ☐

The NPV is positive, therefore the project is viable because it earns more than 11% per annum.

13 (a) A   If x = 8, y = 690.24 – (2.75 × 8) = 668.24

Forecast = trend + seasonal component = 668.24 – 25.25 = 642.99 = 643 (to the nearest unit)

If you selected option B, you calculated the forecast for the seventh period and deducted the seasonal component of the eighth period.

If you selected option C, you correctly forecast the trend for the eighth period but forgot to deduct the seasonal component.

If you selected option D, you simply calculated the trend for the seventh period instead of the eighth period.

(b) D   I   Provided the seasonal variation remains the same in the future as in the past, it will not make forecasts unreliable.

II   Provided a multiplicative model is used, the fact that the trend is increasing need not have any adverse effect on the reliability of forecasts.

III   If the model being used is inappropriate, for example, if an additive model is used when the trend is changing sharply, forecasts will not be very reliable.

IV   Forecasts are made on the assumption that everything continues as in the past.

III and IV are therefore necessary and hence the correct answer is D.

(c) A   I   With an additive model, the weekly component represents the average value of actual production minus the trend for that week, so a component of +9 means production is 9,000 units above the trend.

This is the only correct statement.

If you selected option B, C or D, you have confused the additive variation of –4, +5 and –6 (actually –4,000 units, +5,000 units and –6,000 units respectively) with the multiplicative variation of –4%, +5% and –6% respectively.

(d) A

		Quarter			
	1	*2*	*3*	*4*	*Total*
Unadjusted average	1.09	0.93	1.17	0.78	3.97
Adjustment	0.0075	0.0075	0.0075	0.0075	0.03
Adjusted average	1.0975	0.9375	1.1775	0.7875	4.000

4 – 3.97 = 0.03

We therefore need to add 0.03 ÷ 4 = 0.0075 to each average.

From the table above, it can be seen that the first quarter adjusted average is 1.0975 as per option A.

If you selected option B, you added the entire deficit of 0.03 to the second quarter average instead of spreading it across all four averages.

If you selected option C, you subtracted the entire deficit of 0.03 from the third quarter average rather than sharing it across all four averages.

If you selected option D, you have subtracted the deficit of 0.0075 from each quarter's average, instead of adding it.

(e) B   As this is a multiplicative model, the seasonal variations should sum (in this case) to 4 (an average of 1) as there are four quarters.

Let x = seasonal variation for quarter 4.

$$0.45 + 1.22 + 1.31 + x = 4$$
$$2.98 + x = 4$$
$$x = 4 - 2.98$$
$$= 1.02$$

If you selected option A you subtracted the sum of the seasonal variations from 3 instead of 4.

If you selected option D, you forgot to subtract the sum of the seasonal variations for quarters 1-3 from 4.

(f)

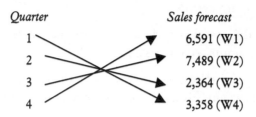

Quarter	Sales forecast
1	6,591 (W1)
2	7,489 (W2)
3	2,364 (W3)
4	3,358 (W4)

Workings

(1) The trend changes from 4,500 to 5,300. The growth rate is 5,300/4,500 = 1.178 = 17.8%.

Expressed per quarter (there are four quarters) this is $1.178^{1/3} = 1.056$ or 5.6% per quarter.

Therefore, in quarter 1, the forecast for actual sales = $5,300 \times 1.056 \times 0.6 = 3,358$.

(2) The trend changes from 4,500 to 5,300. The growth rate is 5,300/4,500 = 1.178 = 17.8%.

Expressed per quarter (there are four quarters) this is $1.178^{1/3} = 1.056$ or 5.6% per quarter.

Therefore, in quarter 2, the forecast for actual sales = $5,300 \times 1.056^2 \times 0.4 = 2,364$.

(3) The trend changes from 4,500 to 5,300. The growth rate is 5,300/4,500 = 1.178 = 17.8%. Expressed per quarter (there are four quarters) this is $1.178^{1/3} = 1.056$ or 5.6% per quarter. Therefore, in quarter 3, the forecast for actual sales = $5,300 \times 1.056^3 \times 1.2 = 7,489$.

(4) The trend changes from 4,500 to 5,300. The growth rate is 5,300/4,500 = 1.178 = 17.8%.

Expressed per quarter (there are four quarters) this is $1.178^{1/3} = 1.056$ or 5.6% per quarter.

Therefore, in quarter 4, the forecast for actual sales = $5,300 \times 1.056^4 \times 1 = 6,591$.

14 (a) D   The formula for the product moment correlation coefficient is provided in your exam. There are no excuses for getting this question wrong.

$$r = \frac{n\Sigma XY - \Sigma X\Sigma Y}{\sqrt{[n\Sigma X^2 - (\Sigma X^2)][n\Sigma Y^2 - (\Sigma Y)^2]}}$$

$$= \frac{(4 \times 57) - (10 \times 22)}{\sqrt{[4 \times 30 - 10^2][4 \times 134 - 22^2]}}$$

$$= \frac{8}{\sqrt{1,040}} = +0.25$$

(b) D

	Critic 1 Rank	Critic 2 Rank	d	d^2
Captain Corelli's guitar	2	1	1	1
Debbie Jones's diary	1	3	2	4
The songs of a bird	4	7	3	9
Cold love in a warm climate	6	5	1	1
Raging wars and peacefulness	5	6	1	1
Charlotte Black	3	2	1	1
The name of the tulip	7	4	3	9
			$\Sigma d^2 =$	26

$$R = 1 - \left[\frac{6\Sigma d^2}{n(n^2 - 1)}\right]$$

$$= 1 - \left[\frac{6 \times 26}{7 \times (49 - 1)}\right]$$

$$= 1 - \frac{156}{336}$$

$$= 0.536$$

(c) C   The independent variable is denoted by X and the dependent one by Y. Statement III is therefore correct. You should have been able to eliminate options B and D straightaway.

The variable to be forecast must always be Y. Statement I is therefore not true.

In calculating the correlation coefficient, it does not matter which variable is X and which is Y, and a totally different regression line equation will result if X and Y are interchanged. Statement II is therefore not true.

Scattergrams are used to show whether or not there is a relationship between X and Y and it does not matter which variable is associated with a particular axis. Statement IV is therefore not true.

All statements (except for III) are not true. The correct answer is therefore C.

(d) D   Where y = a + bx

$$b = \frac{n\Sigma XY - \Sigma X\Sigma Y}{n\Sigma X^2 - (\Sigma X^2)}$$

$$= \frac{(7 \times 587) - (21 \times 184)}{(7 \times 91) - (21^2)}$$

$$= \frac{245}{196}$$

$$= 1.25$$

$$a = \overline{Y} - b\overline{X}$$

$$= \frac{184}{7} - \frac{(1.25 \times 21)}{7}$$

$$= 22.5$$

The correct answer is therefore D.

(e) C   The sample of only six pairs of values is very small and is therefore likely to reduce the reliability of the estimate. Statement I is therefore true.

With such a small sample and the extrapolation required, the estimate is unlikely to be reliable. Statement II is therefore not true.

Since a correlation coefficient of 0.9 would be regarded as strong (it is a high value) the estimate would be reliable. Statement III is therefore not true.

When X = 20, we don't know anything about the relationship between X and Y since the sample data only goes up to X = 10. Statement IV is therefore true.

(f)

(2, 3) (3, 4.5) (4, 6)	?	Perfect positive correlation ✓ Perfect negative correlation Uncorrelated
(2, 3) (3, 1.5) (4, 0)	?	Perfect positive correlation Perfect negative correlation ✓ Uncorrelated
(2, 3) (4, 0) (4, 6)	?	Perfect positive correlation Perfect negative correlation Uncorrelated ✓

Workings

(i)   If these points were plotted on a scatter diagram, all the pairs of values would lie on an upward-sloping straight line with a gradient of +1.5. [Gradient $= \frac{6-3}{4-2} = \frac{3}{2} = 1.5$]. This would be indicative of PERFECT POSITIVE CORRELATION.

(ii) If these points were plotted on a scatter diagram, all the pairs of values would lie on a downward-sloping straight line with a gradient of –1.5. [Gradient $= \frac{0-3}{4-2} = \frac{-3}{2} = -1.5$]. This would be indicative of PERFECT NEGATIVE CORRELATION.

(iii) If these points were plotted on a scatter diagram there would not be evidence of any correlation existing since when x = 4, the corresponding y values are equal to 0 or 6.

Index

BPP
PUBLISHING

REVIEW FORM & FREE PRIZE DRAW

All original review forms from the entire BPP range, completed with genuine comments, will be entered into one of two draws on 31 January 2003 and 31 July 2003. The names on the first four forms picked out on each occasion will be sent a cheque for £50.

Name: _____   **Address:** _____

_____

How have you used this Text?
(Tick one box only)

☐ Self study (book only)

☐ On a course: college (please state)_____

_____

☐ With 'correspondence' package

☐ Other _____

Why did you decide to purchase this Text?
(Tick one box only)

☐ Have used BPP Texts in the past

☐ Recommendation by friend/colleague

☐ Recommendation by a lecturer at college

☐ Saw advertising

☐ Other _____

During the past six months do you recall seeing/receiving any of the following?
(Tick as many boxes as are relevant)

☐ Our advertisement in CIMA *Insider*

☐ Our advertisement in *Financial Management*

☐ Our advertisement in *Pass*

☐ Our brochure with a letter through the post

☐ Our website www.bpp.com

Which (if any) aspects of our advertising do you find useful?
(Tick as many boxes as are relevant)

☐ Prices and publication dates of new editions

☐ Information on product content

☐ Facility to order books off-the-page

☐ None of the above

Which BPP products have you used?					
Text	☐	MCQ cards	☐	i-Learn	☐
Kit	☐	Tape	☐	i-Pass	☐
Passcard	☐	Video	☐	Virtual Campus	☐

How did you/will you take the exam for this paper? (Tick one box only)

Written exam ☐

Computer-based assessment ☐

Your ratings, comments and suggestions would be appreciated on the following areas.

	Very useful	Useful	Not useful
Introductory section (Key study steps, personal study)	☐	☐	☐
Key terms	☐	☐	☐
Quality of explanations	☐	☐	☐
Examples	☐	☐	☐
Questions and answers in each chapter	☐	☐	☐
Chapter roundups	☐	☐	☐
Quick quizzes	☐	☐	☐
Exam focus points	☐	☐	☐
Question bank (paper-based exam)	☐	☐	☐
Queston bank (computer-based assessment)	☐	☐	☐
Answer bank (paper-based exam)	☐	☐	☐
Answer bank (computer-based assessment)	☐	☐	☐
Index	☐	☐	☐
Icons	☐	☐	☐
Mind maps	☐	☐	☐

Overall opinion of this Study Text   Excellent ☐   Good ☐   Adequate ☐   Poor ☐

Do you intend to continue using BPP products?   Yes ☐   No ☐

On the reverse of this page are noted particular areas of the text about which we would welcome your feedback. Please note any further comments and suggestions/errors on the reverse of this page as well. The BPP author of this edition can be e-mailed at: lynnwatkins@bpp.com

Please return this form to: Nick Weller, CIMA Range Manager, BPP Publishing Ltd, FREEPOST, London, W12 8BR

TELL US WHAT YOU THINK

Because the following specific areas of the text cover tricky topics, your comments on their usefulness are particularly welcome.

- The normal distribution (Chapter 10)

- Financial mathematics (Chapters 11 and 12)

- Forecasting (Chapters 13 and 14)

Please note any further comments and suggestions/errors below.

See overleaf for information on other
BPP products and how to order

CIMA Order

To BPP Publishing Ltd, Aldine Place, London W12 8AW
Tel: 020 8740 2211. Fax: 020 8740 1184
www.bpp.com Email publishing@bpp.com
Order online www.bpp.com

Mr/Mrs/Ms (Full name) _____

Daytime delivery address _____

Postcode _____

Daytime Tel _____ Email _____

Date of exam (month/year) _____

	7/02 Texts	1/02 Kits	1/02 Passcards	9/00 Tapes	7/00 Videos	Virtual Campus	7/02 i-Pass	7/02 i-Learn	7/02 MCQ cards
FOUNDATION									
1 Financial Accounting Fundamentals	£20.95	£10.95	£6.95	£12.95	£25.95	£50	£24.95		£5.95
2 Management Accounting Fundamentals	£20.95	£10.95	£6.95	£12.95	£25.95	£50	£24.95		£5.95
3A Economics for Business	£20.95	£10.95	£6.95	£12.95	£25.95	£50	£24.95		£5.95
3B Business Law	£20.95	£10.95	£6.95	£12.95	£25.95	£50	£24.95		£5.95
3C Business Mathematics	£20.95	£10.95	£6.95	£12.95	£25.95	£50	£24.95		£5.95
INTERMEDIATE									
4 Finance	£20.95	£10.95	£6.95	£12.95	£25.95	£80	£24.95	£34.95	£5.95
5 Business Tax (FA 2002)	£20.95 (10/02)	£10.95	£6.95	£12.95	£25.95	£80	£24.95	£34.95	£5.95
6 Financial Accounting	£20.95	£10.95	£6.95	£12.95	£25.95	£80	£24.95	£34.95	£5.95
6i Financial Accounting International	£20.95	£10.95	£6.95	£12.95	£25.95	£80	£24.95	£34.95	£5.95
7 Financial Reporting	£20.95	£10.95	£6.95	£12.95	£25.95	£80	£24.95	£34.95	£5.95
7i Financial Reporting International	£20.95	£10.95				£80	£24.95	£34.95	£5.95
8 Management Accounting - Performance Management	£20.95 *	£10.95	£6.95	£12.95	£25.95	£80	£24.95 *	£34.95	£5.95 *
9 Management Accounting - Decision Making	£20.95 *	£10.95	£6.95	£12.95	£25.95	£80	£24.95 *	£34.95	£5.95 *
10 Systems and Project Management	£20.95	£10.95	£6.95	£12.95	£25.95	£80	£24.95	£34.95	£5.95
11 Organisational Management	£20.95	£10.95	£6.95	£12.95	£25.95	£80	£24.95	£34.95	£5.95
FINAL									
12 Management Accounting - Business Strategy	£20.95	£10.95	£6.95	£12.95	£25.95				
13 Management Accounting - Financial Strategy	£20.95	£10.95	£6.95	£12.95	£25.95				
14 Management Accounting - Information Strategy	£20.95	£10.95	£6.95	£12.95	£25.95		11/02 □ 5/03 □		
15 Case Study (1) Workbook	£20.95			£12.95			11/02 □ 5/03 □		
(2) Toolkit		£19.95 (For 11/02: available 9/02. For 5/03: available 3/03)							
Learning to Learn (7/02)	£9.95								

* For paper 8 and 9, separate editions are available for the November 2002 and May 2003 exams. Please tick the exam you will be sitting.

POSTAGE & PACKING

Study Texts

	First	Each extra
UK	£3.00	£2.00	£ __
Europe***	£5.00	£4.00	£ __
Rest of world	£20.00	£10.00	£ __

Kits/Passcards/Success Tapes

	First	Each extra
UK	£2.00	£1.00	£ __
Europe*	£2.50	£1.00	£ __
Rest of world	£15.00	£8.00	£ __

MCQ cards £1.00 £1.00 £ __

CDs each

UK	£2.00
Europe*	£2.00
Rest of world	£10.00

Breakthrough Videos

	First	Each extra
UK	£2.00	£2.00	£ __
Europe*	£2.00	£2.00	£ __
Rest of world	£20.00	£10.00	£ __

Grand Total (Cheques to *BPP Publishing*) I enclose a cheque for (incl. Postage) £ __

Or charge to Access/Visa/Switch

Card Number _____

Expiry date _____ Start Date _____

Issue Number (Switch Only) _____

Signature _____

Total _____

We aim to deliver to all UK addresses inside 5 working days. A signature will be required. Orders to all EU addresses should be delivered within 6 working days. All other orders to any